Marketing and Consumption in Modern Japan

This book explores the development of marketing and consumerism in Japan throughout the twentieth century. It shows how Japan had a long established indigenous traditional approach to marketing, separate from Western approaches to marketing, and discusses how the Japanese approach to marketing was applied in the form of new marketing activities, which, responding to changing patterns of consumption, contributed considerably to Japan's economic success. The book concludes with a discussion of how the Japanese approach to marketing is likely to develop at a time when globalisation and international marketing are having an increasing impact in Japan.

Kazuo Usui is a Professor in the Faculty of Economics at Saitama University, Japan, and a Visiting Professor at the University of Edinburgh Business School, UK.

Routledge Studies in the Growth Economies of Asia

Marketing and Consumption in Modern Japan

Kazuo Usui

LONDON AND NEW YORK

First published 2014 by Routledge

2 Park Square, Milton Park, Abingdon, Oxon OX14 4RN
711 Third Avenue, New York, NY 10017, USA

Routledge is an imprint of the Taylor & Francis Group, an informa business

First issued in paperback 2016

British Library Cataloguing in Publication Data
A catalogue record for this book is available from the British Library

Library of Congress Cataloging in Publication Data
Usui, Kazuo.
  Marketing and consumption in modern Japan / Kazuo Usui.
    pages cm.—(Routledge studies in the growth economies of
    Asia; 122)
  Includes bibliographical references and index.
  1. Marketing—Japan—History—20th century. 2. Consumers—
  Japan—History—20th century. 3. Consumption (Economics)—
  Japan—History—20th century. 4. Economic development—Japan—
  History—20th century. I. Title.
  HF5415.12.J3U768 2014
  339.4'70952—dc23
                                                    2013029449

ISBN: 978-0-415-32313-0 (hbk)
ISBN: 978-1-138-20598-7 (pbk)

Typeset in Times New Roman
by RefineCatch Limited, Bungay, Suffolk

Contents

Figures

Tables

Acknowledgements

This is my second book published in English. I could not have completed it without the much appreciated help of many people. Because English is not my mother tongue, I asked several native speakers to read my draft. Especially, I would like to express my heartfelt thanks to Ms Alison Bowers, a freelance professional editor in Edinburgh. She undertook the demanding work of checking my English expressions in detail, just as she did for my first publication, *The Development of Marketing Management: The Case of the USA c.1910–1940* (Ashgate, 2008). Ms Kathleen King, Edinburgh, and Mr Tim Bolt, Southampton, were also committed to this work in the very early stages of the project.

I appreciate the support of Emeritus Professor John Dawson, who greatly encouraged me to conduct this project. He also hosted me at the University of Edinburgh, a role which Professor David Marshall has taken over now. I thank the members of CHARM (Conference on Historical Analysis and Research in Marketing), including: Professor D. G. Brian Jones, Quinnipiac University; Professor Terrence Witkowski, California State University; Professor Eric Shaw, Florida Atlantic University; Professor William Keep, The College of New Jersey; and Professor Mark Tadajewski, Durham University. I presented some early drafts at CHARM and received many insightful suggestions.

I am grateful for Grants-in-Aid for Scientific Research (C) from the JSPS (Japan Society for the Promotion of Science) Nos 19530381 (FY2007–8) and 21530433 (FY2009–11). Chapters 3 and 6 of this book are part of the results from this grant, and the project was also funded by the Saitama University Research and Development Bureau in both FY2010 and FY2011.

And most of all, I would like to thank my wife, Fumiko, and four children for their support.

Kazuo Usui
Saitama and Edinburgh,
August 2013

Introduction

The winner of the 1994 Nobel Prize in Literature, the author Kenzaburo Oe, gave as his acceptance speech the paper 'Japan, the ambiguous, and myself'.

> After a hundred and twenty years of modernisation since the opening up of the country, contemporary Japan is split between two opposite poles of ambiguity. ... The modernisation of Japan was oriented toward learning from and imitating the West, yet the country is situated in Asia and has firmly maintained its traditional culture.
>
> (Oe 1995: 117)

There is, of course, no society on which foreign cultures have exerted no influence. Modern Japan has been shaped under intense influences, latterly Western but dating back to the Chinese from around the sixth century. This Chinese influence has been modified and localised over a long historical time, and has become an essential part of so-called Japaneseness. In contrast, the Western influence has been accepted in modern Japan in an artificially hurried and radical manner, so that, as Oe described, it has created an 'ambiguity' concerning the relation between the West and the Japanese Self even for many Japanese.

Still, westernisation was established practically in a very Japanese way. No matter how rapid and drastic the process of westernisation, it could not establish an unadulterated Western-style society in Japan, but incorporated the localised Western culture into the Japanese tradition: a complex hybrid. As the social historian Fernand Braudel wrote:

> As early as the sixth century, in fact, there was what might be called 'a Chinese Japan'; and since 1868 there has been a highly successful 'Western Japan'. Nevertheless, both these key influences have merged into a 'Japanese' Japan. ... In this country of miniature gardens, tea ceremonies and flowering cherries, even Buddhist religion, brought in through China, has been remodelled to suit the Japanese. And this Japanese version of Buddhism is even further removed from the original than the Chinese variant was and is.
>
> (Braudel 1994: 276)

Focusing on the arena of marketing and consumption, this book will explore how such a hybrid of the West and Japan actually developed.

The discourse of westernisation and the role of marketing

The discourse of westernisation was a main driving force for modernisation in Japan. For many Japanese, the West can be defined as the model for Japan to emulate and even transcend by getting rid of its conventional ways. The 'ideal' West is, however, the kind that no one could ever reach. Although the real Western world is full of diversities, Japanese people tend to ignore the differences between North, East, Middle, West and South Europe, or even Europe and North America, and construct the West in their imagination. In this sense, the concept of the West was a Japanese creation.[1]

The immersion into the discourse of westernisation brought Japan to remarkable socio-economic successes not only once, but twice, in history: sudden emergence as a single industrialised country in the Far East in the early twentieth century, and miraculous economic growth after the Second World War. It was natural that as the discourse of westernisation was spreading and gaining strength, the counter-discourse of anti-West also grew. The Second World War regime presented an extreme form. Nevertheless, in most periods of modern Japan, the discourse of westernisation was the mainstream. The two historical socio-economic success periods changed Japan to an enhanced and developed society, adding to the credibility of the discourse.

However, it is important to note that the discourse of westernisation itself could not automatically mobilise people to westernise every dimension of their life. Often referred to as the 'revolution from above', the movement of modernisation came down from the upper echelons of society by way of politico-economic decisions by the government, enactment of constitutions and laws, and advocacy for new philosophy and culture by social leaders. Such strong leaderships by the elite social classes could initiate social changes, but were not enough to permeate Western factors into everyday life of ordinary people. It was marketing that could mediate between the discourse and ordinary people's daily life. The commercialised arena of selling and buying goods and services was a main stage on which various aspects of westernisation were seen and could be assessed by ordinary people. Marketers, seeking to distribute the new Western-style products and services, attempted to lure consumers by new marketing strategies. When consumers, who of course could refuse these goods and services by preserving familiar traditional manners, began to accept them enthusiastically, the new Western factors began to penetrate society and shape new consumer culture.

It should also be underlined that the mediating activities by marketing promoted the hybrid features of modern Western factors and traditional Japan. This process was twofold: first, marketers often invented modern but Japanese-type marketing strategies by mixing Western and traditional Japanese ideas; and second, consumers' continuous acceptance of new goods and services that marketers provided came to form the Japanese version of modern consumer life and consumer culture. This book will explore such interesting processes and show how the so-called 'Western Japan' was merging into the 'Japanese' Japan.

Before actual explorations in following chapters, this introduction explains the analytical framework of the book: the concepts of macromarketing, the consumption pattern, and the modern formats in retail marketing.

An analytical point of view on marketing and consumption

Analysis as macromarketing

Marketing is usually recognised as a business discipline. Its aim is to plan, implement and control marketing strategies in order to achieve success for an individual business.

According to this managerial paradigm of marketing, marketers should identify consumers' needs and wants through marketing research, select a particular market segment as a target, and arrange a marketing mix strategy composed of sub-strategies concerning products, prices, places and promotion (the so-called '4Ps'). Such marketing strategies depend on the particular circumstance, called the 'macro-environment', which is composed of political/legal, economic, technological, demographic, cultural and natural factors. While marketers acknowledge that they cannot control the macroenvironment, they monitor and respond to it to realise the goal, satisfying consumers and making profits. One of the shortest definitions of marketing is 'meeting needs profitably' (Kotler and Keller 2009: 45): this managerial idea became the mainstream in marketing discipline after the Second World War, and was expanded to include the non-profit organisations and even the individual person, especially after the end of the 1960s (see Kotler and Levy 1969, Kotler 1972).

The marketing discipline, however, is not confined to managerial ideas. It also includes societal discussions, which are now called macromarketing in order to distinguish them from micromarketing or marketing management. Germinating in the start of modern marketing thought at the turn of the twentieth century (see e.g. Jones and Monieson 1990), research in marketing from the societal perspective created a new school of marketing as macromarketing in the latter half of the 1970s. When this school started, the definition, scope and methodology of macromarketing were eagerly discussed in order to differentiate them from the widespread managerial paradigm of marketing or micromarketing. The discussions concerning how macromarketing could establish a scope and an integrated theory are still continuing (e.g. Fisk 2006, Nason 2006, Layton and Grossbart 2006, Peterson 2006). This book refers to a definition of macromarketing adopted at its inception by the *Journal of Macromarketing* (JMM 1982: 3): (1) the impact and consequences of micromarketing actions on society (marketing externalities), (2) the impact and consequences of society on marketing systems and actions (social sanctions), and (3) the understanding of marketing systems in the aggregate dimensions (macrosystems analysis). Regarding the first item, although micromarketing thought considers the macroenvironment as uncontrollable for individual marketers, macromarketing assumes that micromarketing actions/strategies exerted, in many cases unintentionally, significant external influences on society or the macroenvironment by an aggregation of many marketers' actions/strategies, or even by those of a single powerful marketer such as Coca Cola or McDonalds.

Drawing on this definition, the analysis of this book will explore (1) how new modern marketing strategies or micromarketing actions exerted external influences, in many cases unintentionally, on Japanese society, (2) why and how Japanese society sometimes wanted to regulate some new marketing strategies (especially in Chapter 4), and (3) how the new modern retail formats (defined below), spread in the sector-wide scale of retailing.[2]

The concept of consumption patterns: consumers as social beings

In order to explore how marketing strategies actually encouraged changes in consumers' lives under the discourse of westernisation, it should be necessary to recognise consumer behaviours as macro phenomena (different from the usual perspective on consumer behaviours as the sub-discipline of micromarketing or marketing management) and to identify the structural relationship between marketing strategies and consumption patterns.

The act of consumption – selection, purchase, use, maintenance and disposal of goods and services – shows a particular pattern in a particular historical time and place. The discussions of so-called 'macro consumption' (Firat 1977, 1987, Firat and Dholakia 1982, 1998) suggest that consumption patterns include 'consumption choices' (pack sizes, brands, products, product classes and consumption patterns) and four 'dimensions' of each of them (the social relationship, the domain of availability, the level of participation and the human activity). By modifying and expanding these discussions, consumption patterns are defined as a composition of consumption choices and the consumption mode. This idea is shown in Figure 0.1.

The consumption choices include (1) the offerings, i.e. product classes, product items, the kind of services and brands, (2) the place of purchase, i.e. retail formats and service establishments, (3) the way of use, and (4) the way of disposal. These choices are the consumer's own decisions, but are made on the basis of the consumption mode in society, which in turn is composed of the domain of availability for consumption choices and the social relationships of consumers with others during the act of consumption and with consumption itself.

The domain of availability for consumption choices, although it is superficially decided by marketers, has its fundamental sources in the macroenvironment as well as its history. It depends, for instance, on the level of technology (e.g. availability of computers, or shopping at vending machines), regulations and laws (e.g. non-availability of particular retail formats in residential areas or of 24-hour shopping), cultural traditions (e.g. availability of chopsticks or sticky rice) and the natural environment (e.g. the necessity for overcoats in cold areas but not in the torrid zone). The broadening of control of market exchange, 'commodification' (e.g. Corrigan 1997) or commercialisation, increases the availability of products, services and institutions for purchase (e.g. the box lunch that used to be made by

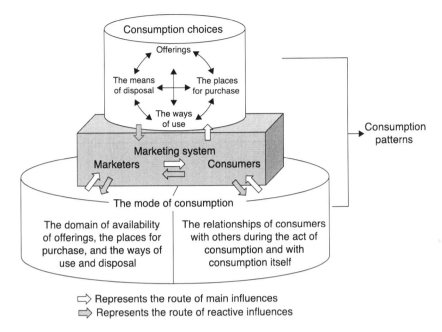

Figure 0.1 The concept of consumption patterns.

Note: The consumption pattern is composed of the mode of consumption and consumption choices. The marketing system mediates between the mode of consumption and the consumption choice, by taking and utilising some elements from the mode of consumption and shaping attractive marketing strategy.

mother is now sold at convenience stores, or advice on diet previously offered by friends is becoming a paid service). As a rule, this expansion comes with economic development. This book will focus on westernisation, modernisation and industrialisation as the important factors expanding the domain of availability.

It should be noted that the domain of availability in society does not directly influence the consumer's choice of consumption; but it is mediated by the system of marketing, as shown in Figure 0.1. It is marketers who recognise the potential changes in availability and actually provide the offerings to consumers, who may accept or refuse them. Not all factors are easy to recognise and utilise. The domain of availability is the social ground for marketers, but does not subordinate their behaviours on a one-to-one basis. It is rather a bundle of possibilities, which allows marketers to pick up and utilise some of them on their own initiative; in this sense, the domain of availability can be called the 'affordance' (Gibson 1977) in the marketing system.

The relationships of consumers with others during the act of consumption are also influenced by macroenvironmental factors, for instance, a cultural tendency of individualism or collectivism (Hofstede 2001), and cultural ways of socialisation in everyday life, communities and organisations. The relationships of consumers with consumption itself are social constructs as well. A consumer's attitude within buying and consumption is a typical example of these relationships. Some findings on consumption from socio-cultural research in the economy, such as Veblen's ([1899] 1994) 'conspicuous consumption' as a means of displaying social status, consumption of 'signs', not of objects, by Baudrillard (1998), and 'modern hedonism' as a day-dreamy, self-illusory quality of experience by Campbell ([1987] 2005), are among the components of the relationship of consumers with consumption itself. Again, the marketing system mediates between the relationships of consumers with others in the act of consumption and with consumption itself as a set of social factors and consumption choices by individual consumers.

Modern marketing and retail formats

In order to explore marketing as mediation between the mode of consumption and individual consumption choices, this book will focus on the arena of retailing, the stage where marketers and final consumers encounter directly. To this end, this book considers two types of marketing, that is, manufacturer-led and retailer-led.

As has been shown by research in business history (e.g. Chandler 1990, see also Porter and Livesay 1971, Chandler 1977), in a modern economy manufacturers take the initiative in mass marketing on the basis of the mass production system, resulting in many influences on final consumers. They use every means of marketing strategy; for instance, they differentiate their own from the competitors' products by developing new items, whether fundamentally innovative or improved in details, or changes to the physical appearance of the products, pre-packaging, putting on brand names and brand marks, and by heavy advertising and publicity via mass media to stimulate pre-selling effects (usually called 'pull strategy'). In addition to these measures described in many marketing textbooks, Japanese manufacturers have often used *keiretsu* retail networks, which had important influences on final consumers.

The term '*keiretsu*' is defined in this book as the exclusive network of merchants organised by a manufacturer by establishing subsidiaries and/or by making contracts with independent merchants (see theoretical note on *keiretsu* relationships). The term '*keiretsu* retailing' shows that this arrangement is adopted on the retail stage, on which organising contracted retailers is more usual than setting up exclusive retail stores as the subsidiary. By doing so, the manufacturer directly takes charge and controls the retail activities the affiliated retailers undertake. In this *keiretsu* retailing system, the manufacturer requires essentially two factors, that is, exclusive dealing and resale price maintenance, although the extent of these requirements is varied, ranging from the explicit requirements clearly defined in contracts to tacit requirements as part of natural business practices. Some factors are often demanded in addition, whether explicitly or implicitly again, such as defining sales territories, providing rebates according to certain standards, dispatching salespeople, and appointing specific merchants as suppliers to retailers.

These requirements sometimes came into conflict with anti-monopoly law which was enforced in 1947; there are long-standing discussions as to whether or not these practices are anti-competitive (e.g. JFTC 1975, 1980, 1991, Ishida [1983] 1995, see also Morishita 1974: 155–58). It should be noted, however, when *keiretsu* retailing emerged in the 1910s to 1930s, no anti-monopoly law existed in Japan; therefore exclusive dealing and resale price maintenance were never problematic in terms of the law. Rather, vertical cooperation and harmony, illustrated by the manufacturers, familiar slogan 'mutual coexistence and mutual prosperity (*kyo-zon kyo-ei*)' (e.g. see Ishihara 2004), were considered virtues that fit with traditional Japanese values. As will be shown in chapters 1, 2, 3 and 6 as exemplified by the field of sweets, cosmetics and household electric appliances, the arrangement of *keiretsu* retailing played an essential role in manufacturer-led marketing and exerted strong influences on consumption in modern Japan.

An important component in retailer-led marketing is 'retail formats (*kouri gyotai*)' or retail institutions, as exemplified by department stores, chain stores, supermarkets, convenience stores, and so forth. The retail format is defined in this book as a particular pattern, a bundle of benefits the marketers deliver through the retail marketing mix, a combination of such factors as store locations, types and designs of the stores, images and atmosphere of the stores, and/or non-store selling (place), width and depth of product assortments (products), retail price levels (prices), and over-the-counter or face-to-face selling plus providing special services and/or selling by self-service (promotion). Dawson (2005) emphasises the relationship between retail 'format' and 'formula'.

> The formats are the generic delivery vehicles of retailers, for example, hypermarket, department store, convenience store, mail order catalogue, vending machine, etc. and the formula is the branded version of the format that is created by a particular firm. Thus, a hypermarket is the format and the Tesco hypermarket, Casino hypermarket, Carrefour hypermarket, and Real hypermarket are the different formulae.
>
> (Dawson 2005: 96)[3]

In the modern history of Japanese retailing, Japanese marketers observed and studied a particular 'format' that had been already generated and prevailed in Western countries, and attempted to follow it. In this introduction process, however, each Japanese marketer, consciously or unconsciously, revised it and pursued his own 'formula' to approach Japanese consumers appropriately within Japanese society and culture. As will be seen in chapters 4, 5 and 7, however, the formulae that Japanese marketers created shared some common features. The result they produced can be called the Japanese version of the format.

From such perspectives, this book will explore how the Japanese version of modern Western marketing and consumption developed in Japan. The book is divided into two major periods: from c.1905 to 1937 (Part I) and from the end of the Second World War to the present (Part II). Each part will open with a brief description on the historical settings of the period concerned.

A theoretical note on *keiretsu* relationships

The *keiretsu* phenomenon this book will explore is usually called 'distribution *keiretsu* (*ryutsu keiretsu*)'. The Japanese term '*keiretsu*' has been famous for representing features of the Japanese economy and business especially since the talks on the structural impediments to trade between Japan and the USA (RITI 1990). Nevertheless, the term tends to cover quite a wide area and be vague even in Japan.

A popular view of *keiretsu* has divided it between the horizontal and the vertical. The horizontal *keiretsu* refers to the so-called 'corporate groups or conglomerates (*kigyo shudan*)'; that is, Mitsui, Mitsubishi and Sumitomo, which originated in the so-called *zaibatsu* groups in the interwar period, and the new groups of Fuyo, Daiichi-Kangin and Sanwa organised in the postwar period. The defining feature is cross-industrial; they have been called 'one-set groups'. Each group, despite some differences, has banks (city and trust type) as its core members and includes many companies across the sectors: commerce (export and import), mining, construction, foods, textiles, paper, chemical, petroleum, ceramics, steel, nonferrous metal, machinery, electrical apparatus, automobile, precision machine, real estate, maritime and land carriage, warehousing industries, and so forth (see, e.g., Okumura 1978, 2000, Shimotani 1993). It is well known that some measures, such as mutual shareholding among the member companies, preferential financing to members or the so-called 'main bank' system, regular luncheon/dinner meetings of presidents and chairmen, and systems of mutual dispatches of executives among members, have served to maintain cross-industrial groups, although the details of actual arrangements and their effects are debatable. The term *keiretsu* began to be used to indicate such arrangements in early analysis that was on the basis of oligopoly or market power theory (e.g. Tamaoki 1957: 190–1, Miyazaki 1966: 48–56, Hadley 1970: 257). This horizontal *keiretsu* phenomenon may have been the most popular outside Japan.

It should be noted, however, that not all important Japanese corporations belong to such horizontal or cross-industrial groups; some companies, such as Panasonic and Sony, started and remained independent of such arrangements. Furthermore, strong doubt has been expressed on the use of *keiretsu* for horizontal relationships (Okumura 1990: 80). This is because such horizontal relationships are based on an equal footing, while vertical ones are not. Shimotani (1993: 220) defines *keiretsu* as the relationships characterised by the fact that (1) the inter-firm trades are not one-off, but continuous and long-term, and (2) asymmetrical power exists among the participant firms, one of which takes the lead. This book follows this usage of *keiretsu*. *Keiretsu* retailing apparently shares these features.

It can be assumed that the vertical *keiretsu* is composed of three kinds of relationships: (1) the corporate group in an industry, (2) the subcontracting relationship between the manufacturer and the subcontracted producers, and (3) the marketing channel relationship between the manufacturer as a marketer and merchants (*keiretsu* wholesalers and *keiretsu* retailers).

Regarding the first of these relationships, Shimotani (1993) distinguishes the '*keiretsu* corporate groups (*keiretsu kigyo*)' from the cross-industrial corporate groups or horizontal *keiretsu*, and defines them as groups composed of the parent company (the shareholding company or the company as the head office) and its subsidiaries within an industry, as exemplified by the Panasonic group or the Sony group. This type of group is recognisable both outside and inside the cross-industrial corporate groups.

The second type is usually called 'production *keiretsu* (*seisan keiretsu*)', in which the manufacturer tends to manage a network of subcontracting manufacturers (*shitauke*) who provide half-finished products to the manufacturer as part of the production process.

The third type of relationship is called 'distribution *keiretsu* (*ryutsu keiretsu*)'. This includes two parts: the wholesale and the retail stages. At each stage, the manufacturer (either as the head office or its subsidiary) organises wholesalers and/or retailers as the members of affiliate organisations (called transaction- or contract-based *keiretsu*), and/or establishes the companies (called capital-based *keiretsu*) as the manufacturer's network. Thus, *keiretsu* wholesaling and *keiretsu* retailing are defined as the networks of wholesale or retail firms organised by the manufacturers, although the actual arrangements are multiform.

Some explanatory theories on the reason why manufacturers adopt distribution *keiretsu* have been submitted in Japanese academia, such as the critical model of monopolistic market behaviours (JFTC 1975, 1980, 1991, Ishida [1983] 1995, Morishita 1974), the power-conflict model (e.g. Ishii 1983), the relationship marketing paradigm (e.g. Ozaki 1998, and transaction-cost economics, agency theory and game theory (e.g. Nakada 1986, Maruyama 1988, Aruga 1993, Naryu 1994, Naryu and Torii 2000). This book, however, will explore the *keiretsu* relationship as a historical phenomenon. Although abstracted theoretical models tend to ignore it, the *keiretsu* relationship was produced in a particular historical context; this suggests that it was rational in that situation, but may lose rationality as that context is transforming and disappearing.

Notes

1   Bonnet (2004: 1) pointed out, 'the West is not merely a Western creation but something that many people around the world have long been imaging and stereotyping, employing and deploying'. As is well known, Said (1979: 3) criticised in his seminal book the customary view of the East and the West as the 'Western style for dominating, restructuring, and having authority over the Orient'. Nevertheless, the discourse of the West was also created outside the Western countries and utilised in a various manners; an example was Chen's (1995: 8) analysis on Occidentalism as 'a powerful anti-official discourse using the Western Others as a metaphor for a political liberation against ideological oppressions' in Post-Mao China.
2   Defining the industry-wide or sector-wide aggregate level as macromarketing may be controversial because some scholars recognised it as only 'meso-macro' (e.g. Arndt 1982, Hunt and Burnett 1982). This book, however, considers it as a macro phenomenon because this level is aggregate enough to represent a Japanese feature in marketing rather than an individual feature of a marketer.
3   See also Dawson 2001a, 2001b, Messinger and Narasimhan 1997, Burt 2010.

Part I

Marketing and consumption from c.1905 to 1937

Historical settings

Modern Japan was stimulated by the discourse of westernisation from the outset. Soon after overthrowing the feudalistic Tokugawa regime (1603–1868), which had maintained national isolationism for well over two hundred years (1633/39– 1854), the Meiji[1] government launched the movement of modernisation and westernisation called 'Civilisation and Enlightenment (*bunmei kaika*)'. With the watchwords 'Change everything (*hyakuji go-isshin*)' and 'Scrap outmoded conventions (*kyuhei daha*)', the government took a strong lead in transforming Japan into a modern and westernised society in every dimension. This movement was part of the nationalistic programme to transform Japan into a modern, wealthy and powerful nation that could rank with the Western countries dominating the world, as directly represented by the slogan to build the 'Wealthy Nation with the Strong Army (*fukoku kyohei*)'.

Soon after capturing power in 1868, the new government dissolved the old regime by replacing more than 260 feudal domains called '*han*', which had been fragmentally ruled by local lords, '*daimyo*', who had their own armies and treasuries, and establishing local prefectures ruled by prefectural governors (1871). The social ranking system, which had defined the warrior class (*samurai* or *bushi*) as the top, followed by peasant, craftsman and merchant classes, was abolished with the declaration of 'equality of all four classes' (1871), although only a small number of people (former local lords and court nobles) were appointed to the nobility (*kazoku*). The scrapping of the social ranking system meant breaking up the warrior class that was the prop and stay of the former regime. This was completed by the universal conscription system for men (1873), which denied the hereditary right to a military career monopolised by the warrior class, and by the law banning sword wearing (1876), which had been afforded only to that class, and the ordinance requiring the cutting off of the topknots (1873) that had been their symbol.

Such a breathtakingly rapid change in the political order was accompanied by policies to modernise Japan by borrowing many Western ideas and attitudes. These policies were accelerated especially after the return home in 1873 of the so-called Iwakura Delegation, which was composed of top leaders of the new government, and about 60 students (who were to be left to study abroad and actually became involved in modernising Japan in various fields later). The Delegation was originally dispatched to revise the unequal treaties which the former regime concluded in 1858, but this proposal was refused by many countries involved. Instead, the Delegation derived wide knowledge and information by their observations of many modern institutions and practices during their travels in the USA and 11 European countries, such as parliaments, government offices, factories, schools and hospitals. The strong impressions and the profound respect which the Delegation derived for the values and ideas that had caused these Western countries to progress, merged into the driving force toward westernisation.

At the same time as transforming the political order, the Meiji government started the modern school system, and introduced modern infrastructures and an economic system receptive to modern technologies and social institutions. The government implemented these ideas often by hiring Western engineers and specialists (called '*oyatoi*') on high salaries.

The government set the Educational Rule (*gakusei*) in 1872 and began primary schooling for every child. The attendance ratio increased from 28.1 per cent at more than 12,500 schools (incl. public and private) in 1873 to 51.0 per cent at more than 30,000 schools a decade later. Although the attendance of female pupils was much lower than male at first (67.2 per cent of boys and 33.6 per cent of girls in 1883), it quickly increased around the turn of the century to surpass 90 per cent in 1903 (in the case of boys this occurred in 1900). In 1912, the last year of the Meiji Era, the attendance ratio reached 98.2 per cent on average at more than 25,000 schools, 98.8 per cent of boys and 97.6 per cent of girls (SB 1988b: 212–15).

As for development of infrastructure and the economic system, the government introduced not only telegraph services (1869), postal services (1871), railway services (1872), gas street lighting (1872), telephone (1877) and electricity services (1882), but also the new monetary system with the gold standard (1870–71), a bank system based on the national law (1872–73) and the joint-stock company system (1873). Furthermore, the government built model mines and factories, such as silk reeling and cotton spinning factories, glassworks and shipbuilding yards. These premises and factories were then sold to private firms. As a result of these policies, from 1886 onward many private stock-holding companies were established in the industries such as railways, cotton spinning and coal mining – this movement is called the 'rapid increase of firms (*kigyo-bokko*)' (Takamura 1992) – and this has been generally recognised as the start of the period of the so-called Industrial Revolution in Japan. While economic historians have differed in their estimate of the completion of this period, depending on how they recognised the concept of Industrial Revolution itself, it can be considered complete by around 1900 or 1910 (Oishi 1975: 10–13). The Industrial Revolution established machine-based manufacturing not only in the light industries such as silk reeling and cotton spinning, but also in the heavy industries such as iron production, ship building and machine-tool manufacturing, and served to lead the Japanese economy to capitalism. This achievement is seen in the emergence of Japan as the single industrialised state in the Far East.

Such a dazzling reform naturally exerted many visible effects on the everyday life of ordinary people. For instance, new townscapes appeared with the introduction of new technologies and Western-style buildings. The new night views of

Tokyo illuminated by gas street lights (1874), and later arc street lamps (1882), attracted many people and made them recognise that the 'enlightenment' was bright. The opening ceremony (1872) of the railway service between Shimbashi Tokyo and Yokohama was a celebration for the country, encouraging recognition that the 'civilised' life was speedy and had a regular style according to the time-table. The government supervised the development of Ginza in Tokyo (1872–77) after a major fire, with brick-built constructions in the style of Regent Street in London (see Figure I.1), exhibiting a totally different townscape the westernisation movement could recognise.

With regard to food and drink, unfamiliar products suddenly appeared before people's eyes, such as beer, wine, milk, coffee, ice cream and beef. In the sphere of clothing, after the military adopted Western-style clothes and shoes (1866), a court suit and a court dress were defined in Western-style (1872), and the government selected a Western-style uniform for national officers, police, railway officials and post-office clerks (1870–72). The providers of these new products were adventurous entrepreneurs. They were the first marketers who scented the new possibility of the 'domain of availability of offerings' (see Introduction, Figure 0.1) expanded by the westernisation movement. While some examples will be explored in the following chapters, here is the famous instance of 'beef cooked in a pan (*ushi-nabe*)' (Hattori [1914] 1992: 89–95, Ishii 1936: 697–708,

Figure I.1 Brick-made buildings in Ginza, Tokyo.

Note: Ginza Street became a landmark in terms of the movement of civilisation and westernisation in the 1870s. After a major fire, the street was reconstructed in Western style with a row of brick buildings (1872–77), imitating Regent Street in London. Many of the original buildings were then gradually renovated or rebuilt, but the whole street was destroyed in the Great Kano Earthquake in 1923. As a result, this townscape completely disappeared.

Reproduced courtesy of Chin-ya, a restaurant of *sukiyaki* established in 1880 in Asakusa, Tokyo. (Picture was drawn in 1873)

Okada 1968: 18–42, Research Laboratory on Food Science 1971: 7–10, Yumoto 1996: 286–7). For more than a thousand years, the Japanese had widely observed a taboo in their meat diet which is believed to have come from the vulgarisation of a tenet of Buddhism; now, as early as 1862, a brave restaurateur called Isekuma overcame his wife's strong opposition and began to offer beef to foreign people in the residential area of Yokohama. The Meiji government itself powerfully supported this new dietary habit, by publicising in 1872 that the Emperor officially ate beef. Thus, 'beef cooked in a pan', although seasoned with typical Japanese flavourings, soy sauce (*shoyu*) and sugar (*sato*) (Yumoto 1966: 286), became a symbol of the westernisation movement; as a popular novelist, Kanagaki Robun ([1871] 1995: 5), described, 'without distinction of which class they used to belong to, the warrior, the peasant, the artisan or the merchant, without distinction of age or sex, and without distinction of the rich and the poor, any folks who dare not eat beef cooked in a pan are neither civilised nor enlightened'.

It should be noted, however, that the alterations fundamentally came from the upper echelon of society. This meant that no matter how practical these revolutionary changes were, it took a long time for them to penetrate every dimension of daily life for almost all Japanese consumers. The consuming habits people had acquired over time were not easily changed. Some adventurous consumers explored new products and services, but changing overall consumption patterns to Western ones, or more precisely, to a Japanese form of them, needed time. There were plenty of interesting stories of interplay between marketers, who solicited consumers to accept unfamiliar products and services, and consumers, who tried them timidly at first, and enthusiastically welcomed them in the end. This will be the focus of Part I.

The dazzling transformation of society brought about by importation of many Western things was supported by the view that the 'essence of being a Japanese patriot was to embrace change' by the early 1880s, but questions arose about the Japanese identity (Gordon 2003: 111). Criticisms of 'Westernisationism (*ookashugi*)' grew, censuring the accommodating attitude to the West. A target of this criticism was the events at Rokumei-kan (a Western-styled two-storey house made of brick constructed by a British architect in 1883), which was the setting for a series of Sunday evening balls to invite foreign dignitaries and Japanese women wearing bustle-style dresses. The events were sponsored by the Foreign Minister and aimed at amendment of unequal treaties (McClain 2002: 181, Tanabe 2010: 305–6). Conservatives also increasingly insisted on the necessity of 'preservation of nationality (*kokusui hozon*)', although as Pyle (1969) described, some leading advocates of this concept were not the hardliners, but open-minded nationalists who had already gained westernised education and recognised the value of Western civilisation. Furthermore, especially after the victories in the First Sino-Japanese War (1894–5) and the Russo-Japanese War (1904–5), a chauvinistic mindset spread in society.

This narrow-minded, aggressive version of nationalism did not wholly sweep across the country until 1937 when the Second Sino-Japanese War was ignited and the wartime regime, which was to lead to the Pacific War (1941–45), was established. Rather, the years from c.1905 to 1925 have been called the period of 'Taisho democracy'[1] (see Shinobu 1954, 1958, 1959, Matsuo 2001, Narita 2007), when various types of liberalistic ideas and movements developed in Japanese society, such as the idea of democracy (called '*minpon-shugi*'), the movement towards universal suffrage, the labour movement, the women's movement, local residents' campaigns, etc. Along with the political movements, 'Taisho democracy', 'Taisho modernism (*Taisho modern*)' and 'Taisho romanticism (*Taisho roman*)' were recognised in a new awareness of a modern sense of the self and individuality and a recognition of free love which threw off the yoke of traditional relationships. European art movements became popular, such as Aestheticism, Art Nouveau, Expressionism or Dadaism, with popularisation of illustrations, pictures and music. Mass media such as newspapers, magazines and radio became popular, and town-scapes were transformed with Western-style buildings, billboards and crowded shopping streets. The cities welcomed the employment associated with modern entertainments such as cafés, beer saloons, ballrooms, theatres, movies and department stores, although the gap widened between urban life and rural life and between the haves and the have-nots. While Japan borrowed many influences from the West, she assimilated and made them Japanese, not only during the 'Taisho' period described above but through several decades of the early twentieth century.

Many of these changes, though not all, had strongly to do with the interplay between the marketers and the consumers, as Part I of this book illustrates. The years from c.1905 to 1937, that is, roughly from the end of the Russo-Japanese War to the establishment of the wartime regime, saw the westernisation movement begin to penetrate for the first time into the everyday life of ordinary consumers on a massive scale, far beyond their experience so far. These changes progressed on the basis of the establishment of capitalism, in which many marketers recognised the scope of expansion in the goods they could offer (see Figure 0.1) not only provided by westernisation itself but also by the progress of industrialisation, and created their new marketing strategy to attract consumers to accept unfamiliar Western-like products and services. Part I will focus on some interesting stories about this process.

Notes

1 The name 'Meiji', also the name 'Taisho' that will appear below, originated in the names of imperial eras. Japan adopted this system for the first time in 645, following the system in China. Modern Japan has had the following era names:
The Meiji Era: 1868 to 1912
The Taisho Era: 1912 to 1926
The Showa Era: 1926 to 1989
The Heisei Era: 1989 (to current time).
2 The period called 'Taisho democracy', as well as 'Taisho romanticism' and 'Taisho modernism', is not exactly the same as Taisho Era, which the period of imperial era name defines. These words only suggest that Taisho Era was the main period for these tendencies.

1 'Reeks of butter and milk'?

Marketing of Western-style sweets through the *keiretsu* retail network

Food and drink are among the most familiar materials in the everyday life of consumers. Although the westernisation movement being initiated from the upper echelons of society was accompanied by various fragmented attempts to offer Western-style diet by innovative individuals, it was not until the 1910s that mass marketing could win consumers' support on a large scale. This chapter will show how such modern marketing progressed in the food and drink sector, especially by focusing on marketing of confectionery. The reason for this focus was that the first immense success was achieved by a manufacturer of Western-style sweets, Morinaga.

Confectionery in Japan is distinguished between Japanese-style sweets (*wa-gashi*) and Western-style sweets (*yo-gashi*) according to the everyday termi-nology, although the distinction tends to be somewhat vague. What are usually called Japanese-style sweets originally came from China, tracing their import as far back as around the eighth century (Sakurai and Adachi 1973: 211–17), but had been adopted, modified and incorporated into the Japanese diet over a long time. In contrast, Western-style sweets were introduced around the Meiji Restoration; they appeared in front of people's eyes as part of the westernisation movement. However, the consumers' preferences had been adjusted to the traditional sweets, so the consumers often resisted the unfamiliar Western tastes. An amazing success of marketing by Morinaga provided representative evidence of changes in the preferences of Japanese consumers, that on a massive scale, people were begin-ning to enjoy modern Western-style tastes in their everyday life.

Before consideration of Morinaga's case, this chapter will explore three issues. The first part will take an overview on the historical conditions in which *keiretsu* retailing appeared in Japan, because Morinaga's success depended on the full use of the *keiretsu* network. While the definition of *keiretsu* was given in the Introduction, historical analysis of this format can be useful for a preparatory work not only for the consideration of this chapter, but also for the following chapters.

Second, while the success of Morinaga was the first case of mass marketing in the food sector, some innovative small- and medium-sized marketers were also emerging. Their influences were limited, but some urban consumers occasionally experienced their new marketing strategies. Increasing numbers of such marketers in the specific urban areas helped to shape the social atmosphere spread by modern Western-like eating habits, and indirectly encouraged the mass marketing of Western-style sweets. Here will be examined three innovative cases of attempts by small-sized marketers in the fields of restaurant and food retail.

The third part will investigate bread marketing by the small- and medium-sized marketers. The reason for taking the case of bread is that Japanese consumers had a tendency to accept bread as part of Western-style sweets rather than goods for staple meals, because they had eaten rice as their staple diet, so that bread tended to conflict with the position of rice in their everyday meals. Marketing and consumption of bread and Western-style sweets progressed hand in hand in the early years of modern Japan. The exploration in this part will provide a wider picture of marketing and consumption of Western-style sweets.

Chain stores and *keiretsu* retailing: manufacturers take the lead

Emergence of what is now called *keiretsu* retailing can be identified as part of the introduction process of the modern concept of chain stores or multiples to Japan from the USA and the UK.

Despite the rapid progress of industrialisation, development in the retail sector was largely delayed; the great majority of retailers remained in their traditional state. While the self-sufficient system of everyday necessities still remained in the rural areas (e.g. Yamamoto 1999: 3), there existed many traditional fairs to which people gathered bringing something to sell and markets that were run privately all over Japan, even in the 1910s[1] (Nakamura 2002: 39–87). There were many street stalls especially in the poor areas (e.g. see Mizu'uchi 2004), and many tiny stores depending on the traditional operations such as intimate face-to-face selling, credit sales with later collections and visiting customers regularly to take orders.

Under such conditions, the concept of chain stores or multiples, which had already developed well in the 1910s–20s in the USA and in the UK (see Lebhar 1959, Jefferys 1954), was introduced to Japan for the first time in the 1910s. Teiitsu Kuwatani, who was an editor of *The Business World* (*Jitsugyo-kai*), one of the early business journals – started as *The World of Commerce* (*Shogyo-kai*) in 1904 and re-named in 1910 (Sugihara 1990: 228) – and soon changed his profession by joining Nakayama Taiyo-do (one of the leading cosmetics manufacturers, see Chapter 2), explained as early as 1912 the new concept of 'linkage store (*renkei shoten*)', which was 'corresponding to what are called "multiple stores" in the UK' (Kuwatani 1912: 112). According to him,

> The linkage store is the system, in which the goods that the central organisation, *i.e.* the head office, buys (or produces) in huge quantities – and therefore at lower prices – are sold separately through its own retail shops located at various places. Perhaps, the name of the linkage stores (*renkei sho-ten*) appears here in this sentence for the first time in Japan.
>
> (Kuwatani 1912: 112, see also 1913: 389)

Current academics (e.g. AOEB 1983: 230, Yahagi 2004: 220, Kono 2005: 72, Hirano 2008: 175–6) recognise that this commentary by Kuwatani was the first introduction of the concept of chain stores into Japan. Kon Enjoji, a contemporary commentator who was occasionally mistakenly credited with the first introduction of this concept, admitted himself in 1917, 'Mr Teiitsu Kuwatani . . . introduced quite a while ago the concept of chain stores the author wants to introduce now', and emphasised, 'What is called chain stores in the USA is corresponding to what is called multiple stores in the UK' (Enjoji 1917: 228). Following their introductions, some other opinion leaders in business (e.g. Shimizu 1920, 1924, 1928, Kuramoto 1924, Otsuka 1926) advocated this concept by translating the term as '*rensa-ten*' or '*chain store*' in *katakana* characters. Around the late 1920s, this concept was frequently mentioned in articles in newspapers (e.g. *Chugai Commercial New*s 1927, 1928, 1931b, *Osaka Mainichi Newspaper* 1929, *Kobe Yushin Daily News* 1929, *Osaka Asahi Newspaper* 1930).

Based on such recommendations, some pioneering attempts started in the 1920s–30s. However, development of any variants of chain stores was slow and limited – whether the corporate chain (the network of retail shops owned by one retail company), the retailer cooperatives (organised contractually by independent retailers by establishing their mutual buying offices) or the voluntary groups (the retail networks sponsored by a wholesaler).

In the case of corporate chains, which were often called the 'genuine chain (*junsei chain*)' in Japanese at the time or have been called the '*regular chain*' in Japanese English thus far, the number and the size were limited, covering only a few specific regions such as the areas of Tokyo, Osaka and/or Nagoya. The investigation in 1935 by the Ministry of Commerce and Industry (MCI 1935a) recognised only eight chains as the 'genuine chain'. These existed in the fields of food, restaurants, clothing, hats and shoes, drugs, and stores selling with limited prices (usually called variety chains), and the number of their branch stores was about 10 to 100 at the largest. As a contemporary commentator pointed out, 'it would be safe to say that the genuine chain stores in our country were still at the infant stage as a whole' (Nasu 1935: 13).

Regarding the retailer cooperatives and the voluntary groups, these were lumped together as the 'spontaneity chain store (*nin'i rensa-ten*)', 'comrade chain store (*doshi rensa-ten*)' or '*voluntary chain*' in *katakana* characters. This type of chain stores was especially recommended as a 'measure for rescuing the poverty-stricken retailers (*kouri kosei saku*)' (e.g. Taniguchi 1933, Ito 1934a, *Osaka Jiji News* 1934, Manda 1935, 1938) in the 1930s under the severe depression of business conditions. The retailer cooperatives were organised in the trades of traditional Japanese foods and Western-style clothing, stationery, shoes, drugs, and cosmetics and everyday items (*komamono Kesho-hin*). Nevertheless, these organisations were generally not large, with membership between 10 and 70. As for the voluntary group as currently defined, there was only one organisation identifiable in the trade of Western-style shoes with only ten member stores in Tokyo.

It should be noted that the *keiretsu* retail networks defined by this book were also included in what was named 'spontaneity chain store', 'comrade chain store' or '*voluntary chain*' in *katakana* characters.[2] Table 1.1 shows the actual examples

Table 1.1 Manufacturers' *keiretsu* retail chains

Name	Starting year of chain	Maximum number of participating retailers (year)	Parent manufacturer	Features
Western-style medicine				
Hoshi Chain Store	1911	35,000 or 50,000	Hoshi Pharmaceutical Co., Ltd.	Stores were granted franchise, and served through exclusive wholesalers.
Taisho Coexistence Association (later, Taisho Chain)	1928	3,492 (1936)	Taisho Pharmaceutical Co., Ltd.	Retailers owned the shares of Taisho Pharmaceutical.
Hyotan-ya Pharmacy SS Chain Store	1929	1,500	Hyotan-ya Pharmacy Co.	The manufacturer provided rebates to affiliated retailers.
Arita Drug Store	1931	500	Arita Drug Co.	Exclusive retailers. Arita Drug Co. also had 50 own stores.
Daimai Home Drug Chain Store	n.a.	2,000	Manufacturing Agent of Osaka Mainichi Newspaper Co.	Tobacco retailers joined the chain organisation to provide cheap home medicine, served through agencies.
Western-style sweets				
Morinaga Candy Store [A] Morinaga Belt-Line Store [B]	1923 [A] 1928 [B]	45 [A] 4,000 [B]	Morinaga & Co., Ltd.	Manufacturer's own retail shops [A], and exclusive retailers [B]; both served through wholesale companies.
Meiji Seika Confectionery Sales Outlet	1923	51 (1935)	Meiji Seika Kaisha Ltd.	Manufacturer's own retail stores served through Meiji Shoji, the wholesale stage.
Western-style cosmetics				
Shiseido Chain Store	1923	7,000 (1932)	Shiseido Co. Ltd.	Exclusive retailers served through wholesale companies.
Club Chain Store	1925	10,000 (1935)	Nakayama Taiyo-do	Served through 250 affiliated wholesalers. The manufacturer is now called Club Cosmetics.

(Continued)

Table 1.1 Continued

Name	Starting year of chain	Maximum number of participating retailers (year)	Parent manufacturer	Features
Electrical products				
Authorised Dealer [*beiri-ten*] of Mazda Lamp	1932	49 (1933)	Tokyo Electric Co., Ltd.	An authorised dealer was organised in each prefecture. Also, 350 Mazda Associations gave support to retailers.
To-Lamp Chain Store	1933	1,000 (1935)	To-den Electric Lightbulb Co., Ltd. (electric lightbulbs)	Exclusive retailers granted franchise. The manufacturer was a subsidiary of Tokyo Electric Light Co., Ltd.
Matsushita Associate Store [*Renmei-ten*]	1935	10,000 (1941)	Matsushita Electric Industrial Co., Ltd. and its subsidiaries (battery lamps, radio sets, etc.)	*Keiretsu* retailers organised by Panasonic [Matsushita]. These stores served through affiliated wholesalers.
Traditional split-toe socks				
Fukusuke Association	1934	n.a.	Fukusuke Tabi Co., Ltd.	The retailers who sold more than 2,000 split-toe socks could join. The association provided educational services and mutual exchanges of information on business.

Sources: The Retail Shop World 1929a, 1929b, 1935, Ministry of Commerce and Industry 1935a, Association for Open Education of Business 1967: 179–84, 1983: 228–35, Suzuki 1980: 141–6, Ozaki 1989, Nagao 2002, Kono 2005: 74, Hirano 2007: 179.

of *keiretsu* networks organised by manufacturers at the time. As many of these networks suffixed 'chain store' in *katakana* characters to their names, the manufacturers recognised their networks as a variant of the format of chain stores. In the case of Morinaga Belt-Line Store, which is a focus in this chapter, although the name did not take the words 'chain store', Hanzaburo Matsuzaki, who was responsible for marketing by Morinaga, laid emphasis on the necessity for improvements for traditional retailers to join the *keiretsu* network: 'Today there is a growing tendency to introduce chain stores to Japan; the fated day for improving the old sweets stores seems to be approaching' (Matsuzaki 1923b).

Importantly, the number of stores in these *keiretsu* networks generally reached some thousands or even more, in sharp contrast with 100 at the most that were organised as other types of chain stores by retailers themselves. Thus, only the networks of retailers led by the manufacturers developed on a huge scale. This fact suggests that some manufacturers, who were confronted with the necessity of nationwide distribution of their products, rushed for organising retailers, who were still generally in the traditional state and did not have ability (business resources and knowledge) enough to develop the mass marketing channels by themselves.

Table 1.1 shows that the industries in which the *keiretsu* networks developed were related to modern Western products; that is, Western-style medicine, sweets, cosmetics and modern electric goods, with the only exception of traditional split-toe socks.[3] As will be explored below,[4] the manufacturers of these products needed the modern retail outlets that could diffuse their products efficiently on a large scale as soon as they established the mass production system. Encountering resistance by traditional merchants to the trading terms that the manufacturers offered, initial hesitation of consumers to adopt these products, and keen competition with other manufacturers after consumers began to accept these products, positively encouraged the manufacturers to develop their exclusive networks. It was through these *keiretsu* retail networks that they promoted mass consumption of modern Western-like products by Japanese consumers. This and the following chapters will explore these examples in depth.

Innovative small-sized chain stores in the food sector: cases of restaurants and a meat retailer

Mass marketing of Western-style sweets did not succeed alone, but was supported by wider ongoing changes in food habits, which were being solicited by many small-sized marketers. Some of them were innovatively attempting to take on board the new concept of chain stores. On some occasions, their networks contained traditional features.

There was a tradition in Japan of replicating store names; therefore, there were originally many organisations presenting stores made to look similar to chain stores. The systems were the 'bestowing the store name (*noren-wake*)', in which the master awarded the privilege of setting up a branch with the same prestigious store name or store brand ('*noren*') to the senior clerks after they had served the shop as apprentices for a long time, and the 'cadet families (*bun-ke*)', in which brothers, sisters and relatives were allowed to have independent houses under the same family name. These traditional systems of replicating store names were not classified as chain stores by contemporary commentators (e.g. see Enjoji 1917: 239–40, *Chugai Commercial New*s 1929a). Nevertheless, several instances that were recognised as modern chain stores sometimes included some traditional features as well. Therefore, Masami Shimizu (1924), a contemporary opinion leader who encouraged modernisation of retailing by publishing a popular business journal, *The Retail Shop World* (*Shoten-kai*) from 1920 (see Nishimura 1999), called these organisations the 'quasi-chain store (*jun-chain store*)' and indicated that there were many such cases in food and restaurant chains; e.g. Nakamuraya Bread Stores (sweet buns, see below), Fugetsudo (Japanese- and Western-style sweets, see below), Eitaro Sweets (Japanese-style sweets), Toyo-ken (restaurants), Seiyo-ken (restaurants), and Mikado (restaurants) (Shimizu 1924). The following are a few advanced cases in the food sector; one was in tradition, while the others were disconnected from the traditional systems.

Miyoshino (see *Chugai Commercial News* 1929b, *The Retail Shop World* 1929a: 72, 1929b: 98–101) was known as a transitional case with a mixture of the old and the new ideas. This was a restaurant chain serving *shiruko*, a traditional sweet porridge made of red beans (*azuki*) with rice-flour dumplings. This restaurant started in 1909 in Tokyo, and developed the network to more than 40 by 1923 and to around 100 by 1929, mainly in the Tokyo area, while nine restaurants were located in local cities or foreign territories. The network was organised at first based on the traditional system of bestowing the store name. As the network expanded, however, the new members could participate in the organisation by buying the store name, Miyoshino, without any apprenticeship. They could join the Miyoshino League (*Miyoshino Domei-kai*) with monthly payment of membership fees. The head office and the leading officers of the Miyoshino League decided the store location, storefront appearance, procurement of raw materials, product quality and prices, while each restaurant was operated by its own account with its own cooking, with some exceptions delivered from the head office. In due course, menus were expanding to include Western-style cakes, soda water and coffee. A news reporter put it, 'I don't know for certain, but I feel the atmosphere inside the restaurants of Miyoshino is gradually modernising' (*The Retail Shop World* 1929b: 101).

In contrast, the restaurant chain, Hongo Bars (see *Chugai Commercial News* 1929a, *The Retail Shop World* 1929a: 71, 1929b: 66–71) was recognised as 'one of the most similar examples to the chain organisations' (*Chugai Commercial News* 1929a) in Western countries. They started a small-sized restaurant around 1916–17 after some trial and error attempts, and developed the network of subsidiaries as a corporate chain of 36 in Tokyo, one in Yokohama and five in Sendai, by 1929. Each restaurant hired employees responsible for management, accounting, cooking and serving. Every morning, the head office delivered food materials to be cooked at each restaurant by car to its premises within Tokyo. The head office bought ingredients in large quantities by cash to procure them at cheaper prices, and even ran a piggery with 4,000 to 5,000 pigs in a suburb of Tokyo as part of their sourcing business.

Hongo Bars served cheap 'Western-style dishes (*yo-shoku*)', such as a dish for a croquette (*korokke*) at 5 *cen*, a pork cutlet at 8 *cen*, a curry with rice (*curry rice*) at 15 *cen*, and beef cooked in a pan (*ushi-nabe*) at 25 *cen* ('*cen*' is the old monetary unit, representing one hundredth of a '*yen*'). These recipes represented the progress of the Japanese approach to Westernised cuisines (see MP 1954: 211–12, Higuchi 1960: 251–3, Yumoto 1996: 294–5), in that these were cooked with Japanese flavourings by utilising what people recognised as 'Western ingredients' (pork and beef, eating of which were taboo before modern Japan, and curry, which powder was imported for the first time from a British company, Crosse &

Blackwell) and a dish of Western origin such as pork cutlets and croquettes. These recipes for Western-style dishes are often recognised as part of the history of so-called 'Taisho modernism', while these are so popular in everyday life nowadays that many people might be tricked into thinking they were Japanese in origin.

An example of one of the most advanced attempts was Tokyo Meat Stores (see *Chugai Commercial News* 1931a, Suzuki 1980: 135–6). This was a corporate chain in Tokyo composed of 14 meat shops by 1931. These stores procured meat at its buying office in Qingdao China, and sold it only at limited prices: at 30-, 50- and 80-*cen* or at 20-, 30- and 50-*cen*. This pricing policy was perhaps influenced by an emergent variety chain, Takashima-ya 10- and 20-*cen* Stores organised by a leading department store of that name, which was an exceptional case in chain stores led by a modern retailer with plentiful resources and knowledge (see Chapter 3). Another progressivity was the introduction of a streamlined way of selling. Their stores were located at busy places such as in front of the stations of street railways; the customer paid for the meat at a cash register first and received a ticket, then handed it to a clerk who wrapped the meat that had already been cut and served on each plate. It was reported with amazement that it took less than one minute for the customer from paying cash to possessing the package.

Thus, some small-sized marketers in the food sector began to try adopting the new concept of chain stores with their innovative spirit. Although their direct influence was limited and occasional, they were the advanced marketers among the increasingly small, personal and individual restaurants and stores offering Western-style food.

Marketing of bread as part of Western-style sweets

Marketing of sweet buns: Kimuraya and its bestowing the store name

Focusing on the field of confectionery, the long history of Japanese-style sweets had produced many traditional wholesalers and retailers. Their real number is, unusually, readily available in this industry because the government needed the data in order to impose the confectionery tax on each establishment between 1885 and 1896. According to these statistics, in FY1885 there were 7,038 wholesalers and 103,392 retailers, and in FY1896 there were 9,318 wholesalers and 161,949 retailers (CSB [1887] 1963a: 160, [1896] 1963b: 526). Amazingly, these numbers were quite a bit larger than their current counterparts: as of 2007, there were 6,001 wholesalers of bread and/or sweets and only 66,177 retailers (METI website 1). However, unlike the current data, almost all merchants in the nineteenth century dealt with Japanese-style sweets.

Among them a few pioneers began to deal in Western-style sweets. For instance, Fugetsudo, who had been a prestigious producer-cum-retailer of Japanese-style sweets since the mid-nineteenth century, began to produce biscuits, bonbons and cakes in 1868 (Ishii 1936: 709, Fugetsudo website). In the case of biscuits and ship's biscuits, the demand was politically created by their adoption as food rations for the military forces instead of rice because of easy preparation and portability.

Nevertheless, the demand remained generally small. Fugetsudo introduced British machinery for producing biscuits for the first time in Japan in 1889, but it is reported that the number of biscuits baked in a single day surpassed the demand in Tokyo for an entire month (NBA 1951: 59–60). Fugetsudo, nevertheless, continued its business by serving both Japanese- and Western-style sweets based on craftsmanship; the enterprise developed to nine stores by 1929 under the rigid system of bestowing the store name that awarded the name only to apprenticed employees (*Chugai Commercial New*s 1929c).

In the meantime, bread was becoming popular as part of Western-style sweets. As mentioned above, bread was in conflict with rice as the traditional staple in everyday meals. Although several pioneers such as Tsutamoto (Ishii 1936: 709) started a bakery in the early 1870s, general resistance against westernisation in this sphere was quite strong, as exemplified by the statement that those Japanese who preferred bread rather than eating rice were ranked as 'the champion (*oozeki*) of foolish people in the present time' (Ishii 1936: 709, APB 1970: 33). As a result, bread tended to be consumed as part of sweets, what has been called 'sweet bun (*kashi-pan*)', rather than part of everyday meals.

A well-known example was Kimuraya (see APB 1970, GPB 1987, Kimuraya General Head Store Co., Ltd. 1989, Ooyama 2001), a small-sized bakery originally called Bun'eido established in 1869 by Yasubei Kimura, a former member of the warrior class. In 1874, this bakery invented *an-pan*, a bun (*pan*) stuffed with traditional sweet bean paste (*an*), utilising melted rice rather than flour. At the same time, Kimuraya opened its main store on a street in Ginza in Tokyo (see Figure 1.1), which was developing into a Western-style row of brick-made buildings. When in the following year the Emperor ate *an-pan*, Kimuraya was elevated to the status of a purveyor to the Imperial Household. Kimuraya also invented *jam-pan*, a bun with a layer of jam inside, in 1899, while Nakamuraya (Nakamuraya website), another famous bakery established in 1901 by Aizo Soma, invented *cream-pan*, a bun with custard cream inside, in 1904. From that time to the present, *an-pan*, *jam-pan* and *cream-pan* have been the most popular sweet buns.

It is reported (MP 1954: 203) that *an-pan* became well known in many local areas around the turn of the twentieth century. This was due in part to journeys undertaken by Gishiro Kimura, the grandson of the founder, to teach large numbers of merchants how to bake *an-pan* (Kimuraya General Head Store Co., Ltd. 1989: 32), in part to the developing system of bestowing the store name, and in part to the increasing imitation of the recipe by bakeries. The imitators had originally no relationship with Kimuraya, but often proclaimed themselves 'Kimuraya' without any permission. According to the 1894 Commercial Directory in Tokyo (Gashu 1894: 361–9, see also APB 1970: 169), ten of 30 bakeries were named Kimuraya. In order to untangle the confusion, the Association of Hereditary Members (*seshu-kai*) of Kimuraya – later called the Organisation for Mutual Friendship (*mutsumi-kai*) – was established in 1902 by the legitimate members who had been awarded the store name. Kimuraya also opened six of its own stores in 1907 (Kimuraya General Head Store Co., Ltd. 1989: 61). However, these stores were burnt down by the Great Tokyo Earthquake in 1923, and the idea of a network of subsidiary stores did not develop after that. As

Figure 1.1 Advertising for the Kimura Bakery in Ginza, Tokyo.

Note: Kimuraya opened its main store on a street in Ginza in Tokyo in 1874. Ginza was a symbolic place for the movement of civilisation and westernisation because after the great fire in 1872, the street was rebuilt to resemble a Western-style row of brick buildings. This advertising shows the bakery area of Kimuraya attached to the store.

Reproduced courtesy of Kimuraya General Head Store.

a result, the confusing situation combining legitimate and imitation stores was not sorted out. *Chugai Commercial News* (1929b) reported in 1929 that in the Tokyo and Yokohama area, there were about 100 Kimuraya as legitimate members, but also about 300 that simply imitated the store name without any contact with the General Head Store.

The idea of the chain store network in bread marketing was developed by Maruki-go, as will be seen below, which was not originally rewarding former apprentices of Kimuraya, but the company awarded it an honorary store name using a trade mark combining the character '*ki*' within a circle ('*maru*'), designed to signify some relationship with Kimuraya (Kimuraya General Head Store Co., Ltd. 1989: 38).

Development of corporate chains for bread marketing, and beyond

As industrialisation progressed, the mass production system in manufacturing was established also in the infrastructure industries for production of bread and sweets. In the flour milling industry, the traditional system of water milling began to be replaced by machine mills, firstly by government-run factories, and then by private companies. The large-sized manufacturers, such as Nippon Flour Mills Co., Ltd. established in 1896 and Tatebayashi Mills Co., Ltd. in 1900 (which changed to Nisshin Mills Co., Ltd. in 1908), took a lead in production, and supplanted imported flour for bread and sweets with their own Japanese products especially after the First World War. In the sugar refining industry also, large-sized companies, such as Nippon Sugar Refining Co., Ltd. established in 1895 (changed to Great Nippon Sugar Refining Co., Ltd. in 1906), Taiwan Sugar Refining Co., Ltd. in 1900, and Meiji Sugar Refining Co., Ltd. in 1906, began to provide good quality sugar in large quantities. Such development of infrastructural industries became the basis for the widespread acceptance of *an-pan* and sweet bun production.

Nevertheless, a bread diet for everyday meals was not easily accepted, other than by such people as foreigners staying in Japan, students who came back from studying abroad, and pupils studying at private schools based on Christianity (which mission was officially allowed in 1873 by removing the long-standing bans from 1587). The bread diet only drew public attention when the price of rice increased rapidly. The nationwide rice riots (*kome sodo*), which broke out spontaneously on 23 July 1918 among housewives in a local city protesting at the soaring prices of rice, rapidly expanded and continued to 11 September all over Japan, involving several million people (Inoue and Watanabe 1959), acted as a stimulus for increased interest in an alternative diet of bread.

Maruki-go Bread Stores (see *The Retail Shop World*, 1929a 73, 1929b: 88–90, 1935: 14, MCI 1935a: 3–8, AOEB 1967: 173, 1983: 254–7, APB 1970) took full advantage of this occasion. This company has been generally recognised as the very first corporate chain in Japan (*The Retail Shop World* 1935: 14, MCI 1935a: 3, AOEB 1967: 173). Established as a small-sized bakery in Osaka in 1905 by Masajiro Mizutani, a broker of flour, Maruki-go opened three subsidiary shops in 1912 employing two sales clerks in each. Although the founder was not apprenticed to Kimuraya, he awarded an honorary trade mark combining the character '*ki*' within a circle ('*maru*'), designed to suggest some relationship with Kimuraya (Kimuraya General Head Store Co., Ltd. 1989: 38). On the occasion of the rice riot, Maruki-go Bread Stores held back prices of bread, so that many consumers crowded around the stores. The company expanded the store network to 37 by 1929 and 49 by 1938 in the Osaka area, becoming the leading bakery there. The stores were located near the stations of suburban railways or the crossroad stations of street railways, so that the customers belonging to the working middle class bought bread on the way home or their wives travelled from home to buy it. Each store carried a big roof signboard, but had a traditional exterior representing Japanese houses, and included many glass cases displaying bread samples at the front of the store. Customers put money on any glass case displaying their chosen bread, and then the sales clerk wrapped that bread. Thus, the operation looked fairly efficient.

In the meantime, the owner, Masajiro, made an observation tour to the USA and European countries in 1924; this was the first observation tour by the head of a bakery in the Osaka area, and produced plentiful results. Firstly, he began to utilise baking yeast, at first by importing it, then by producing it for the first time in Japan. Maruki-go earned a good reputation for their yeast bread. Secondly, he decided to introduce machinery for baking. Kimuraya had first attempted to produce bread by machine around 1902, but without success. Maruki-go established the first full-scale factory in Osaka equipped with three travelling ovens and other machines in 1926 (APB 1970: 393–5). Bread was delivered from the factory to each store every morning by trucks. It is clear that Maruki-go was growing from a producer-cum-retailer with craftsmanship to a mass producer of bread with operating factory management. In this sense, the feature of this store network was transforming from a corporate chain by a retailer to a *keiretsu* retail network led by a manufacturer.

Shikishima Baking Co., Ltd. (see *The Retail Shop World*, 1929a 73, 1929b: 80–87, AOEB 1983: 257, APB 1970, PASCO website) expanded the Maruki-go way. This company was established in 1919 in Nagoya as a subsidiary of Shikishima Flour Milling Co., Ltd., which was founded in 1899. Inviting a skilful baker from Germany, Shikishima Baking Co., opened its own retail store in 1920. The company introduced machinery in 1928, and established a factory using electric ovens in 1932. Along with this development, the company organised not only a network of its own retail stores numbering five by 1929 and 12 by 1933, but also about 120 contracted retailers, who were originally sweets retailers, by 1929 in the Nagoya area. These stores dealt in bread and cakes produced by Shikishima Baking under the same red signboard presenting 'Shikishima'. Thus, as Shikishima became a mass producer of bread and organised its affiliated network, its stores can also be evaluated as a *keiretsu* network, rather than a corporate chain, although the operating area still remained regional.

Both Maruki-go and Shikishima not only sold bread, but also offered Western-style sweets such as Shikishima's cream puffs; Maruki-go's established an in-store milk bar promoting bread and sweets. These ingenuities reflected a campaign to increase consumption of bread. After the Second World War, bread-based school lunch was introduced and bread-based breakfast was gradually spreading. Nevertheless, bread could not eventually replace rice as a staple of everyday diets. It can be said that bread consumption as part of sweets rather than for everyday meals was a Japanese feature.[5]

Mass marketing and mass consumption of Western-style sweets: the role of *keiretsu* retailers in the case of Morinaga

From negative to positive images of butter and milk

Morinaga developed a national network of *keiretsu* retail shops. This company did not get involved in bread production, but confined its business to the confectionery area. Morinaga's marketing was a representative case in the industry of Western-style sweets before the Second World War, inducing changes in the consumption pattern of sweets.

Taichiro Morinaga, the company founder (Morinaga & Co., Ltd. 1954, 2000), had been trained in the production of Western-style sweets in the USA for 11 years, and set up a small shop, named Morinaga Mill of Western-style Sweets (*Morinaga Seiyo-kashi Seizo-jo*), on a side street in Tokyo's Akasaka district in 1899. The macroenvironment was favourable: the government, which had regained the right to set tariffs which it had lost when it first drew up treaties with foreign countries, imposed a 40 per cent import duty on sweets in the same year. This high tariff substantially encouraged the domestic production of Western-style sweets.

An early factor paving the way for Morinaga to become a mass marketer was its definition in the distributive channel not as a producer-cum-retailer, but as a producer or a producer-cum-wholesaler (Tamaki 1967: 337–9). Unlike other pioneers such as Fugetsudo and Kimuraya, which produced and sold perishable products within a specific region, Morinaga's positioning had a potential for advancing mass marketing by overcoming geographical limitations in distribution. At first, Morinaga provided perishable sweets such as cakes and pies in accordance with individual requests, but the product lines were gradually shifted to sweets with a long shelf-life, like marshmallows and candy, appropriate for a producer-cum-wholesaler. In 1905, Taichiro invited Hanzaburo Matsuzaki to become his right-hand man with responsibility for marketing, while Taichiro was responsible for production. In 1909, the company entered into mass production of sweets by establishing a factory with a steam engine, and became publicly listed in the next year.

However, early growth was slow. Japanese consumers traditionally disliked unfamiliar smells of milk and butter, and believed that 'biscuits stink with soap' (APB 1970: 273). Taichiro himself believed that some Western ingredients like caramel would never suit Japanese tastes given that it 'reeked of milk and butter' (Morinaga & Co., Ltd. 1954: 62). This negative image was so strong for the Japanese that it is believed that the Japanese slang term '*bata-kusai*', showing a negative image of Westerners explicitly, can be traced back to the 'reek of butter'. Therefore, Morinaga had to persuade hesitant consumers carefully while they improved products to make them more acceptable. Early advertisements emphasised the suitability of Western-style sweets for the Japanese physical constitution: 'It will never cause any stomach diseases no matter how many sweets you eat' (1906 advertisement).

In 1914 there was major progress. Morinaga put Milk Caramels – 20 pieces of caramel candies wrapped individually with wax paper and contained in a paper case with the trademark of Angel, selling at 10-*cen* – onto the market and caused a great stir among consumers. Morinaga's biannual report stated, 'Orders for Milk Caramel continually flooded in and surpassed the existing production capacity, so that delivery of these ordered products tended to be much delayed. It was after the second factory hurried to start its operation in late July that the orders only just managed to be fulfilled on time' (Morinaga & Co., Ltd. 1915: 228–9). This boom suggested that the Western smell came to be accepted by Japanese consumers; rather, it became a promotional factor in marketing. The strong influence of this product on Japanese consumer society is shown by the fact that since then, for many Japanese consumers, the word '*caramel*' in Japanese *katakana* characters has basically meant caramel candy or hard caramel such as Milk Caramel, rather than the broad range of confections derived from the caramelisation of any type of sugar.

The boom in Milk Caramels raised Morinaga to the lead in the Western-style sweets industry. Based on this success, Morinaga began to adopt the full-line product policy by diversifying into the so-called 'five major product lines'; that is, chocolates, biscuits, drops and milk-related products, in addition to caramels. To pursue this diversification strategy, however, Morinaga again confronted a difficulty due to consumers' hesitation. Especially in the case of chocolate, a popular sentiment was that 'chocolate is too bitter for Japanese tastes'. In order to overcome this negative sentiment, Morinaga expanded the brand Milk Caramel to Milk Chocolate, so that it suggested mild rather than bitter. Morinaga put an advertisement in the trains in 1919 emphasising that chocolate was a proud new taste of the Japanese, 'Morinaga's Milk Chocolate, On behalf of modern Japanese tastes'. Morinaga started mass production of chocolate in 1918 for the first time in the history of Japanese chocolate-making, 'an epoch-making year' (JACC 1958: 13).

The idea that one mass producer should offer a full line of sweets composed of 'five major product lines', rather than specialising in a particular product line, was devised by Hanzaburo Matsuzaki as a result of observations of the sweets market in Western countries. He wrote in his retrospective that, although many sweets manufacturers in Europe and the USA specialised in production of one class of sweet such as chewing gum, biscuits or chocolates, 'I believe a Japanese company could not follow such specialised production because the Japanese market for Western-style sweets was still too small'. Therefore, 'I judged our company had to take the full-line management policy' (Matsuzaki 1954: 154–5). This full-line product policy became the basis of establishing the network of exclusive wholesalers and retailers, because if Morinaga specialised in production of only one product line similar to many Western manufacturers, the exclusive dealing requirement would not be acceptable for merchants.

Organising the keiretsu *network of wholesalers*

The philosophy of organising the network of marketing channels was also raised by Hanzaburo Matsuzaki: production and sales were 'an inseparable pair of wheels' (Matsuzaki 1923a: 4, 1954: 108). This meant that the manufacturer should not only be concerned with production or products, but should also focus on consumers. 'We originally expect that the sales of our products are not targeted at the wholesaler, but should be centred on the consumer' (Matsuzaki 1924a: 9).

> What I have always emphasised – from the manufacturer to the consumer – does not necessarily mean the manufacturer should actually sell directly to the consumer. This is an emphatic expression to show that the manufacturer cannot provide a good quality product at a cheap price until they take an attitude as if they serve the consumer directly.
>
> (Matsuzaki 1924b: 5)

Thus, this idea was to be brought about by retailers. For this to work, the wholesale sector would have to be organised because the national distribution which bypassed the wholesale step would prohibitively increase distribution costs. Around 1915, when the success of Milk Caramel became apparent, Morinaga launched an initiative to organise exclusive wholesale agents (*senzoku tokuyaku-ten*) based on a contract. An event in 1917, however, gave Morinaga a strong motive to strengthen the *keiretsu* wholesale network. In September of that year, some exclusive wholesalers in the Tokyo and Northern Japan regions proposed, even if they sold competing brands with Morinaga, to continue reselling Morinaga's products as before. The reaction by Hanzaburo was strict: 'I will never accept it. We must part with each other because our friendship is now doomed to die' (Matsuzaki 1954: 110). Thus, the talk between Hanzaburo and wholesalers broke down.

The background of this event was that some leaders of exclusive wholesalers had already established a competitive company, which was believed to be aimed at 'usurping the market share of Morinaga' (Tamaki 1967: 352), and had begun to sell imitations of candy caramel, branded Monarch Caramel and King Caramel (Japan Provisions Newspaper Co., 1967: 152). This company, Meiji Seika Co., Ltd. (now Meiji Co., Ltd.), a subsidiary of a sugar refining manufacturer, Meiji Sugar Refining Co., Ltd, became in 1924 a powerful rival of Morinaga. The breakdown of the talks occurred as this strong rival producer was emerging.

After this event, Morinaga decided to replace the contract-based wholesale agents with its own wholesale companies, called 'sales companies (*hanbai kaisha*)'. These companies were established with co-investment by Morinaga (with less than 10 per cent investment) and the former exclusive wholesale agents. In 1922, the first wholesale company was established in Osaka and by 1927 there were 16 wholesale companies established throughout Japan, accompanied by the disbanding of the network of exclusive wholesale agents (Oogushi 1929: 16). These wholesale companies were expected not only to deal exclusively, but also to engage in vertical marketing campaigns together with Morinaga and the retailers. Matsuji Oogushi, the Head of the Domestic Sales Department of Morinaga, emphasised that the ideal wholesalers should:

> always strive to enrich the assortments at the retail stores utilising legs, brain and heart, visit the retailers every day, help the retailers whenever they are busy, and hurry to the retailers as soon as a new product comes to market in order to show it, explain it and encourage them to sell it.
>
> (Oogushi 1924: 5)

Such painstaking support was a feature inside the Japanese *keiretsu* networks.

Toward modernised retailers

Based on this *keiretsu* wholesale system, Morinaga also began to organise the retail stage. Three different attempts were identifiable in this sphere.

First of all, Morinaga started opening its own retail shops, named Morinaga Candy Stores, from 1923, soon after the *keiretsu* wholesale companies began to be established. The first one was opened inside a building near Tokyo Station, with the network expanding to a total of 45 shops by 1939. These were the demonstration shops to represent the ideal Western-style stores to which Morinaga wanted the traditional retailers to transform. These stores had modern exteriors, Western-like decorative display windows, space for both the retailing of sweets and a soda fountain inside the store and good service from sales girls wearing hygienic uniforms.

Secondly, Morinaga set up the organisation for affiliated sweets retailers, called the Morinaga Society for Mutual Prosperity (*Morinaga Kyoei-kai*) in 1924. Unfortunately, no official record exists to show how many retailers actually joined this society, but Morinaga solicited many traditional sweets retailers to join this organisation. The statutes of this society (*Morinaga Monthly* 1924a) did not explicitly define the exclusive dealing; rather, Morinaga wanted to encourage modernisation of traditional sweets retailers through this society. The house newsletter circulated among member merchants, *Morinaga Monthly*, was a medium for spreading knowledge of modern marketing through its various articles. Several articles were intended to teach retailers how to calculate the turnover of capital and profits to promote 'scientific management in retailing' (e.g. Yano 1923a, 1923b).

The newsletter also taught retailers how to decorate the window displays, as shown by the example presented in Figure 1.2. In order to encourage the spread of such window displays, Morinaga's wholesale companies in the Tokyo region organised a 'Shop Window Decoration Contest' for their approximately 500 retailers (*Morinaga Monthly* 1925a, 1925b). Western-imaged window displays for small-sized sweet shops created a new atmosphere on the shopping streets and gave a new representation of Western-style consumption to the general public no matter whether they became real customers or not.

Furthermore, Morinaga eagerly recommended that retailers refurbish and modernise their stores (e.g. *Morinaga Monthly* 1925c). *Morinaga Monthly* often showed actual examples of making sweet stores more Western through refurbishments, as exemplified by Figure 1.3. Both the exterior and the interior of these stores gave a strong impression of modern Western stores for traditional Japanese consumers at the time. Thus, the introduction of new store designs was changing the townscape to a modern outlook. The Society for Mutual Prosperity was a medium for knowledge transfer on modern retail marketing from the manufacturer to traditional sweets retailers.

The Morinaga Belt-Line Stores as a pivot for modern vertical marketing

Finally, Morinaga started to organise the network of exclusive retailers, called Morinaga Belt-Line Stores, from 1928 onward. Morinaga recruited the first-class confectionery shops for its members, with consideration of the distance from existing members. The members increased to around 4,000 stores before the Second World War.

The pledge included an article on price maintenance; 'Shall keep strictly the retail prices Your Company [*i.e.* Morinaga] defined' (section 4), and the exclusive dealing article; 'As far as the five major lines of Morinaga (caramels, chocolates, biscuits, drops and milk products), shall not deal in similar products of other

Figure 1.2 How to decorate a display window: education for retailers by Morinaga (1924).

Source: Morinaga Monthly 1924b.

Notes:
1   This picture was carried in the article, 'How to decorate display windows'. The title of this decoration was 'School Excursion'. The Japanese letters at upper left say, 'Morinaga's Sweets as part of a School Excursion'.
2   The window display for small-sized retailers was a quite new idea. The schoolgirl and the school excursion were also modern images because these were outcomes of the movement of westernisation and modernisation led by the government.
3   The article indicated how to decorate the display window in detail. For instance, 'All the grounds should be fresh-coloured', 'The letters of "Morinaga's Sweets" should be black', 'The letters of "as an Attendant of School Excursion" should be white', 'The cloth of the girl should be green like an olive', 'The dog should be black', 'Indirect lighting should be provided at night', and so forth.

Reproduced courtesy of Morinaga & Co., Ltd.

companies' (section 3) (Manda 1938, p. 147). Although maintaining retail prices looked to be quite difficult, partly due to the price war of caramels caused by the depression in the 1930s, and partly due to surplus of sweet shops (more than 178,000 confectionery retailers existed in 1939 reported by the Cabinet Statistics Bureau 1939) intensifying price competition, the exclusive stipulation was

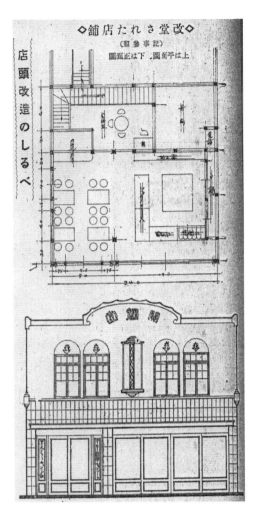

Figure 1.3 An actual example of modernised refurbishment of a retail sweet store based on the instruction by Morinaga (1925).

Source: Morinaga Monthly 1925d.

Notes:
1 *Morinaga Monthly* often introduced an actual example of refurbishment which they recommended. This is the retail store named 'Kaiki-do', located in front of the Ootsuki Station of the Chuo Line, in the suburbs of Tokyo.
2 The lower figure shows the front exterior, which gave an impression of a modern Western-style store. The upper figure shows the ground plan, which also gave a quite modern impression. The store inside had both retail space equipped with display cases and a café called a 'cocoa hall'.
3 The inner space on the upper right is the 'living room' and the stairway connected it. The upper floor, not included in this drawing, was the owner's residence.

Reproduced courtesy of Morinaga & Co., Ltd.

basically effective. In an investigation by the Ministry of Commerce and Industry, Kazuharu Manda, the Head of the Department of Belt-Line Stores, commented this stipulation was 'the most important' (Ministry of Commerce and Industry 1935b: 6, see also Manda 1934: 36).

In return, each Belt-Line Store was given a variety of support for vertical marketing campaigns, as well as a standardised store plan with a standardised sign on the roof and a metal board, standardised wrapping paper, and a uniform and a sanitary white cap for sales clerks (see Figure 1.4).

Based on the network of Belt-Line Stores, Morinaga launched various vertical marketing campaigns (Manda 1934, 1938, Ministry of Commerce and Industry 1935b, Morinaga & Co., Ltd. 1954, 2000). The company arranged the 'Morinaga Belt-Line Day' with special sales campaigns on the first day of each month. On that day, Morinaga both placed advertisements in newspapers and hoisted an advertising balloon. In addition, on the 1st and 15th of every month, Morinaga provided a 'special product (*tokusen-hin*)' such as Morinaga Belt-Line Chocolate, which could only be sold at member stores. In coordination with these campaigns, Morinaga held a nationwide competition called the Caramel Art Festival, which invited craftworks by primary school children with recycling of the empty paper packages of caramel and chocolate. Morinaga also often organised 'Special Days' in cooperation with the member stores in a specific region. It should be noted that such campaigns by Morinaga were not confined to metropolises, but reached many provincial cities, as Kazuharu Manda described: 'when we hold a Special Day in a city with less than 100,000 residents, it always becomes overwhelmingly popular and creates a so-called "sensation" there' (Ministry of Commerce and Industry 1935b: 21).

To support these marketing campaigns, Morinaga began to dispatch a team of demonstrators, called 'Sweet Girls', from 1932. The original idea was suggested by a leading department store, Takashimaya (see Chapter 4), which introduced a female demonstrator, called a 'mannequin (*manekin*) girl', to an exhibition in 1928. In the next year, Chieko Ueno, a leader of the mannequin girls, organised the Japan Mannequin Club, membership of which was composed of female demonstrators-cum-fashion models, resulting in the start of a new profession (Komiya 2005a: 143). In 1932, Morinaga began to recruit the Sweet Girls as its demonstrators. Despite Morinaga's strict requirements – 18–20 year old girls who had graduated from high school, who grew up in a harmonised and severely disciplined family, who were good-looking, who were suited to Western-style clothes, who were highly cultured with a modern sense, and who spoke standard Japanese rather than dialects, etc. – more than 600 girls applied, and only five were selected. After being trained for about a month, these girls began to be dispatched, firstly, to Morinaga Candy Stores as well as some department stores and then to Belt-Line Stores. This endeavour acquired enormous publicity from newspaper and magazine articles, and people came in hordes to the spots where these girls were dispatched. Therefore, recruitment of the girls became an annual event and high standards were maintained (Komiya 2005a: 144–6). Morinaga's attempt received favourable attention from the public who began to enjoy the Western-style

Figure 1.4 A Morinaga Belt-Line Store.

Note: The store has a modern appearance with a small window display (on the left side), and carried a standardised metal board, MB standing for Morinaga Belt-Line. The sales clerk (perhaps the owner) shown in the middle wore a sanitary uniform and a white cap, also giving a modern image.

Reproduced courtesy of Morinaga & Co., Ltd.

commercialised atmosphere shaped by these demonstrators. This policy exerted a strong influence on Shiseido, a cosmetics manufacturer (see Chapter 2).

Furthermore, Morinaga organised the MB Club (*MB-kai*) for end consumers. In order to qualify, the consumer had to pay a subscription fee of 50-*cen* per month. In turn, he/she would receive products dispatched directly from the factory twice a month. In addition, the consumer would be invited to special events such as dances, musical evenings with records, trips to hot springs, theatre trips, lectures on cooking, washing or dancing and so forth. In the meantime, the exclusive retail stores could utilise the member lists of consumers for their local business promotions. It has been reported that 15,000 consumers had joined by 1935 (Ministry of Commerce and Industry 1935b: 14). This was one of the earliest attempts at a relationship marketing or club marketing programme in modern marketing history in Japan. The idea was also followed by Shiseido on a more expanded scale (see Chapter 2).

As is seen, the network of Morinaga Belt-Line Stores functioned as a pivot to develop modern marketing by Morinaga and spread not merely the national brands of Western-style sweets, but also modern Western images, atmospheres and townscapes with consumers' everyday shopping.

Marketing philosophy by Hanzaburo Matsuzaki

The operations in these *keiretsu* stores reflected Hanzaburo's philosophy (Matsuzaki 1923b: 9): ' "how to sell the products" was considered previously as a kind of technique or art, but recently as an academic discipline or science'.

According to him (1923b: 9), 'Providing the consumer with satisfaction (*manzoku*) and pleasant sensation (*kaikan*) must be the greatest and an indispensable assumption for a distributor to do his business'. 'Satisfaction' should be 'gained when the consumer realises the good quality of the product and feels this is reliable', and 'pleasant sensation' should mean 'comfortable feelings arisen from extremely kind and polite attitudes and treatments to the customers of the store by sales clerks and others, much less from the perfect facilities of the store'.

Furthermore, Hanzaburo (1923b: 9) made a distinction between 'selling widely' and 'selling deeply'. He emphasised that 'wide sales' or where 'consumers buy a product only once' can be attained by a number of tricks, but 'this is not real sales'. 'Creating real demand' or 'continuing and maintaining sales', in other words 'deep sales', must be attained by 'trust and reputation showing that people stick to this particular product rather than others'. Thus, Hanzaburo's marketing philosophy can be evaluated as an early form of consumer orientation and relationship marketing.

The long-term relationship was not sought only with final consumers but also with *keiretsu* retailers. Morinaga Belt-Line Stores were supposed to be partners who could carry on this idea in cooperation with Morinaga. Therefore, Morinaga chose 'leading and first-class confectioners' as the member stores, rather than ordinary stores 'which are much less certain in the future', and defined these as 'the unit retail stores (*tan'i-ten*)' for Morinaga. The stores would adopt Morinaga's pattern, in contrast to previous seller/buyer relationships, and would carry out Morinaga's plan as a team (MCI 1935b: 6–7). This was an identifiable, early version of marketing concept and relationship marketing in modern Japan.

Epilogue: after the Second World War

The Second World War and the anti-westernisation movement disrupted Morinaga's marketing. In 1942 Morinaga Belt-Line Stores was forced to dissolve due to wartime controls.

After Japan's defeat in the War and the lifting of the controls on the industry, Morinaga restarted the organisation of their affiliated retail stores as the 'Morinaga Angel Stores'. This network was established through Morinaga Trading & Co., Ltd. (*Morinaga Shoji*) in 1949 as a nationwide wholesale company instead of the sales companies before the War. This company organised the retail stores as members of the Angel Association. The number of member stores throughout Japan reached 4,500 in 1955. Although exclusive dealing and price maintenance were not officially required this time because the Anti-Monopoly Law was already enforced in 1947, the status of *keiretsu* retail store as the partner of marketing by Morinaga was inherited from the status of Morinaga Belt-Line Stores before the War.

Nevertheless, the *keiretsu* retail store arrangement came to face a serious difficulty when the new retail format, the Japanese *super*, rapidly took hold (see Chapter 5). These *super* with wide assortments including competing brands under the self-service system undermined the *keiretsu* retail stores that dealt in narrow assortments, substantially the Morinaga brands only. The official history book of Morinaga describes this situation.

> Many large-sized *super* came out one after another, so that it became difficult to continue the Angel Association as the policy containing whole dimensions of distribution led by only one manufacturer. Therefore, being proud of the excellent results in 'nurturing model retail stores' which were attained, the Angel Association ceased its activities in the summer of the 47th year of Showa [in 1972].
>
> (Morinaga & Co., Ltd. 2000: 171)

Thus, *keiretsu* retailing completed its role and disappeared. This event suggests that when an innovation in the retail format occurred through accumulation of practical knowledge and exploitation of business resources on the retailer side, the *keiretsu* network organised by the manufacturer could be undermined. A similar event will be described in Chapter 6 in the industry of household electric appliances.

Conclusion

The pioneering marketers of Western-style foods and sweets, whether they were the small- and medium-sized or the large-sized, contributed in aggregate to changes in everyday consumption patterns of ordinary consumers. The progress of westernisation and industrialisation brought these pioneering marketers opportunities to recognise the expanding domain of availability of offerings (see Introduction, Figure 0.1), while they figured out new strategies to attract consumers to their new products and services. The success in this interaction combined to exert influence on changes in the consumption pattern and consumer culture.

As the offerings of foods and sweets had mixed features of the traditional Japanese and the modern Western ingredients and images, new Western-style eating habits were never purely Western, but a hybrid of the West and Japan. Marketing strategies, including organising store/restaurant networks, also more or less combined the traditional and the modern Western way. The *keiretsu* retail network in particular was a Japanese modification of the modern Western idea on retail format of chain stores or multiples. Morinaga's case was historically the first full-fledged successful form of mass marketing in the confectionery industry.

Confronting dominance by merchants of traditional Japanese-type sweets, Morinaga arranged their *keiretsu* network both on wholesale and retail stages and infused the idea of what they considered modern into it. In this sense, the organisation of a *keiretsu* network served as a medium for transfer of knowledge on modern retail marketing from a manufacturer to *keiretsu* retailers. Morinaga's exclusive chain stores operated their shops in the most advanced way at the time. The mass marketing through *keiretsu* retailers was providing modern Western-styled shops, townscapes and shopping atmospheres on the national scale. They spread Western-style sweets to the consumers beyond a few major metropolises to many provincial cities, although unlike the period of High Economic Growth after the Second World War, modern consumer life had not yet captured the majority of rural households. In addition, the success of Morinaga's marketing gave an impetus to development of manufacturers specialising in Western-style sweets, with no history of bread production, such as Meiji (Meiji Co., Ltd.) and Grico (from 1921, Ezaki Grico Co., Ltd.). Although they became rivals of Morinaga, the competition among them encouraged the spread of Western-style sweets among Japanese consumers.

Finally, it should not be ignored that even if the *keiretsu* network played a role in the transfer of modern Western retailing, the actual operation of the network bore a very Japanese feature, shown by the relentless support for *keiretsu* retailers by *keiretsu* wholesalers. Similar systems will be recognised in chapters 3 and 7. Heavy human involvement can be seen as a feature of Japanese marketing.

Notes

1 The government began to promote the public retail markets of everyday necessities after the rice riots in 1918, to solve the problem of inefficiency in the distribution system for the labourers residing in the urban areas (see Usui 1995: 159–60). In order to do this, the government investigated the overall conditions of fairs and markets. According to this, there existed 287 fairs and 1,377 private markets, as well as 136 public markets, in all Japan as of September 1918 (Nakamura 2002: 41 Table 1).

2 As the classification of chain stores, Hirano (2008) defines what this book calls the *keiretsu* retail networks as the franchise chains. As far as the retail stage is concerned, this indication sounds to be reasonable, although the marketers did not clearly recognise this name in the 1910s to 1930s. Dicke (1992: 2–3), a historian of the franchise

system, explains; 'In a franchise system one large firm, often called the parent company, grants or sells the right to distribute its products or use its trade name and processes to a number of smaller firms. The boundaries of the relationship and the ultimate basis for control are established by contract. Contracts typically either have no fixed terms or run from three to twenty years, but once a franchisee signs on, the conditions under which either termination or nonrenewal can legally occur are limited as long as performance is satisfactory. . . . For the system to work, the franchise holders, although legally independent, must conform to detailed standards of operation designed and enforced by the parent company'. In addition, Dicke (1992: 3) classified the franchise system into product franchising ('a manufacturer markets its output almost entirely through highly specialised retailers, who, in turn, rely on the manufacturer for most of the products they sell') and business-format franchising (where the outlet itself, together with a comprehensive package of services to support it, is the product). It should be possible to interpret that the Japanese manufacturers attempted to create similar organisations to the franchising system though unintentionally, because they tried to sell unfamiliar Western-style or modern technological products often with an orientation to provide some business package and some standard format for outlets.

3   The Fukusuke Association of traditional split-toe socks shown in Table 1.1 was organised by Fukusuke Tabi (now Fukusuke Corp.). This company was established in 1882 by Fukumatsu Tsujimoto as a wholesaler, named Maru-Fuku, of traditional split-toe socks (*tabi*) in Osaka. The company introduced the machine-made process to produce split-toe socks with some improvements thanks to use of Singer sewing machines. The advertising copy, 'the quality of split-toe socks made by machine-sewing is better than that by hand-sewing', was adopted in 1895. Launching nationwide marketing, the company gradually established contracted wholesale agents on the basis of one agent per prefecture. In 1930, the company persuaded these agents to establish Fukusuke Sales Companies with their own investments; as a result, 418 agents all over Japan were reduced to 31 wholesale companies and 97 agents. In addition, the company organised the Fukusuke Association in 1934, in which those retailers who sold more than 2,000 split-toe socks per year participated. Through this Association, Fukusuke provided series of retail management lectures to the retailers and the opportunity to exchange business information (see Kaneko 1942, AOEB 1983: 234, Fukusuke Corporation website). Clearly, the rapid progress of mass production of split-toe socks met conflicts with the traditional distribution channel of split-toe socks, leading to the *keiretsu* network.

4   The main reason for excluding the case of medicine was that the *keiretsu* network disappeared soon after 1925 although it was established firstly in Japan (see Usui 2009). The outline of this story is as follows.

Japan had a long tradition of Japanese and Chinese medicines (*wa-kan yaku*), which can be traced far back to about the seventh century: there had been many traditional doctors of Chinese medicines (*kanpo-i*); medicine had generally been produced in the home and the dispensing work had often been kept secret as a family tradition; the distribution of the medicines both for medical doctors and general consumers had been controlled by traditional pharmaceutical wholesalers (*yakushu ton-ya*) (see Jinbo 2008: 6). Hoshi Pharmaceutical, started by Hajime Hoshi in 1906 as a manufacturer of new Western-style household medicines, organised *keiretsu* retailers called 'special retail stores (*tokuyaku-ten*)' all over Japan, whose number increased from about 700 stores in 1910 to 4,000 in 1913 and 15,000 in 1915, reaching 35,000 stores in 1923 (Jinbo 2008: 12), although the brochure published in 1923 by the company stated the number was about 50,000 (Hoshi Pharmaceutical Co., Ltd. 1923: 11). This network of *keiretsu* retailers was a way of capturing retail outlets dealing in mass produced medicines by bypassing traditional wholesale distribution channels.

The *keiretsu* stores of Hoshi Pharmaceutical were recruited not from traditional pharmacies, but rather from peripheral and miscellaneous merchants, including the stores run as a sideline by farmers, merchants of sundries, shopkeepers, kimono fabric and drapery merchants and pawnbrokers, and new merchants who changed their jobs to Hoshi special retail stores from careers such as post-office clerks, primary school teachers, employees of foreign trade companies and rice merchants. These stores either dealt exclusively with Hoshi's products, or sold other manufacturers' medicines concurrently (Jinbo 2008: 12). Hoshi Pharmaceutical chose only one store per district (a village or a town) to secure the franchise. The company provided these merchants with signboards and gave marketing support through national advertising of Hoshi brands. The prices were rather cheaper than the competitors in order to introduce the products to final consumers, who were generally not yet familiar with Western-style medicines. Hoshi Pharmaceutical provided these special retail stores with incentives and educational information through in-house bulletins circulating among special retailers and the conventions for the special retail stores (Hoshi Pharmaceutical Co., Ltd. 1923: 25–26, Jinbo 2008: 19–20). Furthermore, the company established a boarding school named Hoshi Pharmaceutical Commercial School in 1921 as an educational institution for the owners of the special retail stores and their heirs. The School also provided a two week course for the owners (Hoshi Pharmaceutical Co., Ltd. 1923: 12–16). By doing this, Hoshi Pharmaceutical could bypass the wholesale step that was dominated by traditional wholesalers and sell directly to these retailers. As the number of *keiretsu* retailers and the areas they covered expanded, however, Hoshi recognised the necessity of the wholesale step to distribute the product on the nationwide scale to avoid a prohibitive increase in distribution costs. Therefore, the company chose principally exclusive wholesalers from the special retail stores, and established two layers of the wholesale system: the wholesalers covering a prefecture and the wholesalers selling in cities, towns or local districts (Hoshi Pharmaceutical Co., Ltd. 1923: 11, Jinbo 2008: 13–16).

Nevertheless, such a distinguished first example of *keiretsu* retailing crashed and disappeared soon after 1925, when a politically motivated scandal accused Hajime Hoshi of illegal opium usage, although he was later found not guilty (see Ooyama 1959, Hoshi 1978). Now only Hoshi Pharmaceutical University (see Hoshi University website) remains as a legacy; the manufacturing company and *keiretsu* organisation totally disappeared.

5   After the Second World War, mass producers' marketing of bread further developed through a nationwide *keiretsu* retail network established by Yamazaki Baking Co., Ltd. The company was formed in 1948 and started mass production of bread at a factory from 1955. It developed Yamazaki Shops as a franchise chain of bread, food and beverages (see Yamazaki Shop website) and Daily Yamazaki as a network of convenience stores (see Daily Yamazaki website) recruited by its subsidiary. As of December 2010, the number of Yamazaki Shops is 3,719 and that of Daily Yamazaki is 1,964. Nevertheless, Yamazaki sells their products to many other retail channels such as *super* (see Chapter 4), other conveniences stores and various retail stores. Therefore, the percentages of sales through *keiretsu* shops is fairly small: Yamazaki Shops account for 4.9 per cent and Daily Yamazaki 2.5 per cent, whereas *super* account for 40.6 per cent, other convenience stores 23.2 per cent and other retail stores 25.4 per cent (Yamazaki Baking Co., Ltd. 2010, see also Yamazaki website).

Interestingly, even in the case of Yamazaki, the percentage of sales volume of bread for meals in this company is relatively small. According to Yamazaki Baking Co., Ltd. December 2010 data, sales of loaves of ordinary bread (*shoku-pan*) account only for 15.3 per cent, and filled or garnished bread (*chori-pan*) 6.6 per cent although these were the original area of this bread company. In contrast, the percentage of sweet buns (*kashi-pan*) reached 46.6 per cent, Japanese-style sweets 10.8 per cent, Western-style sweets 13.4 per cent and others 7.3 per cent (Yamazaki Baking Co., Ltd. 2010, see also Yamazaki website). This means that although Yamazaki is popular as a mass producer of bread, the company heavily depends on bread as sweets, rather than bread for everyday meals.

2 'Miss Shiseido'

Marketing an image with the help of *keiretsu*

Following the previous discussion, this and the next chapters will explore the historical role of *keiretsu* retailing in depth. This chapter will consider the cosmetics industry with a special focus on the leading marketer, Shiseido.

Similar to confectionery, cosmetics also distinguish between the Japanese-style and the Western-style. The Japanese-style cosmetics, such as Japanese rouge (*beni*), white powder (*oshiroi*) and hair oils (*bintsuke abura*), had attained full maturity before modern Japan, based on the traditional Japanese fashion including clothing (*kimono*), hairstyles and sandals (*zori*), and on the traditional sense of female beauty. Under this circumstance, demand for Western-style cosmetics was not easily stimulated. The spread of Western-style cosmetics basically depended on how new Western-style fashion penetrated into the everyday life of consumers. Despite strong recommendations to adopt it by the Meiji government and social leaders as part of the Movement towards Civilisation and Enlightenment (*bunmei kaika*), it took a long time for ordinary people to adopt the Western-style in every dimension of their life.

This chapter will explore how female fashion and use of cosmetics were changing hand in hand. It will be composed of two sections. The first section will consider the period between c.1868 and around the turn of the twentieth century, in which the fashion changes were generally slow and partial. This section will investigate the conditions around changes in fashion and how pioneering marketers attempted to provide their cosmetics. The second section will focus on the period of c.1905 to 1937, in which various aspects of Western types of women and fashions were becoming conspicuous. After an overview on these changes, this part will focus on marketing by Shiseido, an emergent leader despite being a latecomer to the cosmetics industry, and consider how their *keiretsu* retail network played a pivotal role.

The early stage of Western-style fashion and cosmetics after the Meiji Restoration

The early attempts to change fashion and cosmetics

Despite the strong recommendation of Western-style fashion from the upper echelon of society, the rate at which it was accepted varied greatly for the different components of fashion, among men and women, for official/working environments or in private homes, and between social classes. The fastest adoption was among men's fashion in the higher class on official or work occasions, such as the Emperor's official costume (1872) and the uniforms of military forces, national officers, police, railway officials and post-office clerks. In the private sphere at home, however, the men usually wore Japanese-style clothing, so an image spread that Western-style clothing was for official occasions, while Japanese-style clothing was for the private (Tanabe 2010: 296).

Regarding the female fashion, the changes were more limited and slower because women had generally less opportunity to appear on the official or public sites. Some exceptional cases included the Empress's fashion (1873), the ceremonial Imperial Court dresses described as 'robe montante' and 'robe décolleté' (1886) (PRI 1986: 16, Imai 1999b: 124), and noble women's dresses for the waltz at *Rokumei-kan* or the Hall of the Baying Stag (see Part I Historical settings). The supply of Western-style cosmetics for these unusual occasions depended on the importation from the Western countries. The foreign cosmetics, including perfume, scented oil, lotion and cosmetic soap, had a totally different presentation in terms of bottles, packages and labels from the traditional Japanese-style cosmetics.

The occasions at the Hall of the Baying Stag, however, produced the contrary effect: criticism against 'Westernisationism (*ooka-shugi*)'. It is also reported (e.g. Kon [1968] 1972: 326–8) that especially in the 1890s and 1900s, the reverse trend was identifiable, with wearing of traditional Japanese clothing rather favoured by people, in line with the increasing nationalistic mood due to victories in the First Sino-Japanese War (1894–5) and the Russo-Japanese War (1904–5). Such a reluctance to change in fashion was a cause of the slow spread of Western-style cosmetics.

Despite this antagonistic mood, some components of women's fashion were relatively fast changing. The introduction of what was called the 'bundled hairstyle (*soku-hatsu*)' was a case in point (the description below of the hairstyle is based on Aoki 1971: 28–51, Shiseido Co., Ltd., 1972: 34–35 and 54, PRI 1986: 98–103, Haruyama 1989: 246–56, Yumoto 1996: 276–7, Ootake 2001: 158–62). The traditional Japanese coiffure (*nihon-gami*) was tied strictly by putting the traditional hair oil (*bintsuke abura*) in long black hair, combing it down and dressing it up by using a paper cord (*moto-yui*), and composed of four parts: the forelock (*mae-gami*), the hair on the temples (*bin*), a chignon (*mage*), and the overhanging hair in the back (*tabo*) (Ootake 2001: 158), with many variants according to marital status and age. In contrast, the 'bundled hairstyle' meant that the chignon was changed to braided hair in order to eliminate usage of a lot of traditional hair oils, which was unhygienic due to the oils collecting dust, as well as to reduce the wasted time for hairdressing and inactivity due to the heavy and vulnerable hairstyles (Ootake 2001: 160). There were actually many variants to these hairstyles, such as what was called the 'English-style knot' at which the chignon was changed to braiding hair in three strands, 'Western-style up-rolling' or twisting a bundle of long hair and rolling it up on the top, and others.[1] In 1885, the Association for the Bundled Hairstyle for Women (*Fujin Soku-hatsu Kai*) was organised under the leadership of a military medical doctor, Kanae Watanabe, and emphasised that the Japanese coiffure was insanitary because it made hair hard to wash. Soon after the campaign by the Association started, *Osaka Asahi Newspaper* (1885) reported the bundled hairstyle was 'in vogue' 'around the Tokyo area'.

This bundled hairstyle had often been called the 'Western hairstyles (*yo-hatsu*)' (Aoki 1971, Chapter 2), although the 'Western hairstyle' came to indicate more usually the new hairstyles introduced later in interwar Japan, as will be seen below. The bundled hairstyle was distinct from the traditional Japanese coiffure, but still appropriate with a traditional *kimono* for a female; in this sense, it was in transition to the Western styles.

Adopting the bundled hairstyle reduced the consumption of traditional hair oils (*bintsuke abura*) and increased hair washing opportunities with rising demand for 'hair washing powders (*kamiarai-ko*)' composed of various ashes, which were replaced by soap later. The advertisements for hair washing powders inserted by small-sized marketers were identifiable, for instance, in 1878 and 1881 in *Yomiuri Newspaper* (1878a, 1878b, 1881) and in 1883 in *Osaka Asahi Newspaper* (1883). In the meantime, soap, although it had been introduced around the 1530s–50s from Spain (Kobayashi and Hattori 1940: 143–8), was not popular before modern Japan. Isoemon Tsutsumi established the first factory to produce soap based on Western chemical knowledge in 1873 in Yokohama (Kobayashi and Hattori 1940: 206, Kao Soap Co., Ltd. 1971: 106), but his factory was forced out of business in 1890 facing business depression. From 1877 onwards, however, domestic production of soap increased (Kobayashi and Hattori 1940: 237), enough to surpass the quantity imported in 1885 (Yumoto 1996: 170). Around then, soap for cosmetic use also began to be provided by domestic manufacturers. For instance, Nagase Store (now Kao Corporation) started its business in 1887, and began to sell high-quality cosmetic soap, branded Kao Soap, in 1890 (Kao Corporation website). Thus, the marketers of cosmetic soap were emerging.

As for female costumes, the students of 'women's higher schools (*koto jo-gakko*)', the institutes of secondary education dedicated for women, were emerging as a kind of icon. As female attendance in elementary schools increased around the turn of the twentieth century (see Part I Historical settings), some girls began to consider secondary education.[2] Despite the traditional opinion that women had no need of education, and much less 'higher' education, some advanced educators began to establish specialised institutions for women. While an American teacher, Mary E. Kidder, started a small private Kidder's School (now Ferris University) in Yokohama as early as 1870 (see Ferris University website), the Meiji government founded the National School for Women (*Kanritsu Jogakko*) in Tokyo in 1872, the Teacher's School for Women in Tokyo (*Tokyo Joshi Shihan Gakko*, now Ochanomizu University) in 1875, and established the Annexed Higher Women's School (*Fuzoku Koto Jogakko*) in 1882 (see ME 1972a: 212–4; Ochanomizu University website). Although these early schools were not initially clearly defined as institutions of secondary education for women, the government began to set rules for women in 1891 by amending the Order of

Secondary Schools originally set in 1886, and issued the Order of Women's Higher Schools (*Koto Jogakko Rei*) in 1897 (ME 1972a: 346–50).[3] The number of private and national higher women's schools and their students rapidly grew from five schools with 286 students in 1882 to 209 schools with 64,871 students in 1912 (the final year of the Meiji Period). It further increased in the interwar period resulting in 880 schools with 518,684 students in 1940 (ME 1972b).

The idea of secondary education for women was quite new, and their clothing fashions attracted attention. At first, these women students wore *kimono* with *hakama* (loose-legged pleated trousers as the traditional formal wear). However, *hakama* was originally designed for men, not for women; a compromise style composed of *kimono* for women and *hakama* for men seemed to confirm their resolution when women appeared for the first time in a public place of secondary education like men (Ochanomizu University 1984: 46–7, Koyama 2008: 202–3, Tanabe 2010: 310–11). In due course, a style of *hakama* specifically for woman was designed. As the government suggested *hakama* for these female students, wearing *kimono* with maroon-coloured *hakama*, as well as choosing a bundled hairstyle and Western-style shoes, and studying at the Western-style school houses, was becoming symbolic for female students in the early twentieth century (Tanabe 2010: 314–15) (see Figure 2.1, the left-hand picture). In interwar Japan, the uniforms for higher women's schools changed further to Western-style costumes. It was in 1919 that the first Western-style uniform was adopted by Yamawaki Higher School for Women in Tokyo as a one-piece dress made of deep-blue serge with white collar and a wide-brimmed hat called capeline (Imai 1999b: 128). In the 1930s the Western-style costume was spreading as uniform, (Kuroba 1994: 126–8) as seen in the right-hand picture in Figure 2.1.

According to the investigation in 1907 by *Yomiuri Newspaper* (1907) of several cosmetics shops in the Hongo and Kanda Ryogoku areas in Tokyo into what kind of cosmetics were demanded by the students of women's higher schools, 'expensive cosmetics have sold well for these few years'; imported soap and perfume were preferred; cosmetic cream used for foundation to white powders was becoming the vogue, and the students tended to choose imported rather than made-in-Japan products because of the quality issue. Among them, however, some domestic products also began to be selected, such as Misono White Powder and Royal Lotion (by Club Cosmetics), as will be seen below. Because the background of female students of higher women's schools was still confined to the upper class at the time, their preferences basically reflected the favourites of high society. Nevertheless, the products Japanese marketers offered were building a presence.

Early marketers of Western-style cosmetics

In the early years of modernisation, imported foreign cosmetics were dealt in by the trading houses (*shokan*) at settlement ports, and distributed by wholesalers or agents (*nakagai*), via secondary wholesalers, to retailers. Because the merchants who handled the Japanese-style cosmetics had been called 'everyday items dealers

Figure 2.1 Historical school uniforms of Ochanomizu University around 1902 (left) and after 1932 (right)

Note: The left-hand picture: the school uniform around 1902 when the university was called the Teacher's Higher School for Women in Tokyo. The student wore a Japanese-style *kimono* with traditional splashed patterns of arrows, maroon-coloured *hakama*, which followed the heritage of *hakama* as traditional and official trousers for men but was newly designed for women, and Western-style black shoes rather than traditional Japanese sandals (*zori*). She has the bundled hairstyle tied by a ribbon, which was called 'Margaret' representing at the time an atmosphere of the modern Western-style. The girl holds marguerites in her left hand, perhaps to reflect her hairstyle.

The right-hand picture: one of the two school uniforms after 1932. The students wore a sailor uniform, which was a popular design. The picture shows the progress of wearing Western-style clothing by female students in the 1930s. Her hairstyle also became what was called the Western-style in interwar Japan.

Both painted by Seiran Sakauchi (1897–1969).
Reproduced courtesy of the Digital Archive, Ochanomizu University.

(*komamonoya*)', the merchants who sold the Western products became known as 'foreign or Western-style everyday items dealers (*hakurai- or yo-komamono sho*)'. These merchants dealt in quite a wide range of product lines, including not only Western-style cosmetics, but also other products such as Western-style umbrellas, matches, candles, tobacco, wine, tea, sugar, sauce and miscellaneous products (JCIA 1995: 82–85).

The traditional Japanese-style cosmetics continued to be provided by domestic manufacturers even after the Meiji Restoration because the demand was still stable. One of the important items was white powder. A change came about, however, with the introduction of knowledge on modern Western chemistry. The traditional production of white powder included lead, so warnings that leaded white powder was harmful to health were repeatedly made from the 1880s. Nevertheless, this dangerous custom remained for a while. The government issued a rule to eliminate lead in 1900, but this rule allowed leaded powder to remain in use 'for some time' because there were too many brands which included white lead being sold in the market (JCIA 1995: 61–62). An investigation by the Metropolitan Police Department in Tokyo revealed that there was three times as much leaded white powder as lead-free white powder. It was not until 1934 that the production and sale of leaded white powder was totally banned (PRI 1986: 21 and 46).

The first lead-free white powder appeared in 1878, and several brands followed (JCIA 1995: 66). However, these brands were unsuccessful in gaining popularity. It was the Imperial Misono White Powder introduced in 1904 that eventually become strong enough to drive the traditional leaded brands out of the market. The above-mentioned investigation by *Yomiuri Newspaper* in 1907 showed that this brand won the favour of female students. This product was created by a medical doctor, Nakahiko Hasebe, a chemist who had studied in France. He presented the lead-free white powder to the Imperial Court and it was accepted as an article for Imperial use in 1900 (Hirao 1929: 743, JCIA 1995: 64–65, Mizuo 1998: 48–49). The sign of 'Imperial use (*goryo*)' had a strong influence which enabled popularity to trickle down for this brand. Hasebe established a company named Ito Butterfly Garden (*Ito Kocho-en*) with his friend, Sakae Ito, in 1904 (the succeeding company, Tsumura Cosmetics, was liquidated in 1997).

This lead-free product was followed by other prominent brands such as Lait White Powder by Hirao Sampei Store in 1905, Maple (*Kaede*) and Flower (*Hana*, this brand name was soon changed to Spring [*Yayoi*]) by Shiseido in 1906, and Club White Powder by Nakayama Taiyo-do in 1910. All these products are mentioned below. In the meantime, social debates occurred about whether it should be banned for female students to wear white powder at women's higher schools (PRI 1986: 21). An advertising message for Higher School White Powder (*Daigaku Oshiroi*) provided by Yano Fragrant Garden (*Yano Hoko-En*) asked, 'why is the use of white powder prohibited for female students?' and insisted that lead-free white powder should be recommended rather than banned (see JCIA 1995: [122]). Competition in advertising between Imperial Misono White Powder and Higher School White Powder became much talked about among consumers (Mizuo 1998: 55–56).

White powder was, however, originally part of the Japanese-style cosmetics. Domestic production of Western-style cosmetics started around 1872 by imitating imported perfume (PRI 1986: 23). A famous pioneering producer was Hirao Sampei Store, founded in 1878 (the company was closed in 1954). Its business started as a pharmacy, and sold medicine prescribed by a famous medical doctor, Jun Matsumoto, who studied Dutch medical science at the Nagasaki port before the opening up of Japan and became the inspector general of army surgeons of the Meiji government (JCIA 1995: 39–40). In 1878, the year of its founding, this store introduced 'Komachi Lotion (*Komachi-mizu*)' ('Komachi' connoted the historical beauty, Ono-no-Komachi, in the ninth century), which was used as foundation for white powder and nutrition for the skin. This was also prescribed by Doctor Jun Matsumoto based on modern knowledge of medicine and chemistry. This brand became popular, and the company established factories in Tokyo and Osaka to produce not only lotion, cosmetic cream, perfume and white powder, but also soap, washing powder, tooth-powder, etc. (Hirao 1929: 18–24). From 1906, this company adopted the brand name 'Lait' for its cosmetics (see Hirao 1929: 101–5), and became a dominant marketer in the field of Western-style cosmetics before the First World War.

Another leading company was Nakayama Taiyo-do (now Club Cosmetics Co., Ltd.). This was founded in Kobe in 1903 by Taichi Nakayama as a retail store named Nakayama Taiyo-do, which handled imported miscellaneous products including cosmetics/sanitary products such as cosmetic cream, soap, washing powder and toothpowder, Western trousers and shirts, razors, combs, and so forth. The company expanded its business to the manufacturing sector and began to sell washing soap powder under the brand name 'Club' in 1906 (Club Cosmetics 2003: 10–19). By expanding the product lines to include unleaded white powder (1910) and cosmetic cream (1911), and by establishing good relationships with emergent department stores (Club Cosmetics 2003: 30–31, 40–41 and 22–23), the Club brand rapidly grew to be another dominant marketer. Thus, 'Lait in Eastern Japan and Club in Western Japan' were called the 'two major brands' in the 1910s (see Kohara 1994: 36).

Compared with these early leaders who were successful in making a quick use of the expanding domain of availability due to gradual penetrations of Western-style make-up and mediating it with individual consumption choices, Shiseido's growth was slower in the cosmetics field although it had started earlier. Shiseido was founded as a pharmacy for Western-style prescription medicines in 1872. The store located one block from the west end of the developing row of brick-made buildings on a street, as pictured in the introduction to the company (Shiseido Co., Ltd. 1972: 14). The founder, Arinobu Fukuhara, had studied Western pharmacology and had worked as the director of the Naval pharmacy, where Western-style medicine (*yo-yaku*) was popular although the traditional Japanese and Chinese medicine (*wa-kan-yaku*) were still generally favoured in ordinary society (see Usui 2009: 280). Arinobu founded Shiseido Pharmacy, which was named by A. Fukuhara and Jun Matsumoto, who was also committed to the start of Hirao Sampei Store as a pharmacy and to the prescription of Imperial Komachi Lotion as mentioned above (Mizuo 1998: 36).

In 1888, Shiseido entered the field of hygiene products and became the talk of consumers by introducing toothpaste, which was in a ceramic container, for the first time in Japan (Shiseido Co., Ltd. 1972: 36). And in 1897, Shiseido produced and sold cosmetics for the first time, which were lotion, perfume and hair oil (Shiseido Co., Ltd. 1972: 36–43). The lotion, branded 'Eudermine', became a particular symbol of Shiseido's cosmetics as 'red-coloured water' in a well-designed bottle (Takase 1997). The company also introduced in 1906 lead-free cosmetic powder, which, however, was not white, but skin-coloured. This introduced a change in the traditional concept that cosmetic powder should be simply white, although the powder was not commercially successful (Shiseido Co., Ltd. 1972: 52, PRI 1986: 22–23, Mizuo 1998: 51–52). Despite these efforts, the main product lines of Shiseido at first were toothpaste and tablets for anti-beriberi (sold from 1893) (Shiseido Co., Ltd. 1972: 46). It was not until 1915 that Shiseido came to focus on the cosmetic business when Shinzo Fukuhara, who was a son of Arinobu and studied pharmacology at Columbia University in the USA, and experienced work in a pharmacy and a cosmetics factory (1908–13), took over his father's business (Shiseido Co., Ltd. 1972: 56). The decision responded to the decisive changes in the mode of consumption in the 1910s–30s.

Development of Western-style fashion and cosmetics: the role of the *keiretsu* retail network in interwar Japan

'Moga' (modern girls) as avant-garde in Western-style fashion

As historians (e.g. Young 1999, Sato 2003, Molony and Uno 2005) have been increasingly focusing attention, the new consumer culture of women, including changes in their fashions, became conspicuous in interwar Japan.

As the modern industrialised economy progressed, new professions for men and women emerged. Men appeared as new white-collar workers, who became known as 'wedged people (*hokyu seikatsu-sha*)' or 'salaried men' (*salary man* in *katakana* characters) (Maeda 1928a, 1928b). The census data showed the 'clerical and related workers' were 958,092 or 3.2 per cent of 'the total number gainfully employed' (including those 14 years old and under) in 1930, and 2,044,540 or 6.3 per cent in 1940 (1940 data includes people originating in Korea, Taiwan and others) although this data includes both males and females (SB 1987: 405). Many of the 'salaried men' wore Western-designed suits at their offices as a de facto uniform, although it was still the usual custom for them to change into traditional *kimono* without *hakama* when they returned home.

'Professional women (*shokugyo fujin*)' also began appearing. They were nurses, teachers, office workers, typists, telephone operators, bus conductors (called '*bus girls*'), sales clerks and elevator operators (called '*elevator girls*') at department stores and demonstrators called '*mannequin girls*' (called simply *manekin* in *katakana* characters) (see Chapter 1). The 1930 census data on occupation reported that the number of women engaging in nursing was 82,535, primary school teachers numbered 93,751, general clerical workers 51,319, typists and stenographers 6,353, shop salespersons and sales clerks 405,099, telephone operators 35,557, and conductors in transportation 6,185 (SB website 1). While some of them, for instance telephone operators, still wore Japanese-style *kimono*, other women, especially those who worked in public jobs, such as bus conductors, sales clerks, elevator operators and demonstrators, wore Western-style clothing as their uniforms even though this was 'to facilitate difficult business transactions and attract male customers' (Sato 2003: 119). In the meantime, young factory girls (*joko*), who had been hired since the middle of the Industrial Revolution in such industries as cotton spinning and silk reeling and had worn the *kimono* with a band of cloth (*tasuki*, used for holding sleeves out of the way) during their working hours, began to be required to wear the Western-style clothing with a cap made of cloth and a white apron as their uniforms from the point of view of efficiency, safety and health (Nasu 1969: 386).

Sato (2003) identifies the 'self-motivated middle class housewife' as another type of woman who enjoyed the new consumer culture through reading women's magazines. As a matter of fact, several mass-circulated magazines targeting women attained widespread popularity, such as *Woman's World* (*Fujin Sekai*) published from 1906, *Woman's Companion* (*Fujin no Tomo*) from 1908, *Women's Sphere* (*Fujo-kai*) from 1910, *Woman's Review* (*Fujin Ko-ron*) from 1916, *Housewife's Companion* (*Shufu no Tomo*) from 1917, and *Woman's Club* (*Fujin Club*) from 1920. These mass-readership magazines captured as their readers the middle class and even the lower middle class women (Sato 2003: 79–81). Although many Japanese publishers did not officially announce circulation figures, it was reported that *Housewife's Companion* had a monthly circulation of about 600,000 with a rate of 0.5 to 1 per cent in unsold, returned copies, *Women's Club* achieved 550,000 with a return ratio of 5 to 10 per cent, *Women's Sphere* sold 350,000 with a return ratio of 25 per cent, *Woman's Review* monthly circulated 200,000 with a return ratio of 15 per cent, and *Woman's World* had a monthly circulation of 120,000 with 45 per cent returned (Minemura 1931: 77, see also Sato 2005: 123, fn. 1). It is believed (Takahashi 1999: 96–101) that the circulation of *Housewife's Companion* was the second largest, following the first *hoi polloi* magazine, *King*, from 1925. According to Sato's (2003: 100–111 and 189, fn. 4, 2005: 99) analysis, as these magazines encompassed middle class women, the topics they published developed beyond the tastes of higher school students fascinated with fiction and the issues related to privileged young ladies, such as a lady's virtue and the mental stability to keep peaceful households, down to the topics much appealing to the masses, including practical issues such as cooking, cleaning and sewing for family, fashion trends, and the so-called 'confessional articles (*kokuhaku kiji*)' composed of letters from the readers and advice to them regarding such problems as love, marriage and various social relationships. The articles about trendy fashions, as well as advertisements in the magazines, also 'acquainted readers with fads in fashions, hairstyles, accessories, and even the latest dance steps' (Sato 2003: 104). As such, these women's magazines were directly or indirectly the promoters of fashion changes.

The mainstream philosophy on women's role at the time was to become the 'good wife and wise mother (*ryo-sai ken-bo*)' (Nakajima 1984, Koyama 1999, Uno 2005), based on the aim of higher women's schools to cultivate 'womanly virtues'. Nevertheless, radical philosophy emerged to advocate women's emancipation in the 1910s (see Lowy 2007). The new theatre drama, 'A Doll's House (Et Dukkehjem)' by Henrik Ibsen, with the actress Sumako Matsui playing Nora, gained public favour in 1911, making a strong impression on the new type of personality. In the same year, the magazine *Blue Stockings* (*Seito*), edited only by women, began to be issued to emancipate women from the rule of patriarchy (banned from sale in 1915 and ceased in 1916). The famous leader, Raicho Hiratsuka ([1913] 1983a), usually called Raicho, declared the 'new woman (*atarashii on'na*)'; these words became popular to designate the new independent women. Raicho wore the Japanese-style *kimono* at first; but from 1920 when the Association of New Women (*Shin Fujin Kyokai*)[4] was officially organised, she began to wear dark blue suits made of serge with a short-cut hairstyle and travelled around Japan giving public lectures (Hiratsuka [1955] 1984: 302–4, Imai 1999b: 127–8, Habu 2004: 157–8). Thus, Western-style clothing became a symbol for the emancipation of women, even although this was not necessarily Raicho's intention.

In the meantime, corresponding to the vogue in Western countries (Aoki 1971: 69–72), the short-cut or bobbed hairstyle, called '*danpatsu*', spread among avant-garde women from the mid-1920s to the early 1930s (Takahashi 1999). Raicho herself had bobbed hair in 1923 because she felt her hair was bothersome, causing 'headaches due to fatigue', and gave the impression 'she is the leading edge of fashion' (Hiratsuka [1926] 1983b). Almost at the same time, the new fashionable women, called 'modern girls (*modern girl*)' (Kitazawa 1924, Kiyosawa 1926), or more frequently abbreviated to '*moga*' in Japanese abbreviation, came to be recognisable on busy shopping streets in metropolises. These girls dressed in Western-style clothes, often wearing a boater with a striped ribbon with the bobbed hairstyle (Imai 2000: 125) and roamed around popular places in cities such as movie theatres, dance halls, revues, cafes and bars. The girls' equivalent, the boys wearing the Western-style clothing, were called 'modern boys' or '*mobo*'. While these people were variously talked about and considered (see e.g. Sato 1991, 2003: Chapter 2, Shin 2003), it should be noted that they were a new type of consumers who were different from suffragists such as the group of *Blue Stockings* and the 'new woman' (Kiyosawa 1926: 215–18). An early article refer- ring to 'modern girls' indicated:

> Then, what does the modern girl mean? The person I call the modern girl here is not the so-called new woman. She is not the awakened woman; nor the feminist, and much less the suffragist . . . . The new women in the former era realised and stirred up because they recognised that they were no more the slaves of men and they were the same human being. In contrast, the modern girls do not think they were originally the slaves of men . . . The former new women insisted that women had the same right to drink as men had, and they drank even if they did not want to drink . . . The modern girls are not inter- ested in whether they have the same right or not as the men. They drink just because they want to. The behaviours of modern girls start from natural

wants, not from the consciousness of what they should do ... The modern girls were created by the spirit of the modern age. In this sense, they have the legitimate reason of their existence ... [The modern girls] insist on their wants and behave freely because they respect themselves ... Thus, the modern girls do not have any traditional concept at all. They are the completely new women who respect themselves before everything.

(Kitazawa 1924: 227–30)

It can be said that the emergence of the modern girls showed changes in the relationships of consumers with others during the act of consumption and with consumption itself in the mode of consumption (see Introduction, Figure 0.1). They can be evaluated as the first consumers who embodied hedonistic or individualistic consumption, and this type of consumption mode appeared for the first time in the modern history of Japan.

Nonetheless, this trend should not be overvalued. As Figure 2.2 shows, just next to the modern girls, there were women who still wore traditional *kimono*. It

Figure 2.2 Modern girls (*moga*) in a busy shopping street in Osaka (1925).

Note: Two women in the centre, wearing Western-style costumes and sharing a Western-style parasol, were called '*moga* (modern girls)'. They were state-of-the-art in westernised fashion. A man on the left wearing Western-style clothes was called a '*mobo* (modern boy)'. Interestingly, however, two women on the right still wore the traditional *kimono*, although their hairstyles were not traditional. This picture shows Japan was still in transition in terms of fashion.

Reproduced courtesy of Osaka Mainichi Newspaper

was this duality, or a sort of juxtaposition, that characterised Japanese consumer society at the time.

As a matter of fact, Wajiro Kon, a pioneer of the study of modern social phenomena, or what he called 'modernology (*kogen-gaku*)', investigated fashions worn by pedestrians walking on a Ginza street (between Kyobashi and Shinbashi) for four days in May 1925. He found that only 1 per cent of women wore Western-style clothes, while 99 per cent wore the traditional *kimono*. In contrast, regarding the men's fashion, 67 per cent wore the Western-style clothes with 33 per cent in the traditional *kimono* (Kon 1925). A follow-up investigation on female costume was made under the direction of Wajiro Kon, simultaneously in 19 cities (including four overseas territories) from 3 pm to 4 pm, 1 May 1937. The number of women investigated was 26,002. The average of those who wore Western-style clothes was still only 26 per cent. The investigation in Tokyo revealed that the rates were 39 per cent on the street in Maru-no-uchi (there were many 'professional women' because of the famous location of business offices), 27 per cent in Shinjuku (there were many female students because of the amusement area), 24 per cent in Ginza (the fashionable street) and only 9 per cent in Asakusa (the famous traditional shopping street) (*Friends of Women* 1937).

The duality was also apparent in the census data on occupation. Even though the 'professional women' became conspicuous and attracted the public eye, the overwhelming majority of working women were engaged in traditional or manual labour. According to calculation by this author based on the 1930 census data (SB website 1), among the 10,589,403 female labourers (which was about half of women 15 years or older), 6,350,138 or 60 per cent worked as 'farmers and sericulturists', 1,482,042 or 14 per cent were factory workers, 697,116 or 6.6 per cent worked as 'domestic service workers', and 363,623 or 3.4 per cent were 'servants and waitresses'. Regarding the factory workers, 911,538 or 8.6 per cent were employed as 'silk reel and textile workers', 2.5 times the number of male workers in these fields.

Thus, although the female consumers were more and more enjoying the Western-style fashion and even the avant-garde or hedonistic mode of consumption in the metropolitan areas, the majority of women still maintained the traditional fashion, many even wearing traditional *kimono* even in busy shopping streets in Tokyo and Osaka. It was this disparity that encouraged the marketers of Western-style cosmetics to create strategies to penetrate Western-style fashion and cosmetics. The strategies by Shiseido were the most remarkable and brought this company into the lead in the cosmetics industry.

Marketing of Western images and knowledge by Shiseido

One of the outstanding strategies by Shiseido was to promote the new hairstyle called the 'covering ears' (*mimi-kakushi*), a representative form of the Western hairstyle at the time.

Soon after Shinzo Fukuhara took over his father's business, he opened a cosmetic store in 1915 as the Cosmetic Department in a three-story building made of brick in Ginza, and set up the Departments of Beauty Care, Beautiful Hair and Children's Clothing on the second floor of this building in 1922 (Shiseido Co., Ltd. 1972: 56–57). The Beautiful Hair Department (*bihatsu-ka*, now Shiseido Beauty Saloon) invited an American hairdresser, Helen Grossman, to be its head, who created the new hairstyle called 'covering ears (*mimi-kakushi*)' (Shiseido Co., Ltd. 1972: 58, Shiseido and Shiseido Beauty Saloon websites). The issue on who was the first was historically controversial as there are different opinions as to who invented the 'covering ears' shape in 1922, that is, Ms Yu Misu who worked for Shiseido's Design Department and transferred to work for a competitor, Nakayama Taiyo-do, and Ms Moto Ina, a theatre hairdresser (PRI 1986: 104–6). Nevertheless, it is undeniable that Shiseido was eagerly involved, and had sufficient influence to spread the 'covering ears' style. In fact, Ms Grossman introduced this hairstyle at many demonstration meetings travelling around many cities.

This hairstyle marked a historical turning point from the transitional bundled hairstyle (*soku-hatsu*) to what became known as Western hairstyle (*yo-hatsu*) in interwar Japan, in two features. First, the traditional hairstyles including the bundled hairstyle were symmetric, but the 'covering ears' style split the forelock seventy-thirty. Although 'covering ears' was not the first style to adopt an asymmetric shape (the 'actress hairstyle' had also split the forelock to seventy-thirty or sixty-forty although it did not become popular (PRI 1986: 104), 'covering ears' became the first asymmetrical hairstyle that won popularity. Second, in contrast with the traditional shape that piled the hair high up on the head, this style let the hair fall naturally to cover both ears, and pressed a light wave by using a pair of tongs (Ootake 2001: 162–3, Shiseido Beauty Saloon website). In the same year of exhibiting this style, Chieko Yamane, who had studied hairdressing skills in the USA, opened up an independent beauty salon and introduced waving or curling hair by the hair iron or the so-called 'Marcel waves' (named after a French innovator of a curling iron, Marcel Grateau). In the mid-1930s, the permanent wave machine was also introduced (PRI 1986: 108–9 and 114–18), resulting in the spread of permed hair or what was called '*den-patsu*', meaning the electrified hairstyle. Shiseido's work ran parallel with this. The 'covering ears' hairstyle was rapidly accepted by many women because the shape was new, but still suitable for the *kimono* as well as with Western-style clothes, and became the representative Western hairstyle (*yo-hatsu*) by the early 1930s, accompanied by the 'uncovering ears' style (PRI 1986: 112–14). These styles were much more popular than the bobbed hairstyle (*dan-patsu*) mentioned above, because this was considered too radical. The investigation directed by Wajiro Kon in 1937 showed that 48 per cent of women on average had the Western-like hairstyle (*yo-hatsu*), i.e. 'covering ears' and 'uncovering ears', and their variants, while 20 per cent still had the bundled hairstyle (*soku-hatsu*), 8 per cent had bobbed hair (*danpatsu*), and only 3 per cent had the Japanese-style coiffure (*nihon-gami*); the rest were other styles (*Friends of Women* 1937: 102).

Shiseido was also the eager promoter of elaborate Western images. Image-oriented appeals had been emphasised in previous years also; however, 'Komachi Lotion' by Hirao Sampei Store and Club Washing Powder by Nakayama Taiyo-do, for instance, which had gained popularity before Shiseido's products, had depended heavily on the Japanese image corresponding to the social atmosphere at the time, typically shown by women wearing traditional *kimono*. These competitors gradually became involved in appealing for Western images, but Shiseido was at the forefront. Shinzo Fukuhara, although he had studied pharmacy in the USA, was also an artistic photographer with a profound sense of art himself. Soon after he took over his father's business, he established the Design Department (*isho-bu*) in 1916 (Kakizaki 2001: 19), and began to hire young and energetic artists such as Sue Yabe, Mitsugu Maeda, Reika Sawa, Takeo Yamamoto and Ayao Yamana. The design motif of this Department assimilated the Art Nouveau Style. While Yamana tended to blend it with Art Deco, the Art Nouveau Style was the origin of design policy in Shiseido (Shiseido Co., Ltd. 1993: 157–63), on which various creations developed into posters, advertisements in newspapers and magazines, packages and window displays (see Figure 2.3). Thus, what became called the 'Shiseido's Style' (Saito 1996: 20) was established in its early stage. As will be seen in the next chapter, while the modern Western buildings of emergent department stores adopted the magnificent Renaissance Style, the Art Nouveau Style of Shiseido was a major advance in artistic appeal.

Based on these efforts to promote Western-style fashion and images, Shiseido began to organise *keiretsu* retailers from 1923, designed to play a pivotal role in spreading Western images and knowledge of how to use Western-style cosmetics with maintenance of retail prices and protection of brand images. This attempt was rather earlier than Morinaga's (see Chapter 1). The idea came from Noboru Matsumoto, who studied in the USA for eight years, gained a Bachelor of Commercial Science degree from New York University, and met Shinzo Fukuhara there. After experience at Mitsukoshi, Matsumoto joined Shiseido in 1916 and was responsible for the marketing field of the company (RGBA 1957: 232–51, Shiseido Co., Ltd., 1972: 56). Also, around 1921, Shiseido defined the so-called 'five principles (*5-dai shugi*)' as the company's philosophy (Shiseido Co., Ltd. 1972: 68, Sasaki 2009: 67); that is,

1   The principle of product quality orientation
2   The principle of mutual prosperity with distributors
3   The principle of retail orientation
4   The principle of steady business
5   The principle of respecting virtue.

The third principle was replaced later by the principle of consumer orientation. Organising the retail *keiretsu* network reflected these principles.

The direct incentive to organise the *keiretsu* network was to protect their emergent brands from aggressive price cutting, what was called 'abusive discounts (*ranbai*)', by petty retailers. This threat became real especially in the depression after the First World War and the social disorder after the Great Kanto Earthquake on 1 September 1923. Nakayama Taiyo-do and Hirao Sampei Store made statements regarding the need to correct 'abusive discounts' in November and

Figure 2.3 Poster ad by Shiseido: 'Makeup for Spring by Shiseido's White Powder' (1925).
Reproduced courtesy of Shiseido Co., Ltd.

December 1923 (JCIA 1995: 170–4). The response by Shiseido was more real-istic. In the same December, Shiseido declared the launch of a programme to organise 'chain stores' composed of exclusive independent retailers, called Shiseido Chain Stores. 'Why is the organisation of chain stores required?' asked Shinzo Fukuhara (1924) himself in the first volume of *Shiseido Monthly*. 'It is firstly because we want to make the prices of Shiseido's products the same anytime anywhere.' Fukuhara emphasised that selling the products 'with the same spirit as Shiseido' could bring mutual prosperity between the manufacturer and the retailers and lead to the consumer's 'feeling of assurance' (cited from Kohara 1994: 42, Sasaki 1995: 121). Shiseido Chain Stores would represent the virtue of justice and sincerity, mutual prosperity, steady business and retailer (and consumer) orienta-tion by protecting prices and product quality.

Contrary to most predictions that only a small number would do this because Shiseido was still a newcomer, about 3,000 retailers applied to join the organisa-tion (RGBA 1957: 115). The number increased to 7,000 by 1929 (Shiseido Co., Ltd. 1972: 76). In order to support these *keiretsu* retailers, Shiseido also began to replace contracted wholesalers with sales companies that were established through joint investments by Shiseido and contracted wholesalers from 1927. The number increased to 33 companies by 1934 (Otsuka 1934: 103–5). As a result, the Shiseido *keiretsu* channel was composed of *keiretsu* wholesalers and retailers, which was quite similar to that of Morinaga. Nevertheless, the result of price control can be seen to be more effective than for Morinaga. This was because the number of cosmetics retailers was rather smaller than confectionery shops, as shown, for instance, by the data that the number of cosmetics retailers was almost one-tenth of sweet retailers (Cabinet Statistic Bureau 1939). Therefore, with the percentage of retailers in the *keiretsu* relationship officially reported as 10 per cent by the company, this was sufficient to maintain the policy of restricted sales-outlets (Furo 1994: 40), in which 'only the *keiretsu* chain stores can deal with the products that cannot be dealt with at other shops' in certain territory (Otsuka 1934: 105).

Shiseido's competitors followed this method, but their attempts were much more modest. For instance, Nakayama Taiyo-do started in 1925 to organise 'Co-prosperous Associations' (*kyoei-kai*) for retailers in many areas, members of which were required to maintain retail prices under clear sales terms. The prod-ucts sold by the members were called Yang-class Cosmetics from 1926. In the meantime, a company established in 1925, the Dou-class Cosmetics (named after cosmetics only sold at Doujima Assembly Hall, called Dou Hall, in 1924), sold only through special *keiretsu* retailers, appointed on the basis of one retailer per prefecture. The latter case was much stricter in terms of resale price maintenance, but the sales volume reached only a tenth of that of Yang-class products (Club Cosmetics Co., Ltd. 1983: 58–62, 2003: 68–69, 82–85 and 88–89, Nagao 2002). Hirao Sampei Store also required retailers to maintain retail prices (Hirao 1929: 229–262, Nagao 2002), but its effect was also quite weak. In contrast, Shiseido made full use of *keiretsu* retailing not only for price maintenance to protect its emergent brands from aggressive price cutting, but also to spread knowledge of Western-style cosmetics.

In order to run the *keiretsu* retailer network smoothly, in 1935 Shiseido organised lecture seminars, called Shiseido Chain Store School, at which the members of Chain Store boarded together in Tokyo for a week and studied cosmetics, sales tactics and the application of make-up. The School then developed into the Moving School, which visited each local area independently and provided four days of lectures, resulting in the training of 2,600 people. At the same time, from 1935, Shiseido began to circulate a monthly magazine, *Research in Chain Stores*, among retailers (Shiseido Co., Ltd. 1972: 103–4).

In addition, Shiseido launched two important policies that directly related to the final consumers. Both ideas had originated in Morinaga, but Shiseido expanded them to play a significant role. The first was to dispatch demonstrators, which followed the example of Morinaga's Sweet Girls from 1932 (Komiya 2005a). From 1933, Shiseido began to organise demonstrators, called 'Miss Shiseido'. Similar to Morinaga, the hiring requirement was strictly limited to 'daughters of good families'. The role of Miss Shiseido was, however, much more important than for Morinaga staff because they were the actual educators on how to use Western-style cosmetics, as well as being demonstrators.

In its first year, Shiseido chose nine girls from 350 applicants, and trained them for seven months to demonstrate products and perform as actresses in a 'modern beauty drama' taking about one and a half hours, in which cosmetics were actually used (Komiya 2005a). From 1934 these girls travelled around major cities, performed the 'modern beauty drama', and after the drama gave consumers advice on applying make-up.

Miss Shiseido created a sensation. The recruitment was undertaken every year until 1937, then the name was changed to the Girls of the Beauty Department (*biyo-buin*) (Komiya 2005b: 139). After the first format, the focal point of activities by Miss Shiseido was changed to 'Moving Beauty Salons', in which they demonstrated how to use Western-style cosmetics and gave advice to the consumers, who were brought together by the *keiretsu* Chain Stores (Komiya 2005a: 158–62, 2005b: 132–5). Figure 2.4 shows an example of a Moving Beauty Salon held in 1934. Interestingly the picture shows that even in the 1930s, many women, who sat directly on the *tatami*-mats in the Japanese manner and gazed intently at the demonstration, still wore the traditional *kimono*: westernisation of everyday life was still at a half-way stage at the time. Miss Shiseido taught knowledge of Western-style cosmetics, which most Japanese mothers could not teach their daughters, much less be learned in schools. Miss Shiseido played a key role in this.

The second initiative was the consumer club, such as the 'Flower of Camellia Club (*Hanatsubaki-kai*)', which started in 1937. 'Flower of Camellia' (*Hanatsubaki*) had been used as the uniformed brand of Shiseido since 1915. The precedent was again the MB Club by Morinaga, but the size and the role were largely different. Although the MB Club had membership fees, the Flower of Camellia Club was free. As a result, the number of the members was estimated to have been about one million even before the Second World War (Fujioka 2000b: 102). Each consumer who bought Shiseido products was classified into one of three levels (the regular, the special and the honoured members) and given invitations to the beauty courses,

Figure 2.4 Summer Moving Beauty Salon (1934).
Reproduced courtesy of Shiseido Co., Ltd.

a free monthly magazine, *Flower of Camellia*, and coupons. The coupons were valid only when the customers bought at the same store, and each *keiretsu* retailer managed the list of members (Fujioka 1999, 2000a). This can be evaluated as an early attempt at relationship marketing or a club marketing programme to secure final consumers for Shiseido's cosmetics and its *keiretsu* retailers.

These two attempts were direct contacts with final consumers by manufacturers to expand the use of their brands, and in turn expanded the Western-style fashion, by transferring images and knowledge of the new cosmetics to the consumers. These attempts became effective because they were implemented by full use of *keiretsu* marketing channels.

Epilogue: development after the Second World War

As will be mentioned in Chapter 5, almost all the population began to wear Western-style clothing after the Second World War, so the new cosmetics spread widely. Opportunities to use traditional Japanese-style cosmetics had been sharply decreasing along with opportunities to wear *kimono*. As a result, when consumers simply mention 'cosmetics', it usually means the Western-style cosmetics nowadays.

Shiseido kept its leading position, and the *keiretsu* retail system further developed, followed by several new competitors. The result was that a unique classification has taken root in the Japanese cosmetics industry; that is, those who market the products through the *keiretsu* networks are called the manufacturers of 'institutional products (*seido-hin*)' and those who sell the products through independent merchants are called the manufacturers of 'general products (*ippan-hin*)', while those who distribute the products through doorstep salespeople are called the manufacturers of 'door-to-door products (*hohan-hin*)'. The 'institutional products' were provided by powerful manufacturers, such as Shiseido, Kanebo (established in 1936 as a soap manufacturer and began in cosmetics from 1961, now part of Kao group), Kosé (established in 1946) and Max Factor (established in 1909 in the USA, entered the Japanese market in 1953, bought by P&G and became P&G Max Factor in 1987).

Recalling the experiences before the Second World War, Shiseido developed a *keiretsu* network composed of exclusively contracted retailers. Shiseido set up exclusive sales counters for these stores and dispatched 'beauty consultants (*biyo buin*)' inheriting the tradition from Miss Shiseido (Yamauchi 1996), at its own expense. When Shiseido sold their products through department stores, the same arrangement applied. This type of strategy looked to conflict with the Anti-Monopoly Law enforced in 1947 especially in terms of resale price maintenance. It should be noted, however, an amendment of this Law in 1953 permitted the exemption of resale price maintenance of cosmetics. As a result, the 'institutional products' sold through *keiretsu* retailers became the mainstream. Fujisawa (2007: 13) indicates that although in 1950–5 the market share of cosmetics was dominated by 'general products' sold through independent retailers (15 per cent for 'institutional products', 75 per cent for 'general products' and 10 per cent for 'door-to-door products'), in the latter half of the 1960s the market share of 'institutional products' sold through *keiretsu* retailers surpassed that of 'general products' (60 per cent for 'institutional products', 20 per cent for 'general products'). At the end of the 1970s, the market share of 'institutional products' stood at 65 per cent, while that of 'general products' was only 10 per cent and 'door-to-door products' was 25 per cent. Thus, the exemption of resale price maintenance was supportive to the *keiretsu* networks, producing an 'overwhelming victory of the powerful manufacturers of institutional products' (Fujisawa 2007: 13).

The favourable legal macroenvironment was, however, only part of the reasons why *keiretsu* retailing continued after the Second World War. The decisive factor was that no innovative retail formats appeared that could challenge the *keiretsu* retail networks. In the case of Western-style sweets explored in Chapter 1, pre-packaged foods were the suitable and important items for the emergent retail format '*super*' (see Chapter 5) that sold them under the self-service system. As this new retail format developed nationwide networks, the *keiretsu* retail network of sweets organised by the manufacturer was becoming obsolete. In the cosmetics industry, in contrast, such innovation did not occur on the retailer's side. Department stores naturally sold many branded and image-oriented cosmetics on their sales floors, but they could co-exist with the *keiretsu* retail strategy by cosmetics manufacturers; the department stores provided a certain space of sales floor for a specific cosmetics manufacturer, where the manufacturer could establish their exclusive sales corner and dispatch their sales clerks.

In due course, some changes appeared. From 1974, the range of the exemption of resale price maintenance for cosmetics was restricted to the products sold at 1,000 yen or less, despite strong opposition from the *keiretsu* retailers themselves and the manufacturers. In addition, in 1997, all exemptions of resale price maintenance, which had been applied to various kinds of products, were finally lifted (Fujisawa 2007: 31–36). Under this legal circumstance, some lawsuits were raised in the 1990s by independent retailers against the manufacturers in terms of obligatory articles in the agreements on the face-to-face sales system (sales activities had to be made in combination with consulting activities provided by dispatched sales ladies). The Fair Trade Commission also issued some notices to a few cosmetics manufacturers, to eliminate the practice of resale price maintenance. The lawsuits by independent retailers provided the evidence that some innovative cosmetics retailers were growing who sold cosmetics under the self-service system with aggressive price cutting of the manufacturers' brands. This progress, however, was blocked by the judgement of the Supreme Court in 1998 that decided the face-to-face sales system of cosmetics was lawful as the manufacturer's marketing strategy (*Nikkei Newspaper* 1998b). As for the resale price maintenance, the manufacturers ceased explicit requirements on it–not in order to abolish the *keiretsu* networks, however, as Shiseido held about 25,000 *keiretsu* retail chain stores in 1998 (*Nikkei Business* 1998a). While the section of the so-called 'cosmetics sold under self-service (*self-keshohin*)' was strengthened corresponding to the increase of sales at independent self-service stores such as '*super*' and convenience stores (*Nikkei Newspaper* 1998b), Shiseido continued to sell the so-called 'cosmetics sold under the counselling services (*counselling keshohin*)' at the *keiretsu* chain stores.

Conclusion

As Harootunian (2000) described, the 'fantasy of modern life' pervaded interwar Japan. In the sphere of fashion and cosmetics, the modern type of consumers, such as professional women, middle class housewives reading the mass-circulated women's magazines and hedonistic or individualistic 'modern girls (*moga*)' enjoyed the new Western-style culture, fashion and cosmetics. Nevertheless, this phenomenon was still limited. Many consumers usually wore traditional *kimono* and lacked knowledge of how to use the new Western-style cosmetics. It was this gap that constituted the background, on which Shiseido developed its *keiretsu* retailing strategy. Because both traditional retailers and final consumers had not sufficient knowledge on Western-style cosmetics, Shiseido's *keiretsu* network served as a medium to transfer knowledge and images of fashion and its products. Protecting retail prices of cosmetics by organising *keiretsu* distributors meant protecting their brand images. Some ideas for *keiretsu* networks, such as dispatched demonstrators and a consumer's club, had originated with Morinaga, as seen in Chapter 1, but Shiseido developed them on their own terms as powerful measures of transforming images and knowledge to consumers.

Unlike the sweets industry, some powerful cosmetics manufacturers developed *keiretsu* retailing even after the Second World War because no competing retail format had emerged against the *keiretsu* networks, as well as the especially preferential treatment of cosmetics by the Anti-monopoly Law.

The *keiretsu* retailing system, however, may have to be altered due to the changes in consumer behaviours and globalisation of the cosmetics business. Unlike the situation in interwar Japan, in which many consumers lacked knowledge and images on the Western-style cosmetics, the current consumers already know Western-style fashion and cosmetics very well, so on many occasions, consumers do not necessarily require introductions and explanations of the products when they buy and use them. This is the reason why the sales of 'cosmetics sold under self-service' have increased. This means that the relationship of consumers with others and with consumers themselves during the act of buying and consumption is changing again; that is, busy consumers buy and use Western-style cosmetics for their daily life, and look to save time at the counter, but they may also want advice on buying and using them on special occasions. Globalisation of the cosmetics business – Shiseido listed 45 per cent sales from foreign business according to the 2010–11 Financial Statements – also provides a totally different context in the mode of consumption (see Figure 0.1). Therefore, the marketing system including *keiretsu* retailing cannot be static, but must continue changing.

Notes

1 During the 1890s–1900s, the reactionary decades in fashion, the Japanese-style coiffure made a strong resurgence under the heavy pressure of nationalism. However, the bundled hairstyle survived this nationalistic mood. Some variants developed, such as the 'peaked hairstyle (*hisashi-gami*)', which curled both the forelock and the hair on the temples around a pad to make an overhanging shape in the front like a peak, and the 203rd Hill', a dramatic version of the peaked hairstyle, which was named for the hard-fought battlefield in Port Arthur in the Russo-Japanese War; this hairstyle suggested the victory of Japan in the War and satisfied the patriotic mood in society.

2 When the modern educational system started in 1872 with the Educational Rule (*gakusei*), primary education was to be provided at normal schools (*jinjo sho-gakko*) composed of the four-year lower primary between six and nine years old and the four-year higher primary between 10 and 13 years old, with the definition, 'Primary schooling is for elementary education which the general population cannot refuse to receive' (Chapter 21, The Proclamation of Ministry of Education). The early primary schools charged tuition fees although the poor were often exempted from payment. The first rule was too idealistic to be appropriate for the real situation, so the rule was relaxed in 1876 to allow the period of primary education to be reduced to three years as the minimum. The 1886 Order of Primary Schools (*sho-gakko rei*) clearly defined, 'Those parents who take care of school aged children have a duty to let them graduate from the normal primary school' (section 20); the 1900 Amended Order standardised the period of compulsory education to four years without tuition fees; and the 1907 Amended Order extended the period of compulsory education at normal primary schools to six years (cf. Ministry of Education 1972a, Ministry of Education website).

3 The Order defined the requirements for admission for women 12 years old or older, who had completed the second year of Higher Elementary School (section 10), and that the standard length of study required for graduation was four years, although this could be expanded or contracted by one year according to circumstances (section 9) (Ministry

of Education 1972b: 134). In 1908 the length of study required for graduation was changed to four or five years and in 1920 basically set at five years with an option to contract this to four years. Although advancing to the normal schools (*shihan gakko*) was another means for women to get secondary education, the women's higher schools aiming at 'higher general education' (section 1) were much more popular and also more prestigious (Sato 2003: 25).

4   The Association of New Women was dissolved in 1922 when Raicho resigned from the movement, and her fellows started the Alliance for Implementation of Women's Suffrage [*Fujin Sansei-ken Kisei-Domei*] in 1924.

3 Lighting as enlightenment

Consumer life with modern Western technologies

Electric lighting also started as part of the Movement of Civilisation and Enlightenment. As already mentioned in the Historical Settings to Part I, the experimental arc street lighting in 1882 in Ginza, Tokyo, was a great success, so electric lighting became part of the modern Western image. Nevertheless, much time elapsed before individual households were wired and accepted consumer electronic products. It was in the 1920s that the new Japanese phrase 'electrification of households (*katei denka*)' was coined and electrical products such as light-bulbs and radio receivers began to be popular.

Unlike sweets and cosmetics explored in the previous chapters, electrical products were historically new; therefore there were no conflicts between businesses for Japanese- and Western-style products. Rather, the centre of competition in this industry was between the subsidiary of an electric power company, which later merged into a company producing heavy electrical apparatus, and companies specialising in household electrical appliances. In this competition process, the system of *keiretsu* retailing was variously used by manufacturers who had different positions in the market. This short chapter will explore the early stage of *keiretsu* retail networks in the household electric products industry, and will serve as an introduction to Chapter 6 on the full development and decline of the system after the Second World War.

Spread of wired homes and early success of electrification before the Second World War

Spread of electric lightbulbs at home

For electrical products to be accepted, the electric power industry had to develop. Initially the industry was highly fragmented, composed of many local companies meeting local demand for electricity (Kurihara 1964: 25–31, Matsushima 1975). The pioneer was Tokyo Electrical Light (*Tokyo Dento*) Co., Ltd. The company was licensed by the Tokyo government in 1883, established in 1886 and started to transmit electricity to a very limited area in Tokyo from a small-sized thermal power plant from 1887 (Yoshida 2005:148–52). Many small-sized power companies followed this pattern in cities such as Tokyo, Osaka and Nagoya. The demand for electric power was not large at first; it was restricted to lighting for limited areas (Kikkawa 2004a: 27).

In the 1900s, technology in high-voltage transmission of electricity from far distant large-sized hydroelectric power stations was introduced, and created the boom in water-power generation in the latter half of the 1910s and the early 1920s (Kikkawa 2004a: 55–57). This caused severe competition for many electric power companies, leading to aggressive mergers and acquisitions, resulting in the 1920s in the electric power industry's domination by the five major power companies – Tokyo Electrical Light, Uji River Electricity, Toho Power, Daido Power, and Nippon Power (Kurihara 1964: Chapter 4). While the competitive attitude among the five turned to a cooperative one in the early 1930s (Kikkawa 2004a: Chapter 3), their dominance continued until 1939 when the Japan Electric Generation and Transmission Company (*Nippon Hassoden KK*) was established for wartime control. This development contributed to an increase in industrial usage of electric power in the late 1900s to the early 1930s (Kikkawa 2004a: 62–64). The 'electrification of factories (*kojo denka*)' was the driving force in the development of the electric power industry.

Initially, Japanese consumers quickly accepted the electric lightbulb. Although most lightbulbs were imported at first, Tokyo Electric (*Tokyo Denki*) Co., Ltd., a subsidiary of a power company, was successful in producing its own. This company was one of the predecessors of Toshiba Corporation, a leader in the field of electric machinery and a strong rival of Panasonic. Tokyo Electric arranged a technological alliance with General Electric in the USA in 1905, and began to sell tungsten filament lightbulbs under the brand Mazda Lamp in 1911. The name was connected with Ahura Mazda, the God of Light in Zoroastrianism. The sales of Mazda Lamps in Japan rapidly increased with the demand to replace short-life carbon filament lightbulbs. The success of Tokyo Electric induced many other manufacturers to enter the lightbulb market, including Osaka Electric Lightbulb aligned with the German firm AEG (*Allgemeine Elektrizitäts Gesellschaft*), Imperial Electric Lightbulb, Japan Electric Lightbulb and so forth. By 1913, almost 90 per cent of bulbs were produced domestically in Japan (Takeuchi 1966: 112–13).

The main customers were at first for business use: initially electric power companies themselves, which sold electricity by installing electric lightbulbs, and secondly, the military, government offices, factories, schools, shopping premises and public purposes (Tokyo Shibaura Electric Co., Ltd. 1963: 39). In the meantime, domestic use began to spread in the latter half of the 1900s and rapidly increased during the 1920s. Amazingly, it is estimated that the ratio of electrified households in Japan reached nearly 90 per cent in the latter half of the 1920s (Kikkawa 2004a: 61, Fig. 2-1). This expansion of home use of electricity was encouraged by the change in the system of electric fees from fixed fees to a meter-rate system in 1924 (Hirano K. 2008: 40), and by reducing the prices of electricity through competition among electric power suppliers (Kikkawa 2004a: 110–11).

The term 'electrification of households', which is usually believed to have been coined after the Second World War, had already appeared in some newspaper articles in the 1920s (see e.g. *Osaka Asahi Newspaper* 1921, *Osaka Jiji Shimpo*

1922). *Hochi Newspaper* (1939) proudly reported that at the end of 1936, even many remote and isolated places were electrified. Thus, everyday life with electricity started for Japanese consumers.

The expansion of the household market for lightbulbs was accompanied by an increase in the number of lightbulb factories: from 64 in 1923, 128 in 1930, to 282 in 1937 (Hirasawa 2004: 52, Table 8). Many of these were 'the small-sized manufacturers of light bulbs in town (*machi-kyu gyosha*)'. They contracted to produce with wholesalers, who exported the products at aggressively cheap prices to North America, Europe and Asia. The dramatic increase in the export of cheap electric bulbs from Japan caused the USA to set an anti-dumping tariff in 1933, and some European governments also attempted to control the invasion of Japanese bulbs (Hirasawa 1996, 2004). In turn, the Japanese domestic market became much more flooded with cheap bulbs than ever before. 'There was an overflow of cheap and short-life lightbulbs in the market' (Shimizu 1935: 1), wrote a manager of Tokyo Electric at the time. These lightbulbs were sold by miscellaneous retailers such as general stores, rice stores and liquor (*sake*) stores and others. As will be explored in the next section, *keiretsu* retailing was emerging as an effective measure for retail marketing. The increasing experience with electric lighting by many consumers also became the basis for the rapid spread of consumer electrical products after the Second World War.

Radio receivers and electric fans as consumer products

Compared to the consumption of electric lightbulbs, consumption of other electrical products was generally limited. Radio receivers became a popular item, however. After radio transmissions were started by the Tokyo Broadcasting Station in 1925, the vacuum radio replaced the crystal radio and spread among consumers. Some assemblers, such as Yamanaka Electric, Shichiou Wireless, Hayakawa Electric and Matsushita Electric, expanded production and competed furiously, resulting in a lively market for radio sets (see Figure 3.1). Around 1930, Tokyo Electric, which allied with GE and introduced radio tube technology, began to dominate 70–80 per cent of the radio tube market (Takeuchi 1966: 134). Because of patent problems, some companies in wireless communications had to stop the production of radio tubes and withdraw from the assembly of radio sets. Additionally, in 1935 and 1936, Tokyo Electric aggressively bought shares in the leading assemblers of radio sets, including Yamanaka Electric, Shichiou Wireless and Hayakawa Electric (though not Matsushita), as will be shown below. As a result of this marketing competition, the consumption of radio sets grew, and a new lifestyle blending the modern West and Japan was emerging (see Figure 3.1). The government's medium of choice for wartime information and control of the Japanese people also encouraged spread of the radio sets. A government report shows that 5,668,031 households, or about 40 per cent of the country, were subscribers to radio by 1940 (SB 1988b: 306).

The electric iron was also becoming popular. It replaced the traditional implement called '*hinoshi*', a single-handed copper-made pan with live charcoals,

Figure 3.1 Magazine advertisements entitled 'The New National Radio Set' by Matsushita (Panasonic) in 1932.

Note: The images in these advertisements represented a home of the upper-middle class. These advertisements utilised both Western and Japanese images for their radio set, which was one of their major product lines. Both images, of the Western and the Japanese lifestyles, were normally used, although as the wartime control system progressed, the Japanese image was used more frequently.

(Left Picture) The lady in this ad wore elegant Western-style clothing and sat on a Western-style chair, appealing to an image of a Western lifestyle. The ad copy says, 'Living with lucid sounds and shining with crystalline colour; its name is the New National Radio Receiver'. The brand name 'National' was used for decades by Matsushita (Panasonic) until 2008.

(Right Picture) A magazine ad in the same year for a radio set. In contrast with the ad at left, this appeals with a spring-like Japanese image by presenting a girl wearing *kimono* with bright colours and patterns. The ad copy insists, 'Bright and comfortable: a good start for spring by the new National radio set'.

Reproduced courtesy of Panasonic Corp.

and the box iron with live charcoals that had been introduced in the late nineteenth century. About 3,001,000 households (over 20 per cent), not counting overseas territories (Yamada and Mori 1983: 27), were estimated to have this item by 1937.

Electric fans were also attractive for many consumers because of the heat and humidity during the Japanese summer. Nevertheless, prices were generally so high that they were considered luxury goods. While 652,854 fans were imported from the USA in 1925, only 58,302 fans were produced domestically in 1939.

However, these fans were generally located in public places such as banks, department stores, post offices and train stations. For home use, a new rental system of this product launched in the 1920s (Hirano K. 2008: 41–43).

Many other items, such as electric washing machines, vacuum cleaners and refrigerators, were experimentally imported or produced, but did not spread because of their high prices. In addition, due to the wartime controls, especially the 'Rule of Limitation of Production and Selling of Luxury Items' enacted from 1940, many electrical products were banned from production and consumption.

Competition in electric products through *keiretsu* retailing: three different roles of *keiretsu* retail networks

Authorised dealers by Tokyo Electric

Many electric lightbulbs produced by the small-sized manufacturers in town were sold at miscellaneous shops. In view of this, Tokyo Electric (a predecessor of Toshiba, the originator of tungsten filament lightbulbs in the Japanese market as mentioned above) decided to organise retailers in order to spread their high-quality products in this market because the cheap lightbulbs 'encroached on the market of our Mazda Lamp' (Shimizu 1935: 1). Based on the belief that the Japanese consumer market would become important as it had in the USA as the meter-rate system replaced a fixed-rate system (Shimizu 1935: 1–2), Tokyo Electric began to tackle the home-use market seriously by introducing specialised products for home use and organising *keiretsu* retailers (Sakaguchi 1935, Tokyo Electric Co., Ltd. 1940, Tokyo Shibaura Electric Co., Ltd. 1963, Hashizume and Nishimura 2005). This campaign was the very first *keiretsu* arrangement in electrical products.

In 1930, Tokyo Electric introduced the home-use electric lightbulb, branded Mazda Lamp in a Red Package Box, the price and life span of which was lower than the high-quality lightbulbs for business use, named Mazda Lamp in a Blue Package Box (Tokyo Shibaura Electric Co., Ltd. 1963: 38–39, 1977: 33). Tokyo Electric established four of its own retail shops to demonstrate electric bulbs from 1914 to 1932, and set up 11 companies as new channels to final consumers in Tokyo and several cities between 1930 and 1933; some were committed to both wholesaling and retailing, and others only to wholesaling (Tokyo Electric Co., Ltd. 1940: 207–9). After these transitional attempts, Tokyo Electric began in 1932 to persuade local retail stores to become 'authorised dealers (*benri-ten*)' on the basis of one dealer per prefecture. The term 'dealer' was adopted according to the analysis of the dealer system of Ford in the USA (Hashizume and Nishimura 2005: 82). They were relatively powerful retailers in each area, and had special contracts with Tokyo Electric to sell Mazda Lamps (Tokyo Shibaura Electric Co., Ltd. 1963: 40, 83–84). An example was Sato Saichi Shop, which had four shops in four local cities in Fukushima Prefecture. They had sold about 71,000 lightbulbs per year, but among these only about 11,000 (16 per cent) were Mazda Lamps. The owner's contract with Tokyo Electric undertook to sell 50,000 Mazda

Lamps, and this was realised in the first year (Sakaguchi 1935: 35). This case indicates that authorised dealers were not limited exclusively to sell Mazda Lamps, but were expected to maximise sales to compete with cheap, short-life bulbs produced locally by small manufacturers. 'You will miss out when you use a bad-quality lightbulb even if it is free' was the marketing slogan of Mazda Lamp (Sakaguchi 1935: 15). By May 1933, Tokyo Electric had contracted 49 authorised dealers (Sakaguchi 1935: 4).

In addition to these *keiretsu* retailers, Tokyo Electric organised 350 Mazda Associations (*Mazda-kai*), which were to guide retailers how to deal in the light-bulbs and to nurture the spirit of mutual support and mutual prosperity between the manufacturer and retailers. *Mazda News* (*Mazda Shimpo*), a circulating magazine among merchants, was also an educational medium for them. As for the wholesale step, between 1930 and 1933 their own sales companies were organised, which divided Japan into ten blocks (including foreign territories) and were expected to serve the regional retailers, whether authorised dealers or independents.

In 1934, the sales company in Tokyo began to dispatch assistant salespeople to retailers and developed a good reputation among shop owners. In September of the same year, Tokyo Electric and its sales companies dispatched 105 salespeople to retail shops on a person-per-day basis, responding to requests from retailers. These people made door-to-door sales to customers with the retail shop owners (Sakaguchi 1935: 278). This system of supportive salespeople dispatched from the manufacturer and its sales companies became popular in the industry after around 1965 (see Chapter 6). Here can be found its origin.

Thus the marketing of Mazda Lamp included the attempt to organise *keiretsu* retailers in household electrical appliances. Gradually, however, this retailing became less of a marketing focus for Tokyo Electric. The main reason was that the company strategy was leaning towards product diversification, which included not only household appliances such as washing machines and refrigerators, but also industrial goods such as vacuum cleaners, X-ray equipment, exterior and interior illuminators, watt-hour meters and distributing boards, etc. The company also entered the electrochemical industry from 1936. This meant that Tokyo Electric became less and less dependent on lightbulbs: whereas they represented almost 70 per cent of total sales in 1927, this percentage fell to 40 per cent by 1937 (Tokyo Shibaura Electric Co., Ltd. 1977: 35). In 1939, Tokyo Electric amalgamated with Shibaura Engineering Works Co., Ltd. (*Shibaura Seisaku-sho*) to form Tokyo Shibaura Electric Co., Ltd. (now Toshiba Corporation). Shibaura Engineering Works had started as a pioneering manufacturer of telegraphic equipment named Tanaka Engineering Works (*Tanaka Seizo-sho*) in 1875, and grew to be a leading company for heavy electrical apparatus (such products as dynamos, motors and transformers) as a major member company of the Mitsui corporate group (*Mitsui zaibatsu*). This amalgamation changed the fundamental feature of the company into a manufacturer of heavy electrical apparatus, rather than of household electrical appliances. Tokyo Shibaura Electric made a major contribution to the development of heavy and chemical industries in Japan, including during the wartime regime. *Keiretsu* retailing, of course, became less significant as part of their strategy. The period when this company returned its strategic focus to household electrical appliances was after the Second World War, when almost all Japanese consumers enjoyed these products during the High Economic Growth.

Tou Lamp Chain as an organisation of peripheral retailers

In the meantime, another *keiretsu* retail network was organised as Tou Lamp Chain (AOEB 1967: 184, Toko Electric Co., Ltd. 1984). In 1935, 13 manufacturers of electric lightbulbs in Tokyo and Osaka established Tozai Electric Lightbulb Co., Ltd. as their mutual sales company. While this company arranged cartel agreements with Tokyo Electric on prices and market share (40 per cent for Tozai Electric Lightbulb and 60 per cent for Tokyo Electric in terms of shipped products), Tozai Electric Lightbulb established the unified brand name, Tou Lamp, and began to organise retailers as *keiretsu* chain stores.

The leader in the organisation of Tozai Electric Lightbulb was Toden Electric Lightbulb Co., Ltd. (now Toko Electric Co., Ltd.), which had originally been established as the manufacturing division for electric bulbs by the leading power company, Tokyo Electrical Light in 1928. They established the Tou Lamp brand and applied a *keiretsu* retail system which had begun originally in 1933 (Toko Electric Co., Ltd. 1984: 156–8). Tozai Electric Lightbulb inherited the brand name and its chain store organisation. The target of Tou Lamp was final consumers rather than business users. The company organised 200 contracted wholesale agencies (*haikyu-jo*), which were to resell Tou Lamp to *keiretsu* retailers, named Tou Lamp Chain. The number of the member retailers has been variously reported. While Toko Electric's official history (1984: 65) described 3,000 to 4,000, another commentator has estimated it as about 1,000 (AOEB 1967: 184).

In any case, these *keiretsu* stores were chosen from neighbourhood retailers in residential areas, such as general stores, rice stores and liquor (*sake*) stores. Unlike the authorised dealers of Mazda Lamps, the Tou Lamp Chain was composed of petty, powerless retailers who originally were not involved in the retailing of electrical products. Each store was supplied with electric bulbs based on a system similar to the credit selling system (*kashi-uri*) traditionally adopted by the pharmaceutical business, in which Tozai Electric Lightbulb lent a certain volume of Tou Lamps contained in displayed boxes, and when the Tou Lamps were sold, the same number was re-supplied by wholesale agencies and counted as the sales volume of that shop. Thus, *keiretsu* retailers did not need specific investments to continue the relationships with the manufacturer (Toko Electric Co., Ltd. 1984: 64–65).

Tozai Electric Lightbulb issued the monthly magazine, *Monthly Tou*, as a circular among merchants. The company also arranged short courses of lectures in many places to provide product knowledge, raise morale in sales and inspire mutual loyalty (Toko Electric Co., Ltd. 1984: 65). Furthermore, Tozai Electric Lightbulb felt that relying on only one kind of product was too narrow in terms of retailers' assortment to continue the relationship with them, so the company developed a plan to expand the brand to include miscellaneous goods such as soaps, toothpowders and toothbrushes. Tou Lamp Soap and Tou Lamp Toothpowder were introduced to the market (Toko Electric Co., Ltd. 1984: 66), but these attempts were soon disrupted by wartime controls.

The stores of Retailers' League to compete with the more powerful manufacturer

Independent from the above movements, Matsushita (now Panasonic Corporation) rapidly grew by diversification of its product lines. Matsushita was founded in Osaka in 1918 as a specialised manufacturer of insulator plates by one of the most famous Japanese entrepreneurs, Konosuke Matsushita (e.g., see Kotter 1997, McInerney 2007). Its products included, among others, attachment plugs and two-way lightbulb sockets (1918), bullet-shaped (1923) and then square (1927) battery lamps for bicycles, electric irons (1927), electric foot warmers (1929), vacuum radios (1931), dry cell batteries (1931), storage batteries (1935), electric light-bulbs (1936), electric gramophones (1936), and electric fans (1936) (Matsushita Electric Co., Ltd. 1953, 1968). Alongside this development, Matsushita adopted divisional organisation for the first time in Japan in 1933 (Kotter 1997: Chapter 9). Three divisions – (1) radio sets, (2) lamps and batteries, and (3) heating apparatus, wiring implements and synthetic resins (this was sub-divided to create a fourth division in the following year) – were organised and granted autonomy for produc-tion and sales (Matsushita Electric Industry Co., Ltd. 1968: 111–12). Then in 1935, the company reorganised independent subsidiaries composed of five manu-facturing companies and four sales companies for foreign and domestic trading, resulting in the formation of the so-called Matsushita Corporate Group (Shimotani 1993: 167–71, 1994: 2–4). The group was, however, basically for home-use electrical appliances, not diversified to heavy electric apparatus as with Tokyo Shibaura Electric.

This competitive advantage of Matsushita was brought about through their marketing ability (Takeuchi 1966: 135). When the company was still a local small-sized factory, Matsushita recruited wholesalers as its agents, which dealt with competing products as well as Matsushita's lines. From 1927 to 1932, Matsushita set up sales branches and offices throughout Japan (Ozaki 1989: 139–45), and after 1932, *keiretsu* wholesalers were organised based on divisions of products with contractual restriction to Matsushita products (Ozaki 1989: 145). At the retail stage, Matsushita began to issue a monthly circular for retailers, named Monthly Matsushita Electric, from 1927 to keep direct contact with retailers, and set up the Alliance of Retail Stores (*renmei-ten*) in 1935 (Matsushita Electric Industry Co., Ltd. 1968: 129–35). The member retailers were required to maintain retail prices and buy products from only the one wholesale company indicated by Matsushita. Each retailer was awarded bonuses in accordance with the volume it bought from the designated wholesale company. The number of member stores reached more than 10,000 by 1941 (Ozaki 1989: 147).

The core forces to organise these *keiretsu* stores were the subsidiary manufac-turer of batteries and battery lamps, and that of vacuum radio sets. Batteries and battery lamps were provided by many other small-sized manufacturers, so an aggressive price war developed. In the case of radio sets, the selling activities of these new products needed some technical support (Ozaki 1989: 147–8), so the *keiretsu* retailing of Matsushita directly aimed at price maintenance and support to retailers. However, seen as a whole, the marketing ability through *keiretsu* retailing played a substantial role in protecting Matsushita from competing with the powerful Tokyo Electric. As already mentioned, Tokyo Electric aggressively bought shares in the leading assemblers of radio sets in 1935 and 1936, but Matsushita was an exception. As Takeuchi (1966: 135–6) indicated, Matsushita had already become large enough to prevent a takeover by or merger with Tokyo Electric because the sales of Matsushita Electric were one-quarter that of Tokyo Electric in the mid-1930s. This meant that Matsushita was not a target of acquisition, but rather the major customer for radio tubes from Tokyo Electric (Takeuchi 1966: 136). The marketing ability through *keiretsu* retailing was essential for its existence before the Second World War, and remained so after the War.

Conclusion

In interwar Japan, the wide spread of electrical products, such as lightbulbs and radio receivers, shaped the new consumer life. Nevertheless, the variety of consumer electrical products was still limited. This was in contrast with the USA, in which such products as washing machines, vacuum cleaners and refrigerators, as well as radio sets, penetrated typical homes during the interwar years. In this sense, interwar Japan was still at an introductory stage which would give rise to a more mature stage in the postwar years.

The marketers of electrical products recognised the expanding domain of availability of offering (see Figure 0.1) that was brought about by the progress of technology and of the electric power industry, and attempted to spread the new technological products. In this process, marketers utilised *keiretsu* retail networks for different purposes: for the most powerful manufacturers to penetrate the consumer market by organising superior retailers, for less powerful manufacturers to survive by organising peripheral retailers, and for a developing manufacturer to be able to diversify product lines to protect itself from takeover by a more powerful manufacturer. In any case, the arrangements of *keiretsu* networks expanded the opportunities for consumers to experience and acquire the new electrical products. As soon as a modern consumer life with some electrical goods was about to begin, however, the militaristic regime disrupted this trend.

After the defeat in the War, marketing and consumption of electric products had to start afresh, but soon blossomed in the period of High Economic Growth, as will be explored in Chapter 6. For this rapid progress, the experience of the interwar years was a useful legacy. On the industrial level, without the development of electric power stations, nationwide transmission of electricity to homes and extensive spread of the wired home in the interwar period, the rapid progress of the household electric appliances industry after the War, as will be shown in Chapter 6, could not have been realised. For consumers, the wide consumption of some electrical products such as electric lightbulbs and radio receivers would make it easier for them to accept the new electrical products at home after the War. And for marketers, the use of the *keiretsu* retail networks contributed to recreate this type of network; *keiretsu* retailing became effective in competition and in distributing new products all over Japan.

4 'Tomorrow I'll go to Mitsukoshi'

The department store, a dream or a threat of modernity?

'Today I'll go to Teigeki and tomorrow to Mitsukoshi' was a historically famous advertising catchphrase in the programme brochures of Teikoku Theatre (*Teikoku Gekijo*, abbreviated to *Teigeki*) published by the Mitsukoshi Department Store in 1914–15. This was catchy for upper-middle class women living in the *Yamanote* section or High City of Tokyo, where originally the warrior class resided in the Edo Era (see Seidensticker 1991, Hatsuda 1993 215–22). This advertising copy has been interpreted as a masterpiece reflecting the newly enjoyable lifestyle of the Japanese bourgeoisie.

The department store was a major format that dominated the retail world before the Second World War; it provided modern, Western-style shopping experiences by opening up modern buildings full of modern technologies, introducing modern store operations and inspiring images of the current Western lifestyle, although the products handled were mixed collections of traditional and modern Western styles. This chapter will consider the birth and development of Japanese department stores before the Second World War, mainly focusing on the leading department store, Mitsukoshi. In contrast with the famous 'wheel of retailing' model (McNair 1931, Hollander 1960) (innovative retailers entering the market as low-status, low-margin, low-price operators, and 'trading up' the quality of merchandising handled, to mature as high-cost, high-price merchants), the Japanese department store originally appeared as a high-status, high-price, full-service retailer, and 'traded down' its merchandise in competition with other department stores, resulting in price-conscious marketing. This chapter will explore how the Japanese department store emerged as a high-status retailer who appealed with modern Western images to upper middle class consumers, and how it became popularised and spread beyond both the limited class and the big cities. In the process of development, the department store became the social institution that diffused the new shopping style and experiences to a much wider consumer base and included provincial cities.

This process developed, however, in the face of traditional retailers' antagonism. The extremely rapid progress in modernisation of retail strategies and operations had a strong impact on many traditional petty retailers, who saw a serious menace. The final part of this chapter will describe the conflict between the department stores and the traditional merchants, another aspect of retail marketing in modern Japan.

The birth of the modern department store in Japan

*Large-sized merchant houses (*odana*) as the predecessor*

While it has been indicated (Grossick and Jaumain 1999: 10) that many Western department stores grew from the drapery business, the pioneers of Japanese department stores were the inheritors of large-sized *kimono* fabric stores, called the 'large-sized merchant house' (*odana* in old Japanese).

This type of shop can be traced back to the seventeenth century. They sold silk *kimono* fabrics at a one-storey house mainly in Edo (now Tokyo, especially in the Honcho and Honkokucho area in Nihonbashi), which was a huge consuming metropolis based around the political system in the Edo Era[1]. The head office and sourcing office were usually in the old city, Kyoto, which was the producing centre of *kimono* fabrics represented by *Nishijin* brocade (Hayashi 2001: preface and 2–9) and so they were often termed the 'Kyoto-based merchants who had stores in Edo (*Edo-tana mochi Kyo-shonin*)', although they often originated outside Kyoto[2] (Hayashi 2001: 8). It was reported that in 1735, there were 47 large-sized merchant houses or *odana* in Edo, which had their sourcing offices in Kyoto (Mitsui Bunko 1980: 175). Some of them continued in business into the modern era and transformed themselves into department stores. These included the following examples (see also Table 4.1 below):

- Shirokiya Department Store (bought by Tokyu Department Store in 1967 and closed in 1999): The founder, Hikotaro Omura, whose family came from Koshu, Omi (see note 2), went to Edo (Tokyo) from Kyoto in 1662 to open a small everyday items shop (*komamonoya*), and expanded the products to deal in cotton and silk fabrics. Shirokiya had four *odana* in Edo by 1805, while the basic decision making, sourcing and processing operations continued in the head office in Kyoto (Shirokiya Co., Ltd. 1957, Hayashi 2001: 9–10).
- Mitsukoshi Department Store: The founder, Takatoshi Mitsui, with family roots in Matsuzaka, Ise (see note 2), established Echigoya in Edo in 1673. At the same time, he set up the sourcing office in Kyoto (Nakada 1959). In the latter half of the eighteenth century, Echigoya had four *odana* in Edo and one in Osaka, and the head office with the sourcing function in Kyoto together with three sourcing and/or processing shops. They also had exchange shops respectively in Kyoto, Osaka and Edo, two wholesale offices for threads in Kyoto, and a sourcing office in Matsuzaka (Nakai 1966: 89–90, Nishizaka 1992: 180 1, Ishikawa and Yasuoka 1995: 94).
- Daimaru Department Store: The founder, Hikozaemon Shimomura, whose family came from Kawachi-no-kuni (now Yao City in Osaka), opened a *kimono* fabrics shop, Daimaru, in Kyoto in 1717. By 1819, Daimaru had its

head office and six stores in Kyoto, three in Osaka, two in Edo, one each in Nagoya and Hyogo, as well as two exchange shops in Kyoto and Osaka. The head office in Kyoto took on the function of sourcing (Daimaru Co., Ltd. 1967).

- Matsuzakaya Department Store: The founder, Sukemichi Ito, with family origins in Nagoya, started a small wholesale house of *kimono* everyday items in 1611 in Kyoto. The eleventh heir, Sukesato Ito, progressed to Edo by buying out a retail shop called Matsuzakaya in 1768, which had originally been set up in the late 1700s (1704–10) by Ribe Ota, a merchant from Shiroko, Ise. The store name was retained. Then he started a wholesale shop with cotton fabrics in Edo in 1805 and a similar shop in Nagoya in 1856 (Matsuzakaya Co., Ltd. 1981).

- Takashimaya Department Store: They were latecomers. The founder, the first Shinshichi Iida, whose family came from Koshu, Takashima-gun Omi (see footnote 2), started a used clothing shop in Kyoto, named Takashimaya, in 1831. The next heir changed it to a *kimono* fabrics retail shop in 1854. The third heir was eager to submit artistic fabrics to exhibitions, as well as to start a foreign trade office in Kyoto. The store network expanded to Osaka in 1887 and to Tokyo in 1890, considerably after the Meiji Restoration (Takashimaya Co., Ltd. 1968).

In their development, there are a few innovative factors that can be identified, for example in the case of Echigoya, the precedent of Mitsukoshi Department Store.

First of all, Echigoya introduced the system of 'cash sales at the shop (*tanasaki uri*)' to target random town shoppers as early as 1676 when they started their second store in Edo (Nakada 1959: 84–88, Mitsui Bunko 1980: 24–25). This was quite different from the usual business practices at the time, whereby the retailers visited the houses of high-ranked warrior class people, bringing them samples ('*misemono uri*' or 'selling by samples'), or the products themselves (*yashiki uri* or 'selling at houses'), to get orders on credit. In addition, when Echigoya moved the store to a new location in Edo in 1683 due to a great fire, it distributed an advertisement (*hikihuda*) to private homes to introduce the system of 'selling at fixed prices (*kakene nashi*)', as well as cash sales at the shop (Nakada 1959: 109–13, Mitsui Bunko 1980: 33–34). Thus, cash sales and fixed prices, often considered the key elements of modern retailing (e.g. Walsh 1999: 46), were a historic introduction in pre-modern society. Furthermore, the sourcing houses of *odana* controlled the weavers of *Nishijin* Brocade, the famous brand of silk fabrics woven in the Nishijin area in Kyoto, by advancing payments and materials (Mitsui Bunko 1980: 170). It was reported that 247 contracted craftsmen existed in 1733 (Mitsui Bunko 1980: 166–7). The putting-out system was the source of power for *odana* in terms of marketing of *kimono* fabrics.

Despite these innovative practices, some very traditional aspects of the store operations remained. Figure 4.1 shows the woodblock prints illustrating the outside and inside of the store of Echigoya. The picture at left shows that the store

Figure 4.1 Echigoya as *odana*: the outside and the inside of the store.

Note: These pictures of woodblock prints show the outside and the inside of Mitsui Echigoya in the Edo Period.

(Left Picture) The exterior of the shop. The store put up their store logo on the *noren* curtains, which however blocked pedestrians from looking into the store.

(Right Picture) The inside of the shop. The *tatami*-mats were laid and the customers had to take off their footwear when they entered the shop. The products were not displayed beforehand; a shop boy in the middle is carrying several rolls of *kimono* fabrics to some customers, who kneel on the *tatami*-mats as shown in the back centre. Modern retail features of free entrance, free browsing and window shopping were not yet adopted by the large merchant houses (*odana*).

Reproduced courtesy of Mitsukoshi Isetan Ltd.

was screened by traditional curtains, called '*noren*', which completely secluded the inside of the store from passers-by. It had no exterior display windows, so pedestrians could not see the inside of the store, nor enjoy any window-shopping. In other words, the store did not adopt the free entrance system for browsing without obligation.

The picture on the right-hand side shows the inside of the store. When the customer entered, they had to take off their footwear, Japanese sandals (*zori*) or wooden clogs (*geta*), at the entrance. There were no in-store displays of products. In the middle of this picture, the customers are kneeling on the traditional *tatami*-mats (the rush-covered straw mats), while the shop boy, who is slightly turned towards the arrival of a person entering, is bringing some rolls of *kimono* fabrics, perhaps to the customers. This traditional sales method was called the system of 'sales with kneeling on the *tatami*-mats (*zauri*)'. Customers could not browse the products in a carefree manner. The large retail houses did not have the systems of freely entering the store, and of browsing the merchandise with no pressure to buy, which the modern retail format would usually adopt. In order to transform themselves into modern retailers, this traditional routine had to be changed.

Learning about the modern department store

After the Meiji Restoration, Echigoya and other large-sized merchant houses did not easily change these traditional store operations. They continued the system of sales involving customers' kneeling on the *tatami*-mats.

Although some signs of the revolution in retailing were appearing elsewhere, such as the so-called 'exhibition house' format (called *kanko-ba* or *kansho-ba*),[3] it was not until around the turn of the twentieth century that they set out to transform themselves into modern stores. The basis of this transformation was knowledge about the modern department store obtained by direct observations in the West. In the case of Mitsukoshi, modernisation started when Yoshio Takahashi (1933: 128–32, see also Nakagawa 1996, Mitsukoshi Co., Ltd. 2005: 38–39, Hirano 2005, Kogo 2006) was appointed as the director by Mitsui Bank, the core bank of the Mitsui family's business, in 1895. He had experienced education at Eastman Commercial School in Poughkeepsie, New York, from 1887 to 1888, and had an observation attachment to John Wanamaker Department Store in Philadelphia 'for 45 days' (Takahashi 1933: 131) after his graduation. According to Takahashi's (1933: 253) own account, when he was nominated as director, 'I had an idea that the Japanese retail business should ultimately adopt the method of Wanamaker Department Store in Philadelphia'. Despite fierce resistance by senior employees who went on strike in 1898 (Mitsukoshi Co., Ltd. 2005: 34–35), Takahashi acted decisively to reform the management system as a whole, such as introducing the Western-style book keeping system by abolishing the conventional daybook (called '*daifukucho*'), changing the management organisation to clarify the authorised limits and responsibilities of employees, and altering the design of sales floors and the store atmosphere, which included the store operations as will be mentioned below.

As Takahashi held another post as the director of Mitsui Mining concurrently in 1898, which came to dominate his time, he resigned from Mitsukoshi in 1905 in line with strategic decisions made by the Mitsui Group (Nakagawa 1996: 244). Instead, Osuke Hibi (see Hibi [1908] 1965, Hirano 2005) was dispatched to Mitsukoshi by Mitsui bank in 1898 and inherited Takahashi's reform. Hibi had never experienced department stores, so he visited London in 1906 to observe Harrods and also examined other European countries. Soon after he came back, he declared that the aim of the reform was to become 'a Harrods-like store in the East' (Mitsukoshi Co., Ltd. 2005: 66–69 and 102). The directors' personal observations in the USA and the UK inspired internal revolutions.

Mitsukoshi also dispatched their employees regularly to Western countries to study in detail various department stores; for instance, Tamisuke Yokokawa, an architect engineer, visited the USA to observe stores such as Bloomingdale's, Wanamaker and Macy's in 1896 (Mitsukoshi Co., Ltd. 2005: 39), Ekizo Toyoizumi also went to the USA in 1903 and Kohei Hayasi to Western countries between 1904 and 1906, both to study window displays (Takayanagi 1994: 132 and 155).

Other former *odana* had similar stories. In the case of Shirokiya, the tenth heir of the founder, Wakichiro Omura, studied at Cheltenham College in the UK and observed department stores there from 1887 to 1895 (Shirokiya Co., Ltd. 1957: 285–6). Similarly in Daimaru, the eleventh heir, Shotaro Shimomura, made an observational tour of department stores in the USA, the UK and other Western countries in 1908. Daimaru also frequently dispatched their employees to the USA, France and other Western countries in the 1920s (Daimaru Co., Ltd. 1967: 236 and 361). The young fifteenth heir of Matsuzakaya, Suketami Ito, joined an observational tour of department stores and other businesses in the USA in 1908, and promoted the reform of Matsuzakaya towards the department store by overcoming strong opposition from his father and many relatives (Matsuzakaya Co., Ltd. 1981: 27–29).

Takashimaya (see Takashimaya Co., Ltd. 1968, Yamamori and Kazama 1991: 91, Fujioka 2006) had active experience in the foreign markets. This company eagerly submitted various kinds of artistic *kimono* fabrics, such as *yuzen*-taste printed silk (*yuzsen-zome*), *real-hachijo*-taste striped silk (*honjachijo-jima*), *chichibu*-taste striped silk (*chichibu-jima*) and so forth, to many exhibitions not only in Japan, but also abroad, including Paris (1889), London (1891), Chicago (1893) and Antwerp (1894). Based on these foreign experiences, in 1897 the company appointed G. Gambefort & Cie as the first foreign agent to sell *kimono* fabrics in Lyon, France, and then organised some foreign offices in Lyon (1899), London (1906), Sydney (1909) and New York (1910). Along with these activities, the Department of Foreign Trade of Takashimaya became an independent company in 1905. Despite these experiences, the fourth heir of Takashimaya, Shinshichi Iida, was originally reluctant to reform Takashimaya into a department store because he was proud of *kimono* fabrics trading. When the younger members of the Iida family insisted on reform around 1918–19, he talked with his daughter's husband: 'now a big issue is raised and the opinions are divided between me and other family members . . . the younger members of the Iida Family insisted on changing the method of store operations to that of the department store' (Takashimaya Co., Ltd. 1968: 340, also see Fujioka 2006: 51). Shinshichi, however, compromised in the end. The story suggested that the exceptionally early experiences in the foreign markets of this company, as well as the recognition of the rivals who had already begun the transformation, encouraged their reform.

Birth of the modern department store

The transformation to the department store included abandoning traditional store operations and introducing the modern Western way. Table 4.1 shows how the former *odana* began to adopt change.

The first step in reform was to abolish sales involving customers' kneeling on the *tatami*-mats, and to introduce modern Western-looking display cases in the store and window displays externally, encouraging freedom to browse and window-shop.

In the case of Mitsukoshi, soon after Yoshio Takahashi became the director the change to a showcase system began, and this change was completed in all stores

Table 4.1 Major department stores originating as *odana* which began business in the Edo Period

Store name	Retail shop begun in Edo	The founder and family	Original hometown[1]	Leadership towards department store	Establishment of joint-stock corporation	Discard of kneeling format	Street display windows introduced	Western-style premises built	Shoe caretakers dropped	Stores as of 1934[2]	M² of total sales floors, largest store as of 1934
Shirokiya	1662	Hikotaro Omura (Omura Family)	Nagahama, Koshu (Omi)	Wakichiro Omura (10th heir) Kinjiro Iwahashi (employed executive)	1919	1903	1903	1903: 3-storey (Tokyo) 1911: 5-storey (Tokyo) 1920: 8-storey (Osaka)	1924	8 stores	Tokyo Store with 28,621 m²
Mitsukoshi	1673	Takatoshi Mitsui (Mitsui Family)	Matsuzaka, Ise	Yoshio Takahashi (employed executive) Osuke Hibi (employed executive)	1904	1895	1903	1908: 3-storey (Tokyo) 1914: 5-storey with basement, 13,210 m² (Tokyo)	1924	9 stores	Nihonbashi Muromachi Store in Tokyo with 45,983 m²
Daimaru	1717	Hikozaemon Shimomura (Shimomura Family)	Fushimi, Kyoto	Shotaro Shimomura (11th heir)	1920	1908	1908	1912: 3-storey (Kyoto) 1922: 6-storey (Osaka)	1926	3 Stores	Osaka Store with 40,053 m²
Matsuzakaya	1768	Sukesato Ito (11th heir) (Ito Family)	Nagoya	Suketami Ito (15th heir)	1910	1907	1907	1907: 3-storey (Tokyo) 1910: 3-storey (Kyoto)	1924	8 stores	Nagoya Store with 23,193 m²
Takashimaya	1831	Shinshichi Iida (Iida Family)	Koshu Takashima-gun (Omi)	Young members of Iida family, allowed by Shinshichi Iida (4th heir)	1919	1896	1896	1912: 3-storey (Kyoto) 1922: 7-storey, 9,917 m² (Osaka)	1927	4 stores	Nankai Store in Osaka with 29,977 m²

Sources: Matsuzakaya Co., Ltd. 1981, Shirokiya Co., Ltd. 2005, Daimaru Co., Ltd. 1957, Mitsukoshi Co., Ltd. 1968, Takashimaya Co., Ltd. 1968, AOEB 1983: 200–3, and website of each company.

Notes:

1 Merchants from Ise (now the northern and the middle part of Mie Prefecture) and Omi (now Shiga Prefecture) had a historical reputation as progressive merchants.

2 The number excludes a station stall (in the case of Shirokiya) and a restaurant (in the case of Daimaru), but includes medium-sized branch stores.

in 1900 (Mitsukoshi Co., Ltd. 2005: 34–35 and 37–39). Shirokiya also began this introduction in 1903 (Shirokiya Co., Ltd. 1957: 287–8), followed by Matsuzakaya when they began an experimental trial at the reopened Ueno store in 1907 (Matsuzakaya Co., Ltd. 1981: 27), and by Daimaru in 1908 when the store in Tokyo was renovated (Daimaru Co., Ltd. 1967: 247).

Along with this reform, exterior plate-glass display windows (see Takayanagi 1994, Tajima 1999) were introduced to show the products and store image to the pedestrians on the streets, replacing the traditional *noren* curtains and plastered storehouse walls. While some shops with imported Western products in a few port towns such as Yokohama and Nagasaki had introduced these display windows (Takayanagi 1994: 45–99), it was the department stores that began to attract people's attention with them. Takashimaya introduced the display windows to the newly renovated Kyoto store in 1896 (Takashimaya Co., Ltd. 1968: 366, Takashimaya website, see also Tajima 1999: 258). This was followed by Mitsukoshi (Mitsukoshi Co., Ltd. 2005: 37, see also Takayanagi 1994: 130–2) and Shirokiya (Shirokiya Co., Ltd. 1957: 293–5) in 1903, Matsuzakaya at the Ueno Store in 1907 (Matsuzakaya Co., Ltd. 1981: 27), and Daimaru in 1908 (Tajima 1999: 258).

These developments expanded the use of mannequins for the display windows, which were gradually supplied by domestic manufacturers from around 1900. The stores began to organise designers who were responsible for the display windows under the section/department of advertising, display or design (Tajima 1999: 259–71). Although mannequins in these windows often wore Japanese-style *kimono*, the display windows contributed to the modern, commercialised shopping streets, where many consumers began to enjoy going around window-shopping. The event in which Morinaga began to teach how to present display windows for its small-sized *keiretsu* sweet shops, as described in Chapter 1, was an attempt to expand this movement into their *keiretsu* retailers.

The decisive step towards the modern department store was to expand the range of assorted products and to construct a modern building with departmentalised sales floors. At the end of 1904, Mitsukoshi's publicity featured the famous 'declaration of the department store' as the organisation became a joint-stock company:

> We will increase the variety of products our store handles, will provide customers with any items as far as clothing and ornaments are concerned under one roof, and finally end up with what is called a department store in the USA.
>
> (cited from Mitsukoshi Co., Ltd. 2005: 362)

Mitsukoshi also rewrote section 5 of the certificate of incorporation in 1907: 'The purpose of the company is to carry on the business of exhibiting and selling goods, which means the business of what is called "department store" in the USA' (Mitsukoshi Co., Ltd. 2005: 363). From around this time, Mitsukoshi began to expand their assortments. Although they had begun selling Western-style clothing at Mitsukoshi as early as 1888, inspired by the events at *Rokumei-kan* or the Hall of the Baying Stag, this was stopped in 1895 because the company judged the selling of such clothing as 'premature' (Mitsukoshi Co., Ltd. 2005: 33 and 67). In 1906, it was restarted. Mitsukoshi also began to sell Western-style cosmetics, hats and children's accessories in 1905, and further expanded the variety of assortment to include such items as Western-style shoes and umbrellas, travelling goods, toys, bags and combs, miscellaneous goods, jewellery, stationery, furniture, sets of dolls for female festivals, etc., and provided restaurant services, photo studios and exhibitions by 1907 (Mitsukoshi Co., Ltd. 2005: 65, 68, 70 and 72; see also Hatsuda 1993: 95).

In 1908, Mitsukoshi demolished the old storehouse that had been a popular *odana* and constructed a 'temporary store (*kari eigyo-jo*)' as a three-storey Renaissance style building made of wood with 5,210 m² total floor area. In 1914, Mitsukoshi completed 'the central store (*honten*)', which was a ferro-concrete five-storey building with a basement. The building was equipped with four lifts and an escalator, and totalled 13,210 m² of sales floors; Mitsukoshi were proud of owning 'the largest building in the world east of the Suez Canal' (Mitsukoshi Co., Ltd. 2005: 70, 75, 82 and 84–85). Thus, the full-fledged modern department store was finally established as shown in Figure 4.2. Although this store was burnt down when the Kanto earthquake occurred in 1923, the reconstruction of the central store was completed in 1927. In the meantime, Mitsukoshi expanded the store network by setting up the Osaka branch store in a seven-storey, one-basement building with 9,250 m² total floor area in 1917, and the Shinjuku branch store in Tokyo in a five-storey, one-basement building with 3,300 m² total floor area in 1925.

Other former *odana* progressed in a similar way. Matsuzakaya opened up a three-storey building as an experimental store in Ueno, Tokyo in 1907 and a three-storey shop made of wood in Nagoya in 1910 (Matsuzakaya Co., Ltd. 1981: 27–30). It introduced the department system to handle a wider range of products in 1917. The departments were composed of six (Tokyo) and eight (Nagoya) floors, but 90 per cent of sales still concerned *kimono*-related goods. It gradually added new departments, however: miscellaneous products in 1920, art and craft products, photographic equipment and musical instruments in 1924, restaurants, studios and barbers in 1926, and sales of bed linen, ceramics and kitchenware in 1927 (Matsuzakaya Co., Ltd. 1981: 31–32). Matsuzakaya further opened a Ginza store in Tokyo with an eight-storey, one-basement concrete steel building in 1924, a Nagoya store with six storeys and two basements in 1926, and so forth (Matsuzakaya Co., Ltd. 1981: 42–43).

In the case of Shirokiya, after constructing a three-storey building in 1903 that was a blend of Japanese and Western styles, where they sold fabrics such as wool and muslin delaines for Western-style clothing, Western-style cosmetics, toys, miscellaneous products, etc. in addition to *kimono*-related products, the company extended this to a five-storey building equipped with a lift in 1911. Shirokiya also built an eight-storey building in Osaka (Shirokiya Co., Ltd. 1957:287–9, 293–7 and 345–8). Similarly, Daimaru constructed a three-storey Saracen-style building made of wood in Kyoto (where its headquarters had moved) in 1912, and a six-storey ferro-concrete building in Osaka in 1922 (Daimaru Co., Ltd. 1967: 281–2

Figure 4.2 The modern building of Mitsukoshi Department Store in 1914.

Note: This Mitsukoshi Department Store was completed in 1914. The upper picture shows the outside of the building. The lower pictures show the central well-hole inside the store.

Reproduced courtesy of Mitsukoshi Isetan Ltd.

and 329–30). Takashimaya built a three-storey storehouse-style construction in Kyoto in 1912, and opened up a modern seven-storey ferro-concrete building with a basement in Osaka in 1922 (Takashimaya Co., Ltd. 1968: 12 and 19–20, Takashimaya website).

The emergence of such multi-storey concrete steel buildings was evidence that the modern department store was finally established in Japan. The external appearance was modern and Western at a glance, although each store adopted various styles of design, such as the Gothic, the Renaissance, modernism and art deco, and a style with some Japanese features (Hashizume 1999: 285–7). These buildings became a symbol of commercialised shopping streets in major cities, and changed the Japanese cityscape to something like the Western one.

The institution to promote the Japanese version of the West

Although the appearance of these buildings was modern and Western, at first the stores still operated in a traditional way.

A typical example was the shoes caretaker (*gesoku-ban*) system: when customers entered the modern department store buildings, they were still required to take off their shoes and leave them to the shoes caretakers or put covers on them. This was a vestige of store operations in *odana* as mentioned above. A few Japanese intellectuals who knew foreign department stores well complained about this system:

> In the department stores in London and any other countries, entrances and exits are quite convenient . . . I wish 'the Japanese department stores could follow that soon'. Needless to say, foreign people put on shoes and are not required to put covers on their shoes [when they enter the stores] as Japanese department stores do . . . In Japan, people are required to put covers on shoes, and when people wear *geta* [Japanese wooden clogs], they have to take them off and leave them, so they have to walk with their bare feet or almost bare feet with *tabi* [traditional split-toe socks] inside the stores . . . Exits are also troublesome. The *geta* caretakers receive the number tickets, match them to the *geta* respectively, sometimes clean up the *geta* with superficial kindness, and arrange them . . . Department stores even in China and Singapore do not have such a system. Why do only Japanese stores need such an annoying system?
>
> (Shimizu 1924b)

It was not until 1924, ten years after the modern Western-style building was constructed, that Mitsukoshi abolished this system (Mitsukoshi Co., Ltd. 2005: 110–11). Other department stores also began to give it up after the Kanto earthquake in 1923. Takashimaya abolished it in 1927 because when they reconstructed the building after the earthquake, they did not adopt carpeted floors (Takashimaya Co., Ltd. 1968: 21). Similarly, Shirokiya introduced the system of walking into the store with shoes on (*dosoku nyujo*) in their Osaka store in 1924, when they changed to linoleum flooring (Shirokiya Co., Ltd. 1957: 377). Matsuzakaya abandoned the removal of shoes when the Ginza store was opened in 1924, soon after the earthquake (Matsuzakaya Co., Ltd. 1981: 42). In the case of Daimaru, the Osaka Store advertised in 1926, 'Please visit Daimaru with your shoes on'. Despite some disputes in the company over whether *kimono* silk fabrics would be badly stained with shoe dust, the company recognised that the abolition of this system increased the number of visitors around threefold (Daimaru Co., Ltd. 1967: 336–7).

The department stores delivered various types of modern Western atmosphere to Japanese people and began to function as the social institution through which many Japanese met Western-style novelty in their everyday life. The following is an example from Mitsukoshi (see Mitsukoshi Co., Ltd. 2005: 68–105).

In 1909 Mitsukoshi organised a Boys' Music Band which played Western wood and brass instruments. According to Osuke Hibi's philosophy, the department stores were to be 'the stores for society and the public' (Hibi 1911: 247). This departure was similar to house concert events played by the employees' orchestra at Bon Marché in Paris (Miller 1981: 169–73) although it is not clear if Hibi was influenced by this Western counterpart's event. The Boys' Music Band at Mitsukoshi was a fanfare to announce that the department store could introduce something new. It exerted some influence on the Japanese business world: Shirokiya Department Store organised a Girls' Music Band in 1911, in which the girls wore traditional *kimono* but played Western instruments such as violin and guitar (Shirokiya Co., Ltd. 1957: 308–11), and as will be mentioned below, the Takarazuka Revue, which held its popularity until recent times, also started under the influence of Mitsukoshi's Music Band (Kei-Hanshin Kyuko Electric Railway Co., Ltd. 1959: 137).

The interior and the operations of the department store were full of novelty. For instance, Mitsukoshi began to install free lounges decorated and stocked with luxurious Western-style furniture (see Figure 4.3 [A]) as early as 1900, even before the modern building was built. It was 'a beautifully decorated small room with [Western-style] tables, in which waitresses served teas and cakes for customers' relaxation or while waiting for others', as Mitsukoshi's historical record reported. At first, however, 'the customers were hesitant to enter these rooms; they only peeped into the rooms and talked with each other about how gorgeous the furniture was' (Mitsukoshi Co., Ltd. 2005: 39, see also Jin'no 1994: 88–90). Other contrivances at this early stage included a Western-style restaurant in the store (1907), an observation floor called a 'float garden' (1907), a group of messenger boys who wore a UK-styled uniform and delivered orders by bicycle (1909, see Figure 4.3 [B]), and receiving telephone orders (1911). When the store's new building was completed in 1914, it was also equipped with many new features suggesting a modern Western atmosphere to the customers, such as the central well (see the lower pictures in Figure 4.2), lion statues cast by a British artist set at the entrance, and the lifts and escalators signifying modern technology (see Figure 4.3 [C]). It was natural that each sales floor exhibited many modern Western-style products and expanded these assortments in due course to include Western-style clothing, cosmetics, umbrellas, shoes, socks, cameras, liquors like wine, whisky and brandy, furniture, travel goods and children's products. It also sold electrical products,

[B] The messenger boys (1909), who delivered orders. The boys wore a UK-style uniform and used a bicycle: a modern, Western means of transport.

[A] The free lounge (1900). It was reported that many customers were hesitant to use it due to its looking too gorgeous.

[D] The sales floor for electric products (1925). As explored in Chapter 3, electric products signified new modern life.

[C] The escalator provided in the new modern building (1914). Some customers still wore *kimono*.

Figure 4.3 Mitsukoshi: the Western ambience.

Reproduced courtesy of Mitsukoshi Isetan Ltd.

which began to spread in the 1920s, as explored in the previous chapter (see Figure 4.3 [D]).

A historian of Japanese department stores, Jin'no (1994, 1999a), emphasised that exhibiting Western-style furniture diffused the new 'taste (*shumi*)' which the department stores encouraged. As part of the so-called Taisho modernism (see Historical settings to Part I), the purely Japanese-style houses owned by the upper and upper-middle classes began to introduce a Western-style sitting room fitted with appropriate furniture, mainly to meet guests. This compromise in home style or 'the Japanese way of modernism (*nihon-teki modernism*)' (Jin'no 1994: 106) was encouraged by the promotion of the West through the department stores.

Recent historical research (Jin'no 1994, 1999a, 1999b, Nishizawa 1999, Fujioka 2006) also focused on the role of small-sized groups organised by the department stores themselves in order to study fashion and to attempt to take the lead in shaping it. In 1905 Mitsukoshi launched the Research Association on Vogues (*Ryuko Kenkyu-Kai* or *Ryuko-kai*) by asking the advice of scholars, artists and newspaper reporters as members (Mitsukoshi Co., Ltd. 2005: 65). The Association had regular research meetings on fashions, hosted prize contests to improve designs, held exhibitions of artistic works, and arranged series of public lectures (see Jin'no 1994: Chapter 3). Takashimaya also (see Nishizawa 1999: 68–73, Fujioka 2006: 74–82) started the Association for Selecting the One Hundred Most Beautiful (*Hyakusen-kai*) in 1913 by organising artists, scholars, poets and critics. The Association ran design prize contests by setting themes such as 'the new Japanese-style design (*shin yamato moyo*)' and 'sapphire colour', and held exhibitions of prize-winning works. Many manufacturers observed and followed the trends in design exhibited by Takashimaya's Association (Fujioka 2006: 79–80). Daimaru also started to hold the 'Meeting to Study Colours (*ken-sai-kai*)' from 1916 (Daimaru Co., Ltd. 1967: 317), and Shirokiya launched similar organisations around 1922 (Shirokiya Co., Ltd. 1957: 358–9).

The designs these organisations focused mainly on were for *kimono* fabrics because many women still usually wore *kimono* in their everyday life. As Jin'no (1994: Chapter 3) explored in the case of Mitsukoshi, the fashions that the Research Association on Vogues often took part in were the reactionary tendencies, e.g. the 'Genroku taste' (the Genroku Era, 1688 to 1704, was a sub-period of the Edo Period) and the 'Edo taste'. Nevertheless, there was a tendency that 'the Japanese-style introduced the Western tastes, and the Western-style was carried in the Japanese tastes' (Jin'no 1994: 211); for instance, *kimono* fabrics accepted the modern secessionism designs, while the neckties only used for Western-style clothing adopted the traditional patterns employed by *kimono* fabrics (Jin'no 1994: 211–2). Thus, the blending of Western and Japanese tastes was progressing even though *kimono* fabrics were still the important item for department stores.

The blended atmosphere of the West and Japan was typically represented by the advertising posters of Mitsukoshi, shown in Figure 4.4, drawn by Hisui Sugiura, who is judged as one of the early Japanese designers who was influenced by the style of art nouveau and created the Japanese equivalent (Un'no 1978). The art nouveau style picture at left was to announce the opening of the new building. The picture on the right was drawn by him in the same year. The atmosphere created by these posters suggested the social role of the department store as the medium to foster the Japanese way of westernisation and modernisation.

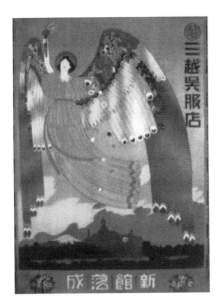

Figure 4.4 Advertising posters of Mitsukoshi by Hisui Sugiura (1914).

Note: These advertisements were painted by Hisui Sugiura, who was hired by Mitsukoshi. He was influenced by the style of art nouveau and is now praised as one of the early Japanese designers who created the Japanese version of art nouveau (Un'no 1978). It is known that the art nouveau style originally had some influences from the so-called Japonisme, that is, the tendency of many Japanese woodblock prints or *ukiyo-e* drawn in the Edo Era appearing especially in France in the late 19th century; Japanese artists tended to have a greater affinity with the art nouveau style.

(Left Picture) The poster to announce the opening of the new department store in October 1914.

(Right Picture) The poster painted for the spring sales in the same year.

Reproduced courtesy of Mitsukoshi Isetan Ltd.

Popularisation of department stores alongside politico-economic conflicts

Development of department stores by new entrants

In the 1920s and 1930s, competition among the department stores was becoming tough, so they turned increasingly to the low-price appeal. This meant that the Japanese department stores originally targeting the upper- and upper-middle classes were starting to 'trade down' their sales to the massive middle class in urban areas.

Bargain sales were becoming popular among department stores. In the case of Mitsukoshi, the Osaka branch store decided for the first time to set four special bargain days, called 'prosperity days (*sakae-bi*)', from 1 October 1919 to sell *kimono* fabrics aimed at the masses and daily goods for practical use; and Mitsukoshi in Tokyo ran what they called 'cotton days (*momen day*)', for three days from 3 November 1919 (Mitsukoshi Co., Ltd. 2005: 94). These bargains were doing a roaring trade, so Mitsukoshi expanded their assortments to turn to the mass market. Shirokiya in Tokyo followed, setting up a bargain space on the fourth floor in 1922 (Shirokiya Co., Ltd. 1957: 349–50).

In 1926 Takashimaya in Osaka opened a bargain space on the fifth floor to sell any 100 items at a uniform price of 10-*sen* (*sen* was an old monetary unit) (Takashimaya Co., Ltd. 1968: 394), followed in 1931 by the establishment of the sales floor dedicated to selling at uniform prices (Takashimaya Co., Ltd. 1968: 398). The idea further developed into the network of Takashimaya 10-*sen* Store (the name was later changed to the 10- and 20-*sen* Store, and then the 10-, 20- and 50-*sen* Store), an exceptionally large corporate chain numbering 106 stores by 1941 (Suzuki 1980: 136–40, Hirano 2008: 181–4, see also MCI 1936). This chain is evidence of a diversification policy of the department store into the extremely low-price market.

The intensified price competition among department stores was stimulated by new entrants to the department store format, which had three different origins. One source was the latecomers in *kimono* fabric stores (*gofuku-ya*), which arose after the Meiji Restoration in 1868. Matsuya Department Store (see Matsuya Co., Ltd. 1969) developed from Tsuruya, which began as a store selling cotton for *kimono* in Yokohama in 1869. The company bought Imagawa Matsuya in 1889, which had been a *kimono* fabric store since 1776 in Kanda Tokyo, and continued the store name, Matsuya, which reflected its historic lineage better than Tsuruya. It built a Western-style three-storey building in 1907, and opened up a modern department store in 1925 in Ginza Tokyo, occupying about 4,472 m² for sales from the first to the sixth floors of an eight-storey building with two basements. Because Tsuruya's origin was soon after the Meiji Restoration and it bought the traditional *kimono* fabric store started in the Edo Era, Matsuya was sometimes considered part of the orthodox department stores as the inheritors of *odana*. In the meantime, Isetan Department Store (see Isetan Co., Ltd. 1990) opened a magnificent store in 1933 in Shinjuku Tokyo with a total of 14,444 m² floors in a seven-storey, two-basement building. This store originated in Iseya Tanji *Kimono* Fabric Store (*Ise-ya Tanji Gofuku-ten*) started in 1886 in Kanda Tokyo.

The second source of newcomers was the department store at the railway station, which was called the 'terminal department store (*terminal departo*)'. This idea grew up in the 1920s, based on the development of the networks of private railways in the great cities. While the railway service was started in 1872 under government operations, a private company started horse tramway services in 1882 and railway services in 1883 (Wakuda 1993: 1). The number of private companies increased to 410 by 1930; in terms of the length of track, by 1930 the state company held 14,487 kilometres, while the private companies held 7,018 kilometres in total (SB website 1). As for metropolitan areas such as Tokyo, Osaka and Nagoya, large-sized private (electric) railway companies developed after Tobu Railway Co., in Tokyo, which originally began in 1899, but the Railway

Nationalisation Law in 1906 resulted in the nationalisation of the 17 major private railway companies.[4] The new idea of the 'terminal department store' was introduced by Hankyu Electric Railway (Hanshin Kyuko Electric Railway) in Osaka, which started as Mino-Arima Electric Railway Track Co., in 1907 after the original company, Han-Tsuru Railway, was nationalised by the above Law.

The president of Hankyu Electric Railway, Ichizo Kobayashi, began terminal department stores as part of an excellent business strategy. The company developed not only the railway network in suburban areas, but also many wide housing lots adjacent to the railways, in which Hankyu constructed numerous houses and sold them to consumers who would automatically become the passengers of the railway. Initially the company built 200 houses in 1910, including both Japanese and Western-designed homes, on a site about 109,157 m² in total, and sold them by instalment payments for ten years. The process continued until 1944, creating 24 housing lots with about 3,952,800 m² in total (Kei-Hanshin Kyuko Electric Railway Co., Ltd. 1959: 116–25; see also Nishikawa et al. 1993, Noda et al. 1993, Yasuda et al. 1998, Otani et al. 1998). The company was also involved in the electricity supply business, not only for the operation of electric trains, but also private houses and factories in areas adjacent to the railways through its transformer stations, which received power both from its own thermal and water power plants and from other companies' plants (Kei-Hanshin Kyuko Electric Railway Co., Ltd. 1959: 85–92). The sales volume of the power supply business was the second largest in Hankyu's revenues after the sales volume of the transportation business (see Terauchi and Haneda 1993, Haneda and Terauchi 1993).

As part of this business strategy, Hankyu Electric Railway opened up a hot springs resort in Takarazuka on the Umeda-Takarazuka Line to attract the passengers. Here the Takarazuka Revue became popular, which first started in 1927 following the Mitsukoshi Boys' Music Band, but developed a dedicated music school in 1933 and a dedicated revue theatre with 4,000 seats in 1938 (Kei-Hanshin Kyuko Electric Railway Co., Ltd. 1959: 135–53). Takarazuka Revue is still popular today, and can be seen as a typical Japanese version of a Western-style revue.

The store at the railway terminus, Hankyu Department Store (see Kei-Hanshin Kyuko Electric Railway Co., Ltd. 1959: 166–77, Hankyu Department Store Co., Ltd. 1976), was also part of this strategy. Ichizo Kobayashi built a five-storey building in Umeda Osaka in 1920, and invited Shirokiya Department Store to its first floor in order to observe how the store operated and what products were saleable, while Hankyu ran their own restaurant on the second floor and used the third to fifth floors as their office. In 1925 when the contract with Shirokiya expired, the so-called Hankyu Market was opened, occupying the second and third floors to sell foods, cosmetics and household articles, while the first was renovated as a waiting space for passengers at Umeda Station; the fourth and fifth floors were used for their own restaurants. On the strength of this experience, Hankyu Department Store was begun in 1929 in a new ferro-concrete building with eight floors and two basements and 10,605 m² total floor space, built for a new Umeda Station of the Hankyu Electric Railway. In this building, the first floor was used for ticket gates for trains, while the second to sixth floors and the first basement were sales floors and the seventh and eighth were restaurants. These were the first attempts to create the so-called 'terminal department store'.

The strategy of Hankyu group as a whole can be evaluated as an early version of relationship marketing, or lifestyle retailing, which geared people up to a common lifestyle by residing in similar grades of private houses located in planned residential lots, utilising the same private railway services in their everyday life, enjoying the same entertainments such as Takarazuka Revue, and shopping at the terminal department store of Hankyu.

The great success of the first terminal department store rapidly spread the idea that the store could be used to capture travelling passengers as customers. Some private railway companies followed Hankyu's method of developing adjacent housing lots, while others only picked up the idea of terminal department stores. In Tokyo, inspired by the good reputation of Hankyu Market, when Keio Electric Railway built the new Shinjuku station building in 1927, Musashinoya (inaugurated in 1879) opened up the Shinjuku Store by using the second to fifth floors (AOEB 1967: 127–9, Suzuki 1980: 6). Although this attempt failed due to the bankruptcy of Musashinoya in 1928, the idea continued to be followed. In 1931, Matsuya Department Store rented the new terminal building of Asakusa Station, Tokyo, from Tobu Railway Co., which had seven floors and one basement with a huge 37,500 m² of total floor space. It started a branch department store by devoting six floors to selling products and two floors for restaurants and events, while the ticket gates were located in the basement (Matsuya Co., Ltd. 1969: 214–18). 'Terminal department stores' continued to be established, such as Keihin Department Store at Shinagawa Station (Tokyo) by the Keihin Kyuko Electric Railway in 1933, Hanshin Department Store at Umeda Station (Osaka) of Hanshin Electric Railway in 1933, Toyoko Department Store at Shibuya Station (Tokyo) by Tokyo Yokohama Electric Railway in 1934, Kiku-ya Department Store at Ikebukuro Station (Tokyo) by Musashino Electric Railway in 1940, etc. (see Suzuki 1980: 6–7, Tobu Department Store Co., Ltd. 1993: 17). These developments gave strong encouragement to the popularisation of department stores, and this type of store was the main driving force in accelerating the price competition and 'trading down' of the department stores.

The final source of new entrants to the department store industry was the provincial department store. In some provincial cities, such as Yokosuka, Shizuoka, and Hiroshima (Suzuki 1980: 84), progressive provincial retailers began to challenge the department store business, following the pattern in major cities. For example, in Sapporo City in Hokkaido Island, Marui-Imai Department Store, which began an everyday items store (*komamonoya*) in 1872 and became a cotton fabric store for *kimono* in 1874, started imitating the trend to department stores as early as 1916 with a three-storey modern building of about 4,165 m² of total floor space (Marui Imai Co., Ltd. 1992: 52, 59 and 98). The founder had observed emergent department stores in Tokyo and Osaka, and his son and a right-hand man had studied them in the USA for three years from 1898 (Marui Imai Co., Ltd. 1992: 87–8, 94 and 104).

In Sendai City in the north-east (Tohoku) region, Fujisaki, which can trace its origin back to a cotton *kimono* fabric store started in 1819, opened a department of

Western-style clothing in 1914, then in 1919 a store with a two-storey wooden Western-style building of about 660 m^2 of total floor space, and in 1932 a three-storey reinforced concrete building with a basement and about 2,800 m^2 of total floor space (Fujisaki Co., Ltd. 1990: 22, 86, 92–93 and 110–11). The fourth heir of this store, the fourth Saburosuke, who grew up with an American private teacher and had twice undertaken world tours, became an entrepreneur; he launched trade with Brazil, Argentina, India, Burma and Taiwan, as well as entering the production field by operating textile factories (Fujisaki Co., Ltd. 1990: 48–106). The modernisation of his store was part of his innovative businesses.

In Fukuoka City in Kyushu Island, Iwataya Department Store, which also originated from a *kimono* fabric store started in 1754, established a 'terminal department store' at Tenjin, the location of Fukuoka Station of the Kyushu Railway, in 1936. The store had eight storeys and a basement with about 15,000 m^2 of total floor space, and a three-storey and basement annex with about 2,400 m^2 (Iwataya Co., Ltd. 1967: 1 and 37–54). Although Fukuoka was a local city, it had a population of about 300,000, and a few department stores had already appeared such as Tamaya (changed from an old *kimono* fabric store in 1925) and Matsuya (a different store from Matsuya in Tokyo; this Fukuoka store was changed from Matsuya Muslin Store in 1935 with aggressively attractive low prices) (Iwataya Co., Ltd. 1967: 32–33 and 65). Iwataya Department Store was established to compete with these.

Thus, although the actual conditions of their emergence varied, the retail format of the department store was certainly spreading beyond the major cities.

Dominance by the department store

The upsurge of new entrants naturally increased the weight of sales by department stores in the retail sector and enlarged people's opportunities to utilise them. Although a nationwide census of commerce was not conducted until 1952 in Japan, five major local authorities,[5] i.e., Tokyo, Yokohama, Nagoya, Osaka and Kobe, conducted their own censuses in the 1930s. According to these surveys the weight of department stores in each city can be calculated, as shown in Table 4.2.

In the Old Tokyo City – the centre area composed of 15 Wards (*ku*) – sales by the department stores, only 0.03 per cent of all retail stores, took more than 32 per cent of total retail sales (the sum of sales by retail stores and retail sales by wholesale-cum-retail stores). In all areas of Tokyo City (later known as 'Greater Tokyo (*Dai-Tokyo*)' to include the original 15 Wards plus 20 Wards in New Tokyo), the department stores represented 25 per cent of total retail sales. While the data in other cities were not as high as in Tokyo, it was apparent that the department stores, with 0.01 to 0.03 per cent of the total number of retail stores, still reached almost 10 to 15 per cent of retail sales. The new format of department stores was shaping the oligopolistic structure of the market in these major cities.

The reliability of these census data is debatable in whether the weight of the department stores was exaggerated; contemporary scholars (Hon'iden and Nakanishi 1938: 91) noted that the percentage of department stores especially in Tokyo looked 'excessively high', and a historian (Suzuki 1980: 117) suspected

Table 4.2 The weight of department stores in five major cities (1931–1935)[1]

City	Year of investigation	Number of stores			Sales volume			Number of employees[2]		
		All retail stores	Department stores	% of dept. stores	All retail sales[3] (yen)	Department stores	% of dept. stores	All retail stores	Department stores	% of dept. stores
Greater Tokyo[4]	1931/32	128,303	36	0.03	944,151,554	235,678,169	25.0	311,126	15,980	5.1
Old Tokyo	1931	58,602	18	0.03	656,699,134	211,818,050	32.3	154,831	14,128	9.1
New Tokyo	1932	69,701	18	0.03	287,452,420	23,860,119	8.3	156,295	1,8852	1.2
Yokohama	1933	17,931	4	0.02	92,546,772	10,503,974	11.3	42,720	1,225	2.9
Nagoya	1933	25,680	5	0.02	128,557,039	19,875,974	15.5	48,857	1,991	4.1
Osaka	1935	73,141	7	0.01	780,716,221	108,456,316	13.9	180,931	14,133	7.8
Kobe	1933	18,709	6	0.03	128,525,461	13,086,200	10.2	41,647	1,440	3.5

Notes:

1 This table is according to the census survey of commerce in each city, which was conducted by each local government based on the recommendation by the Ministry of Commerce and Industry. The survey divided merchants' establishments into three industries; that is, the retail, the wholesale-cum-retail, and the wholesale industries. The major part of sales by the establishments in the wholesale-cum-retail industry was generally for wholesale, so data of the numbers of retail stores and employees excludes the wholesale-cum-retail industry.

2 'Number of employees' in this table includes both self-employed people and employed workers.

3 'All retail sales' in this table includes both retail sales by the retail stores and retail sales by the wholesale-cum-retail premises. Only in the case of Osaka, retail sales were calculated in all three industries; so 'all retail sales' in Osaka are the sum of retail sales made by retail premises, wholesale-cum-retail premises and wholesale premises.

4 'Old Tokyo' started as 15 Wards (ku) in 1878 and was defined 'City' in 1889. It absorbed surrounding areas of 20 Wards in 1932, which was called 'New Tokyo'. The 'Greater Tokyo (Dai Tokyo)' meant the total areas of Tokyo. The 'Greater Tokyo' was, however, almost equivalent to the current 23 Wards (from 1947), which is now recognised as the heartland of Tokyo.

that not all of the small-sized merchants would have been counted. Even so, the dominance of department stores in the retail field was undeniable in itself.

Regarding provincial cities, a unique strategy called temporary sales exhibitions (*shuccho hanbai*) adopted by the major metropolitan department stores, as well as some emergent provincial department stores as already mentioned, exerted a strong impact on provincial retailers. The metropolitan stores, such as Mitsukoshi, Shirokiya, Matsuzakaya, Daimaru, Takashimaya and Matsuya, frequently held temporary sales exhibitions in provincial cities, usually for a few days per exhibition (Hori 1934: 137), by pre-advertising, dispatching sales clerks and the products to be sold, such as *kimono* fabrics, Western-style haberdashery, everyday items, miscellaneous items and foods (Hori 1933a: 113), and renting exhibition venues such as public halls, theatres, Japanese-style hotels, temples, private residences, etc. (Hori 1933b: 126–7, 1934: 136).

This sales method began in the early development of department stores. In the case of Mitsukoshi (see Mitsukoshi Co., Ltd. 2005: 36), the Osaka Branch Store started dispatched sales in five provincial cities in Kyushu Island as early as 1898, and the Tokyo headquarters began in two provincial cities in Niigata Prefecture in 1900. After these experiences, Mitsukoshi regularly opened temporary sales exhibitions in many provincial cities, every spring and autumn. Shirokiya started temporary provincial sales in three cities in Niigata Prefecture in 1905 (Shirokiya Co., Ltd. 1957: 657). The spread of this method became significant after the 1920s, as shown in Table 4.3.

Shin'ichi Hori, Professor at Kyushu Imperial University, who studied economics of commerce in depth and recognised the temporary sales exhibitions at provincial cities as 'the unique retail format developed only in Japan' (Hori 1937: 137, see also Hori 1933a: 102), conducted a questionnaire investigation in 1932 of provincial city governments with a population of 8,000 or more. As Table 4.3 shows, this investigation found that 64 to 69 cities accepted temporary sales exhibitions by department stores in 1923–32, and the medium-sized provincial cities with a population of 10,000–50,000 were the main target of these exhibitions. One city often had many sales exhibitions held by various department stores; for instance, Wakayama City in Wakayama Prefecture had sales exhibitions 13 times

Table 4.3 Local cities with temporary sales exhibitions (*shuccho hanbai*) by department stores (1912–1932)

Population of cities	Before 1912	1913–1917	1918–1922	1923–1927	1928–1932	Total
8,000–10,000	2	3	5	9	9	28
10,000–20,000	5	4	11	19	32	71
20,000–50,000	1	2	3	25	19	50
50,000–100,000	8	4	2	8	5	27
More than 100,000	4	2	3	3	2	14
Total	20	15	24	64	67	190

Source: Data from Hori 1933a: 109, 1937: 159.

in 1931 alone, composed of two by Mitsukoshi, Matsuzakaya and Shirokiya respectively, three by Takashimaya and four by other department stores (Hori 1933a: 112, 1337: 163).

These temporary sales exhibitions had double-edged effects on society. On the positive dimension, they introduced modern ways of retailing, such as selling the products displayed beforehand at fixed prices and with attractive service, into provincial cities (Hori 1933a: 106, see also Hirano 1999: 104). The sales functioned as 'the stimulant or the teacher of new sales methods and new business strategies to provincial retailers' (Hori 1935b: 127, see also Hori 1937: 510). Also, for the provincial consumers, the temporary sales exhibitions inspired a dream of modern department stores and made them alert to the superiority of modern retail marketing:

> The store brands of department stores (*hyakkaten no mark*) are sort of like a dream that provincial people are longing for. While provincial retailers like mediaeval merchants adopted the flattering sales method according to the customer, the solid methods of sales by exhibition, fixed prices, attractive service, and advertising provided by department stores . . . . brought a great hope to provincial people, who had fewer stimuli in their everyday life . . . . Thus, the temporary sales exhibits developed based on the requirements of provincial consumers, as well as on the necessities of department stores.
>
> (Hori 1933a: 106)

The rapid spread of these exhibitions, however, was accompanied by an unintentional negative effect.

The anti-department store movement and its result

The fast growth of department stores rapidly increased the gap between them and traditional merchants, resulting in antagonism against department stores.

The first declaration of complaints against the department store (see AOEB 1967: 216, 1983: 142–7) was as early as 1925 by the retailers of muslin *kimono* fabrics in Shitaya Ward (now part of Taito Ward) in Old Tokyo, which had the highest concentration of department stores as shown in Table 4.2. The resolution was passed by 19 retailers, who saw the modern department store as a threat. The resolution was handed over to the Matsuzakaya Department Store located near these retailers. They decided to expand their anti-department store movement and appealed to 25 shopping streets in Tokyo in 1928. In the meantime, the Trade Associations of Merchants of Cotton/Linen-made *Kimono* Fabrics (*Gofuku Futomono-sho Dogyo Kumiai*), composed of retailers who had directly suffered from the threat of department stores, embroiled the Chamber of Commerce and Industry in Tokyo, a core organisation in the business world established in 1878, in the conflict (Yamamoto 1980b: 58–59), so 'the problem of department stores' became widely recognised. Because of the distress of petty merchants due to the severe financial panic in 1927 and the so-called Showa Depression in 1930 influenced by the 1929 Great Depression, the years of 1931 and 32 saw the anti-department store movement reach its peak, evidenced by a series of developments: the spread of the movement to some provincial cities (AOEB 1983: 172–4), the establishment of a few political parties aimed at protection of retailers (Yamamoto 1980b: 73–74, AOEB 1983: 168–71), the formation of the All Japan Federation of Neighbourhood Store Associations (*Zen Nihon Shoten-kai Renmei*) which demanded enactment of the department store law and became a core force of the movement later by influencing the Chamber of Commerce and Industry (Yamamoto 1980b: 80–81 and 89–90), and even a shop owner's suicide by disembowelment in front of Mitsukoshi Department Store to protest over the oppression of department stores (11th June 1932) (AOEB: 176–80).

The protesters blamed various factors, but the main issues included:

- Non-participation in trade associations: an early criticism was raised against the behaviour of department stores in that they did not join the trade associations of merchants of such as cotton fabrics, shoes, everyday items and chests of drawers, and did not observe the control by these associations (Yamamoto 1980b: 48–58, AOEB 1983: 107–14).
- The issue of goods vouchers: each department store made sales in advance by issuing many goods vouchers (*shohin-ken*) that were only valid at individual department stores, while the issuing of goods vouchers commonly valid to many independent stores was banned as quasi-bank notes (Suzuki 1980: 99–101, AOEB 1983: 115–20, 145, 148 and 150–3).
- Free pickup buses: independent merchants were angered by the free pickup bus services organised by department stores – e.g. between Tokyo Station and the head store by Mitsukoshi, and between Shinbashi Station/Yurakucho Station and the new store in Ginza by Matsuzakaya, etc. – that carried the customers directly to the department stores, bypassing independent stores (Suzuki 1980: 93–94, AOEB 1983: 136 and 145).
- Restaurants, advertising, special events, free delivery services offered by department stores: traditional retailers also recognised new contrivances adopted by department stores to attract customers as measures to monopolise sales. The restaurants operated inside the department stores were often the target of blame (Suzuki 1980: 94–99). The earliest movement in 1925 handed to Matsuzakaya the resolution that required abolition of the restaurants and the free pickup buses (AOEB 1983: 145).
- Bait-and-switch sales: the trend towards aggressive price competition among department stores based on popularisation and 'trading down' was recognised as 'bait-and-switch sales (*otori hanbai*)' or 'abusive discounts (*ranbai*)' by traditional retailers (AOEB 1983: 136–8).
- Expansion of branch stores and the temporary sales exhibitions: the opening up of new branch stores and the increasingly widespread temporary sales exhibitions in provincial cities were seen as a direct menace (Suzuki 1980 90–95, AOEB 1983: 121–33 and 139–41).

The disputes about these issues at the time showed the lack of adequate competition rules for marketing among the actors involved in retail competition at this early stage of the capitalistic economy in Japan. Many traditional merchants recognised these issues as a 'menace' because the measures the department stores introduced were incredibly new, modern and powerful enough to dissolve the merchants' long-term way of business, and the change depleted their sales volume.

In addition, it is generally recognised that the field of retail often functions as a reservoir which unemployed people flew into. This tendency became revealed at the time in Japan, worsening the retailers' conditions and encouraging the movement of anti-department stores. In fact, Yamamoto (1980a: 8–9) indicated that the population engaged in commerce (wholesale and retail) increased by 1.24 million or 34 per cent from 1920 to 1930 according to the Census of Population, and included more than half of the people who had an occupation. The high ratio of new entrants into the merchant field was also recognised at the time; the 1931 Census of Commerce in the old Tokyo City area pointed out that as many as 5 per cent of unincorporated merchants emerged within three and a half years, and 87 per cent of them were retailers; 'this tendency looks to expose how fast the old and the new retailers were metabolising, reflecting that some were appearing while others were going out, and how disastrous they were' (Tokyo City 1933: 23).

As a result, the so-called 'surplus' and 'distressed' conditions of petty retailers were widely recognised by the mass media (e.g. *Osaka Jiji News* 1930, *Osaka Asahi Newspaper* 1933). In order to improve these conditions, the national government drafted 'The Plan to Reform the Retail System (*Kouri-seido Kaizen Saku*)' in 1929, which recommended that old-fashioned petty retailers should be supported to modernise, without blocking the development of progressive department stores (Yamamoto 1980b: 61–62, AOEB 1983: 154–7). Nevertheless, activist groups, even including the Chamber of Commerce and Industry in Tokyo, strongly opposed this plan, and claimed that they had several ways of controlling the operations of department stores.

The politics thereafter progressed in a very Japanese way. The government enacted the Law of Control over Important Industries in 1931, which allowed competitive companies to form cartels or monopolistic behaviours in cooperation with 'important' industries such as steel, electric power generation, spinning, cement, etc. (Matsushima 1975b) to overcome the depression in the 1930s and compete with foreign companies; the mass media raised a clamour, however, about 'the law for promotion of cartels quite unique in the world' (*Chugai Commercial News* 1931c) or the change 'from free competition to control over firms' (*Tokyo Asahi Newspaper* 1931). Then the government announced that they were preparing the Law of Department Stores (*Tokyo Asahi Newspaper* 1932, *Chugai Commercial News* 1932a). This was apparently part of its regulation-oriented plan for the industries (Yamamoto 1980b: 81).

Confronted with this announcement, 11 major stores, which led the Japan Association of Department Stores, signed up the Self-Constraint Agreement (*Jisei Kyotei*), including abolition of temporary sales exhibitions in provincial cities, suspending the opening of new branch stores for a while, adoption of three closing days of the stores per month, etc. (*Osaka Asahi Newspaper* 1932a, Yamamoto 1980b: 82, AOEB 1983: 185). In return for this voluntary restraint, legislation of the Department Store Law was put off (*Osaka Asahi Newspaper* 1932b); instead, the Law of Commercial Union (*Shogyo Kumiai*) was enacted to encourage establishment of trade associations dedicated to merchants.[6] The Commercial Union of Department Stores (*Hyakkaten Shogyo Kumiai*), changed from the Association of Department Stores in accordance with this law (*Osaka Asahi Newspaper* 1933), tried to bring the department stores under the control of the Union, but this control proved insufficient because not all of them were members. Thus the groundswell for the legislation of the Department Store Law arose again (Suzuki 1980: 308–9). By 1936, ten bills of this law were submitted by several organisations including some political parties, the Federation of Business Unions in Tokyo, the All Japan Federation of Neighbourhood Store Associations, and the Chamber of Commerce and Industry in Tokyo and all of Japan, as well as the Ministry of Commerce and Trade (Taniguchi 1936: 65–69). The Commercial Union of Department Stores declared an objection to the law by insisting that 'the oppression of department stores would bring disadvantages to consumers and wither the manufacturing industries', and that it 'would not be the right way to revitalise the retailers' (JCUD 1936: 1 and 3–8). Nevertheless, the Department Store Law was finally enacted in 1937.

The Law and its enforcement regulations defined the department store as a store with 3,000 m² or more of sales floor space (estimating 95 per cent of the total floor space as the sales area) in six major cities, and with 1,500 m² or more in other cities. The Law and the enforcement regulations defined rules mainly as follows:

- The licensing system: those who want to operate a department store should have a licence from the Minister of Commerce and Industry.
- The approval system for expanding sales floor space and operating a temporary sales exhibit: setting up any branch stores, branch sales offices and delivery centres, expanding any sales floor spaces, and operating any temporary sales exhibitions must have the approval from the Minister.
- Regulation of operating hours and closing days: all department stores should be closed by 7.00 pm from April to October and by 6.00 pm from November to March, and should have three closing days per month in major conurbations and one closing day per month in other cities.

The Department Store Law clearly exerted fairly strong governmental control. The year 1937 saw the outbreak of the Second Sino-Japanese War, and the National Mobilisation Law was enacted in the following year. Japanese society was caught up in wartime control fever, which ruined any efforts to modernise consumption patterns.

Conclusion

The department store was the only dominant format of modern retailing that was created by independent retailers, rather than manufacturers, before the Second World War. This format provided Japanese consumers with a modern,

Western-style shopping venue. This new possible domain (see Figure 0.1) was recognised by the marketers who could observe Western department stores directly. These marketers were the scions of wealthy merchants, *odana*, so they had enough business and financial resources to carry out these observations and introduce them into their organisations even though they confronted tough conditions due to radical changes in society. The transformation process from *odana* to the modern department store included cutting off some unique traditions of retail operations and introducing modern Western-style ways of retail business.

The innovative Western-style goods and the new services the department stores provided were also based on the utilisation of the new selling space, and encouraged customers to dream of a different world of consumption. In addition, some department stores attempted to create new fashion trends and intentionally combined artistic designs even in Japanese-origin products like *kimono* fabrics.

The progress of department stores induced new entrants to this format, accompanied by 'trading down' with attractive price competition. The terminal department store was a new type of this format. A private electric railway company introduced a new marketing model that combined railway services with selling many houses adjacent to the railways, providing electric power, developing entertainment venues and opening up a department store at a main station. This new type of department store rapidly spread in metropolitan areas. In the meantime, while provincial department stores grew in some smaller cities, the major department stores increasingly also held their temporary sales exhibitions in many of these cities; the influence of department stores was spreading beyond the limited number of metropolitan centres, diffusing awareness and understanding of the method of modern retail marketing, such as sales of displayed products at fixed prices, as well as inspiring a dream of the department store brands in great cities.

The rapid spread of department stores, however, also encouraged a negative response among petty traditional merchants. Confronted with modern, capitalistic marketing competition for the first time, they saw it as a menace. As a result, the Department Store Law, and the regulation of large-sized retail formats, became another feature of retail marketing in modern Japan. This feature continued until the year 2000 with some changes; while the first Law was abolished in 1947 when the Anti-Monopoly Law was enacted, the so-called second Department Store Law became effective from 1956 to 1974, and the Large-scale Retail Store Law from 1974 to 2000. In all of the laws, the operating hours and dates of department stores or large-sized retail stores were regulated; meanwhile, as will be explored in the final chapter, a new format of convenience store was encouraged by the regulation of operating hours and dates of large-sized stores.

After the Second World War, the leading role in the retail world formerly held by the department store was usurped by the new Japanese-type format of '*super*'. While the department stores enjoyed establishment status and focused on fashionable products, the aggressive tendency to expand store networks was taken over by the newly emergent '*super*'. This book will explore in depth the new retail formats of '*super*' in Chapter 5.

Notes

1   Edo (Tokyo) was the place where the Tokugawa government (Tokugawa Shogunate) was located. The Shogunate compelled all local lords (*daimyo*), who ruled their own local fiefs (*han*), to an alternate-year residence in Edo (called the *sankin kotai* system), and their wife and children were always forced to live in Edo (the *saishi zaifu* system) as a sort of hostages to the Tokugawa Shogunate. Their residences in Edo required many subordinates also to stay there. These people belonged to the warrior class; in other words, the purely consuming class based on the collection of land taxes mainly accepted as rice. Development of Edo was encouraged by this political system at first. Demand for silk fabrics for *kimono* also came from these people. In due course, however, purchasing power by the townspeople, who were outside the ruling class, was increasing and the use of silk-made fabric by these townspeople became permitted from the latter half of the seventeenth century (Nishizaka 1992: 183). As a result, while the old merchants traded only with the warrior class, the new merchants were able to sell the silk fabric to the rising townspeople (Hayashi 1992a: 55).

2   Many of these merchants came from Ise (the northern and middle part of Mie Prefecture) or Omi (almost identical to Shiga Prefecture). The 'merchants from Ise (*Ise shonin*)' or 'those from Omi (*Omi shonin*)' had the principal family house (*honke*) in their hometowns, and developed store networks in Edo and other metropolitan areas. These merchants often recruited their principal employees from their hometowns.

3   The so-called 'exhibition house (*kanko-ba* or *kansho-ba*)' began in 1878 in Tokyo as the place to sell goods that had been exhibited at the Domestic Exhibition for Promotion of Industries. The first exhibition house (see AOEB 1967: 57–60, Hatsuda 1983: 125–8, 1993: 8–18, Tanaka 1986: 22–27, Suzuki 2000: 2001: 34–83, 2002: 233–5) was run by the government of Tokyo City, and then was entrusted to merchants from 1880. It covered a huge area of about 16,959 m^2, including a few houses connected by corridors and a garden, in which 1,518 retailers set up their shops. As this first attempt proved successful and popular, exhibition houses were opened almost every year from 1880, reaching a total of 27 houses with 2,140 exhibitors in Tokyo in 1902 (Hatsuda 1983: 7, Suzuki 2002: 137) and spreading to other cities such as Sapporo, Sendai, Shizuoka, Osaka, Yokohama and Fukuoka (AOEB 1967: 67–68). These premises were usually owned by private individuals, who rented a particular space to exhibitors for deposit and monthly exhibition fees. Each house had its own rule, but all goods were sold at fixed prices. The exhibition houses sold everything except foods, including traditional Japanese-style and new Western-style products (AOEB 1967: 61–62). This format can be seen as an early version of the shopping centre in Japan.

  The customers were free to enter the houses and browse each store inside without any pressure to buy. In addition, some exhibition houses began to allow the customers to walk into the houses with their shoes or sandals on from around the mid-1880s, although the early houses required removal of the footwear at the entrance (Hatsuda 1983: 130–1). Some exhibition houses had a conspicuous outward exterior, such as a Western-style brick construction or a building with a clock tower or a penthouse (Hatsuda 1983: 131–2, 1993: 49–59), creating a new townscape in shopping streets in the 1880s–1910s and a transitional stage between the traditional and the modern retail institution.

  The exhibition houses decreased rapidly in number from the turn of 1902 and almost disappeared by the 1930s (Hatsuda 1993: 30). The merchants who exhibited their shops in the houses were traditional merchants and had little knowledge and concept of modern retailing. The exhibition house itself could not control the products these merchants sold either. As a result, the reputation of 'products at exhibition houses (*kankoba mono*)' dropped to become cheap and inferior (AOEB 1967: 69–70), and lost consumer trust. In turn, the modern format of department stores replaced these exhibition houses.

4   There was historical controversy over whether the railway services should be offered by the state or by private companies. While the Private Railway Rule in 1887 and the Private Railway Law in 1900 gave the basis of law for their construction, the Railway Nationalisation Law in 1906 decided that the state should buy 17 major private railway companies. This nationalisation, however, did not target all private railways. Many local railways were operated by independent companies; this situation was authorised by the Narrow-Gauge Railway Law (1910–19) and the Local Railway Law in 1919. This picture changed radically only in 1987 when the national railway services were privatised.

5   The Japanese often referred to the 'six major cities (*6-dai toshi*)' including Kyoto in addition to the five cities mentioned. Kyoto City ([1937] 1989) also conducted this sort of survey in 1936. However, the data did not include sales volume or the number of employees of department stores. Therefore this book excludes the data on Kyoto City. Tokyo City was the first to survey: all following surveys were conducted by local governments with 'commission by the Ministry of Commerce and Industry'.

6   At the same time, the Law for the Control of Goods Vouchers was also enacted. It required obligatory deposits from department stores in order to secure voucher holders and block the unlimited issue of vouchers (*Chugai Commercial News* 1932b).

Part II

Marketing and consumption, High Economic Growth to the present

Historical settings

Although the anti-Western discourse, which insisted on 'overcoming modernity' and defined the West as the 'sickness' or the 'poison' for the Japanese (Harootunian 2000: 35, see also Bruma and Margalit 2004: 2), reached an extreme under the wartime regime, the defeat of Japan made it quite clear for many Japanese that this discourse would be disastrous. They felt that not only the neighbouring Asian people, but also the Japanese themselves, were the victims of the war and their militaristic government. 'There were nothing but burnt-out ruins as far as eyes could see', was a cliché when people looked back at the situation at the end of the War.

Dower's *Embracing Defeat* (2000) is an accurate description of the courageous survival of Japanese civilians at the time. The postwar life started with the occupation by the American army, which established the GHQ-SCAP (General Headquarters of Supreme Commander for the Allied Powers). Instead of the distorted images of savage America that many Japanese held as a result of manipulation by the militaristic government, information on the astoundingly wealthy American way of life flowed into Japan through the American army itself, especially via the PXs (post exchanges) of the army; the army also brought in vital new medicines such as penicillin, and broad mass media including newspapers, magazines, radio programmes, and of course American movies. A radio programme, 'The Letters from America (*America dayori*)', sent by a Japanese journalist living in the USA from 1926 (Hayashi 1997), was an instance. It was broadcast from 1948 to 1952 and inspired a wonderful image of the American lifestyle. Thus, the discourse of westernisation, in essence Americanisation at this time, was strongly revived in Japan as the form that people aspired to, to catch up with the wealthy 'American way of life'.

Under the supreme power of the GHQ-SCAP, the so-called Postwar Reform (*sengo kaikaku*) was achieved. The components of the Reform were those that could have never been achieved by Japanese efforts, such as:

- female suffrage (1945);
- labour reform (1945–47) that granted the rights of workers to organise, bargain collectively and hold a strike;
- agrarian reform (1945–50) that demolished the tenant farming system by forced acquisition of farmland from landowners and its distribution to peasants at a cheap rate;

- democratisation of the economy (1945–47) that dissolved the *zaibatsu* conglomerates to eradicate the economic basis of Japanese militarism, while paving the way for the anti-monopoly law;
- educational reform (1946–48) that eliminated the militaristic content of education such as the Imperial Rescript of Education and stipulated the principle of separation of religions such as Shintoism from public education;
- family-law reform (1948) that amended the Civil Law to abolish the system of male head of a family and the system of inheritance by the eldest son only; and
- the new Constitution (1947) that defines sovereignty of people, fundamental human rights and eternal renunciation of wars, by removing sovereignty from the Emperor and setting Him as the symbol of the unity of the state.

The reactions of the Japanese naturally varied. Some people likely complied with anything as a direct result of defeat and considered that the Reform enforced by the supreme power could be repealed after the end of the American occupation (see Dower 2000: 226), although this vision has not been realised; the Abe government elected in 2012 claimed to support it, however. Many other Japanese overwhelmingly welcomed the Reform because they strongly felt it denied the militarism from which they had suffered. The so-called 'generation of postwar democracy' especially, including Kenzaburo Oe, found in the Reform an element of 'the concept of universal humanity' (Oe 1995: 120) or 'the idea of democracy and determination never to wage a war again' (118–19). Therefore, even if they had been able to consider that the Reform 'reflected an agenda inspired by heavy doses of liberal New Deal attitudes, labour reformism, and Bill of Rights idealism of a sort that was in the process of being repudiated (or ignored) in the United States' (Dower 2000: 26), this generation would mostly have welcomed this development.

In any case, the liberal and idealistic attitude of the Americans had changed radically by the time they left Japan in April 1952, as they began to require Japan to be 'a subordinate Cold War partner' (Dower 2000: 23). The change in politics of American occupation accompanied the change in economic policy from the simple restraint of Japanese economic power by recognising it as the basis of Japanese militarism to the encouragement of rebuilding it, including the heavy chemical industries to respond to the start of the Cold War in 1948 (Yoshikawa 1997: 136–8). New technologies and new investments were introduced to revitalise Japanese economy. The Japanese government established the 'Policy of Rationalisation of Industries (*sangyo gorika seisaku*)' in 1949 (MITI 1957: 10–14) in order to encourage replacement of deteriorated machinery and facilities which had been overused and not replaced due to the war, through measures such as a special exemption from import taxes for important machinery, permission for accelerated depreciation and financing by the Japan Development Bank established in 1951 (Nishino 2006: 109–11). Taking an opportunity of the economic boom due to the Korean War in 1950, many raw materials industries, such as steel and chemicals, started huge-scale investments to introduce new technologies and new production equipment, resulting in a supply of high-quality goods at low prices. This prompted major investment in consumer product industries, such as consumer electric goods and private cars, accompanied by the rapid expansion of consumer markets, composed of the many consumers who adored the American way of life and whose incomes were gradually increasing. Thus, the phenomenon of what was called 'one investment induced many other investments (*toshi ga toshi o yobu*)' exploded, and the High Economic Growth (*kodo keizai seicho*) began.

The period of this Growth is usually defined as the years from 1955 to 1973. Figure II.1 shows the annual growth ratios of GDE (Gross Domestic Expenditure) – equivalent to GDP (Gross Domestic Product) by adjusting the statistical discrepancy – and Domestic Final Consumption Expenditure of Households according to official government data. The remarkable economic growth was evident from the fact that the average growth ratios between 1955 and 1973 were 15.5 per cent in GDE and 14.2 per cent in Domestic Final Consumption Expenditure per Household on the current prices basis, and 9.2 per cent and 8.7 per cent respectively on the constant prices basis in the year of 1990. Furthermore, the economic progress at the time achieved a world-class result. Historical research on GDP of 56 countries in the world by Maddison (1995) shows that Japan's GDP on a constant price basis surpassed any countries in Europe during this period, resulting in the second largest GDP among the capitalist nations after the USA, although the per capita GDP was still behind many countries of Europe and North America. High Economic Growth rapidly transformed Japan from a defeated country of burnt ruins to one of the wealthiest countries in the world.

The rapid economic progress brought the consumption pattern closer to a modernised and westernised/Americanised one; and marketing mediated the changing modes of consumption and individual consumption choices. This was not the first such experience for Japan. As was explored in Part I, Japan had already had a similar experience in the interwar period. The essential difference between the two periods was that while before the Second World War the modern and westernised consumption pattern was basically limited to the urban areas and the affluent classes, after the War it spread, in contrast, to every corner of Japanese society. As a result, the modern and Western/American ways of marketing and consumption pattern took a firm hold in Japanese society.

The westernisation/Americanisation was again, however, a hybrid with the unique Japanese way. This will be described in Part II. Chapter 5 will explore how Japanese consumption of everyday necessities including clothing and food (as well as dwelling) was changing to the Japanese reflection of modern Western-style hand in hand with development of the Japanese version of self-service chain stores, called 'general *super*'. Chapter 6 will describe how consumption of house-hold electric appliances spread, supported by the Japanese style of *keiretsu* retail system that was inherited from the pre-war period.

Around the end of High Economic Growth, new phenomena appeared in the economy and consumption. The industrial structure began to shift to the so-called

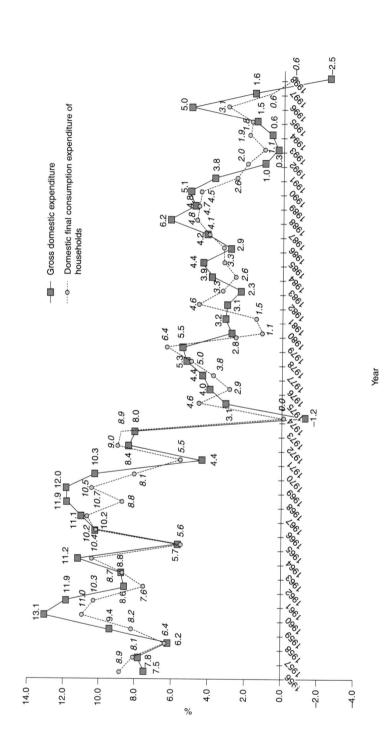

Figure II.1 The annual growth ratios of Gross Domestic Expenditure and Domestic Final Consumption Expenditure of Households (1956–98).

Source: The ratios are calculated from the data by Statistics Bureau, Ministry of Internal Affairs and Communications, Historical Statistics of Japan (SB websites 1 and 2).

Note: The data is on the calender year basis according to the System of National Accounts 1968 (SNA68), and on the constant price at market price of 1990.

tertiary industry, and consumption began to swing to services or intangible products. The change in the industrial structure was shown by the 1974 Labour Force Survey that indicated the ratio of the working population in tertiary industry surpassed 50 per cent for the first time, as shown by Figure II.2. The *White Paper on Economy* was issued by the government (EPA 1977: 213–9; 1979: 314–31) and many commentators became interested in this sector. The survey by the government also revealed the steady increase in expenditure for intangible goods or services, as shown by Figure II.3.

These social changes attracted great attention, combined with the influence of several translations of Western intellectuals, such as D. Bell's *The Coming of Post-Industrial Society* (1973, trans. 1975), R. Barthes' *Empire of Signs* ([1970] 1982, trans. 1974, 2004, describing the impressions on Japan based on his visit in 1966), J. Baudrillard's *The Consumer Society: Myths and Structures* ([1970] 1998, trans. 1979), and A. Toffler's *The Third Wave* ([1980] 1981, trans. 1982). Eager attempts to describe the new features of society included labels such as 'matured society (*seijuku-ka shakai*)', 'post-industrial society (*datsu-sangyo shakai*)', 'service-centred society (*service shakai*)', 'intangible values directed society (*soft-ka shakai*)', 'information-centred society (*joho shakai*)', 'postmodern society (*postmodern shakai*)', and 'consumer society (*shohi shakai*)' (e.g. *Nikkei*

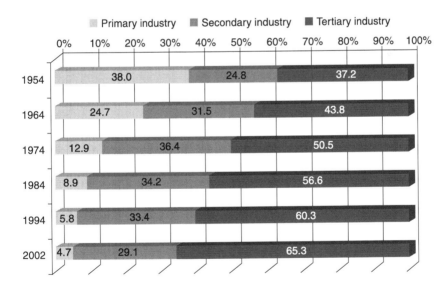

Figure II.2 Changes in the component of the labour force in the primary, secondary and tertiary industries (1954–2002).

Source: Data from *Labour Force Survey* by the Statistics Bureau (website 1).

Note: *Labour Force Survey* is a sample survey. The 5-year population also revealed that the labour force in the tertiary industry surpassed 50% in 1975. The percentage are among the people of 15 years old and over and those who are engaged in works.

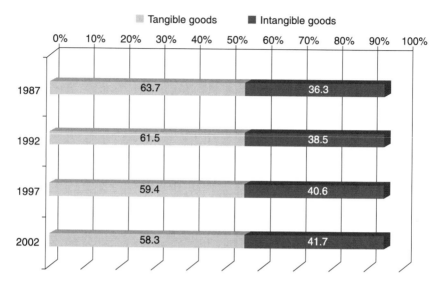

Figure II.3 Changes in the composition of consumer expenditures between tangible and intangible goods (1987–2002).

Source: Data from *Family Income and Expenditure Survey* by the Statistics Bureau (website 2).
Note: Divided into tangible and intangible goods based on 'the classification by items (*hinmoku-betsu bunrui*)' of consumer expenditure. The categories of 'pocket money (*kozukai*)', 'money gift (*zoyo-kin*)', 'other social expenses (*ta no kosai-hi*)' and 'remittances (*shiokuri-kin*)' are excluded.

Newspaper 1976b, EPA 1985: 166–71, Mamada 2005, 2007). Several business commentators coined Japanese words around the mid-1980s to point out the new features in consumers' choices, such as the 'divided masses (*bun-shu*)' (Hakuhodo 1985), 'small-sized masses (*sho-shu*)' (Hirajima 1985), 'class-oriented consumption (*kaiso-shohi*)' (Ozawa 1985) and 'hidden mass (*kakure taushu*)' (*Nikkei Business* 1986). The sense was broadly shared that Japan had stepped up to a new historical era.

Along with these changes, some institutions of retail marketing that had largely contributed to High Economic Growth were having to confront difficulties. The exploration of this aspect will be included in Chapter 5 as the problem encountered by general *super*, adopting diversification strategy, and their failures, and in Chapter 6 as the problem faced by *keiretsu* retailers of being undermined by independent retailers, who appeared in quick succession. Chapter 7 will investigate marketing by convenience stores as newly dominant retail marketers in the new circumstances. These tendencies in marketing developed together with the maturity of the Japanese-type consumer society, which intensified Japanese features on the basis of reshaping westernisation/Americanisation.

5 'Discount is my philosophy'

Consumption of everyday necessities from *super*

The progress of High Economic Growth (1955–73) transformed Japan from defeated ruins to a wealthy, modern and Western-looking society, accompanied by changes in buying and consumption habits of everyday necessities. These changes were mediated by a new retail format, incorporating the ideas of self-service and chain store networks. Before the Second World War, most small- and medium-sized retailers did not have enough knowledge and business resources to create a new retail format that could undertake the mass marketing matched with mass production since developed by modern manufacturers; therefore, the networks of retail stores had to be developed as *keiretsu* stores organised by manufacturers themselves (see chapters 1–3). In contrast, after the War some independent retailers gained the ability by their own efforts to develop nationwide store networks with self-service systems.

This chapter will explore how retail marketing progressed via self-service stores that provided everyday necessities during the period of High Economic Growth, and what followed after. The first section of this chapter will discuss changes in the living conditions after the War, which became the foundation of a new everyday life. The second and principal section will investigate the unique Japanese format of self-service stores, which is usually called '*super*' in Japanese *katakana* characters. The name is originally an abbreviation of 'supermarket' in English, but quite different from the American counterpart. This section will investigate how the self-service stores were born and how such a unique retail format developed in Japan, mainly by using the new top retailer Daiei as an example. *Discount is my Philosophy*, published by Isao Nakauchi (1969) the founder of Daiei, was a publicity-seeking declaration about the role of the new retail format. The exploration of Daiei will reveal the state-of-the-art activities in retail marketing during the High Economic Growth period. The final section will be an overview of the story of what happened in the *super* after that period, focusing on the diversification strategy of retail formats that *super* undertook in order to match changes in consumer preferences, which led to clear successes and failures.

The whole chapter will study the influences of the second wave of westernisation, in essence Americanisation, on marketing and consumption of everyday items and how the Japanese way of westernisation progressed in reality.

Domestic migration bringing about a new way of life: the basis of postwar style consumption

Urbanisation and suburbanisation by demographic changes

Figure 5.1 shows a scene of 'group migration in order to get jobs (*shudan shushoku*)' in the Tokyo metropolitan area. The migrant group is composed of new graduates of secondary schools, who had been appointed to new jobs. The train, often specially arranged, is just leaving a hometown, and their families and friends are sending them off. This annual migration by train became a special feature of the graduation season in March from about 1954 to around the mid-1960s; in other words, the first half of the period of High Economic Growth. The employers of these migrants were mainly the small- and medium-sized firms in the metropolitan area (Yoshikawa 1997: 110, Kato 1997: 143–67), and as it proved, the frequency of migrants changing their jobs was quite high; around one-fourth working for medium-sized establishments hiring 30 to 99 employees left their jobs within a year (Kato 1997: 181). However, many of them did not go

Figure 5.1 A migrant group just leaving a rural station of Fukushima (1 April 1956).

Note: The picture shows a migrant group composed of new graduates, who have appoint-ments for new jobs in the Tokyo area, just leaving their hometown, Fukushima. Their families and friends have got together to send them off. This train was specially arranged for these group migrations.

Reproduced courtesy of The Mainichi Newspapers.

back to their hometowns, but instead got other jobs and stayed in the metropolis (Yoshikawa 1997: 111–16), resulting in an increase in the population of metropolitan areas.

The 'group migration' was only one symbolic feature of urban migration in this period. Not only these youngsters but also many other types of workers were absorbed into urban areas as the economy swiftly grew, accompanied by rapid urbanisation and suburbanisation. While the progress of industrialisation had induced urbanisation even before the Second World War, it began on a large scale after 1945. According to the quinquennial Census of Population started in 1920, while the proportion of the population residing in the legally-defined 'cities' increased from 18.0 per cent in 1920 to 37.7 per cent in 1940, the proportion after the War swelled from 37.3 per cent in 1950, 56.1 per cent in 1955, 75.9 per cent in 1975 to 76.7 per cent in 1985 (and 86.3 per cent in 2005). The Census of Population redefined 'densely inhabited districts' in 1960 to show the real numbers of urban population because the areas administratively titled 'cities' were themselves growing by merging with neighbouring areas and being newly established. The proportion residing in these districts also grew from 41.0 per cent in 1960 and 54.5 per cent in 1975 to 57.5 per cent in 1985 and 63.4 per cent in 2005 (calculated from SB website 1).

The abrupt urbanisation was soon followed by suburbanisation. The data of 'net domestic migration', which the Census of Population defines as the changes in population less the 'natural changes' due to childbirth and death, show that in all areas of Tokyo, i.e. the central 23 wards roughly equivalent to the former Greater Tokyo, plus all suburbs within the metropolis, the change in proportion of this type of migration decreased from 21.1 per cent between 1950 and 1955, to −2.8 per cent between 1965 and 1970. In contrast, this figure in the dormitory areas surrounding Tokyo increased; during the same period, in Saitama Prefecture it grew from −1.5 per cent to 19.0 per cent; in Chiba Prefecture from −3.1 per cent to 17.2 per cent; and in Kanagawa Prefecture from 10.0 per cent to 14.4 per cent (data from SB website 1).

The process of rapid urbanisation/suburbanisation was accompanied by the process of splitting traditional large-sized or three-generation families to resemble the nuclear family. Census data show that the number of people per household decreased from 4.05 in 1960 and 3.27 in 1975 to 3.14 in 1985 (now 2.54 in 2005). The ratio of the number of nuclear families (except one-person households, see Chapter 7) in all households increased from 53.0 per cent in 1960, 59.5 per cent in 1975 to 60.0 per cent in 1985 (calculated from SB website 1). The increase in the proportion of nuclear families encouraged people to abandon the traditional large-sized families and to adopt the new urban lifestyle, while the increase in number of households simply raised demand for some kinds of consumer goods that were needed in each separate household, such as electrical appliances (Yoshikawa 1997: 125–6). These demographic changes provided the basis for changes in consumption for everyday life.

'Danchi *tribe' enjoying a dream modern dwelling*

The rapid domestic migration was accompanied by changes in living conditions. Housing was already in desperately short supply due to the disasters of war. Soon after the defeat, the Japanese government announced that about 4.2 million families were in need of shelter (Nishiyama 1989: 290–1). The beginning of rapid migration from the rural to the urban areas served as another sharp warning on shortages of housing (called '*jutaku-nan*'). The Bureau of Construction of the Tokyo Metropolitan Government estimated in 1952 that about 400,000 houses were needed and confessed, 'it is almost impossible for the supply of housing to catch up with the increasing population' (*Asahi Newspaper* 1952). According to the macro data (JPCH 1981: 1 and 98), the shortage in the number of houses/ apartments was not solved until 1973, that is, the final year of the period of High Economic Growth.

The urban and national governments began to tackle the problem of housing as their social policy. The Japanese government established the Government Housing Loan Corporation (*Jutaku Kinyu Koko*) in 1950 (now Japan Housing Finance Agency, *Jutaku Kinyu Shien Kiko*), which provided low-interest home loans for those who had the ability to buy their own houses. In addition, public apartments/ houses began to be let at low rents, based on the Public Housing Act in 1951. These apartments caused a tremendous stir. When the Tokyo Metropolitan Government offered 285 public apartments for the first time in 1953, applications were immediately over-subscribed by a factor of 170 (Tokyo Metropolitan Government website). When the government began to provide rental apartments/ houses through the Japan Public Corporation of Housing (*Nihon Jutaku Kodan*, simply called '*Kodan*') established in 1955 (now Urban Renaissance Agency, *UR Toshi Kiko*), it also attracted wide attention. The Corporation began to supply the housing complex called '*danchi*' from 1955. Again the number of applicants was so large that the residents were chosen by lottery. The success rate was forbiddingly low; for example in 1961 only one in thirty-one applicants on average in all of Japan (Kitagawa 2002: 3). The much-envied winners became known as the '*danchi* tribe (*danchi-zoku*)' (Maeda 1985, Yoshikawa 1997: 62).

As shown in Figure 5.2, the *danchi* complex was a group of purpose-built apartments, made of reinforced concrete in line with a regulation restricting construction to non-combustible materials against fires and earthquakes. Although the *danchi* buildings were not the first reinforced concrete buildings in Japanese history,[1] many *danchi* dwellers were living for the first time in such modern constructions. In addition, the *danchi* apartments were equipped with new facilities, such as Western-style balconies, modern indoor bathrooms (although the regular visit to the public baths was still popular at the time), and Western-design toilets, replacing the traditional Japanese and septic-tank-style toilets especially from around 1960 (Maeda 1985: 38–40). It was the *danchi* apartments which introduced the image of a new modern Western dwelling to many people.

Among the new facilities of *danchi* apartments, the most attractive feature was the inner space of what was called '*dining kitchen*' or '*DK*' in Japanese English.

Figure 5.2 A large-sized housing complex, *Hibari-ga-Oka Danchi*, in Tokyo (1959) and observation by the Crown Prince and Princess (upper right 1960).

Note: Hibari-ga-Oka is one of the earliest large-sized housing complexes (*danchi*) created by the Japan Public Corporation of Housing in 1959. The location was in Tanashi City (now Nishi-Tokyo City), a suburban area in Tokyo Metropolis. The premise of this complex included a primary school, green parks, a branch office of the city government, tennis courts, and a playground for baseball. In addition, Seiyu opened their first self-service store consisting of a one-storey house with about 529 m² sales floor space in 1959 following the request by the Japan Public Corporation of Housing, although it was closed soon after because Seiyu did not yet have concrete knowledge on the self-service system at the time (Yui 1991: 140, Tatsuki 1991: 384). In any case, this premise was called a model housing complex, so many people, including the Crown Prince and Princess (appearing on a modern-looking balcony in the picture on the upper right), came to observe. The buildings have become dilapidated, so a reconstruction project, *Hibari-ga-Oka* Park Hills, began in 2004.

Reproduced courtesy of Osaka Mainichi Newspaper.

This was a combined space for cooking and eating. As Nishiyama (1989: 347) indicated, this space was 'the fundamental innovation that completely changed the room arrangement' from the traditional Japanese-style: the floor of the *dining kitchen* was not covered by traditional *tatami*-mats, but by wooden flooring, encouraging residents to replace the traditional low-height dining table called '*chabudai*', which family members sat around by kneeling on *tatami*-mats, with Western-height dining tables and chairs, as shown in Figure 5.3. Although as was mentioned in Chapter 4, some wealthy people had already introduced the Western-style rooms without *tatami*-mats as a drawing room to their residences before the Second World War, the introduction of such a space to the residences of ordinary people was quite new.[2] The enviable *dining kitchen* became 'an indispensable factor for modern dwellings' (Nishiyama 1989: 347) in Japan. Since that time, wooden flooring has widely replaced *tatami*-mats in Japanese homes.

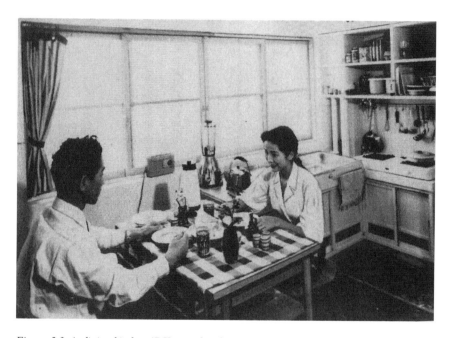

Figure 5.3 A *dining kitchen* (*DK*) at a *danchi* apartment (1956).

Note: The picture shows the newly designed *dining kitchen* at a *danchi* apartment in Kanaoka Housing Complex (*Kanaoka Danchi*) in Osaka in 1956. This complex offered 900 *danchi* apartments, each of which had 2DK (two rooms and a *dining kitchen*) with a total space of 40 m², of which the *dining kitchen* measured about 7 m². The picture shows a young couple eating Japanese food while sitting on chairs by a Western-styled table of higher height, and not kneeling on *tatami*-mats as before. Behind the lady, there is a stainless steel sink, two small gas ranges and a cupboard on the right-hand side, which also gives an impression of a new image of the modern Western lifestyle.

Reproduced courtesy of UR (Urban Renaissance Agency).

What was recognised as the 'modern' and 'Western' way of life at *danchi* apartments at the time was, however, essentially a mixed composition of the traditional and the new. The standard type of *danchi* apartments had, in addition to the '*dining kitchen*', usually two other rooms, floored with *tatami*-mats. In these rooms, residents would sleep with the traditional *futon* (thick mattress with cover) spread directly on the *tatami*-mats, and not with Western-style beds. In the *dining kitchen*, people continued to use chopsticks and eat traditional rice, miso soup, and other foodstuffs and seasonings: the new lifestyle at *danchi* apartments essentially meant a new version of the Japanese way of modern Western life. Many of the daily consumer items, not only food but also cheap dining tables and chairs, non-luxury curtains, practical kitchenware, clothing, etc., had to be bought at nearby stores. The Japanese-type self-service stores provided everything in mass-produced form. Although the longing for *danchi* life diminished after the end of the High Economic Growth period when the absolute shortage of housing was resolved,[3] the new lifestyle had become ingrained in the everyday habits of many ordinary consumers during that period.

Emergence and development of general *super*: the role in changing consumption of clothing and food

Birth of self-service stores in Japan

Soon after the defeat in 1945, urban consumers procured their everyday necessities from black market stalls. As the turmoil gradually subsided, they bought these products from small-sized traditional neighbourhood merchants such as greengrocers (*yaoya*), fishmongers (*sakanaya*), butchers (*nikuya*), cheap sweet shops (*dagashiya*), ironmongers (*kanamonoya*), hardware stores (*aramonoya*), and tailors and dressmakers (*shitateya*). In the meantime, some business people attempted to introduce new methods of retail marketing from the West, especially from the USA, to provide the increasing mass of urban consumers with everyday necessities. Self-service retailing was a major topic in these circumstances.

The idea of self-service retailing was not entirely new in 1945. Some commentators (e.g. Shimizu 1923a, 1924b, *Kobe Yushin Daily News* 1929, Kitada 1931: 401–2) had mentioned the self-service method as early as the 1920s, although even recent Japanese historians of retailing, except Suzuki (1991: 316) who mentioned it in Kitada's book, have almost forgotten these early works. Shimizu (1924b), for instance, described Piggly Wiggly Stores, which is now known as one of the earliest self-service stores opened by Clarence Sunders in Memphis, Tennessee in 1916 (see e.g. Mayo 1993: 89), as 'shops without sales clerks' in his series of 48 newspaper articles describing his observations on retailing around the world. Nevertheless, these early references had only a limited influence. It was not until the 1950s that the self-service idea gained wide interest and began to be realised in the actual business scene.

The first Japanese self-service store has generally been acknowledged to be Kinokuniya, opened in 1953 in Aoyama, Tokyo, although it has been controversial whether or not this store was appropriate to be called the first supermarket in Japan. Kinokuniya was originally a fruit shop started in 1910, but was closed in 1941 due to wartime control and burnt down in the air strike in 1945 (Hiramatsu 1989: 13–20). Tokuo Masui, the founder's son, restarted the business from around 1947. The products sold included vegetables that were native to the West, such as lettuces. This store was accredited by the Tokyo Metropolitan government to sell clean, quality vegetables (Hiramatsu 1989: 45–46), and they also sold these vegetables to the PXs (Post Exchanges), the stores inside the bases of the American occupational army. Through supplying the PXs, Masui and his subordinates happened to observe a self-service food store, named Commissary (Hiramatsu 1989: 67–71). Masui attempted to follow some of the methods of this store in order to attract American army officers and their families living on the neighbouring streets to his shop; for instance, in 1950 he installed an open-shelved type refrigerator to store fruit and vegetables (Hiramatsu 1989: 72–77).

Meanwhile, NCR Japan, established in 1920 as the Japanese subsidiary of NCR Corporation in the USA, began to support the introduction of self-service stores in order to sell their cash registers to retailers (Nagato 1991: 3–13). The American headquarters invited the Japanese manager, Tsuyoshi Nagato, to the USA in 1952–53 to study the actual self-service systems and supermarkets operating there. By overcoming many scruples inside the company, such as that the self-service system would not suit Japanese conditions or that Japan was not mature enough to adopt it, Nagato and NCR Japan decided to choose Kinokuniya as a possible model case and proposed the idea directly to its owner, Masui, in 1953 (Masui 1963: 171–3). Kinokuniya held study meetings with NCR Japan for about ten months and prepared many new factors untried by traditional Japanese retailers, such as gondolas to display goods, price tags, shopping bags made of craft paper, shopping carts, and sales floors made of terrazzo that could cope with the weight of shopping carts. As a result of these efforts, the first self-service store was opened on 28 November 1953 with 132 m^2 sales floor space (Hiramatsu 1989: 77–94, Nagato 1991: 14–17).

In the next year, two additional self-service stores were opened up (Tateno 1994: 5–6); that is, in June a store of the consumer cooperative society in Kikuna, Yokohama, with 49.6 m^2 sales floor space, and in December Ootomo in Kyoto, with less than 19.8 m^2 sales floor space, (Kanei 2000: 177–80). The former store was part of the consumer cooperative movement, which revived under the difficult conditions of obtaining food after the War, becoming protected and regulated by the Law of Consumer Cooperatives in 1948 and then developing in urban areas to support the working class (AOEB 1981: 192–204). Ootomo was a dealer in dried foods, who had used an NCR cash register, and was also recommended by NCR Japan to observe and follow the ways of Kinokuniya (Kanei 2000: 188–9). In the meantime, the mass media began paying attention to the self-service method (e.g. *Nikkei Newspaper* 1953, 1954). Nagato of NCR Japan also publicised the self-service method in a newspaper article (*Yomiuri Newspaper* 1953).

As a result, the number of self-service stores gradually increased in the latter half of the 1950s. According to the report of the Supermarket Association of Japan (now New Supermarket Association of Japan) established in 1958 by Masui of Kinokuniya (NSAJ website), the number of self-service stores increased from 40 in 1955 to 139 in 1956, 283 in 1957, 562 in 1958, 1,036 in 1959, and 1,442 in 1960 (Okuzumi 1958: 36, 1960: 38). The mass media also increasingly made a big deal of 'the self-service age' (*Nikkei Newspaper* 1958a) or 'the supermarket age' (*Yomiuri Newspaper* 1958a, *Nikkei Newspaper* 1958b).

In this early stage, some developments appeared which supported the spread of self-service. Significant in this was the Movement of Housewives' Stores (*Shufu no Mise Undo*), launched by Hideo Yoshida (1982, see also AOEB 1981: 244–63, Tateno 1986: 61–62, Suzuki 1991: 317–18, Yahagi 1997: Chapter 1). Yoshida started the self-service store, Maruwa Food Centre, with about 397 m^2 sales floor space in the provincial city, Kokura, in Kyushu Island, in 1956 under direct influence from Nagato of NCR Japan. Some commentators (e.g. Kuramoto and Atsumi 1960: 50–52, AOEB 1981: 247, Yahagi 1997: 36) insist that it is this Maruwa Food Centre, rather than Kinokuniya, that should be honoured as the first 'supermarket' in Japan, because while the assortment of Kinokuniya was limited to fruits and vegetables, Maruwa Food Centre sold all foods in general, and also because while Kinokuniya's main customers were wealthy foreign people related to the occupational force and did not seek discounted prices, Maruwa Food Centre targeted ordinary consumers and emphasised lower prices. In any event, Yoshida of Maruwa Food Centre had an opportunity in 1957 to report his experiences at a national meeting sponsored by the Open Research Group of Business (later changed to the Association for Open Education of Business). This group was launched by Minoru Kitamura in 1949 initially to tackle the taxation issue for retailers, and later shifted its activities to support modernisation of retailers (Yahagi 1997: 48–49). Yoshida emphasised that the introduction of self-service could reduce costs and increase sales volume, and this talk attracted the audience. With Yoshida's support, the first Housewives' Store was opened in 1957 in the provincial city Ogaki, in Gifu Prefecture. Then the Movement of Housewives' Stores developed as a loose network of self-service retailers, reaching 25 stores by October 1958 (AOEB 1981: 250) under the collaboration of two leaders, Yoshida and Kitamura. This Movement, however, split into two factions in December 1958 due to a conflict between the two leaders (*Yomiuri Newspaper* 1958b); the 'Pinwheel Faction (*kazaguruma-kei*)' led by Yoshida (they used a pinwheel design for their stores) and the 'Open Education Faction (*kokai-kei*)' by Kitamura (their organisation was based on the Association for Open Education for Business), and the influence of both factions was gradually lost.

Development of super *as a Japanese method in self-service stores*

At the initial stage, almost all self-service stores were food stores. Soon, however, newcomers emerged who came from anything but the food sector, and became the mainstream in self-service retailers in Japan.

The top runner was Daiei. When Daiei opened its first store, it called itself 'Daiei Headquarter Osaka, the Housewives' Store' under the influence of the

Movement of Housewives' Stores (UMDS 2006: 120–4). Despite this banner, however, the enterprise was neither a food nor a self-service store. Isao Nakauchi, the founder of Daiei, had some experience as a drugs broker soon after the defeat of the War because his father's business before the War was pharmaceutical. Therefore, when he started his first retail store in September 1957, he opened up a drugs store. The store had only 97 m² sales floor space with 13 sales clerks, located in front of Senbayashi Station of Keihan Electric Railway in Osaka (Daiei 1992: 15), and almost 90 per cent sales were of medicines and toiletries/cosmetics (UMDS 2006: 125). Confronted with discounting by rivals, however, this store began to sell cheap confectionery, which soon contributed nearly 50 per cent of sales (UMDS 2006: 126). In December 1958 Nakauchi opened up a second small store in San'nomiya in Kobe, near the JR San'nomiya station, and replaced it with a third store nearby in April 1959, which had been an old two-storey warehouse with 562 m² floor space. Daiei used only the first floor of 330 m² for sales space (Daiei 1992: 25–26). It was this third store that introduced the self-service method for the first time (Daiei 1992: 26, UMDS 2006: 126).

This store gradually expanded the assortment of products. According to Nakauchi's own reminiscences (UMDS 2006: 132–42, see also Daiei 1992: 32–34), the idea of expanding their assortment was gained directly from customers' opinions on each individual item. For instance, when Nakauchi heard from some customers that they wanted beef, he purchased dressed meat in a week or so and sold it at 39 yen per 100 grams, beating the usual price of 60 yen per 100 grams. This cheap beef promoted awareness of Daiei among the people. Sales of apples, bananas and underwear produced by Gunze (established in 1896 as a silk reeling company and producing underwear from 1946) started in a similar way (UMDS 2006: 151). Thus, at first there were no grand strategies to decide in which direction the store would expand the assortment of products.

As the San'nomiya store (the third store) was becoming popular, Nakauchi bought a movie theatre located diagonally across from the store, and the store operated from both bases from 1961. The old store had two sales floors totalling 1,190 m², with foods, toiletries/cosmetics and drugs on the first floor, and electrical appliances and everyday items on the second floor; and the new premises had two sales floors and a basement totalling 1,258 m², providing men's clothing/articles and women's underwear on the first floor, women's clothing/articles on the second floor, and children's and babies' clothing/articles in the basement (Daiei 1992: 29). The stores were essentially approaching the format later known as '*super*' – or 'general *super*' to distinguish it from the self-service store focusing on food (called 'food *super*'). This development was based not on theory but on trial and error. This was evident from a research interview of the founder Nakauchi in his later years, conducted by a few Japanese business historians: they asked, 'about when did you have the concept of general *super* in your mind, Mr Nakauchi?'; and Nakauchi's answer was quite simple, 'Well, I rarely considered the concept of general *super* in my mind, in effect' (UMDS 2006: 158). This remark suggested that at this early stage, the emergent format did not have any proper model.

In the meantime, the concept of the Self-service Discount Department Store (SSDDS) (see Yahagi 1998: 128–34, 2004: 237) emerged, and soon began to illustrate the objective for emergent Japanese self-service stores. The concept was advocated by Uichi Kitazato (1962, 1963), a pen name of Hajime Sato, who also worked for NCR Japan and moved to Seibu Department Store from 1963 (Sato 1974: 333–4); later he became the head of the Research Institute of the Distribution Industry (*Ryutsu-Sangyo Kenkyujo*) sponsored by the Seibu Group (later Saison Group). In studying the practice of US retailers, Kitazato was inspired by the development of E. J. Korvette. This store was started by Eugene Ferkauf, the son of Rumanian immigrants, as a discount retailer of luggage in Manhattan in 1948, and developed the chain network composed of 17 discount department stores from 1954 to 1962 (Silberman 1962a: 99, see also *Business Week* 1962: 72), a format described as 'part supermarket, part department store, part carnival' (*Time* 1963: 47). It created a great stir when it invaded Manhattan's Fifth Avenue, the most prestigious shopping street, in 1962 by occupying a seven-storey building (*Business Week* 1962, Silberman 1962a, 1962b, *Time* 1963). Echoing the praise for Ferkauf by M. P. McNair (Silberman 1962a: 99, *Time* 1963: 46), a professor celebrated for being the originator of the theory of the 'wheel of retailing', Kitazato (1962: 18–19) wrote,

If we could recognise supermarkets, which were born in the 1930s and merged into the American way of life as far as eating habits are concerned, as the flag-bearer of the first commercial revolution, it is the SSDDS that should be the real champion of the second commercial revolution.

(Kitazato 1962: 8)

According to Kitazato, the SSDDS dealt in the 'full range of products equivalent to department stores and sold en masse at discounted prices' (Kitazato 1962: 8). It sells 'as many as 7,000 items of foods and 100,000 to 180,000 items of other general products on sales floors of 100,000 to 250,000 square feet under the self-service method, with low margins and a high product turnover, and by elaborately planning the impulse buying of customers' (Kitazato 1962: 14).

Soon after this introduction, some Japanese retailers swiftly adopted the concept of SSDDS as the format they were looking for. In the case of Daiei, it opened up the first self-declared SSDDS in 1963 in San'nomiya, Kobe. A reportage under the title of 'The SSDDS in Japan' (Kobayashi 1963) enthusiastically reported that this store would give substance to the vogue phrase 'Revolution of Distribution (*ryutsu kakumei*)', which came into fashion in 1962 via books published by Hayashi (1962) and Tajima (1962): '"Revolution of Distribution" is no longer an empty theory used in journalism . . . It is not an exaggeration to say that 1963 is becoming "the year in which Revolution of Distribution is really advancing"' (Kobayashi 1963: 84).

This store embraced the features of the retail format considered to be SSDDS at the time, as shown by Figure 5.4. It occupied a six-storey-with-basement building and sold women's clothing and related specialty products in addition to foods,

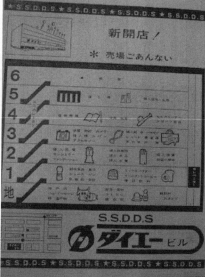

| External appearance of SSDDS | The guide of floor plan hung on the wall of the store |

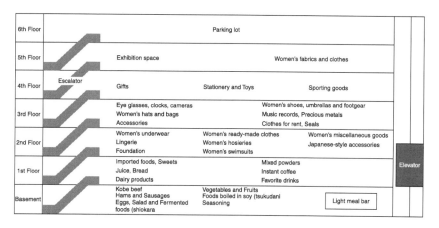

6th Floor		Parking lot		
5th Floor		Exhibition space	Women's fabrics and clothes	
4th Floor	Escalator	Gifts	Stationery and Toys	Sporting goods
3rd Floor		Eye glasses, clocks, cameras Women's hats and bags Accessories	Women's shoes, umbrellas and footgear Music records, Precious metals Clothes for rent, Seals	
2nd Floor		Women's underwear Lingerie Foundation	Women's ready-made clothes Women's hosieries Women's swimsuits	Women's miscellaneous goods Japanese-style accessories
1st Floor		Imported foods, Sweets Juice, Bread Dairy products	Mixed powders Instant coffee Favorite drinks	Elevator
Basement		Kobe beef Hams and Sausages Eggs, Salad and Fermented foods (shiokara	Vegetables and Fruits Foods boiled in soy (tsukudani Seasoning	Light meal bar

Figure 5.4 The first SSDDS and its floor plan of Daiei (1963).

Source: Pictures of the external view (upper left) and the original guide of the floor plan (lower left) are from Nakauchi Memorial Resource Centre. The translation of the floor plan guide into English (right) was done by the author referring to the picture of the original guide.

Note: The external billboard showed 'S.S.D.D.S.', and did the original floor plan, evidence that Daiei emphasised this term as the new concept of the store at the time. The 3rd floor was rented to specialty retailers.

Pictures are reproduced courtesy of Nakauchi Memorial Resource Centre, University of Marketing and Distribution Sciences.

stationery/toys and sporting products and others sold on the departmentalised sales floors. At the same time, the old store at San'nomiya sold men's clothing and electrical appliances as well as drugs and cosmetics/toiletries (Daiei 1992: 81–82). The new store ostentatiously put 'S.S.D.D.S. Daiei' on an exterior signboard and 'S.S.D.D.S. Daiei Building' on the guide map of the store inside.

This concept was not only adopted by Daiei but also by powerful emergent rivals. For instance, Seiyu Store (now Seiyu, see below) opened premises carrying the slogan 'the first SSDDS in Tokyo Metropolis' in September 1962 (Tatsuki 1991: 382–4). Shiro, later merged with Jusco (now Aeon, see below), also started SSDDS in 1962 in Kawanishi, Hyogo Prefecture, while Okadaya, who had already opened Okadaya Department Store in Yokkaichi, Mie Prefecture in 1959 focusing on selling cheap clothing under the self-service system, also merged with Jusco (Jusco 2000: 50 and 30, see below). In addition, from 1964 Ito Yokado decided to develop a chain network of SSDDS by labelling them 'the real SSDDS created in Tokyo Metropolis' (Ito Yokado 2007: 26, see below).

Although 'SSDDS' was replaced in store names by *super* or general *super* in due course,[4] the stores with the full-line assortment of products, not only food but also any other everyday necessities, became mainstream in self-service retailing in Japan by utilising multi-storey buildings with departmentalised sales floors. Self-service shopping for clothes was an essential component of this format. The press clearly recognised this feature: 'defying the common belief that supermarkets are generally food stores, there are so many supermarkets in Japan that deal in clothing in their main assortment of products' (Kobayashi 1963: 84). This feature continued during the High Economic Growth period. The survey of the top 120 *super* companies conducted by the Japan Research Institute of Textile Economy in 1971 identified that in all sales volume clothing accounted for 46.0 per cent, whereas food remained at 33.5 per cent (Nakagome 1975: 148).

This aspect was brought about directly by the founders of general *super*, whose background came from anything but the food sector. As well as Daiei's background in the pharmaceutical sector, other rivals came from the clothing sector or a subsidiary of department stores; that is:

- Ito Yokado started its business as a retail shop selling Western clothing/ haberdasheries in 1920 under the name of Miyogaya in Asakusa Tokyo (Ito 2003: 63–74, Ito Yokado 2007: 2–27);
- Jusco (now Aeon) was formed by an agreement in 1968 to merge three clothing retailers, Okadaya, Futagi and Shiro (Okada 1983, Jusco 2000: 3–54);
- Seiyu (started as Seiyu Store, now under the umbrella of Walmart) started as a subsidiary of Seibu Department Store in 1956;
- Nichii (later Mycal, merged with Aeon in 2006) was formed in 1963 by a merger of two clothing retailers, Self Hatoya (known as the earliest clothing store in Osaka that introduced the self-service method, in 1955) and Okamoto Store, and two clothing wholesalers, Yamato Kobayashi Store and Erupisu (Yamazaki 1988: 25, Yahagi 1997: 81–85); and

- Uny was established in 1971 also on a merger of two clothing retailers, Hoteiya and Nishikawaya (Yahagi 1997: 91–93, Uny website).

It is apparent that buying and selling of clothing was easier for these merchants, compared to those who were originally food retailers. More essentially, however, the feature of selling clothing as the main assortment of products at general *super* was brought about by the changes in the domain of availability of clothing and changes in consumer behaviours in terms of the relationships of consumers with others during the act of consumption of clothing.

Changes in marketing and consumption of clothing

Completion of transformation to Western-style clothing

As was explored in Chapter 2, Western-style clothing (*yo-fuku*) had been adopted before the Second World War, but its diffusion was yet limited to particular social strata and to particular occasions. The wartime regime strongly disapproved of Western things, but ironically, it decisively deprived people of traditional Japanese clothing in their everyday life. Under the wartime control, men outside the military forces were forced to wear the 'wartime uniform (*kokumin-fuku*)', which was essentially based on Western-style designs similar to the Japanese military uniform, although the current dogma supporting the war insisted on its bearing original Japanese features (Inoue 2001). Women were also subjected to strong social pressure to have 'working pantaloons (*monpe*)', which were sewn at home often by altering the kimono, but were quite unlike the traditional design. 'Political power approved the Western-style by patching this style up with a decor of 'standard' and 'Japanese-like'; the fact was that traditional Japanese-style clothing was officially turned away' (Yokota 1999: 57).

After the defeat, people never returned to the traditional Japanese design. Due to severe difficulty of getting food, many people had to visit farmers and exchange expensive *kimono* for food although the farmers were often reluctant to do this simply because *kimono* could not be eaten (see retrospect such as *Asahi Newspaper* 2006, *Tokyo Newspaper* 2010 etc.). Meanwhile, people continued to sew their clothing at home by modifying various kinds of traditional clothes, because of the absolute shortage of fabric. An astonished observer (Yoshida 1955: 13) reported that as early as the mid-summer of 1946, many women on busy streets were changing from 'working pantaloons' to Western-style skirts and blouses. In the meantime, the articles in magazines appeared to recommend women to wear Western-style clothing (Kajima 1996: 10, Mori 2008), while foreign movies stimulated Western-style fashion. These were part of the westernisation/ Americanisation movement soon after the War. A sudden boom in sewing Western-style clothing (*yo-sai boom*) occurred in 1948–49 and about 2,000 dress-making schools were hastily established with attendance of almost 200,000 female students (Shimokawa 1997: 200). This was evidence of widely spreading interest in Western-style clothing at the time. Many of these students did not intend to be professionals, but studied it as training for homemaking before their weddings (Okumura 1979: 44). In the summer of 1950, Wajiro Kon, a famous observer of modernology (see Chapter 2), reported his surprise in recognising in his travels how widely Western-style skirts and blouses or one-piece dresses had spread over many parts of Japan:

> Amazingly, at any out-of-the-way hamlets I visited, almost all women wore Western-style clothing; not only the youngsters, but also the middle-aged ladies and old women. Only one or two in one hundred still wore *kimono*, but I recognised they were quite exceptional. . . . These changes could never have been predicted by anyone before the War.
>
> (Kon 1967: 103)

Thus, the long period of transformation from traditional costumes to Western-style clothing, not only for limited occasions or for specific people in a particular social stratum, but for everyday life of every consumer, was finally completed after the Second World War.

The stability of Western-style clothing in society was encouraged by changes in two factors in the supply side; that is, the spread of ready-made clothing, and synthetic fibre. Regarding ready-made clothing,[5] it became steadily more popular and was reflected in the diminishing popularity of dressmaking schools in the latter half of the 1950s (Okumura 1979: 47–48) and the decline of tailors and dressmakers from 1960 (Nakagome 1975: 61). At first, the products were dogged by negative images of 'things off the peg (*tsurushi*)' (Kajima 1996: 13–14), and the producers were condemned as 'the destroyer of fabrics (*tsubushiya*)' (Nakagome 1975: 166–8). It was reported that many powerful department stores demanded unusual trade practices with weak manufacturers (usually manufacturers-cum-wholesalers) of ready-made clothing, such as the 'sales-or-return system of unsold goods (*henpin-sei*)' from department stores to vendors, and the system of 'dispatching sales clerks (*haken-ten'in*)' onto the sales floors of department stores at the expense of vendors (see Takaoka 1997). Some manufacturers, such as Kashiyama, Renown and Tokyo Style, however, used the stores' demands cleverly as an effective measure for getting information on the actual saleability of products in the market (Ejiri 1979: chapters 5 and 6, Usui 1992: 46, Takaoka 1997), and this assisted their development into eminent manufacturers (Kinoshita 2004, 2011) who became known as 'apparel manufacturers' (*apparel maker* in *katakana* characters) instead of 'the destroyers of fabrics'. A group of marketers composed of department stores and apparel manufacturers, who were basically fashion oriented, was growing from the 1960s onwards. As demonstrated below, general *super* perceived a different market segment that this group targeted, that is, those who consumed clothing for practical uses on a mass scale.

Introduction of synthetic fibres as new materials for ready-made clothing accelerated their diffusion, especially for practical uses. Differing from the field of sewing or knitting of clothing, the production of synthetic fibre became a structured oligopoly as early as the latter half of the 1950s, composed of the leading textile manufacturers who had existed before the Second World War (Fujii 1971: 9–10). They introduced synthetic fibre technology from foreign manufacturers and strongly stimulated the spread of Western-style ready-made clothing for practical use. For instance, Toray (established as Toyo Rayon in 1926) started the production of nylon under a technical tie-up with DuPont in the USA in 1951 (Fujii 1971: 166–85), leading to the boom in nylon blouses in 1952. Toray and Teijin (established as Works for Artificial Silk of Azuma Manufacturing in 1915) collaborated to introduce polyester technology from ICI in the UK and started mass production under the brand name of 'Tetoron' in 1958 (Fujii 1971: 211–6). Tetoron became widely used in ready-made clothing for practical use; for instance, men's short-sleeved shirts became a boom in 1961 under the name of 'Hong Kong Shirt' (Kajima 1996: 47–48). In addition, the blend of wool and Tetoron allowed clothing manufacturers to access cheaper materials for men's suits in large amounts (MITI 1964: 194). Acrylic fibre was competitively introduced by several large-sized manufacturers under various brands, leading to the 'knit boom' from 1961 (Fujii 1971: 219–23).

The role of super *as a clothing retailer*

The newly expanded domain of offerings of ready-made clothing and synthetic fibre provided an opportunity for general *super* to mediate between these possible offerings and consumers' choices, particularly for mass consumption for practical clothing. Daiei attempted to initiate this mediation (see Daiei 1992: 64–68).

As early as 1962, Daiei began to sell the so-called '*cutter-shirt*' (which in Japanese English meant men's shirts which had no cuffs and collars) under the brand name 'Toyobo Blue-Mountain Cutter-Shirt' (see Figure 5.5[A]). This was a collaborate brand of Daiei with Toyobo, the fourth largest manufacturer of synthetic fibre at the time;[6] and the name 'Blue-Mountain', which had been bought from a vendor of sports clothing, represented the Daiei brand. All products were sewn by an independent manufacturer, Marushin Fuhaku (later Tomiya Apparel). The product was made of a blend of cotton and Tetoron (polyester). At the time, the sizes of shirts were not yet standardised nationally (the first Japanese Industrial Standards [JIS] for shirts were set in 1964 as JISL 4117), so Daiei introduced their own category for neck measurements and sleeve lengths, resulting in about 40 patterns for size. As many housewives, who usually bought clothing for their husbands, were not yet familiar with the size category of ready-made shirts, Daiei displayed them by size in categorised boxes in plastic. Toyobo had sold its nationally branded 'Diamond Shirt' at 1,200 to 1,500 yen; but in contrast, Daiei sold 'Toyobo Blue-Mountain Cutter-Shirt' at 680 yen only with 16.9 per cent of gross margin. This united brand created a sensation. Daiei expanded the variety of thickness of yarns, colours and printed patterns. While the first month's order to the vendor was 6,000 shirts, three years later the sales volume surpassed one million shirts per year. This case was recognised at the time to be representative of the 'revolution of distribution' (Munakata 1963: 15).

[A] Toyobo Blue-Mountain
Cutter-Shirt (1962)

[B] Gunze Blue-Mountain
Underwear (1962)

[C] Venus in collaboration with
Nissin Flour Milling (1962)

[D-1] Bubu, Daiei's private
brand of colour TV (1970)

[D-2] Demonstration of Bubu, selling
at only 59,800 yen (1970)

Figure 5.5 Private brands of Daiei (1960s–1970s).

Reproduced courtesy of Nakauchi Memorial Resource Centre, University of Marketing and Distribution Sciences.

A similar project was undertaken in the field of men's underwear. In 1962 the collaboration between Daiei and Gunze, a large-sized manufacturer of knitted underwear (established in 1896), introduced a collaborate brand, 'Gunze Blue-Mountain Underwear' (see Figure 5.5 [B]) with great success. The sales volume reached 6 per cent of all turnover of underwear in Daiei within three years, and the collaborative branding expanded to include other large-sized manufacturers, such as Kanebo and Unitika (Daiei 1992: 70). The brand name 'Blue-Mountain' was used for all areas of clothing dealt by Daiei until 1968 when the new brand name 'Christie' was introduced for clothing for women (Daiei 1992: 65). The founder of Daiei, Nakauchi, published a book entitled *Discount is My Philosophy* in 1969, which emphasised that 'The destination that the doctrine of Daiei heads for is a consumer-oriented company. . . . Consumer sovereignty is necessary not because of sentimental humanitarianism, but because of a severe requirement from the economic point of view' (Nakauchi 1969: 19–20). Clearly his strong belief was supported by such successful experience in the introduction of private brands.

While the above cases of Daiei were the state-of-the-art marketing at the time, other *super* also tackled selling practical-use clothing by utilising their original background as clothing merchants. As a result, *super* took a firm root as the retail outlets for clothing after the end of the High Economic Growth period. Table 5.1

Table 5.1 Retail channels of clothing (1976)

					Unit: %
	Department stores	Large-sized super[1]	Specialty stores[2]	Neighbourhood stores[3]	Others[4]
Men's clothing					
Sweaters	30.6	26.0	19.4	21.5	2.6
Shirts	32.7	24.0	21.7	18.9	2.7
Trousers	22.7	19.0	33.1	21.9	3.2
Suits	35.9	6.7	41.2	10.4	5.8
Women's clothing					
Sweaters	25.0	18.5	28.8	24.0	3.6
Blouses	25.6	17.6	27.9	25.7	3.3
Skirts	27.5	21.9	28.9	19.3	2.5
Slacks	18.6	24.3	22.4	31.1	3.7
Dresses	37.3	12.6	29.3	18.4	2.4

Source: IWS 1978.

Notes: The ratios are calculated on the basis of prices.

1 Large-sized *super*: super as part of corporate chain, with 3,000 m² and more of total sales floor space, and with 100 million yen and more of turnover of clothing per year

2 Specialty store: specialty stores of men's, women's or children's clothing, tailors, and specialty stores of jeans, shirts or sporting goods.

3 Neighbourhood stores: small-sized *super*, traditonal harberdasher stores, general stores, and school or company shop.

4 Others: Those who have no permanent stores, such as wholesalers, peddlers or mail order houses.

shows the proportion of different retail channels for clothing in 1976, after the end of High Economic Growth. It suggests that in cheaper practical clothing such as men's sweaters and shirts, women's skirts and slacks, the ratios of buying at 'large-sized *super*', i.e. general *super*, were high; in contrast, in the case of expensive clothing or items sensitive to fashion such as men's suits and women's dresses, the ratios bought at general *super* remained relatively low.

It was clear that while expensive clothing made of 100 per cent wool, for example, tended to be bought at department stores, clothing made of synthetic fibres were bought at *super* (IWS 1978: 20). According to survey data in 1976 (IWS 1978: 26–27), for instance, 46 per cent of the cheapest category of men's sweaters (less than 1,800 yen per sweater) and 48 per cent of the second cheapest category (1,800 yen to 2,700 yen) were sold at 'large-sized *super*'. In this case, 58 per cent of the cheapest category and 41 per cent of the second cheapest category of sweaters were made of synthetic fibre. In contrast, 42 per cent of the most expensive category of sweaters (5,100 yen or more) was sold at the department stores, and 47 per cent of this category of sweaters was made of pure wool.

A reputation for retailing practical clothing was, however, a double-edged sword. Whatever the intended use for the clothing, the elements of fashion could not be completely eliminated, and even if ordinary consumers were only beginning to enjoy mass consumption of Western-style clothing, they were also always interested in fashionable trends. Therefore, even before the start of the High Economic Growth period, some leading department stores introduced the mode from Paris and other foreign cities (e.g. Kajima 2006: 35–36). The years of High Economic Growth saw the emergence of another type of marketing actor, that is, modern specialty stores of Western-style fashionable ready-made clothing, such as Suzuya and Tamaya for women's clothing and for men, Mitsumine and Takakyu. They began to expand their store networks from around the mid-1960s by opening shops as tenant retailers at city centres and/or in shopping complexes of railway stations, shopping centres and department stores (Nakagome 1975: 130–4).

The executives of general *super*, of course, recognised such a fashionable aspect of clothing and began to add fashionable and high-quality clothing, such as men's suits made of pure wool (IWS 1978: 20), to their assortment of products. This orientation led to 'trading up' of the products they handled and to the diversification strategy of retail formats, as will be seen in the section below.

Marketing and consumption of food by super

Retaining traditional preference

In the field of buying and consuming food for everyday diet, some traditional features remained for a while despite the progress of High Economic Growth. Especially in the category of perishables, usually called the 'three major categories of perishable foods (*seisen san-pin*)', that is, vegetables/fruits, fish and meat, many Japanese housewives continued to buy in very small amounts several times a week at traditional neighbourhood greengrocers/fruit shops, fishmongers and butchers.

In fact, a survey in Tokyo and Osaka metropolises (JSSA 1975: 60, see also Okada 1975: 355–6) showed that even in 1974, just after the end of the High Economic Growth period, 52.4 per cent of monthly purchases of vegetables/ fruits were still made at traditional shops, whereas only 13.0 per cent were at large-sized *super* or general *super* and 10.7 per cent at food *super*. The opinion was rooted in society at the time that 'the sales section of vegetables and fruits in *super* is weak' (Okada 1975: 366). Similarly, 45.6 per cent of fish (including fresh produce, Japanese-style fish pâtés and salted dry fish) were bought at traditional fishmongers and only 18.9 per cent at general *super* and 22.0 per cent at food *super*. Of meats (including processed meats), 42.9 per cent were bought at butchers, whereas it was 20.7 per cent at general *super* and 20.5 per cent at food *super*.

These data suggested that although *super* rapidly progressed, Japanese house-wives continued to visit neighbourhood shops a number of times a week and bought these foods in small amounts. This was mainly due to the culture of freshness-oriented cuisine, as typically exemplified by Japanese dishes such as raw fish (*sashimi*) and cold bean curd (*hiya-yakko*). The same survey (JSSA 1975: 60, see also Okada 1975: 368) revealed that the housewives referred to 'freshness' as the highest criterion for their choice; 84.0 per cent for vegetables, 81.9 per cent for fish and shellfish, and 70.7 per cent for meat. In contrast, 'constant cheapness' was relatively low as a criterion; only 33.3 per cent for vegetables/fruit, 23.3 per cent for fish and shellfish, and 28.7 per cent for beef and pork.

Super originally did not have a forte for handling the three major categories of perishable foods. This was because these products were less standardised in size, shape and quality, were not pre-packed, and fluctuated in price and the obtainable volumes depending on weather and other conditions. In addition, Japanese *super* faced some demands which they recognised their American counterparts did not have, such as the more sophisticated variety in spices for fish and consumers' preferences for the thinnest slices of meat (see Azuchi 2006: 61–66). As the skills of traditional merchants looked to be more suitable for handling these categories of products than the self-service system, *super* tended to lease floor space to the specialised merchants to sell these products; especially in the early years of the self-service system (Nagato 1963: 184).

Furthermore, the system of public wholesale markets in Japan was more supportive to traditional neighbourhood retailers than to *super*. This system began as far back as 1923, to redress the imbalance between increased demand for perishable foods as everyday necessities by urban labourers and fluctuating supplies, often with soaring prices manipulated by the wholesalers (Fujita 1972, 1986). Public wholesale markets were run under the supervision of local govern-ments and were established in many cities. After the Second World War, the national government decided to expand these public wholesale markets to many provincial cities in order to meet the further progress of urbanisation (Editorial

Committee 1979: 619–735, Kikuchi 2002: 73–75). In these markets, the auction system (called '*seri*') was adopted; however, this was not necessarily suitable for large-sized *super* who looked for economy of scale, because under this system the large-sized orders tended to push up the market prices rather than reduce them (Azuchi 2006: 65–66).

As a result of this combination of factors, traditional greengrocers, fishmongers and butchers kept their positions in the markets during the High Economic Growth period. Figure 5.6 shows the changes in store numbers of these traditional retailers respectively and the total number of retail stores, according to the Census of Commerce; this started in 1952 to investigate all wholesale and retail establishments nationwide every two years (from 1979 every three years, and from 1997 every five years, with supplementation by the simple census survey two years after the main census survey). The graph shows that the numbers of greengrocers and fishmongers steadily decreased from 1976; before that, the numbers had fluctuated. In the case of butchers, the number securely increased until 1979, then

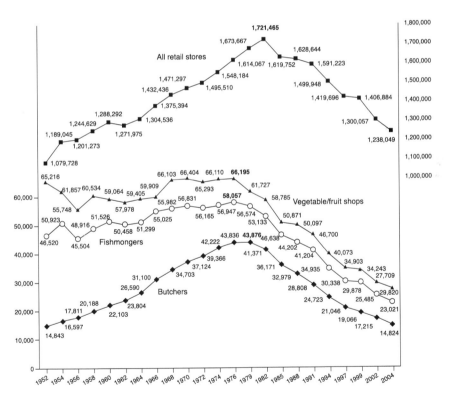

Figure 5.6 Changes in the number of retail stores (1952–2004)

Source: Ministry of Economy, Trade and Industry, *Census of Commerce*.

Notes: The number of all retail stores excludes 'eating and drinking places'. The numbers in bold show the peak numbers in each category.

showed a steady decrease. These data suggest that at least during the period of High Economic Growth, these traditional retailers were able to maintain their positions in the market with consumer support. It should be especially noted that the proportion of household expenditure on meat in the total household expenditure on foods steadily increased from 8.0 per cent in 1962 to 11.7 per cent in 1975, while the ratios of vegetables and fish were rather stable with a little less than 13.0 per cent for vegetables and 11.8 per cent to 14.2 per cent for fish (calculated from SB website 2). The shift to consumption of meat or animal proteins was called 'modernisation' (Yamaguchi 1983: 11, Yamaguchi 1990: 25, Shibazaki 1990: 54) or 'westernisation' (Yoshida 1988) of eating habits ('*shoku no kindaika*', or '*shoku no yofuka*') at the time.[7] The steady increase in numbers of butchers reflected the increase in meat expenditure.

Fitting of super to food retailing

Despite holding firm during the High Economic Growth period, numbers of these traditional food retailers began to decrease steadily after 1976–79. Turning to the total number of retail stores in Figure 5.6, it consistently increased until 1982 before beginning a steady decline until the present due to the significant decrease in non-incorporated, small-sized retailers alongside the increase in incorporated, medium- and large-sized retailers. This meant that despite the famous stereotypical description that most Japanese homemakers prefer convenient and more personal shops in the neighbourhood (e.g. see Kotler and Armstrong 2000: 345–6), the petty retailers found difficulty in continuing their businesses, and the structure of the retail industry had been changing since 1982. Greengrocers, fishmongers and butchers in particular began to decline even earlier than the average. This has been ascribed to tough competition from the powerful *super*, which overcame their disadvantageous position in the food sector by the following measures.

In the field of perishable foods, *super* broke new ground with incremental innovations. In the early days, their consultants (e.g. Kuramoto and Atsumi 1960: 223–43) taught in detail how to pre-pack and tag perishable foods and bulk processed foods on the premises, by using polyester, then a newly emergent material. *Super* also began to try to manage the craftsmen by standardising their operations (Azuchi 1987: 78–85, 2006: 68–91). To increase efficiency in cutting, slicing, combining, packing and tagging perishables, *super* instituted a wide back area behind the sales section (Okada 1975: 17). This space was also useful for cooking various side dishes ('*sozai*') sold via self-service. Some advanced *super* introduced a central packaging system, in which the company set up a packaging centre and delivered the packaged perishable foods to several branch stores (Azuchi 1987: 89–97).

In addition, advanced *super* invested in cold storages, refrigerators and cold showcases to maximise the freshness of perishable goods. The refrigeration equipment was also effective for dealing with frozen foods, which appeared in great quantities at the time, as will be seen below. Although the government began to provide special loans for retailers to have refrigeration equipment (SMEA 1966) based on the so-called 'cold chain (*cold chain*)', which planned to establish physical distribution networks which could deal with keeping lower temperatures (STA 1965, Hirano 1967: 94), the heavy investment in the equipment was clearly financially advantageous for large-sized *super* (see Morishita 1974: 183, Okada 1975: 16–17).

Large-sized *super* also began to bypass the public wholesale markets by procuring directly from producers or from the collection and delivery centres (*shu-hai centre*) run by the National Federation of Agricultural Co-operative Associations (*Zen-No*), a marketing and supply organisation of the Japan Agricultural Cooperative (JA) (Okada 1975: 15). The amendment of the law of public wholesale markets in 1971 encouraged the expansion of public markets on the one hand, but also allowed on the other hand direct dealing ('*aitai torihiki*') between wholesale merchants (*oroshiuri-nin*) in the markets and retail buyers, as an exception to the auction system. There were variations in this direct dealing method, such as lien dealing ('*saki-dori*'), which was preferential selling to particular retail buyers before the auction started, and the advanced agreement on direct dealing ('*yoyaku aitai torihiki*'), which were agreements on dealing in a few months to sell the products with price corrections to some extent (Kikuchi 1995: 250–4, Kidachi 1996: 68–69). Bypassing the public wholesale markets and erosion of the auction system undermined the public wholesale markets themselves and provided advantages for large-sized *super* in retail competition.

In non-perishable foods, the increase in branded processed foods prepacked by manufacturers created a more favourable environment for the self-service of *super* than for traditional retailers. A succession of new types of foods appeared and attracted the eye of many consumers during the High Economic Growth period. For instance, there was the introduction of so-called 'instant foods (*instant shokuhin*)', such as instant coffee or powdered coffee, instant curry or curry roux, instant or powdered soup, and instant or powdered juice. A marked event in this field was the invention of instant Chinese noodles, branded Chicken Ramen, in 1958 by Nissin Food Product Co., (Miura and Koezuka 1997). The concept that people could eat them just by pouring boiling water and waiting only for a few minutes was enthusiastically welcomed by consumers; so many manufacturers entered this field, shaping a huge market for instant Chinese noodles within a year (Sakai 1990: 241). The total production increased to 216,695 tons in 1965, 9.4 times larger than in 1959 (STA 1967). In 1971 Nissin Food Product Co., introduced a revised product, instant Chinese noodles in a Styrofoam cup, branded Cup Noodle, which are nowadays consumed worldwide, especially in East and Southeast Asian countries, in many variations.

Another popular case was the introduction of the ready-meal curry, branded Bon Curry, by Otsuka Foods Co., Ltd. in 1968. This was the first food packed in a retort-pouch, known as 'retort food (*retort shokuhin*)' in Japan. The product was made by sterilisation at high temperature and was vacuum-wrapped in the retort-pouch; consumers could eat the curry just by boiling it a few minutes. Other manufacturers soon followed to provide this new type of instant foods, such as stew (by House Foods Corp.), spaghetti meat sauce (by Yamamori Co., Ltd.), and stewed giblets (*motsu-nikomi*, by Nichiro Corp.); 1971 saw a rush of food manufacturers entering this field (Miura 1990: 442–3). The total production volume of retort-pouch food increased 1.6 times (about 50,000 tons) in 1973 compared to 1971 (Miura 1990: 444). In addition, frozen foods, which there had been attempts to introduce into the market as early as 1930, became popular especially from the late 1950s (Hisa 1990: 454–5). The total production rapidly increased from 1,591 tons in 1958 to 317,772 tons in 1973, or by a factor of nearly 200 (JFFA 2009: 34). Furthermore, many food manufacturers actively introduced nationally branded products such as chocolate, caramel, chewing gum, whisky, beer, cola, canned juice, mayonnaise, pre-packed sliced ham, to name a few, although some of them had been popular before the Second World War, as was explored in Chapter 1.

As a result of the spread of these new products, Japanese homes and dining tables filled with them at this time, a phenomenon called 'diversification or individualisation of eating habits (*shoku no tayo-ka, kosei-ka*)'. A significant point was that these new products introduced by manufacturers were essentially suitable for self-service retailing. While a few advanced manufacturers had to develop *keiretsu* retailers' networks to secure the possibility of nationwide distribution of their products in the 1910s–30s, as shown in Chapter 1, the manufacturers during the High Economic Growth period did not have to do this because independent self-service retailers were emerging in many localities, and some powerful retailers had begun to organise a nationwide network of general *super*. Pre-packaged foods provided by manufacturers gave advantage to these self-service retailers. In other words, development of marketing by processed food manufacturers expanded the domain of availability of offerings, which gave opportunities for the new type of retail format *super* to enhance consumers' choices. In this sense, manufacturers' marketing and *super* progressed hand in hand.

In the food sector, the most advanced strategy was also undertaken by Daiei. Similar to its initiative in ready-made clothing, Daiei began to introduce privately branded food with the collaboration of manufacturers. As early as 1961, Daiei introduced 'instant coffee' under collaboration with UCC Ueshima Coffee Co., Ltd., known as UCC. This company had started the wholesale business of coffee beans in 1933 in Kobe (Ueshima 1990: 1122) and grew to be a leading importer, manufacturer of tinned coffee and developer of the café after the War. Soon after Nestlé introduced instant coffee to Japan for the first time in 1959, Daiei followed two years later when the importation of instant coffee was liberalised. UCC imported non-branded instant coffee from the USA, and Daiei labelled it Red Rose, their symbol at the time, and started to sell it in its stores – Daiei's first attempt to sell private brands. The success of this attempt encouraged the expansion of the scope of private brands to include ramen, powdered juice, margarine, *mitsumame* (a mixture of gelatine cubes, boiled soy beans and fruits topped with treacle), macaroni and spaghetti in 1962, and ground coffee, Ceylon tea and Netherland cocoa in 1963. These products were procured mainly through joint development with small- and medium-sized manufacturers (Nakauchi Historical Resource Centre 2002).

Daiei also cooperated with a leading manufacturer in a project for a private brand of flour. The package of flour, useful for both Japanese- and Western-style recipes, was becoming a popular item in the food section of Daiei, before the company introduced any frozen or pre-cooked foods. Daiei had sold a 1 kg pack of flour at 63 yen, radically cheaper than retailers' usual 75 yen, but the gross margin for Daiei was quite small. Daiei negotiated with Nissin Flour Milling, which had been established in 1900 and was the second largest flour miller at the time, resulting in the agreement that ensured Daiei could buy a minimum volume of flour upfront for three years at a decisively cheaper price. Daiei could procure a pack of 1 kg flour at 51 yen from Nissin and sold it at 59 yen, the most salutary improvement of gross margin for Daiei. This product (see picture C in Figure 5.5) was introduced under the brand name of Venus, with a decorated flower design for Venus and Daiei's logo, and the name of Nissin Flour Milling Inc. printed onto the package surface (the story from Daiei 1992: 61–62, Nakauchi Historical Resource Centre 2002). As with Blue-Mountain shirts and underwear, this product was a huge success as a double-brand between the *super* and a leading manufacturer.

As a result of this series of innovations, the *super* were recognised as an institution for everyday food shopping.

The result of the development of super in the High Economic Growth period

By 1964, when the influences of the self-service system could not be ignored, the Census of Commerce began to investigate the self-service method. According to this, the number of 'retail establishments of general merchandise', which referred to general *super*, accounted for 8.1 per cent of all self-service stores in 1964, and represented 24.7 per cent of sales volume and 19.7 per cent of sales floor space. The proportion increased markedly in the next ten years; that is, in 1974 general *super* with only 8.7 per cent in self-service outlets accounted for 42.4 per cent of sales volume and 38.8 per cent of sales floors (see Table 5.2.1).

Along with this development, the oligopolistic position of general *super* became apparent. As of 1974, large-sized self-service stores with 1,500 m^2 sales floor space or more accounted for 8.1 per cent in the number of stores, but occupied 43.2 per cent in sales volume and 47.2 per cent in sales floor space, although small-sized self-service stores with 100 to 299 m^2 sales floor space still occupied 50.2 per cent in terms of the number of stores but had only 15.1 per cent in sales volume and 13.6 per cent in sales floor space, as seen in Table 5.2.2. The average sales floor space of general *super* grew from 890 m^2 in 1964 to 2,930 m^2 in 1974 (TISI 1983).

Table 5.3 represents changes in the top ten retailers in terms of sales volume: department stores dominated all top ten rankings in 1960, but two *super* had taken their place in 1967, when *Nikkei Newspaper on Distribution* (*Nikkei Ryutsu*

Table 5.2.1 Various types of self-service stores: number of stores, sales volume and sales floor space (1964–1976)

Year	All self-service stores[1]			General super[2]			Food super[3]			Clothing super[4]			Others[5]		
	Number of stores	Sales volume (mil. yen)	Sales floor space (thsnd. m²)	Number of stores (%)	Sales volume (%)	Sales floor space (%)	Number of stores (%)	Sales volume (%)	Sales floor space (%)	Number of stores (%)	Sales volume (%)	Sales floor space (%)	Number of stores (%)	Sales volume (%)	Sales floor space (%)
1964	5,620	392,373	1,342	8.1	24.7	19.4	70.9	51.2	58.9	18.1	21.8	19.5	3.0	2.3	2.2
1966	4,790	581,145	1,557	4.8	11.4	9.1	78.1	68.1	70.3	13.9	17.6	17.9	3.2	3.0	2.6
1968	7,062	1,028,570	2,780	4.4	11.6	10.0	76.4	60.8	63.1	13.1	20.8	20.8	6.0	6.9	6.1
1970	9,403	1,612,459	4,188	6.1	21.9	19.3	78.5	57.5	59.8	11.5	16.9	18.0	3.9	3.7	3.0
1972	10,634	2,447,583	5,587	6.4	24.5	21.6	75.9	54.6	54.9	12.5	16.5	19.1	5.2	4.4	4.5
1974	12,034	4,253,531	7,890	8.7	42.4	38.8	76.3	44.9	46.2	9.7	9.8	12.4	5.3	2.9	2.6
1976	14,543	6,750,221	10,110	9.1	42.7	41.0	80.0	46.7	44.6	8.6	10.0	13.2	2.3	0.7	1.2

Table 5.2.2 Self-service stores by the sales floor space (1964–1976)

Year	Stores with 100 m²–299 m² sales floor space			Stores with 300 m²–599 m² sales floor space			Stores with 600 m²–1,499 m² sales floor space			Stores with 1,500 m² sales floor space or more		
	Number of stores (%)	Sales volume (%)	Sales floor space (%)	Number of stores (%)	Sales volume (%)	Sales floor space (%)	Number of stores (%)	Sales volume (%)	Sales floor space (%)	Number of stores (%)	Sales volume (%)	Sales floor space (%)
1964	63.4	29.2	31.7	22.7	25.0	26.4	11.8	28.8	26.6	2.1	17.0	15.3
1966	64.9	34.4	31.7	23.1	28.7	28.9	10.9	29.9	31.2	1.1	7.0	8.3
1968	60.7	26.4	26.3	23.2	24.1	23.8	13.1	31.0	31.8	3.0	18.5	18.2
1970	58.5	22.5	22.8	22.9	21.2	21.3	14.3	29.9	32.6	4.3	26.3	23.3
1972	50.4	16.9	18.2	25.2	20.0	20.5	18.5	33.8	34.4	5.5	29.3	26.9
1974	50.2	13.6	15.1	25.5	16.1	17.6	16.3	23.0	24.1	8.1	47.2	43.2
1976	49.4	12.8	14.0	25.3	15.2	17.2	16.6	21.9	23.0	8.8	50.0	45.9

Source: Census of Commerce (TISI 1983).

Notes: The Census of Commerce started from 1952 to investigate all wholesale and retail establishments (excluding eating and drinking places) in all Japan every two years (from 1976 every three years; and from 1997 every five years with simplified interim survey every two year after the Census) and began to include the investigation on the self-service method from 1964.

1 The 'self-service method' was defined by the Census of Commerce as the method combining the following three factors: (a) selling pre-packed and pre-price-tagged products, (b) the customers can freely pick up the products by carrying shopping baskets or others, and (c) the customers pay all together at the checkout counters equipped at exits. The 'self-service stores' were defined as those stores adopting this self-service method to 50% or more sales floor space.

2 'General super' is a different reading of the statistical category of the retail establishments of 'general merchandise'.

3 'Food super' is a different reading of the statistical category of the retail establishments of 'foods and beverages'.

4 'Clothing super' is a different reading of the statistical category of the retail establishments of 'dry goods, apparel and accessories'.

5 'Others' is a different reading of the statistical category of the retail establishmnents of 'furniture and household utensils'.

Table 5.3 Top 10 retailers in Japan in terms of sales volume (1960–1999)

Rank	1960				1967				1972			
	Name of store	Format	Sales volume	Number of outlets	Name of store	Format	Sales volume	Number of outlets	Name of store	Format	Sales volume	Number of outlets
1	Mitsukoshi	Dept St	45	10	Daimaru	Dept St	113	4	**Daiei**	***Super***	**305**	**90**
2	Daimaru	Dept St	45	4	Mitsukoshi	Dept St	104	10	Mitsukoshi	Dept St	292	12
3	Takashimaya	Dept St	39	3	Takashimaya	Dept St	99	4	Daimaru	Dept St	213	6
4	Matsuzakaya	Dept St	37	5	Matsuzakaya	Dept St	81	5	Takashimaya	Dept St	199	4
5	Tobu Dept Store	Dept St	30	3	**Daiei**	***Super***	**58**	**34**	**Seiyu Store**	***Super***	**167**	**96**
6	Isetan	Dept St	23	2	Seibu Dept Store	Dept St	50	6	Seibu Dept Store	Dept St	155	10
7	Hankyu Dept Store	Dept St	21	4	Isetan	Dept St	47	2	**Jusco**	***Super***	**155**	**131**
8	Seibu Dept Store	Dept St	19	2	Hankyu Dept Store	Dept St	47	5	Matsuya	Dept St	149	6
9	Sogo	Dept St	15	3	Tokyu Dept Store	Dept St	40	2	**Nichii**	***Super***	**144**	**156**
10	Matsuya	Dept St	12	3	**Seiyu Store**	***Super***	**32**	**35**	Uny	***Super***	**126**	**108**

Rank	1982				1992				1999			
	Name of store	Format	Sales volume	Number of outlets	Name of store	Format	Sales volume	Number of outlets	Name of store	Format	Sales volume	Number of outlets
1	**Daiei**	**Super**	**1,252**	**162**	**Daiei**	**Super**	**2,015**	**255**	**Daiei**	**Super**	**2,205**	**308**
2	**Ito Yokado**	**Super**	**799**	**113**	**Ito Yokado**	**Super**	**1,512**	**143**	**Ito Yokado**	**Super**	**1,509**	**176**
3	**Seiyu**	**Super**	**652**	**161**	**Seiyu**	**Super**	**1,104**	**204**	**Jusco**	**Super**	**1,422**	**347**
4	**Jusco**	**Super**	**652**	**146**	**Jusco**	**Super**	**1,006**	**168**	**Mycal**	**Super**	**1,081**	**123**
5	Mitsukoshi	Dept St	546	14	Mitsukoshi	Dept St	842	14	Takashimaya	Dept St	1,021	18
6	**Nichii**	**Super**	**505**	**150**	Seibu Dept Store	Dept St	808	17	**Seiyu**	**Super**	**875**	**191**
7	Takashimaya	Dept St	467	6	**Nichii**	**Super**	**789**	**150**	**Uny**	**Super**	**774**	**144**
8	Seibu Dept Store	Dept St	456	10	Takashimaya	Dept St	789	10	Mitsukoshi	Dept St	676	12
9	Daimaru	Dept St	435	7	Daimaru	Dept St	570	7	Seibu Dept Store	Dept St	589	22
10	**Uny**	**Super**	**371**	**161**	**Uny**	**Super**	**569**	**119**	Marui	Dept St	481	30

Source: Data in 1960 was compiled by Sato (1974: 195), referring to Annual Report and other materials. Data from 1967 to 1999 referring to *Nikkei Ryutsu Newspaper* and Nikkei Ryutsu Newspaper ed., *Handbook on Economy of Distribution*, Tokyo: Nihon Keizai Shimbun-sha, each year (in Japanese).

Newspaper) started to publish the ranking table of retailing, and the sales volume of Daiei finally surpassed the sales of Mitsukoshi in 1972. This event was epoch-making in the history of Japanese retail because Daiei with only a fifteen-year history overtook Mitsukoshi with its almost three hundred year history from 1673. This Table also shows that while department stores did not eagerly expand their store networks, general *super* positively adopted the principle of chain store networks. As was mentioned above, each outlet of their networks was composed of large-sized SSDDS-type stores; their chain networks became dominant in the retail world. The store networks of general *super* developed in major cities first, and then invaded the medium-sized provincial cities with populations from 50,000 to 100,000 all over Japan, especially from 1970 onwards (Itozono and Deie 1983: 162). As a result, the structure of the top ten retailers was fixed, with general *super* dominant and department stores at the bottom. This feature continued at least until the end of the twentieth century, as shown in Table 5.3. This was the conclusion of High Economic Growth in the retail sector in Japan.

The reasons for the *super* and department stores' different response can be explained by two factors. The first factor was difference in the legal environment. From 1956 to 1973, the expansion of department store networks was regulated by the new Department Store Law; in contrast, general *super* could escape from this regulation because they were not department stores. Although their SSDDS-type stores resembled them, they often registered each floor of one building as an independent company in order to show that they were not legally department stores. Disputes naturally occurred which accused them of being 'quasi-department stores (*giji-hyakkaten*)' (Shirahige 1974: 171–5). In 1974, the Large-sized Retail Store Law was enforced, replacing the Department Store Law so as to regulate any large-sized retail stores no matter what kind of retail format the store had.[8] When the Law was put into force, however, general *super* had already established their presence.

The second factor is the difference of ethos and strategy between department stores and general *super*. The managers of established department stores generally had a stable ethos based on the long standing of their businesses, and their strategy respected the much more luxurious, fashionable and aesthetic aspect of retailing, rather than simple expansion of sales and store networks. In contrast, the founders of general *super* originally embodied a direct, aggressive spirit in expansion of their businesses as younger entrepreneurs, and they continued to pursue opening new stores in many provincial cities under the new Law, even though politico-economic battles broke out between the incoming general *super* and local retailers.

A turning point: failure of the innovation of private-brand colour TV

Around the final years of the High Economic Growth period, an emblematic event occurred to reveal the limitations of the 'simply discounting' strategy of general *super*.

The top player, Daiei, introduced privately branded colour TVs in 1970. As will be explored in the next chapter, the main retailers for household electrical appliances were *keiretsu* stores organised by manufacturers during the period of High Economic Growth, although general *super* were also selling these products. In 1968, the Electric Industries Association in the USA filed a complaint under the Anti-dumping Act against colour TVs imported from Japan, and the dumping was officially recognised in 1970 and 1971. Meanwhile, the Fair Trade Commission in Japan began to investigate large-sized manufacturers under the suspicion of price fixing in the domestic market in 1966, and issued a judgement on unlawful retail price maintenance in 1970. Corresponding to these movements, some organisations of the consumer movement, such as the National Liaison Committee of Consumers' Organisations, the Housewives' Federation, the Japanese Consumers' Co-operative Union, the League of Women Voters of Japan, and the National Federation of Regional Women's Organisations, launched a boycott of colour TVs in 1970. The 'problem on double-standard prices of colour TVs' became a hot issue in Japanese society.

In such an atmosphere, Daiei announced the introduction of privately branded colour TVs with 13 inch screens, named 'Bubu', from 25 November 1970. The retail price was less than 60 per cent of nationally branded products; it was 59,800 yen, but the product, as the founder Nakauchi claimed at a news conference, was equivalent to 99,800 yen colour TVs under national brands. At the time, Daiei had already introduced private brands of electrical products under the name 'Bubu', such as electric fans from April 1970 and black-and-white TVs from September 1970 (Daiei 1992: 127–34, Nakauchi Historical Resource Centre 2002). However, the announcement of private brand colour TVs caused a sensation. A newspaper article (*Asahi Newspaper* 1970a) talked at length about how the leader of general *super* 'challenged' the monopolistic prices defined by the dominant manufacturers.

In order to source this private brand, Daiei had secretly formed an alliance with the medium-sized assembly manufacturer, Crown & Co., Ltd. This company, however, grew scared of facing severe unexpected pressures from other players in the industry after Daiei's news conference, and asked Daiei to put the sales price up about 10,000 yen. Daiei, however, ignored this and decided to introduce it at less than 60,000 yen as promised, and bought out Crown in order to continue the 'Bubu' project. Figure 5.5 (D-1 and D-2) shows the 'Bubu' colour TVs and selling campaign. Daiei expanded the product line to include colour TVs with 18 inch screens in 1971 and with 20 inch screens in 1974. The founder, Nakauchi, stated in a newspaper interview (*Asahi Newspaper* 1972a) that he would like to increase the ratio of private brands from about 20 per cent at that time to 50 per cent by 1975, although it is uncertain if the ratio of private brands at the time he quoted was accurate.

Nakauchi's famous book, *Discount is My Philosophy*, was written and published in this context. As he emphasised in the book (Nakauchi 1969: 62), 'The Revolution of Distribution means to take back control of the power of distribution from the hands of manufacturers, to those who undertake the distribution economy [i.e. retailers]'. This opinion was not unique at the time. Hajime Sato, with the pen name Uichi Kitazato, the advocate of the concept of SSDDS who was also involved directly in the Seibu/Seiyu (later Saison) group, expressed the same view. Sato (1971: Chapter 10; 1974: Chapter 7) underlined that a 'plural distribution system' should be established, composed of both the manufacturers' system and that of the innovative retailers, who were expected to exert 'countervailing power' against the monopolistic manufacturers. Private brands were supposed to be the main measures to establish this countervailing system driven by innovative retailers.

Despite such visionary views on the role of innovative retailers handling their private brands, Daiei's attempt was not successful. Although the announcement to introduce 'Bubu' caught public attention and was enthusiastically welcomed at a rally held by organisations of the consumer movement (Nakauchi Historical Resource Centre 2002), the real sales volume was far below expectations. Daiei had to stop the production of 'Bubu' in 1976 and change its name to 'Crown', requesting technological cooperation with Sanyo Electric, one of the large-sized manufacturers of household electric appliances (*Nikkei Newspaper* 1976a). Daiei finally gave up managing Crown & Co., Ltd. and disposed of it in 1983. This decision was made when Daiei itself registered a loss on the basis of consolidated accounts in FY1982 for the first time in its history (*Nikkei Newspaper* 1983a).

Some explanations have been offered for this failure, such as strong trust and adherence of Japanese consumers to manufacturers' national brands (*Nikkei Newspaper* 1994a), consumers' expectations about price reductions on national brands (see *Asahi Newspaper* 1971c) because of direct guidance by the Fair Trade Commission (*Asahi Newspaper* 1970b) and the Ministry of International Trade and Industry (*Asahi Newspaper* 1971a), keen competition around technological development in fields such as TVs, and retailers' struggle to compete (Yahagi 1991b, *Nikkei Newspaper* 1983a), diversification of consumers' preferences (*Nikkei Newspaper* 1983a), and shifting of those preferences from simply cheap products to better quality and functions (Yahagi 1991b).

In retrospect, it is clear that Daiei began to grope for an alternative strategy to simple discounting around the time when the failure of 'Bubu' became apparent. In 1974, Nakauchi suddenly ceased publication of *Discount is my Philosophy*, although the book was still a bestseller running into a nineteenth impression. It was reported that this withdrawal was based on the following advice by a famous commentator: 'if the executive publishes a book, he will be bound by the book and his decision making will become blunted' (*Sankei Newspaper* 2007). This story suggests that Nakauchi himself began to search for an alternative to the discounting strategy he strongly advocated in his early days.

Beyond High Economic Growth: an overview of the diversification strategy by general super and its results

Diversification to conglomerchants: an overview

After the end of the High Economic Growth period, the features of general *super* were changing.

Although the main assortment of products in general *super* were clothing rather than foods during the High Economic Growth period, as was mentioned above, this was largely changing from the 1980s onwards; the Current Survey of Commerce (calculated by METI website 2) shows the proportion of clothing sales in large-sized *super* severely decreased from 34.0 per cent in 1980 to 13.3 per cent in 2009, while that of food sharply increased from 42.5 per cent to 63.7 per cent. Clearly general *super* were becoming food stores similar to their Western counterparts. As consumer behaviours became more diverse and individual (analysis described these consumers as 'divided masses' or 'small-sized masses', as explained in Historical settings to Part II), the practical clothing familiar in general *super* lost its appeal.

Corresponding to these developments, general *super* were shifting their strategy to diversification of retail formats and of businesses to embrace the various kinds of service sectors. This process was accompanied by moving away from the original price-appeal innovation and trading up of their products handled. Table 5.4 shows how five major general *super* diversified their business by using their related companies: they came to be called 'conglomerchants'. The slogan, 'comprehensive life industry (*seikatsu sogo sangyo*)', which originated in the Saison Group (Saison Corporation 1992: 1) to suggest that they would be involved in every aspect of a consumer's life, was shared by general *super* as an objective for their diversification strategy. Nakano (1995: 676–7) contended that the diversification strategy of general *super* did not have any clear target and vision; rather it progressed in quite an ad hoc way. Nevertheless, there was some individuality recognisable in each group, as shown by the following three cases.

Failure of Daiei: aggressive diversification without profits

The cases of Daiei and Seiyu are now known as examples of the 'loser group' among general *super*. They had, however, quite different characteristics.

The top retailer Daiei sought diversification most aggressively. A problem of their strategy was the heavy burden of interest-bearing debts due to successive mergers and acquisitions (M&A) and over-investments for diversification. This problem became apparent as early as FY1982 when the consolidated account went into deficit for the first time. One reason was the establishment in 1980 of Le Printemps Japan, by agreement with the famous French department store. This was a symbolic trading up of the retail format in the Daiei group. The company rapidly developed three department stores successively in San'nomiya, Kobe (in March 1981 with around 4,000 m² of sales floor space), Sapporo, Hokkaido (June 1982 with 14,000 m²), and Nanba, Osaka (January 1984 with 16,000 m²); and then entered Ginza Tokyo, the heartland of competition among leading department stores, in April 1984 with about 20,000 m² of sales floor space (Nakano 1984: 28). Despite great fanfare, its sales were less than expected. Combined with the deficit in other related companies, deficit on the consolidated account continued for three fiscal years until FY1984. At this time, Daiei managed to clear its deficit by merging three department stores with Daiei itself that was still profitable and by

Table 5.4 Diversified companies held by general *super* (1993)

Parent company	Daiei	Ito Yokado	Seiyu (Saison)	Aeon	Mycal
Retail formats					
General *super*	**Daiei** **Uneed** **Chujitsu-ya**	Ito Yokado	**Seiyu**	**Jusco**	**Nichii**
Food *super*	Seifu **Maruetsu** Sakae	York Benimaru York Mart	**Seiyu**	**Well Mart** **Shinshu Jusco**	—
Convenience stores	Lawson Sun Chain	Seven Eleven	**Family Mart**	Mini Stop	—
Shopping centres	—	—	Palco	Forus	Vivre Saty
Department stores	**Jujiya** Printemps	Robinson York Matsuzakaya	**Seibu Department Store** **Seiyu**	Bon Belta	Dac City Hoyu
Specialty stores	Lobelia (lady's fashion) Roberto (men's fashion) Daiei Drug (pharmaceuticals) Pacific Sports (sporting goods)	Oshmann's (sporting goods) Mary Ann (lady's fashion) Steps (men's fashion)	Polo Ralph Lauren (designer fashion) Asahi Medico (pharmaceuticals) Seibu Automobile Sales (car sales)	**Taka Q** (men's fashion) Blue Grass (apparel) Cox (casual wear) My-land Shoes (footwear) Book Bahn (books)	**Helme** (lady's fashion) Nuno Koibito (fabrics and notions) MacLaud (men's fashion)

Discount stores	Big A Bandol Topos Fashion Depot Half & Top	Daikuma The Price	—	Big Bang	—
DIYs (Home centres)	D Mart	Marudai	Daik	**Make** Keyo Jusco Ishiguro Jusco	—
Service sector Restaurants	**Volks** Big Boy Victoria Station	Dennys Famil	Seiyo Food Systems	Red Lobster Gourmet Dor	Coms
Fast food shops	Dipperdan (ice cream) Red Rooster (roast chicken) Hokka Hokka Tei (Japanese box lunch)	—	Yoshino-ya (Japanese-style beef bowl)	—	Arby's (sandwiches)
Various service companies	Daiei Leisure Land (amusement arcade) Asahi Travel (travel agent) Nihon Dream Tourism (hotels, amusement parks, movie theatres etc.) Recruit (information provider)	—	Cine-Saison (movie production) Ginza Saison Theatre (theatres) Seibu Book Centre (Libro) (bookshops) Libro Port (publisher) Zushi Marina (marina business)	Coms (sports business) Zwei (marriage varrangement services) Jusvel (travel agent)	People (fitness clubs etc.) Japan Maintenance (management services for buildings and equipment)

(Continued)

Table 5.4 Continued

Parent company	Daiei	Ito Yokado	Seiyu (Saison)	Aeon	Mycal
Finance	**Daiei Finance** Daiei Investment Advisor	—	**Credit Saison** Tokyo City Finance Seibu Investment Advisor	—	—
Development and housing	Daiei Real Estate Daiichi Construction	—	Seiyo Environment Developer Seiyo Land Systems	**Diamond City** Aeon Kogyo **Daiwa House Industry**	**Nissan Construction**

Source: Research by the IBJ 1993, 260 (2): 148–9, revised by the author. See also Nakano 1995: 676.

Note: Characters in bold mean the companies listed on the stock exchange or registered on the over-the-counter market.

removing the Ginza store from the consolidated account (*Nikkei Newspaper* 1985b).

However, the problems of heavy debts were not completely solved. Daiei ran more and more into M&A, such as acquiring the Oriental Hotel in Kobe (1987), a company for leisure equipment named Japan Dream Kanko (1988, merging with Daiei in 1993), a baseball team (1988), building a domed baseball stadium, (1990–93) resort hotel and convention centre (1992–95), the food *super* Maruetsu (1991), the publisher and information provider Recruit (1992), 16 stores of Yaohan Department Stores (1997), and merging the three food *super* Uneed Daiei, Chuzitsuya and Daihanba with Daiei (1994) (Daiei 1997). Concerns were often expressed about Daiei's heavy debt burden (e.g. *Nikkei Ryutsu Newspaper* 1992c, 1996, *Nikkei Financial Newspaper* 1996).

In the meantime, Daiei suddenly tried to return to the discounting strategy from the end of the 1980s (*Nikkei Ryutsu Newspaper* 1988). It introduced the hyper-market format from 1989 and expanded to 27 stores, while it renewed the private brand 'Saving' in 1991, which had been introduced in 1980 as a cheap priced brand, by offering one litre packs of the Saving Valencia Orange Juice at 198 yen against the usual price of 320 yen, 4.7 litre packs of Saving Ice Cream Vanilla at 299 yen as opposed to around 500 yen in 1992, and 3.54 litre cans of Saving Cola from the USA at 39 yen, discounting more than 60 per cent of the usual price in 1994 (Daiei 1997: 2–3). These discount activities were widely discussed in the mass media.

Nevertheless, these policies could not sort out the problem. Daiei reckoned up its deficit in FY1995 for the first time in its history due to the damage caused by the Great Hanshin and Awaji Earthquake. In FY1997, the company recorded a deficit both on the basis of its single and consolidated accounts; in 1999, the founder Nakauchi stepped down from the Presidency, taking responsibility for the financial difficulty; and in 2004, the Daiei group was approved for support from the Industrial Revitalisation Corporation of Japan (IRCJ), which was established in 2003 by the government (and existed until 2007) in order to revitalise the Japanese economy after the so-called sluggish 'lost decade' of the 1990s. This story raised a serious question: whether the retail format of general *super* was already obsolete for Japanese consumers (e.g. *Nikkei Newspaper* 1998a, *Nikkei Business* 1998).

Failure of Seiyu: a too ideal 'democracy' in management

Seiyu met a similar fate but in a different business environment. This company was originally run in harness with Seibu Department Store, and became a major member of the Seibu Saison Group from 1985 (the Saison Group from 1990).

This group was strongly influenced by the personal character of the founder, Seiji Tsutsumi, who was not only an executive but also a famous poet and novelist, and had been a left-wing activist when he was a university student. He uniquely defined the distribution industry as existing 'in the boundary between "the logic of capitalism" and "the logic of humanism"' (Tsutsumi 1979: 344, 1985: 301), and believed that in order to respect 'the logic of humanism' retail companies should go beyond retailing itself which simply sold tangible goods; rather it should support the human being as a cultural entity. Therefore, he insisted that retailing should become 'de-retailing (*datsu-kouri*)'. In this respect, Tsutsumi required the general *super*, Seiyu, not to be 'a volume-oriented retailer (*ryo-han-ten*)' but 'a quality-oriented retailer (*shitsu-han-ten*)'. A new brand, called 'Mujirushi Ryohin (high-quality goods with no brand)', known as 'Muji' outside Japan, which originated as a private brand of Seiyu named 'Seiyu Line' in the late 1970s, was introduced in 1980.

In contrast to Daiei's private brands that appealed with dramatically low prices for mass-produced goods, Tsutsumi defined that the brand concept of Mujirushi Ryohin or Muji should seek, firstly, an ideological slant (anti-establishment and anti-mass production), secondly, strong image (unity and consistency in colour, designs and packages), and thirdly, economy-oriented goods (reasonable prices) (Koyama 1991: 464, see also Yui, Tatsuki and Ito 2010: 88). The brand concept denying simple discounts and volume orientation was appropriate for the changing consumer behaviours after the High Economic Growth period.

Muji was not only sold at Seiyu, but at Muji specialty shops and at other department stores and convenience stores. In 1989 Ryohin Keikaku Co., Ltd. was established as a subsidiary of Seiyu to develop original products, and they developed overseas in 1991 including London, Paris and Hong Kong (Yui, Tatsuki and Ito 2010: 89–92). Mujirushi Ryohin was a superior concept that matched with the increasing individualities in consumption and consumers' preferences for simplicity rather than ostentation (Yui, Tatsuki and Ito 2010: 169–80).

Tsutsumi's concept of the retail business is seen as appropriate for the trends in the post-High Economic Growth period. Despite this, his group was also dissolved due to severe financial problems. The recent analysis of the collapse of the Saison Group (Yui, Tatsuki and Ito 2010: 18, 31 and 40) suggested that Tsutsumi's organisational philosophy, such as 'a republican form of business (*keiei kyowa-sei*)' which was to avoid hierarchical dominance by the core companies over the member companies, and 'a rhizome-like organisation (*rhizome-gata soshiki*)' in which each independent company freely shared ideas and connected with each other underground, rather overlooked the situation where nobody knew or controlled the whole body of the Saison Group that expanded so widely. In addition, Tsutsumi himself began to retire from his business from the end of the 1980s and announced it officially in 1991 (Yui, Tatsuki and Ito 2010: 28–30), presumably partially due to his deepening criticism of Japanese consumer society he had previously served (Tsutsumi 1996), and partially due to his focus on his literary and social activities. As a result, nobody could block the reckless operations of some member companies of the Group.

The process of the write-offs of heavy debts by Tokyo City Finance in 1999–2000 placed an unbearable financial burden on Seiyu, which was taken over by Walmart in 2002–08. In addition to the write-offs of heavy loans by Seiyo Environment Development in 2000–01, Seibu Department Store fell into voluntary liquidation due to accumulated deficits in 2003. Millennium Retailing was established in the same year to reconstruct Seibu and Sogo Department Stores, which further came under the umbrella of Seven & i Holdings in 2006 (Chapter 2 of Yui, Tatsuki and Ito 2010 describes this process).

Success of Ito Yokado: rigid management producing profits

In contrast, Ito Yokado has been known as a typical example of the 'winner group'. This company has been known to be management-oriented. It was keenly involved in self-improvement of operations after 1981 when the company seriously recognised the large reduction in profits for the first time. It began to take a lead in introducing EPOS (Electronic Point of Sales) and other information systems into the Japanese retail industry, accompanied by an efficient management system with a high turnover of products and a highly profitable business (Ogata [1986] 1990, Akiba 2003, Ito Yokado 2007).

As Table 5.5 demonstrates, although the sales volume of Ito Yokado was far behind Daiei, its net profit ranged from almost double to more than four times as large as Daiei's. Ito Yokado actively improved its financial footing after 1981, attaining the highest product turnover ratio, return on assets and equity ratio, and the lowest ratio of break-even point and dependency on loan, among the five major general *super*. The improvement continued in the 1990s, realising a gross profit ratio of 28.04 per cent, equity ratio of 73.67 per cent, and dependency on loan of only 1.49 per cent in 1997 (MITI 1998). Meanwhile, Ito Yokado was rather careful when diversifying into the service sector, as seen in Table 5.4 above. In addition, their diversification into the new retail format of convenience stores by establishing a subsidiary, Seven-Eleven Japan, was a great success, and has taken the lead in the Japanese retail industry. The details will be explored in the last chapter.

In 2005, a shareholding company,[9] Seven & i Holdings, was established based on the success of Seven-Eleven and Ito Yokado, and became the top retailer in Japan in terms of sales volume. Jusco was in second position; it had changed its name to Aeon in 2001, merging with Nichii (re-named Mycal since 1996) in 2001–03, and establishing a holding company, Aeon, in 2008.

Conclusion

For a while after *super* or general *super* developed in Japan, many Japanese people, even many business people, did not recognise the uniqueness of general *super*; they tended to think that because the self-service system was brought into Japan from America, Japanese *super* was equivalent to the American supermarket. The fact was, however, that general *super* was quite unique to Japan, in that it handled not only foods but also clothing, electrical products, and many other everyday necessities, in a multi-storey building with departmentalised sales floors. General *super* was essentially what had been known as a SSDDS.

Table 5.5 Financial footing of five major general *super* (1982 and 1987)

	Daiei		Ito Yokado		Seiyu		Jusco		Nichii	
	1982	1987	1982	1987	1982	1987	1982	1987	1982	1987
Sales volume (million yen)	1,232,250	1,550,313	805,568	1,055,005	851,921	866,307	651,836	807,007	304,602	568,508
Ordinary profit[1] (million yen)	13,862	21,303	22,304	62,519	7,395	10,564	16,325	25,126	12,199	19,518
Net profit (million yen)	6,256	6,909	12,335	30,807	3,549	4,731	8,689	12,017	5,970	9,509
Gross profit ratio (%)	21.64	21.68	22.07	26.09	23.04	22.09	19.68	22.24	29.14	30.12
Return on assets[2] (%)	1.78	2.86	6.70	14.36	2.09	2.66	4.63	5.60	3.67	5.33
Product turnover ratio (times per year)	13.96	24.92	17.85	28.12	14.09	21.34	14.80	16.22	11.13	15.34
Equity ratio[3] (%)	15.94	20.64	40.75	56.05	17.36	20.85	25.92	38.21	26.51	34.15
Dependency on loan[4] (%)	61.88	49.47	28.52	15.78	57.72	51.47	29.91	18.85	36.51	29.33

Source: Data from MITI 1982, 1987; *Nikkei Newspaper* 1989.

Notes:

1 'Ordinary profit (*keijo rieki*)': operating profit + non-operating income − non-operating cost. The Japanese accounting system has respected this accounting category as a typical indicator of profit, although this will be changed by introducing the IFRS (International Financial Reporting Standards).

2 Return is calculated through 'ordinary profit'.

3 The equity ratio measures the proportion of total assets that are financed by stockholders and not creditors.

4 The ratio of short- and long-term loans, discounted bills and debentures to the total capital and discounted bills.

This type of retail format was a historical product. The process of High Economic Growth, which rapidly transformed Japan from defeated ruins to a wealthy, Western-looking society, was accompanied by rapid urbanisation/suburbanisation, and the small-sized families concentrated in these areas, separated from the traditional large-sized rural family unit, needed everyday necessities. *Super* provided them with everything. Partly because of a complete transformation in Japanese clothing to the Western-style after the War, and partly because general *super* had not been food merchants but clothing-related merchants, or at least from the non-food sector, clothing remained prominent in the early stages of general *super*. The mass supply of synthetic fibre and spread of ready-made clothing further extended this domain of offerings for mass marketing of clothing. A wide variety of perishable foods, which Japanese housewives preferred to buy frequently in small amounts, was not so easy to fit into the self-service system, so this section was weak for *super* at least during the period of High Economic Growth. By incremental innovations to handle perishable foods and by increase of processed products pre-packed by manufacturers, however, the food section in general *super* was improving; nowadays, the proportion of food on sale at general *super* is quite high.

Low prices, however, were double-edged. Consumers' choice was based on more varied motives than merely prices; they had other values, such as quality despite higher prices, fashion trends, beauty and aesthetics, minute details of products, personal significance, etc. General *super* naturally kept these factors in mind. After the end of High Economic Growth, they diversified their formats to serve all aspects of consumers' lives. Result varied with the individual characteristics of founders and groups.

Even so, however, the role of general *super* was important in the history of modern retail marketing in Japan. This was the first retail format developed by independent retailers, who were originally small-sized innovators, not the heirs of wealthy merchants in the pre-modern period. They developed this format successfully without any support from manufacturers in the form of their *keiretsu* channels. Development of the format undermined the *keiretsu* network by Morinaga, as described in Chapter 1. In this aspect, the general *super* was a pioneering exemplar that many other retailers wanted to follow. In the field of household electric appliances, a similar historical story to Morinaga's can be identified on a larger scale, as will be explored in the next chapter.

Notes

1   The first reinforced concrete apartment was built by Dojunkai (Ogita and Limbon 1989: 34–36), a non-profit organisation formed in 1924 on the basis of public donations to aid sufferers from the 1923 Great Kanto Earthquake. Recognising that traditional wooden houses were highly prone to damage by the earthquake, Dojunkai built 2,492 public apartments made of reinforced concrete in 13 premises in Tokyo and Yokohama from 1925 to 1933 (Nishiyama 1989: 220–5). Except for apartments in Ochanomizu, which were purely American in style (Nishiyama 1989: 222), almost all apartments were covered by *tatami*-mats, and kitchen floors by lattices (*sunoko*) (Kitagawa 2002:

24). Thus, in contrast to *danchi* apartments after the Second World War, the insides of the Dojunkai apartments were basically in Japanese-style. However, the idea of non-combustible construction against earthquakes had already started and influenced the postwar period.

2   It is usually recognised that the idea of such a space as the '*dining kitchen*' came from the apartments for the National Railway officers built in 1950 (Kitagawa 2002: 125–6), in which the design of this space was called '51C'. This was proposed by the laboratory of Associate Professor Yasumi Yoshitake for public apartments in 1951 (Suzuki et. al. 2004), and was also adopted for the apartments for national officers in Togodai, Tokyo built in 1952 (Kitagawa 2002: 134–6). Historical research by Kitagawa (2002, 2006, Kitagawa and Oogaki 2004a, 2004b) shows that the original concept of '*dining kitchen*' can be traced back to a German idea, Living Kitchen (*Wohnküche*), which was introduced as a small-sized room combining living and kitchen space after the defeat of the First World War in Germany. The Japanese version was in order to achieve 'a residence fulfilling the minimum requirements for living', and was led by the architect Miho Hamaguchi, who was influenced by the famous architect and urban planner Le Corbusier via her Japanese teacher before the War. She became an advisor for the Japan Public Corporation of Housing. Kazuhiko Honjo, who also paid attention to *Wohnküche* and became the first senior manager of the design section of the construction department at the Japan Public Corporation of Housing, came to be known as the godfather of the Japanese word '*dining kitchen*'.

3   For the first time, in 1975–76 the number of applications for *danchi* apartments provided by the Japan Corporation of Housing was not fully subscribed (JPCH 1981: 112–15). Many dwellers began to recognise that the *danchi* apartment was not an ideal residence, but a sort of shelter to fulfil the minimum requirements for living. Especially, the space was pretty small; the first typical design of '55-4N-2DK' had an area of only 43 m^2 including the space for *dining kitchen* consisting of 7.97 m^2. Although the average model was enlarged to some degree to 52.9 m^2 by 1964 (JPCH 1981: 138) and some models had begun to include a living room in addition to the *dining kitchen*, it was quite clear that the space still remained absolutely minimal. For those residents who felt uneasy about such a small space, getting away from *danchi* apartments became the next stage of their desire. They looked for their own independent houses even though they were located in far distant dormitory areas from which it took longer to commute to work, or looked for spacious apartments called '*mansion*' in Japanese English, in the urban areas (Maeda 1985: 34–35 and 42). In both cases, many people shared the so-called 'obsession of owning house/land' (see e.g. Yamada 2001, Yamashita 2003), in which their lifelong aim was their own independent house and land, or their own luxury apartment even though they had to pay back a huge loan their whole life. The increasing ratios of 'house and land rents' among all the consumer expenditures in Figure II.1 reflected this tendency.

4   In the USA, the name SSDDS has been discarded, perhaps because Ferkauf himself had to relinquish Korvette in 1966 due to his mismanagement (Kitazato 1967) and because discount department stores lost their power in the US market. Discussing the different fate of the SSDDS format between USA and Japan, Yahagi (1998) pointed out that US discounters inheriting from SSDDS, such as Walmart and Kmart, came to treat foods lightly in order to maintain their difference from supermarkets, while Japanese SSDDS or general *super* continued to sell everything for the everyday life of consumers, including foods, as well as clothing, household electrical goods and miscellaneous home utensils.

5   The suppliers of ready-made clothing appeared as soon as Western-style clothing was introduced in the early years of modernisation, in such forms as importers-cum-renovators, second-hand shops and renovators of military and government officers' uniforms (Nakagome 1975: 129–30). The department stores had also sold ready-made clothing since around the 1920s. The mainstream of ready-made clothing marketers

was, however, the tailors and dressmakers, who made fitted clothing either themselves or by hiring skilful craftsmen, and then retailed them to the consumers. Some of them grew to be clothing manufacturers, who sewed or knitted clothing themselves or sublet to subcontractors and sold their products wholesale. These manufacturers existed mainly in the four major textile cities of Tokyo, Osaka, Nagoya and Gifu, but generally were of peripheral existence, recognised only as part of personal belonging manufacturers rather than of textile manufacturers before the Second World War (Nakagome 1975: 2–3 and 7–9).

6   Toyobo was originally established in 1882 as Osaka Cotton Spinning Co., the first modern cotton spinning company, by Eiichi Shibusawa, who is famous for being 'the father of Japanese capitalism'. In the synthetic fibre industry, the 'big three' manufacturers became dominant as early as the mid-1950s (Fujii 1971: 9–10): these were Toray (introduced nylon in 1951, mentioned above), Teijin (introduced polyester under the brand of Tetoron in collaboration with Toray in 1958), and Asahi Kasei (established as Ammonification and Silk Works in Nobeoka in 1931).

7   What was called 'modernisation' or 'westernisation' of eating habits also included the tendency to break away from heavy dependence on consumption of rice or grain starch. In fact, the proportion of expenditure on rice in the total household expenditure on foods sharply decreased from 20.1 per cent in 1963 to 9.2 per cent in 1975. The school lunch system, which originated in 1899 and was revived in 1946, encouraged this tendency. When the Law of School Lunch was enacted in 1954, it was officially stated that 'the educational purpose' of school meals was to get away from the 'rice-centred meal' or from 'grain-oriented foods (ryusyoku)' and encourage 'powdered foods (funshoku)' in order to 'improve the balance of nutritional intake' from early ages (Kuroda and Mogi 1985: 124). The school lunch system also encouraged the consumption of bread and milk.

8   The Large-sized Retail Store Law defined a store with a sales floor of 1,500 m² or more (3,000 m² or more in the case of 'ordinance-designated cities', that is, metropolises with population of one million and more) as a 'large-sized store'. The Law was strengthened in 1978 to include stores with a sales floor from 500 m² to 1,500 m² (in the case of 'ordinance-designated cities', from 500 m² to 3,000 m²) as the 'second type of large-sized store'. The Law required 'prior coordination': an incoming large store must arrange with local retailers the size of sales floor, the opening date, its closing time, and the number of dates when it would remain closed (called 'four pre-coordination items'). The attitude of the Japanese government fluctuated with regard to application of the Law: until the mid-1980s it favoured stronger regulation, but it turned to deregulation after that. Taking advantage of the report of Japan-US Structural Impediments Initiative Talks (Research Institute of MITI 1990), the Law was finally abolished in 2000.

9   The shareholding company, which aims to hold shares of other companies to domain them, was prohibited by the Anti-Monopoly Law for a long time after the Second World War to eradicate the zaibatsu conglomerates that were recognised as the economic basis of Japanese militarism. However, it was officially permitted by an amendment of the Anti-Monopoly Law in 1997 as part of the deregulation policy of the Japanese government.

6 'Sacred treasures' for every home

Keiretsu vs. independent retailers of electrical products

Everyday life surrounded by various kinds of electrical products was a dream for many consumers after the Second World War. 'People wake up with an electric alarm clock and shave with an electric safety razor', said a popular radio programme, 'Letters from America (*America Dayori*)', sent from a Japanese journalist living in the USA:

> For breakfast, they first drink orange juice or vegetable juice, like carrot and celery juice extracted by an electric juicer, and then butter a piece of bread toasted golden brown. The electric toaster automatically pops the bread out just when it is toasted to a brown-colour. Listening to the news and weather forecast over the radio, the husband drinks coffee and leaves for work. The housewife manages a few chores simultaneously – wiping the table, washing clothes and cleaning rooms. She tosses the sheets, towels, shirts, children's clothes, handkerchiefs and others all together into the electric washing machine in the corner of the kitchen, puts washing powder into it and turns it on with a switch. . . . During this washing work, she vacuums the rooms with the sound of a buzz and finishes it . . . While listening to the radio, the housewife sits on a chair and presses the clothes that have just finished washing with the press device; then she can enjoy her free time . . . Thus, electrification of homes and farms is not a sort of luxury pleasure for the leisured women for whom cost is not an issue, but rather is an everyday routine for ordinary households.
>
> (Sakai 1949: 129–33)

The longing for such a wealthy, modern way of life was an essential part of the discourse of westernisation, which was in essence Americanisation at the time, and drove many people to catch up with the advanced Western countries.

The progress of High Economic Growth realised this dream. Although a few electrical products, such as lightbulbs and radios, had already begun to spread before the Second World War, as was shown in Chapter 3, it was during this period that basic household electrical appliances, such as washing machines, refrigerators, vacuum cleaners, TVs and electric rice cookers, penetrated almost all homes. While general *super* sold some of these products, the main force in retail marketing were *keiretsu* retailers organised by manufacturers. Inheriting the legacy in the 1920s and 30s, the competition among manufacturers in this industry developed, focusing on competition among *keiretsu* retailers, who were almost exclusively organised by each manufacturer individually. Consumers in all corners of Japan bought electrical products mainly at these *keiretsu* retail shops. The first half of this chapter will explore how marketing by *keiretsu* retailers changed the everyday life of consumers.

As marketing and consumption in this industry were progressing, however, the networks of *keiretsu* retailers were gradually undermined. Inspired by the development of general *super*, independent specialty stores of household electrical appliances began to organise their own networks, and then they themselves were defeated by a more powerful second generation of independent retailers. The latter half of this chapter will consider how marketing and consumption of household electrical appliances changed after High Economic Growth until the present time.

Keiretsu retailers as an effective means to link mass marketing and mass consumption

Keiretsu *retailers became the key*

Postwar life started with the removal of blackout curtains and dispensing with the severe restrictions on lighting imposed during the War. The newspaper headline, 'Let's make our everyday life lighter' (*Asahi Newspaper* 1945) typified the general sense of the many Japanese people who began to appreciate peace.

Electricity generation in 1945 dropped to almost 60 per cent of the peak wartime levels in 1943, but peak levels were exceeded as early as 1949 (Kurihara et al. 1964) thanks to supportive planning, as described in the introduction to Part II. The early focus in the electric machinery industry was heavy apparatus, such as hydro and thermal generators, motors, transformers, switchboards and switchgears, which were necessary for revitalising the economy. In this field a few powerful companies, such as Toshiba (see Chapter 3), Hitachi Manufacturing (established in 1920) and Mitsubishi Electric (established in 1921), which had contributed to economic development in pre-war Japan, recovered and became powerful actors.

Unlike the pre-war period, however, the potential of the consumer electrical market became more and more significant. In the pre-war period, the proportion of household appliances in the overall level of electrical machinery production was almost negligible, merely 2.2 per cent in 1935, but it reached 12.9 per cent in 1954 (Nishino 2006: 102). Perceiving the potential, the manufacturers of heavy electric apparatus began to invest in equipment to produce consumer electrical products (Nakano 1974: 2). The entry of these powerful manufacturers created keen competition among the manufacturers specialising in these products, such as Panasonic (seen in Chapter 3), Sanyo Electric (established in 1947 and popular for the jet-stream type of washing machine in 1953) and Hayakawa Electric (now Sharp Corp., established in 1912, originally known for producing belt buckles and mechanical pencils, later entering the radio receiver market in the 1920s and the television market in 1953). It was this competitive relationship between the powerful manufacturers and those who originally specialised in consumer electrical products that developed marketing and consumption of household electrical appliances at the time.

It should be noted that the cornerstone in this competition was not necessarily the technological ability to produce new consumer electrical products. As Japanese economists of industrial organisation (Komiya, Takeuchi and Kitahara 1973: 48–50) confirmed, the barriers to entering this industry due to technological requirements were not high for the manufacturers, because specialists in heavy electrical apparatus had enough ability to develop any electrical appliances, and even if they lacked it, were capable of introducing new technologies under contract with foreign manufacturers. Therefore, each manufacturer did not become a specialised producer of a single product line, but a multi-product manufacturer of consumer electrical lines. In the case of the electric rice cooker, for instance, Toshiba introduced a successful item in 1955, soon followed by other manufacturers, as will be seen below. Technological ability itself could not protect the manufacturer from its competitors.

In view of this, the key in competition was the ability to capture the marketing channels that could directly face the final consumers. This was recognised as important particularly by the manufacturers of heavy electric apparatus because they were quite unfamiliar with those channels, while Panasonic had experienced success in this before the War. Therefore, Hitachi Manufacturing began to capture the *keiretsu* wholesale channel at the outset when the company decided to enter the consumer market in 1955. Hitachi established a wholesale subsidiary, Hitachi Sales Company of Household Electric Products (*Hitachi Katei Denki Hanbai*), and at the same time, encouraged the Agents of Hitachi Motor, who had been wholesalers with high loyalty to Hitachi Manufacturing, to become *keiretsu* wholesalers specialising in household electrical goods. Hitachi Manufacturing also encouraged their independent agents, who already had a transactional relationship with Hitachi Motor, to change their business to *keiretsu* retail stores, named Hitachi Chain Stalls, from 1956. As Nakano (1974: 4) put it, Hitachi Manufacturing 'all at once established large-scale channels [for consumer products] by utilising the relationship with the former channel members to sell heavy electric apparatus and by having plenty of financial resources'.

Other manufacturers who had come from the production of heavy electric apparatus behaved in a similar way. As was seen in Chapter 3, the predecessor of Toshiba was a pioneer of *keiretsu* retailing in the field of electric lightbulbs. When Toshiba re-entered the consumer market, it changed its wholesale subsidiary, Toshiba Trading Company (*Toshiba Shoji*), originally established for the sales of heavy electric apparatus, to a specialised consumer electric products wholesaler. Around 1956, Toshiba decisively increased its investment in changing its former agents to specialists for the sales of home-use products (Nakano 1974: 4, Son 1992: 26). Similarly, Mitsubishi Electric added wholesale responsibility for consumer goods to their former agents who sold electric motors (Nakano 1974: 4–5).

The entry into *keiretsu* channels by powerful manufacturers of heavy electric apparatus strongly motivated Panasonic to strengthen its *keiretsu* network (Okamoto 1973: 240, Nakano 1974: 5–7). Before 1955, Panasonic overcame the difficulty caused by the loss of many merchants during the War and restarted the Matsushita Retailers League, in which members dealt in all product lines rather than particular electric products. Panasonic also started the National Association for Mutual Prosperity (*National Kyoei-kai*) for wholesale agents in 1949, and established their own wholesale companies through co-investment with wholesale agents (Son 1992). However, facing entry by powerful manufacturers with a background in heavy electric apparatus, Panasonic decided in 1957 to develop its *keiretsu* retail network to a much more advanced level (Okamoto 1973: 240–2, Nakano 1974: 5–7). The new strategy was to divide *keiretsu* retailers into three layers, based on the degree of exclusivity in selling Panasonic products: (1) National Shops (the *katakana* name for a Japanese chain where the exclusive ratio was at least 80 per cent sales of Panasonic products), (2) Association of National Stores (*National Tenkai-ten*, 50 per cent or more), and (3) the National League (*National-kai*) or the National Stores League (*National Renmei-ten*, 30 per cent or more).

Panasonic's approach encouraged other manufacturers in turn to expand their *keiretsu* networks to include the retail field. Mitsubishi Electric and Toshiba launched an effort to organise keiretsu *retail* stores in 1958. In the 1960s, the distributive channels for household electrical appliances became dominated by *keiretsu* wholesalers and retailers; Table 6.1 represents the actual situation as of 1964. Panasonic established its dominance in these networks through having the widest coverage, and this gave them the lead in the industry.

It should be noted that these *keiretsu* retailers were generally small-sized and located anywhere from busy shopping districts to residential areas and from large metropolises to small towns. It was through them that many Japanese consumers bought their household electrical products for the first time. These retailers played a pivotal role in demonstrating the new household electrical appliances to such consumers, and providing door-to-door services, such as delivery, installation and repairs. In fact, the 1970–71 survey by the Ministry of International Trade and Industry (1971: 49–50) showed that 77.8 per cent of repair services were rendered by door-to-door activities of *keiretsu* retailers, while only 22.2 per cent were provided on shop premises. The *keiretsu* retailers were the effective support forces for many consumers who were still inexperienced in handling electrical appliances.

Manufacturers required exclusive dealing and maintenance of recommended retail prices from these *keiretsu* retailers, although these requirements were often controversial from various standpoints, such as the anti-monopoly law enacted from 1947 (e.g. JFTC 1975), considerations on competition policy from a socio-economic perspective (e.g. Komiya, Takeuchi and Kitahara 1973), consumer movements as exemplified by the objection to the price fixing of colour TVs in 1970–71 (e.g. MITI 1971, see also the previous chapter), and the critical paradigm in marketing (e.g. Morishita 1974). In return for cooperation, manufacturers provided various support programmes, such as signboards for the shops (86.7 per cent), invitations to business lecturers (69.6 per cent), support for store renovations (68.5 per cent), providing office supplies (60.8 per cent), invitations to sales competitions (60.3 per cent), subsidies for buying automobiles (51.9 per cent), welfare support for employees (49.7 per cent), business consultations (42.6 per

Table 6.1 Keiretsu marketing channels in household electrical appliances (as of 1964)

The 1st wholesale step		The 2nd wholesale step		The retail step	
Wholesalers (Exclusivity ratio)	Number	Wholesalers (Exclusivity ratio)	Number	Name of retail stores (Exclusivity ratio)	Number
Manufacturers specialising in household electric appliances					
Matsushita Electric Industry (Panasonic)					
National Sales (100%)	178			National Shops (80% and more)	10,000
Agents (50% and more)	210	–	–	Associations of National Stores (50% and more)	13,000
National Monthly Instalment Sales (100%)	41			National Stores League (30% and more)	20,000
Sanyo Electric					
Sales Companies (100%)	15				
Agents (50% and more)	67	–	–	Sanyo Superstores (80% and more)	1,000
Sanyo Monthly Instalment Sales (100%)	17				
Hayakawa Electric (Sharp)					
Sharp Electric (100%)	1	Exclusive Agents (50% and more)	90	Friend Shops (50% and more)	1,000
Sharp Monthly Instalment Sales (100%)	1				
Manufacturers producing both heavy electrical apparatus and household electrical appliances					
Toshiba					
Toshiba Trading Company (100%)	1	Agents (100%)	100	Toshiba Stores (80% and more)	2,000
		Toshiba Monthly Instalment Sales (100%)		Toshiba Linkage Store (10% and more)	20,000
Hitachi Manufacturing					
Hitachi Sales Company of Household Electric Appliances (100%)	1	Agents (80% and more)	100	Hitachi Chain Stalls (80% and more)	3,000
Hitachi Monthly Instalment Sales of Household Electric Appliances (100%)	1				
Mitsubishi Electric Industry					
Mitsubishi Trading Company (100%)	1				
Agents (50% and more)	1 per Prefecture	–	–	Diamond Stores (50% and more)	2,500
Mitsubishi Monthly Instalment Sales (100%)	3				

Source: HBJ 1964: 54 with some revisions.

cent), sales supporters dispatched to stores (38.4 per cent), assistance for retailers' events in order to increase retail sales (37.9 per cent) and the dispatch of business instructors (11.4 per cent) (percentages in parentheses represent the proportions of retailers who answered 'yes' to questionnaires sent by the Ministry of International Trade and Industry (MITI 1971); respondents may have included some non-*keiretsu* retailers). Manufacturers awarded many kinds of rebates to *keiretsu* retailers for specific purposes, such as those only given when sales volume targets were met, when product range targets were met, for sales of particular products, cash rebates, and so forth (MITI 1971: 59–61).

It should be underlined that despite the rigid control of the *keiretsu* retailers, retail stores did not all necessarily participate in only one manufacturer's *keiretsu* organisation. According to the 1968 MITI survey, 44.6 per cent of retailers joined just one manufacturer's *keiretsu* system, while 52.3 per cent joined two or more manufacturers' lists resulting in an average of each retailer joining 2.6 such networks. The 1970 survey showed that the share of retailers joining only one manufacturer's *keiretsu* increased to 61.9 per cent, while the share with membership in two or more was 27.5 per cent, resulting in an average of membership in 1.3 networks per retailer (MITI 1971: 26–27). The opportunity for merchants to engage in independent activities became a hotbed for undermining excellent *keiretsu* retail networks after the end of High Economic Growth.

Changes in consumers' everyday life

The household electrical appliances that spread during the period of High Economic Growth fundamentally changed the everyday life of every Japanese consumer. In the earliest stage, the rice cooker, the washing machine and the refrigerator were called 'the big three of white goods (*shiro-mono go-sanke*)', and the washing machine, the refrigerator and the vacuum cleaner were called the 'three sacred treasures (*sanshu no jingi*)' (Japan Society of Lifology 1999: 455). However, from around 1957, the cliché of 'three sacred treasures' was altered to mean the washing machine, the refrigerator and the black-and-white TV, which connoted the indispensable valuables for any Japanese home.

Figure 6.1 shows the rapid increase in ownership of the washing machine, the refrigerator, the vacuum cleaner and the black-and-white and colour TVs from 1958–60 to 1980. The essential feature in this figure is that although the ownership among non-farm households residing in cities with a population of 50,000 and over grew rapidly, those among farm households swiftly caught up with them, resulting in almost all Japanese households possessing these products by the end of High Economic Growth, in contrast to the pre-war period in which modernisation progressed but remained limited to people residing in city areas and in wealthy classes.

The products spreading at this time can be divided into two types: products that could reduce the time and drudgery of housework, such as the electric rice cooker, the washing machine, the refrigerator and the vacuum cleaner, and those that provided new amusements, typically the black-and-white TV.

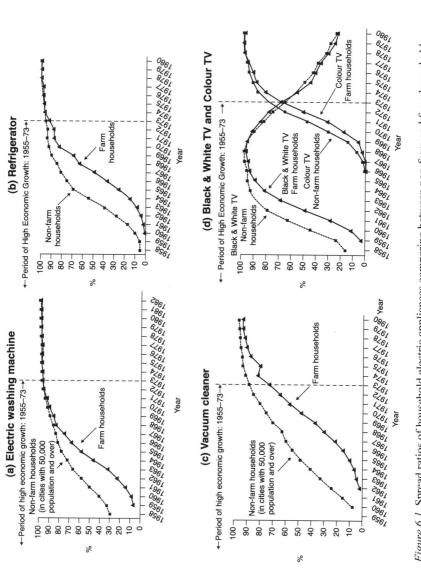

Figure 6.1 Spread ratios of household electric appliances comparing between non-farm and farm households.

Source: SB 1988: 554–5.

To relieve housewives from time-consuming chores, a good example was the rice cooker: although the idea of cooking rice using electricity can be traced as far back as the mid-1910s (Yamada and Mori 1983: 141, Japan Society of Lifology 1999: 457), this type of product became widespread with Toshiba's 1955 launch. Their rice cooker automatically switched off just when the rice was cooked, with the quality of cooked rice as high as that cooked in the traditional manner. Shogo Yamada, who was involved in the development of this product at Toshiba, recalled an immediate hostility among men, who believed that this appliance would make housewives unable to cook rice, which was considered to be a typical role for Japanese housewives (Yamada and Mori 1983: 162).

The housewives, however, were enthusiastic for the product. As shown in Figure 6.2, the traditional manner of cooking rice was time-consuming and painful, demanding the cook's full attention to a large kitchen stove (*kamado*)

Figure 6.2 Rice cooking: the old (1952) and the new (1955).

Note:

(Left picture) The traditional manner of rice cooking. The photo was taken in September 1952 and was reported as the best case of improvement in life amongst farmers' households. The picture shows a kitchen stove (*kamado*) suitable for large-sized families. Rice was boiled in a rice pot (*kama*), and a woman kept fanning in front of the stove to ensure the charcoals were lit, taking a half-sitting posture.

(Right picture) The advertisement for export of the first electric rice cooker developed by Toshiba in 1955. It cooked the rice automatically and eliminated much painful work for the housewives.

Left picture: Reproduced courtesy of The Mainichi Newspapers.
Right picture: Reproduced courtesy of Toshiba Corporation and Toshiba Science Museum.

or a small round charcoal stove (*shichirin*) often placed directly on the bare ground. In contrast, this new device could dramatically reduce the time and labour. A newspaper article in 1957 (Asahi Newspaper 1957) reported that while Toshiba was a front runner in selling about 500,000 rice cookers, Matsushita (Panasonic) and Hitachi Manufacturing were entering this market, and Mitsubishi Electric would also soon be joining; a war among the manufacturers was imminent. By 1965, ownership of electric rice cookers increased to 50.9 per cent of households, reaching 58.3 per cent among non-farm households in cities with a population of at least 50,000 and 35.4 per cent among farm households (EPA 1967: 305). Although official data are unfortunately not available beyond that year, the product became a common item for all Japanese households before long.

The electric washing machine brought about a similar obvious effect. Sanyo Electric introduced the jet-stream type of washing machine in 1953 (Ouchi 2001, 2002). This was square-shaped and small-sized, such that it could easily fit the small Japanese residences, and also had a shorter cleaning time because of its strong action. Manufacturing costs were lower, due to its simple structure. This type of washing machine spread very rapidly, and radically emancipated house-wives from traditional, time-consuming washing by soaping, pressing and scrub-bing clothes, sheets, etc. against the notched washing board in the washtub (*Asahi Newspaper* 1959).

The rapid spread of time-saving electrical appliances and the emergence of so-called 'automated housewives' (Arisawa [1966] 1994: 154) triggered social disputes regarding the role of women at home, which began to be discussed in popular journals from 1955 (see Ueno 1982a, 1982b). The spread of the appli-ances, along with the rapid spread of the popular idea that 'consumption is a good deed', was, in a sense, a straightforward reaction against the symbolic phrase of wartime control, 'we shall never want anything until we have won the War'. The penetration of these products also encouraged many housewives to work outside their homes. Conservative commentators insisted on the importance of the tradi-tional role of housewives, by discussing 'the wrong argument on the emancipation of women' (Fukuda [1955] 1982), the necessity of 'the division of labour between men and women' (Kyu [1957] 1982), or 'the housewife as a manager of the home' (Sekishima [1956] 1982). The appearance of such disputes in itself, however, was supportive evidence that the everyday life of ordinary people had begun to change, although many traditional features still remained in the workplace.

Some electrical products were used as entertainment devices. Figure 5.1[D] above shows how Japanese consumers enthusiastically welcomed televisions; the rise of the ownership ratio of black-and-white TVs swiftly reached more than 90 per cent in the middle of the period of High Economic Growth, and colour TVs quickly replaced them in the latter half of this period. As will be seen in Figure 5.3 below, the spread of the VCR was also rapid, as a TV-related product. Entertainment through TV viewing firmly took root in the daily life of Japanese consumers. According to the five-year periodic survey of TV viewing started in 1960 by Nippon Hoso Kyokai (NHK), the average amount of weekday TV viewing per audience increased from 0.56 hours in 1960 to 2.52 hours in 1965, and surpassed

3 hours in 1970 (Makita 2005: 11–12). This level has largely remained unchanged until the present time (Ogawa and Makita 2005: 253). This is almost equivalent to the USA and the UK, and apparently higher than Northern European countries (Broek 2002, Nielsen 2008).

Thus, the dream of the modern consumer lifestyle surrounded by electrical products rapidly came true during this period. It was through the *keiretsu* retailer that this was realised.

Progress after the High Economic Growth period: increasing variety of products and triumph of independent retailers

Expansion in the variety of household electrical appliances

Despite the historical importance of *keiretsu* retailers, the basis on which they grew was being undermined as marketing and consumption of household electrical appliances further developed after the period of High Economic Growth. An essential factor in eroding their position was the diversification of products, while the decisive factor in disrupting the networks between *keiretsu* retailers and manufacturers was the development of non-*keiretsu*, independent and large-sized retailers. Let us explore the diversification of products first.

As the market for electrical products was increasingly saturated, the mass media (e.g. *Asahi Newspaper* 1966, 1967) began to look for the next big hits which could follow the 'three sacred treasures'. The '3Cs,' standing for colour TVs, cars and air conditioners ('*coolers*' in Japanese English), became generally recognised as the next objectives in consumer durable goods. However, it should be noted that as is suggested in Figure 6.3, except for colour TVs it took a rather longer time for these products to penetrate compared to the 'three sacred treasures'. Many other types of products penetrated into many households, such as microwave ovens, VCRs, CD players, dedicated word processor appliances, personal computers (PC), satellite broadcasting receivers, video camcorders, DVD players, cellular phones and so forth. The variety of 'household electrical appliances (*kaden*)' was expanding remarkably.

The variety was increasing in two ways: first by adding new product categories, so that even products that originally did not fall into the group of 'household electric/electronic products' were merged, such as PCs and dedicated word processor appliances (which will be explained in the next section), which were called 'information-oriented home electronic appliances (*joho-kaden*)' in the new buzzword, and facsimiles and cellular phones, called 'telecommunication-oriented home electronic appliances (*tsushin-kaden*)'. Second, the variety of existing products increased through continuous product differentiation by constant improvements of products to add some enhanced functions. It was the industrial structure which enabled these two forms of increase: technologies of information and telecommunications, as well as of audio and video, were developed and fused by several established players, that is, the manufacturers of heavy electrical apparatus, home electrical products, and communications apparatus. These powerful

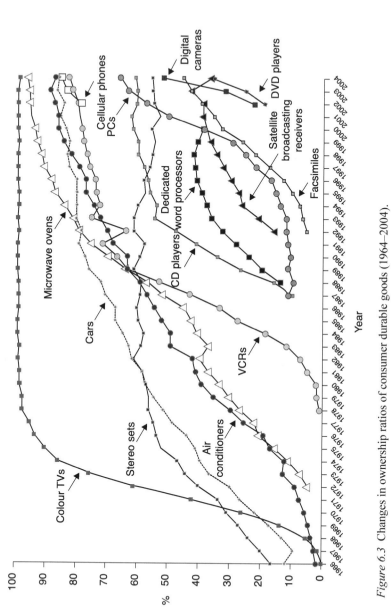

Figure 6.3 Changes in ownership ratios of consumer durable goods (1964–2004).

Source: E-stat website.

manufacturers competed in an oligopolistic structure, keenly introducing basic technologies from Western, especially American, companies and well aware of the trends and achievements of their competitors.

For instance, the large-scale production of mainframe computers started when the manufacturers of heavy electrical apparatus (Hitachi, Toshiba and Mitsubishi Electric), home electrical goods (Panasonic) and communications apparatus (NEC, Fujitsu and Oki Electronic, which were the so-called 'family companies' of NTT) jointly agreed with IBM in 1960 to utilise IBM's basic patents (Takashima 1976: 10–11). Some of these players also took an individual contract with RCA, Honeywell and GE, while others established joint corporations (Takashima 1976: 11, EIAJ 1979: 102).

The new categories of electronic products, such as PCs and word processor appliances, were developed and marketed by these powerful manufacturers. This suggests two dimensions in marketing channels; that is, while the products by the manufacturers who originally arranged the *keiretsu* retailers had the possibility to distribute these new products through their own networks individually, the manufacturers of communications apparatus, such as NEC, Fujitsu and Oki, did not originally have their own *keiretsu* networks so they had to capture outlets to handle their products. PCs and word processor appliances were sold at stores specialising in PC-related products at first, and then were handled by independent and large-sized retailers of electric/electronic products (see e.g. *Nikkei Sangyo Newspaper* 1982b); the story of this development will be explored below. The manufacturers of electrical products tried to sell these products through their own *keiretsu* networks (see the case of Panasonic, *Nikkei Sangyo Newspaper* 1982a) although it was generally hard for the owners of *keiretsu* stores to deal with this new type of products.

This was also the case in marketing of products for telecommunications. From around 1985 when the telecommunications industry was deregulated with the partition and privatisation of NTT, every manufacturer of household electrical appliances began simultaneously to produce telephone handsets with a variety of functions (*Nikkei Sangyo Newspaper* 1985), and tried to distribute them through *keiretsu* channels. However, the large-sized electrical retailers handled them better than the small-sized *keiretsu* retailers, who were not familiar with the techniques in dealing with these products. Thus, an increased variety of product categories was not advantageous for *keiretsu* retailers.

Regarding the increase in variety through diversification of existing products with enhanced functions, introduction of the microcomputer or the programmable one-chip microprocessor provided the strong technological basis for this trend. As the electrical equipment manufacturers were already involved in production of integrated circuits, they naturally moved on to get involved with production of the microprocessors as well. Intel, which invented the microprocessor in 1971, established a Japanese subsidiary in 1976, followed by other American companies like Texas Instruments, Fairchild and Motorola, while the Japanese manufacturers originally producing electric/electronic products, as well as those producing telecommunications devices, launched the production of microprocessors from around 1977. Keen competition among these producers led to radical reductions in prices of microcomputers, leading to nearly 50 per cent reductions in only a year (EIAJ 1979: 162–3, Aoyama 1991: 169, Onishi 1994: 18–19).

Given this background, the embedding of microcomputers into household electric appliances rapidly became common. For instance, there were refrigerators with automatic defrosters, washing machines with an option for the strength of action of the washing motors, TVs with timers for programme setting, air conditioners with automatic three-minute switch off and re-start to protect the machine from a surge of electricity when starting them, microwave ovens with temperature options, and cassette tape decks with an automatic search function, to name a few (MITI 1980: 101). The manufacturers were becoming more and more deeply involved in improvements to functions of existing products, accompanied by an ever-greater increase in the variety of products with minute differences from the previous versions. Kotler, Fahey and Jatusripitak (1985: 108) indicated that the efforts in 'continually improving their product offerings' were the most outstanding feature in Japanese marketing: 'The Japanese are really devoted in their attention to product improvement, especially in quality. The result of this quality consciousness is that Japanese products are accepted as being of higher quality than their counterparts' (1985: 109).

The keen competition pivoting around continuous product improvement by manufacturers did not only increase Japanese consumers' sensitivity to product quality, but ironically it also guided consumers to shop for the products at independent, large-sized retail stores rather than *keiretsu* retail shops, because the large-sized stores concentrated many competing brands on the same sales floors, so that it was easier for consumers to compare the enhanced functions of products.

Developing the individualistic mode of consumption as a Japanese characteristic

Some newly emerging product categories fostered a change in mode of consumption from the household basis to the individualistic and fragmented basis in terms of the relationships of consumers with others during the act of consumption and with consumption itself (see Figure 0.1). This mode could be identified elsewhere in the world, but the transformation in Japan bore some Japanese features. In addition, *keiretsu* retailers were particularly weak in selling these categories of product. The following are typical examples.

Sony Walkman

The individualistic mode of consumption was marked by an epoch-making event in marketing: the sales of Sony Walkman, a headphone cassette tape player, in 1979 (see Morita 1986: 79–83, Sony Corporation 1996: 201–12, Sony Corporate Communications 1998: 270–85, Kuroki 1990, 1999: 71–109, Gay et al. 1997). Despite offering no recording function, this device was accepted by many youngsters who enjoyed listening to high-quality stereo even while walking in town, riding a train, and generally anytime anywhere. Sony deliberately arranged for demonstrators to use this device while taking JR trains, rambling about busy shopping streets and parks, and visiting high schools and universities in Tokyo, rather than choosing mass TV advertisements (Sony Corporate Communications 1998: 202–3, Kuroki 1990: 78–80). The effect of word-of-mouth communication was huge, so popular journals and newspapers began to introduce articles in which some pop singers utilised this device, and so forth. Although some opposition existed inside the company that the brand name 'Walkman' was merely Japanese English, the device spread successfully into foreign countries as well. As a British cultural study discussed the 'use of Walkman and the blurring of boundaries', Walkman disturbed the boundaries between the private and the public world 'by bringing what was conventionally conceived of as a private act – private listening – into public spaces' (Gay et al. 1997: 115). Until it was replaced by Apple's iPod sold from 2001, Walkman was prestigious as the individualistic personal device for listening to music.

Sony was established in 1946 and was known as a technology-oriented company, developing the tape recorder (1950) and transistor radio (1955) for the first time in Japan, and introducing portable TVs (1960) and Trinitron TVs (sets using aperture grille-based CRTs) (1968), etc. Following its competitors' *keiretsu* system of distribution, Sony organised about 3,500 retail stores consisting of the Sony Shop focusing on audio and video equipment and Sony Home Stores selling 'white electrical goods' as well as audio and video equipment, but the percentage of sales through the *keiretsu* retailers was small, about 30 per cent in the early 1980s, significantly less than its competitors (*Nikkei Sangyo Newspaper* 1983b). Youngsters chose to buy personal devices like the Walkman at independent large-sized stores located in busy shopping streets, rather than small-sized neighbourhood *keiretsu* stores (see this issue in detail in the next section).

PCs and dedicated word processors

It was the PC that encouraged the personalised mode of consumption of electronic devices worldwide from the 1980s. The process of spreading these products bore a unique feature in Japan.

As Figure 6.3 shows, the dedicated word processor spread more rapidly than the PC in the 1980s and the early 1990s. This machine, first introduced by Toshiba in 1978, was a variant of PCs, contained word processor software pre-fixed in it with a memory for Japanese *kanji* characters as the read-only memory (ROM); therefore this appliance could be used only for word processing. This was a very Japanese product. The country generally had had no custom of using typewriters in the past; although the typewriter for the Japanese language was invented in 1915, the method of usage was difficult and required experience and skill to operate more than 1,000 to 2,000 pieces to compose *kanji* characters. People now recognised that by using the word processor, they could easily choose and print *kanji* characters (2,965 as Level I, and 3,384 as Level II), plus 453 for *hiragana*, *katakana*, English alphabet characters and others, standardised by the Japan Industrial Standard (JIS) in 1978, and revised in 1983 with some changes of the numbers of *kanji* characters. The advantages of the word processor were clear for many Japanese consumers, while the functions of PCs were still uncertain.

PCs were introduced with an 8-bit central processing unit (CPU) by Sharp and Hitachi in 1978 and NEC in 1979, and with a 16-bit CPU by Mitsubishi Electric in 1981 and NEC in 1982. In those early days, however, the machines needed a special ROM dedicated for *kanji* characters, meaning that Japanese PCs were not compatible with Western PCs. It was not until the latter half of the 1990s that the processing ability of PCs was enhanced enough to replace the special hardware that could process *kanji* characters; and the spread ratio of PCs did not surpass that of word processors before 2000.

As was already pointed out, whether for word processors or PCs, *keiretsu* retailers were not the good suppliers of choice for these products.

From Pocket Bell to i-Mode

In the field of wireless telecommunication devices, a boom in a pager called the 'Pocket Bell', abbreviated to '*Poke-bell*', occurred among Japanese youngsters soon after the NTT was privatised. In 1987, paging services developed the function of displaying messages, though only as numerals. Japanese youngsters figured out a way of numeric punning in order to send their brief notes (see Table 6.2), and exchanging short messages through Pocket Bells soon became a boom among them. The number of subscribers for pagers reached its peak, of about 10.8 million people, in 1996.

The preference for exchanging messages extended from pagers, via cell phone services by the Personal Handy-phone System (PHS) in the latter half of the 1990s where PHS users could exchange 'short messages', to 'i-Mode' services, provided by NTT DoCoMo (an offshoot from the former NTT) from 1999, through which the subscribers could not only exchange email easily, but also access the Internet (Natsuno 2003: Chapter 1, see also Matsunaga 2000). The explosive hit of this Internet-capable mobile phone, 'i-Mode', encouraged the spread of both mobile phones and Internet access among youngsters in the early 2000s. Many Japanese websites began to prepare special pages to adapt for access through mobile phones. As the penetration of PCs had only just exceeded that of dedicated word processors, for many Japanese youngsters, with experience in exchanging messages from the period of pagers, it was rather easier to access the Internet through mobile phones than PCs.

In the mobile phone industry in Japan, the carriers, such as NTT DoCoMo, KDDI and Japan Telecom (which was bought by Vodafone in 2000–01, and by Softbank in 2004), had strong influence and took the lead in deciding the specifics of mobile phone handsets, which were produced for them by individual electronic manufacturers known as original equipment manufacturers (OEMs), such as Panasonic, Sharp, Sony, Toshiba, Hitachi, etc. Each carrier organised new *keiretsu* or exclusive retailers, called the 'official stores (*koshiki-ten*)', such as DoCoMo Shop, to sell to the final consumers. The mobile phone handsets were also sold by independent stores which handled the competing brands, but the competition

Table 6.2 Some examples of numeric punning used through pagers (*pocket-bell*) among youngsters

Numeric punning	Meaning	In Japanese	Explanation for punning
0840	Good morning	ohayo	0 → 'o' 8 → 'ha' abbreviated from 'hachi' meaning 8 4 → 'yo' abbreviated from 'yon' meaning 4 0 ---- 'o'
0906	I will be late	okureru	0 → 'o' 9 → 'ku' meaning 9 0 → 're' abbreviated from 'rei' meaning 0 6 → 'ru' changed from 'roku' meaning 6
14106	I love you	aishiteru	1 → 'ai,' the shape of 1 is similar to I 4 → 'shi' meaning 4 1 → ('i') (voiceless) 0 → 'te' perhaps, the shape of the numeral looks like a paper doll praying for good weather 6 → 'ru' changed from 'roku' meaning 6
222	Stop the long phone call	tsu, tsu, tsu	2 → 'tsu' in a Japanese accent of the English 'two' 222 → 'tsu, tsu, tsu' sounds like the busy signal beep in Japanese telephone services
210000714	I'm bored	tsuman-naiyo	2 → 'tsu' in a Japanese accent of the English 'two' 10000 → 'man' meaning ten thousand 7 → 'na' abbreviated from 'nana' meaning 7 1 → 'i' abbreviated from 'ichi' meaning 1 4 → 'yo' abbreviated from 'yon' meaning 4

Source: Ponytail 1994.

weeded out the weak retailers in due course. Meanwhile, OEMs who produced mobile phone handsets, such as Panasonic, Toshiba and Hitachi, tried to sell them through their own *keiretsu* retailers (see e.g. *Nikkei Ryutsu Newspaper* 1994). The policy did not work well; the official stores were launched on the sales floors of non-*keiretsu*, large-sized retail stores, which will be examined below.

Videogame consoles and software

Finally, videogame consoles (see Shintaku, Tanaka and Yanagawa 2003: Chapter 1, see also Ichikawa 1999, Hamamura 2007) also encouraged the spread of the new personalised, fragmented mode of consumption. Following US pioneers, such as Atari VCS (Video Computer System), which was a huge success from 1977–82 and was imported to Japan despite facing the serious videogame crash of 1983, some Japanese marketers began to offer their own consoles. Nintendo, founded in 1889 and originally a toy manufacturer specialising in decks of Japanese playing cards (*hanafuda*), began to market the videogame console branded Family Computer, abbreviated to '*Fami-Com*', from 1983. This 8-bit console caught on around the mid-1980s, followed by the 16-bit Super Family Computer ('*Super Fami-Com*') in the early 1990s, the 32-bit PlayStation by Sony Computer Entertainment in the later 1990s, Sony PlayStation 2 in the early 2000s, and the recent console, branded Wii, by Nintendo from 2006. Such a succession of hits produced by keen competition between Nintendo, Sony and SEGA (established in 1953 as a manufacturer of jukeboxes, entering the videogame console market in 1983) established the Japanese reputation as world leader in videogames. The spread of videogame freaks ('*game otaku*') focused attention on social disputes attributed to the behaviour and mentality of the 'videogame generation' in society, which were shaping the new consumption mode such as a solitary play without any socialisation and even a violent or a sexually abusive behaviour stimulated by the game contents (e.g. see Koyama 1996, Nakazawa 2004).

Videogame consoles and software were sold mainly at toy stores, specialty stores for these products and large-sized electrical/electronic stores (Media Create 2000: 164–6), and not successfully by *keiretsu* retail shops. The increasing variety of electric/electronic products overall was undermining the basis of *keiretsu* retailers.

The emergence of independent retailers

The decisive factor which undermined the *keiretsu* networks was, however, development of the player who could sell products independently from the manufacturers. These retailers were developing the knowledge and capability of conducting retail marketing by their own efforts.

The first generation appeared as wholesalers-cum-retailers even during the High Economic Growth period. Some of them had compromised, having been involved in the *keiretsu* wholesale networks but quit them because of their unwillingness to be subordinate to the manufacturers, and began to develop their own retail networks (Nakano 1974: 9, Son 1992: 28, Choi 2004: 129 fn. 4). A typical example was LaOX, originally called Asahi Wireless (DTC 1979: 105–113, Son 1992: 31, LaOX website). While this company was a wholesaler of batteries in the 1930s, it restarted as a wholesaler-cum-retailer in Kanda Tokyo soon after the War. Setting up a retail shop in Akihabara, Tokyo, it built a wholesale subsidiary as the *keiretsu* sales company of Sanyo Electric in 1958, but quit this network in 1960. The company also established a *keiretsu* company for Sony in 1962, but again dissolved it in 1970. In the meantime, LaOX established its first subsidiary shop on the shopping streets of Tokyo Station around 1953, built its first suburban-type store in Chiba in 1963, and opened its main large-sized store in Tokyo in 1973. In the last quarter of the twentieth century, LaOX grew into a leading independent chain store dealing in many competing brands. Another instance also originally outside of the *keiretsu* networks was Deodeo, originally named Daiichi Industry (Kubo 1987, DTC 1979: 279–285, Choi 2004: 110–11, Deodeo Website). This company was a local wholesaler of electric appliance parts in Hiroshima Prefecture, which changed to become a retailer in 1952. When faced with discounted sales by Deodeo, in 1953 the local *keiretsu* retailers, who maintained the recommended retail prices, required the manufacturers to suspend shipments of the products to Deodeo. Within the macroenvironment in which the anti-monopoly law was already enacted, however, the Fair Trade Commission decided in 1957 to issue the order to retract the suspension of shipments against Deodeo in order to counter the effects of resale price maintenance agreements.

Thus, independently-oriented merchants gradually emerged. In 1962, LaOX, Deodeo and three other independent retailers held a meeting and decided to establish the 'Research Group on Management by Large-sized Electric Retail Stores in All Japan' (*Zen-Nippon Denki Oogata-ten Keiei Kenkyu-kai*) the following year. Twelve independent retailers joined this organisation. They exchanged information and knowledge, and arranged tours to observe the retail electrical products business in the USA. They were also more or less inspired by the new retail format, '*super*', which had been expanding rapidly during the 1960s. The Sixties saw independent electrical product retailers growing in knowledge and ability through trial and error, by the observation of independent retail networks at home and abroad, and the mutual exchange of knowledge. In 1972, the formation of NEBA (Nippon Electric Big-store Association, *Nippon Denki Senmon Oogata-ten Kyokai*), established as the trade association for independent retailers with a membership of 78 (Akiyama 2006: 88), was evidence of the increasing independence of retailers. In fact, according to the survey by MITI (1971: 27), the percentage of retailers who did not join any *keiretsu* network increased from 3.1 per cent in 1968 to 10.6 per cent in 1970.

Figure 6.4 shows the leading independent retailers as of 1979. The figure demonstrates that although they were generally called 'mass retailers (*ryohan-ten*)', they were mostly medium-sized stores and the chain networks were not national- but regional-based. An essential feature was, however, that these stores were not only located in the largest cities such as Tokyo, Osaka and Nagoya, but also in various provincial cities, such as Obihiro, Aomori, Hachinohe, Furukawa, Maebashi, Shizuoka, Matsumoto, Kure, Hiroshima, Imabari, Kurume, etc., or even in towns such as Tadotsu, as shown in the Figure 6.4. These independent retailers were becoming serious competitors to small-sized *keiretsu* retailers in many places in Japan.

Developing a tripartite relationship: manufacturers, keiretsu *and independent retailers*

Although the manufacturers were keen to develop their own exclusive *keiretsu* retailers, they also tended, as an 'open secret policy', to utilise independent merchants as a balancing factor to absorb overproduction (Nakano 1974: 10, Sato 1974: 164, Ito 1984: 13): when surplus stocks were piled up in the hands of *keiretsu* wholesalers/retailers mainly due to the keen competition among powerful manufacturers with frequent changes in models and styles, the manufacturers and their *keiretsu* wholesalers tended to 'push' these surplus stocks onto independent merchants. These merchants, in return, semi-officially enjoyed discounted sales of these products (see e.g. *Nikkei Ryutsu Newspaper* 1979).

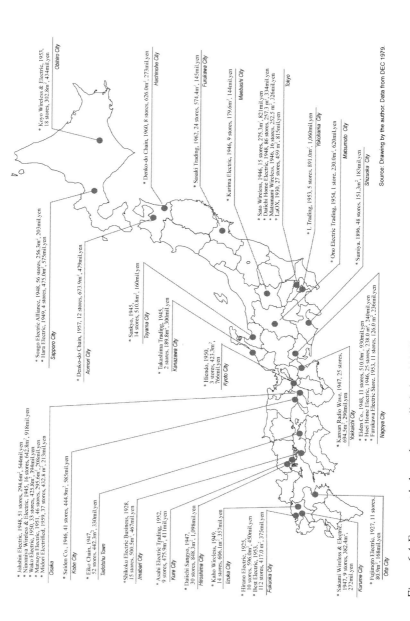

Figure 6.4 Emergent independent retail chains (1979).

Source: Drawing by the author. Data from DEC 1979.

* Koyo Wireless & Electric, 1953, 18 stores, 302.8m², 434mil.yen
Obihiro City

* Songo Electric Alliance, 1948, 56 stores, 256.3m², 203mil.yen
* Hara Electric, 1949, 4 stores, 475.0m², 575mil.yen
Sapporo City

* Denko-do Chain, 1960, 8 stores, 626.0m², 273mil.yen
Hachinohe City

* Sasaki Trading, 1962, 24 stores, 574.4m², 145mil.yen
Furukawa City

* Kurima Electric, 1946, 9 stores, 179.0m², 144mil.yen
Maebashi City

* Sato Wireless, 1946, 15 stores, 275.3m², 821mil.yen
* Daiichi Home Electric, 1948, 86 stores, 257.3 m², 334mil.yen
* Matsunami Wireless, 1946, 16 stores, 252.5 m², 326mil.yen
* LaOX, 1930, 27 stores, 459 m², 815mil.yen
Tokyo

* I. Trading, 1953, 5 stores, 891.0m², 1,060mil.yen
Yokohama City

* Ono Electric Trading, 1954, 1 store, 230.0m², 620mil.yen
Matsumoto City

* Sumiya, 1896, 48 stores, 151.3m², 183mil.yen
Shizuoka City

* Denko-do Chain, 1957, 12 stores, 673.9m², 479mil.yen
Aomori City

* Sankyo, 1945, 14 stores, 510.8m², 160mil.yen
Toyama City

* Takashima Trading, 1945, 2 stores, 189.8m², 300mil.yen
Kanazawa City

* Hiendo, 1950, 3 stores, 423.3m², 766mil.yen
Kyoto City

* Kansai Radio Wave, 1947, 25 stores, 694.5m², 290mil.yen
Yokkaichi City

* Eiden Co. 1948, 11 stores, 510.0m², 930mil.yen
* Hsei Home Electric, 1946, 25 stores, 238.0 m², 340mil.yen
* Funakawa Electric Store, 1953, 11 stores, 126.0 m², 236mil.yen
Nagoya City

* Johshin Electric, 1948, 51 stores, 294.6m², 544mil.yen
* Ninomiya Wireless & Electric, 1945, 16 stores, 642.8m², 918mil.yen
* Waku Electric, 1950, 33 stores, 435.8m², 394mil.yen
* Matsuya Electric, 1951, 46 stores, 295.0m², 208mil.yen
* Midori Electrified, 1959, 37 stores, 432.8 m², 213mil.yen
Osaka

* Seiden Co., 1946, 41 stores, 444.9m², 585mil.yen
Kobe City

* Eiko Chain, 1947, 52 stores, 442.3m², 330mil.yen
Tadotshu Town

* Shikoku Electric Business, 1928, 15 stores, 500.5m², 467mil.yen
Imabari City

* Asahi Electric Trading, 1952, 9 stores, 475.9m², 411mil.yen
Kure City

* Daiichi Sangyo, 1947, 30 stores, 848.3m², 1,098mil.yen
Hiroshima City

* Kabo Wireless, 1949, 14 stores, 606.1m², 357mil.yen
Iizuka City

* Hirano Electric, 1925, 16 stores, 396.0m², 450mil.yen
* Best Electric, 1953, 112 stores, 417.0 m², 375mil.yen
Fukuoka City

* Sakami Wireless & Electric, 1947, 9 stores, 382.4m², 272mil.yen
Kurume City

* Fujimoto Electric, 1927, 11 stores, 80.9m², 168mil.yen
Oita City

Source: Drawing by the author. Data from DEC 1979.

This behaviour was, however, double-edged for the manufacturers. As the sales volumes of these retailers continually increased, discounted sales became increasingly hard for manufacturers to control, but at the same time, it became more and more impossible to ignore the channel of these retailers to secure their high sales volumes. Therefore, the manufacturers began to recognise them officially as their marketing channels. Manufacturers with relatively low market shares and inferior *keiretsu* networks were the first to make the decision. In contrast, Panasonic, which had the top share of the market through its excellent *keiretsu* network, was initially reluctant. Even so, Panasonic eventually approved of the independent channel officially by organising *keiretsu* wholesale companies specialising in independent retailers in 1979–80 (*Nikkei Sangyo Newspaper* 1979, Nakano 1983: 33). Two marketing channels were now operating (JFTC 1980: 401):

- the manufacturer → the *keiretsu* wholesale companies for *keiretsu* retailers → the *keiretsu* retailers → the final consumers, and
- the manufacturer → the *keiretsu* wholesale companies dedicated to independent chain stores → the independent chain stores → the final consumers.

In the case of manufacturers with a background in heavy electrical apparatus, they had their own trading companies intervening between the manufacturers and the *keiretsu* wholesale companies, but these trading companies gradually dropped out of consumer electrical products.

An open secret in this dual operation was the discrimination in selling prices to retailers; naturally, the prices to independent retailers were generally lower. As early as 1963, the *keiretsu* retailers, who maintained recommended retail prices but were exposed to the dangers of price cutting by independent chain stores, organised a cross-*keiretsu* trade union, the Federal Association of Electric Merchants in All Japan (*Zenkoku Denki Shogyo-kumia Rengo-kai*) in the hope of 'normalisation of order in the market' by suppressing discounted sales. They arranged many rallies and even street demonstrations descending on the headquarters of manufacturers (Nakano 1974: 21). The movement of cross-negotiating with the manufacturers rose to a peak in 1975 (e.g. *Nikkei Sangyo Newspaper* 1975a, 1975b, *Nikkei Ryutsu Newspaper* 1996). Although their slogans and their push to maintain recommended retail prices looked doubtful at first glance under the anti-monopoly law, the Federation insisted that discounted sales by independent chains were only possible through loss leaders, misleading price tags, and discrimination in buying prices between the large-sized independents and the *keiretsu* retailers. The Federation aimed to secure legitimate gross margins (30 per cent was required, in contrast with manufacturers' promises of 25–26 per cent) and the full payment of rebates to retailers.

Another requirement by the Federation was to correct the unfair treatment regarding the dispatched sales clerks, called 'helpers', who worked on retailers' sales floors at the expense of manufacturers or their *keiretsu* wholesalers. Although the history of dispatching clerks from the manufacturer to the retailers can be traced back to 1934, when Tokyo Electric (Toshiba) and its sales companies dispatched 105 salespeople to retail shops to make door-to-door sales to customers accompanied by retail shop owners (Sakaguchi 1935: 278), a later example was in the 1965 recession, in the middle of High Economic Growth between the early half and the latter one. At that time, Sharp Corp. began to dispatch salesmen, who were surplus personnel from its factories due to the recession, to its *keiretsu* retailers in order to support them. These salesmen were called the 'Sharp ATOM Force', and became known as an aggressive and hardworking sales force (Suzuki 1978). What were called 'helpers', however, were mainly dispatched to independent retail chains, rather than *keiretsu* retailers, to work on the sales floors especially during weekends and on national holidays. It was reported (*Nikkei Newspaper* 1991b) that the number of these dispatched clerks reached somewhere between 10,000 and 15,000 in the peak year of 1980.

This system is usually explained as the result of the purchasing power of independent chains, which could increase sales at no extra cost to themselves. However, it was also a product of competition among manufacturers on the sales floors of independent chains; when one manufacturer dispatched sales clerks, other competitive manufacturers suspected that they would inevitably recommend the products of their dispatching manufacturers to consumers. Thus, once one manufacturer agreed to dispatch sales clerks, it was hard for others to refuse these requests. As a result, despite the slogan to reduce or abolish the 'helpers' from the early 1980s (e.g. *Nikkei Newspaper* 1982, *Nikkei Ryutsu Newspaper* 1982), and the Fair Trade Commission's order to stop it in 2008, this system has continued to the present time (see *Nikkei Newspaper* 2008a).

New channel policy for keiretsu *retailers*

Although manufacturers could not ignore the mass sales ability of independent retailers, they enjoyed benefits from *keiretsu* retail networks and so they launched a new plan to revitalise them. From 1985, Panasonic, which had organised more than one-third of all electrical retailers, introduced what they called 'the plan for transforming shops (*hen-shin shop keikaku*)'. Panasonic strongly recommended their *keiretsu* retailers to invest in refurbishing their shops to develop from the so-called 'general stores' of electrical products to specialty stores focusing on specialty product lines with an explicit target market. The proposal included four types of model shops: (1) stores specialising in audio-visual equipment targeted at young people (called 'Space 21'), (2) stores specialising in cooking equipment targeted at housewives (called 'With'), (3) electrical stores for families (called 'Bing-Bong'), and (4) electric stores dealing in convenience goods such as batteries, light bulbs, fluorescent lights for homes, and audio and video tapes (called 'Eny'). Toshiba, Hitachi, Mitsubishi and other manufacturers introduced more or less similar plans.

The new plans did not necessarily work smoothly. For instance, Panasonic's 'Space 21' format with its state-of-the-art image was supported most enthusiastically by the second generation owners of *keiretsu* shops in their thirties to forties, but many owners felt that it would be out of place in provincial cities (*Nikkei*

Sangyo Newspaper 1986). Nevertheless, the new plan gave an opportunity for the manufacturers to screen the motivated *keiretsu* retailers, who responded positively to the manufacturer's recommendation on investments for renewal of their shops and on changes in the way their shops were managed: for example adopting long opening hours.

In 1992, Panasonic moved on to the next stage. The company decided to dissolve the *keiretsu* retailers association, Association of National Shops (*National Ten-kai*) which organised 27,000 stores, and established a new organisation called MAST (Market-oriented Ace-Shops Team) instead. The membership fell to about 18,000 shops after Panasonic screened them according to standards of monthly sales volumes (*Nikkei Newspaper* 1992, *Nikkei Ryutsu Newspaper* 1992a). In order to realise this change, the *keiretsu* wholesale subsidiaries had been reduced to 20 companies, named LECs (Life Electronic Corporations). Almost simultaneously, Toshiba started what was called the NASA (New Age Store Action) Plan, which encouraged the leading *keiretsu* stores to organise other *keiretsu* stores into sub-groups within Toshiba's *keiretsu* network, in order to compete with independent chains (*Nikkei Sangyo Newspaper* 1992). Thus, the manufacturers began to abandon attempts to keep all *keiretsu* retailers as their networks and selected only the top-performing ones. As a result, some retailers quit the electrical business and changed to other businesses or closed their shops, while others switched the *keiretsu* network they belonged to for that of another manufacturer (*Nikkei Newspaper* 1995), and others still submitted to independent retail chains as their franchisees (*Nikkei Ryutsu Newspaper* 1992b). The dependency of manufacturers on *keiretsu* channels was rapidly decreasing: it was reported (*Nikkei Ryutsu Newspaper* 2003, *Nikkei Sangyo Newspaper* 2006) that in 2003 the percentage of sales made through them fell to less than 40 per cent in the case of Panasonic and less than 20 per cent in Toshiba and Hitachi, and in 2006 32 per cent in the case of Panasonic and 12 per cent on average of other manufacturers. Many commentators believed that the *keiretsu* retail system had played its historical role and was almost dying out.

Triumph of new independent retailers

This was not the end of the story for electrical retailers. Although *keiretsu* retailers resented the member stores of NEBA because they did not follow the manufacturers' recommended prices, their discounting was not very aggressive. Rather, the members of NEBA adopted the slogan 'normalisation of sales' and tended to resort to non-price competition. A commentator (Yahagi 1991a: 84) evaluated the price competition between manufacturers and the NEBA stores as moderate and favourable in terms of a wholesome market mechanism. Nevertheless, just when such an evaluation was given, some hard discounters outside the NEBA swept across the market and defeated many NEBA member stores. These discounters can be called the second generation of independent retail chains. In contrast to the networks of most member stores of NEBA which were still limited to regional chains, these new discounters developed nationwide networks. Marketing by independent retail chains moved on to a new phase in the 1990s onwards.

Some of these hard discounters, such as Kojima and Yamada Denki, developed their store networks principally in the suburban areas, while others grew from camera discounters such as Yodobashi Camera and Bic Camera, located in front of train stations. The keen competition among them produced frequent changes in the rankings of top retailers of household electric appliances: in terms of turnover, the top retailer was Best Denki from 1900 to 1996, Kojima from 1997 to 2000, and Yamada Denki from 2001 onwards (*Economist* 2007). Confronting these hard discounters, NEBA had to be dissolved in 2005; some of the member stores went bankrupt, others were merged into these new discounters, and others have continued to experience serious difficulties.

The current top retailer, Yamada Denki (Tateishi 2008, *Weekly Diamond* 2008, Yamada Denki website), originally started as a small-sized *keiretsu* retail shop of Panasonic only 26 m², in 1973 in Gunma Prefecture. This shop, however, always advertised its discounted selling, so it caused considerable friction with other *keiretsu* retailers. Yamada Denki decided to leave the *keiretsu* organisation when it opened its second shop in 1982. Because local banks were reluctant to finance them, this company became an over-the-counter traded company in 1989 and began to issue Schweizer Franken- or Euro-dominated convertible bonds in order to procure capital. Using this financing strategy, the company developed a network of large-sized stores all over Japan by aggressive discounted selling: clearly Yamada Denki already had enough knowledge and capability to develop a nationwide network, even though separated from the manufacturer. By March 2008, Yamada Denki had 352 stores, with a sales floor per store of 3,452 m² on average (*Weekly Diamond* 2008). *Nikkei Marketing Journal* (2008) ranked them the third largest retailer in Japan in terms of sales volume in FY2008, following Seven & i Holdings and Aeon. According to the *Stores* (2008) ranking of 250 top world retailers in 2008 (based on the sales volume in 2006), Yamada Denki ranked 58th, while Best Buy (USA) ranked 23rd and DSG International (former Dixons, UK) was 49th.

Not only Yamada Denki was ranked. The same ranking table also showed that Edion was ranked 111th, Yodobashi Camera was 130th, K's Holding was 151st, Bic Camera was 171st, and Kojima 179th: Japanese top retailers of electrical products featured with the other world-class retailers. The result of their growth was the oligopolistic condition of the retail market. *Nikkei Newspaper* (2008b) reported that the market share of the top five retailers increased from about 30 per cent to 50 per cent in the five years to 2008. Intense competition continues, however, so dynamic changes of the top retailers would be quite possible in the future.

Conclusion

A feature of the competitive marketing of household electric appliances in Japan was that manufacturers had great power in terms of business resources, knowledge and technologies.

The manufacturers with backgrounds in heavy electrical apparatus, such as Toshiba, Hitachi and Mitsubishi Electric, were capable of offering the full line of household electric appliances, rather than just a single product line. Those who had specialised in consumer electric products, such as Panasonic, Sharp and Sanyo, had to compete with these companies. An important strategy in their competition was to capture the exclusive or semi-exclusive *keiretsu* retail channel. Under this network, small-sized retailers could operate their electrical shops with various forms of support, incentives and knowledge from the manufacturers and their *keiretsu* wholesale subsidiaries. It was the *keiretsu* shops that spread the domestic electrical products, such as washing machines, refrigerators, rice cookers, vacuum cleaners and TVs, present in almost 100 per cent of households during the period of High Economic Growth. Thus, the longed-for modern everyday life surrounded by many electrical products, the image of Americanisation that inspired many consumers after the War, came true. The *keiretsu* retailers were the social medium to realise this dream.

An alternative system was developing, however, to undermine the *keiretsu* networks. Some independently-oriented retailers began their businesses by following the rapid growth of *super*. Based on the fusion of the technologies for information, telecommunications, audio and video, the factors that disadvantaged the small-sized *keiretsu* retailers grew, such as the diversification of product lines, the keen competition in product differentiation focused on the appeal of enhanced functions, and the appearance of new types of devices for individual use – some forms of them having new Japanese features. As the so-called first generation of independent retailers developed, who operated large-sized discount stores on a regional basis and organised the trade association called the NEBA, the manufacturers could not ignore them and officially recognised them as one of their retail channels. While there was a tripartite relationship among the manufacturers, the *keiretsu* retailers and the independent large-sized discounters were in regular conflict, and a new order of the industry was about to be set. At this moment, the second generation independent retailers, who were hard discounters and developed nationwide networks of large-sized shops, grew rapidly and beat the first generation of independent retailers; as a result the NEBA was dissolved in 2005.

A big question is whether *keiretsu* retailers will totally die out in such a severe environment. Despite many negative assessments, some recent evaluations (e.g. *Nikkei Ryutsu Newspaper* 2006, *Sankei Newspaper* 2006) appreciate that local *keiretsu* retailers were welcomed especially by elderly households, because these retailers frequently visited them and offered personal service such as inspection and repair of products, consultations for replacement buying, and teaching consumers how to use the complicated high-tech products. Especially in the case of Panasonic, the Konosuke Matsushita Memorial School of Commerce (*Matsushita Shogaku-in*), which was established in 1970 and is now part of the Panasonic Marketing School Co., Ltd., has trained about 4,000 inheritors of *keiretsu* retail stores. By strict boarding education for one year full of Japanese-style group behaviourism, the graduates become an active core with an excellent morale among *keiretsu* retailers, especially among the so-called SPSs (*Super Pro-Shops*) which have been selected as superior *keiretsu* stores since 2003 and now total 5,600 stores. Thus, some *keiretsu* retailers are seeking a niche position in the market, despite completely losing their historical role, which was to distribute mass-produced electrical goods from manufacturers in the years when independent retailers were less developed.

7   Convenience stores everywhere

Born in America and revised in Japan

Soon after the end of the High Economic Growth period, a new retail format, the convenience store, began to develop. Small-sized retail shops with a long or a 24-hour operation, seven days a week, became very popular with Japanese consumers, especially young people residing in urban/suburban areas. This retail format was born in the USA and introduced to Japan, but its spread was very rapid and complete in Japan compared with its mother country. For instance, the number of 7-Eleven stores reached 13,233 in Japan on 1 January 2011, far exceeding the sum in North America with about 7,600 stores (website 7-Eleven, Inc.). It was the convenience store that became the representative retail format from the 1970s onwards in Japan. Its appeal was not low prices; rather it provided services such as long opening hours without holiday closures, at convenient locations. In contrast with many Western countries, in which the formats such as the hypermarket and the superstore based on low prices became the main stream in retail marketing in the last few decades of the twentieth century, Japan developed this type of no-price-appeal format.

This chapter will examine how the convenience store format was introduced, and how the operation was changed to the Japanese method even though the basic concept was retained. The exploration will show why the convenience store format became mainstream in Japan.

The early stages of convenience stores

Birth of the concept in the USA

It is generally known that the basic format of the convenience store originated in Southland Ice Company, which was established in Dallas, Texas in 1927 by purchasing four separate ice companies with eight ice manufacturing plants and 21 retail ice stores (Liles 1977: 8 and 19). The company sold bread, eggs and milk, in addition to ice in which demand began to diminish, operating from early in the morning to late night hours and on Sundays (although Sunday operations were criticised as a sacrilege to the holy day), and began to use the totem pole as a trademark, which led to the store name, Tote'm Store, signifying that people 'toted' away their purchases (Liles 1977: 22–23). Overcoming bankruptcy under the depression in 1932, the company had 60 Tote'm Stores in the Dallas – Fort Worth area in Texas by 1939. In 1946, the company decided to change the store name to '7-Eleven' Stores on condition that all the store operators involved in the cooperative programme would agree to stay open from 7.00 am to 11.00 pm seven days a week. These stores sold ice, cold drinks, groceries and drug sundries (Liles 1977: 55 and 67). 7-Eleven reached 74 stores by 1947 and the company changed its name to Southland Corporation in 1948 (Liles 1977: 77), which was incorporated in 1961.

This company rapidly grew by a combination of internal expansion, investing in new stores, takeover of other companies and franchise agreements with independent companies (see Sparks 1995). The 24-hour operation was introduced first in Las Vegas in 1963 and expanded to other states (Liles 1977: 192–5). By the end of 1969, 7-Eleven Stores were open in 31 states, the District of Columbia and Canada, and among 3,537 7-Eleven Stores, 1,286 or 36 per cent were franchised (Liles 1977: 188). Store numbers in USA and Canada reached a peak of 12,719 in 1985 (Kawabe 2003a: 72). The rapid development of this company attracted attention in the Sixties to the general format of convenience stores, and the 1970 estimate was that about 13,250 such stores existed in the USA (see Liles 1977: 191–2).

Introduction of the concept to Japan

At that time, many Japanese business people began to watch the retail trends in the USA, and some of them decided that the convenience store format would be transferable to Japan.

For instance, Yusuke Inagaki, who later organised an early version of Japanese convenience stores, Myshop Chain (see below), became interested in 7-Eleven in the suburbs of Los Angeles in 1962 when he bought cola there (Kawabe 2006: 88–89). Another innovator, Yukio Abe, who originally worked for a large-sized dairy producer, Snow Brand Milk Products Co., Ltd., and became the director of a private research institution focusing on the convenience store format called MCR, sponsored by food manufacturers, remembered that he discovered 7-Eleven for the first time in the mid-1960s when he stayed in a suburban area of Chicago (Abe 1971a: 42–45). However, when Abe introduced the idea of convenience stores for the first time, 'no one showed interest', according to his account (Abe 1971b: 36). In 1968, the Japan Chamber of Commerce and Industry and the Junior Chamber International Japan jointly dispatched a business mission to observe the retail distribution system in the USA. The leader, Shigeo Kitano, published a report and indicated the new format of convenience stores as 'the revival of mom-and-pop stores' (Kitano 1969: 19–22). It was confirmed (Sugioka 1977: 19) that this report gave an opportunity for the Small and Medium Enterprise Agency (SMEA) to gain interest in the format of convenience stores. The SMEA commissioned the Research Institute of the Distribution Industry sponsored by the Seibu group (see Chapter 5) to write a manual for convenience stores in order to support small- and medium-sized retailers. The Institute organised a special committee composed of a marketing professor and business executive men, including a member of staff from Daiei, a leader of Kmart (see below) and Yukio Abe (MITI and SMEA 1972), and published *The Convenience Stores Manual* in 1972. Other organisations, such as the Japan Voluntary Chain Association and the Japan Management Association, also began to study this format from 1970 onwards (Abe 1971c: 3, Takebayashi 1973: 29–30).

In the meantime, the early forms of convenience stores were emerging mainly as part of voluntary chains led by wholesalers (see Sugioka 1977: 28, Deie 1990: 172, 1995: 74–75, Kawabe 2004: 9–10, 2006: 88–90). The examples consisted of Kmart (sponsored by a sweets wholesaler, Kittaka, in Osaka) in 1967, Sun Mart (by a food wholesaler, Marusei, in Kobe) in 1968, Sunflower (by a liquor and food wholesaler, Saihara, in Osaka) in 1969, Seiko Mart (by a liquor wholesaler, Nishio, in Hokkaido) and Coco Store (by a liquor and food wholesaler, Yamaizumi, now Izmic, in Nagoya) in 1971. In addition, a retailer cooperative, Myshop Chain, introduced this format as Convenience Store Myshop Kanzaki Store in Amagasaki, Hyogo, in 1968 and Mammy Toyonaka Store in Osaka in 1969 (Kawabe 2006: 89).[1] In contrast to their American counterpart, many of these convenience stores handled the traditional three categories of perishable foods, that is, vegetables/ fruits, fish and meats. The leaders at the time recognised that this feature suited Japanese shopping and eating habits, so these convenience stores were proudly called 'the Japanese-type (*nihon-gata*)' (Nagata 1972: 32, Deie 1995: 74–75, Kawabe 2006: 90). Nevertheless, the mainstream was soon replaced by convenience stores that excluded handling traditional perishable foods.

Remodelling, Japanese style

Start of the subsidiaries of super

Although the convenience store format aimed at reawakening the 'sleeping mom-and-pop stores' (Nagata 1972: 32), the real growth of this format started when general *super* adopted it as part of their diversification strategy. These stores also had more or less direct contracts with American companies.

The leading company in this field was Ito Yokado. From 1970 its executives (see Ito Yokado 2007: 146–51, also 7-Eleven Japan 1991: 4–8), including Toshifumi Suzuki and others, made frequent observation tours of retailing and found 7-Eleven signboards everywhere. They visited the head office of Southland Corporation and proposed alliance in 1972. At first, the offer was 'almost turned away at the door' as a company in the Far East 'was beneath their notice' (Ito Yokado 2007: 149). Nearly a year later, the alliance proposal was more welcome to Southland Corp., which had dispatched a few managers to Japan in order to observe the Japanese market and the conditions of Ito Yokado. They had reported back a favourable impression to head office (Liles 1977: 221–2). In 1973 the agreement for an international area license was signed and York Seven Co., Ltd. (the name was changed to 7-Eleven Japan in 1978, hereinafter called 7-Eleven Japan) was organised as a wholly-owned subsidiary of Ito Yokado. Although

Southland Corp. originally insisted on a joint venture, Ito Yokado turned this down in order to keep a free hand with regard to everyday decisions (7-Eleven Japan 1991: 12). In fact, 7-Eleven Japan was soon to recognise the real necessity of altering Southland ways to fit, except the following three basic principles: the trademark of 7-Eleven, the format of the convenience store, and the profit-oriented accounting system (7-Eleven Japan 1991: 25–30). Ito Yokado was also successful in reducing the royalty from the harsh 1 per cent of turnover Southland required, to 0.6 per cent of it, as Ito Yokado insisted that the Japanese company would largely have to modify the American or Southland way of business to fit Japanese conditions where national traits, business practices and consumer behaviours were quite different from the USA, as easily exemplified by the manuals that had to be translated entirely into Japanese (7-Eleven Japan 1991: 10–12). The year 1974, when the first Japanese 7-Eleven store was opened, was known as 'the first year of the convenience store age (*coveni gan'nen*)' in Japan.

The top large-sized *super*, Daiei, followed the same pattern as Ito Yokado. It contracted in 1974 an agreement with Lawson Milk Company, Ohio, which was established as a milk shop in 1939, taken over by Consolidated Food Corp. (now Sara Lee Corp.) in 1959, and developed convenience stores (Lawson, Inc. website). In 1975 Daiei established Daiei-Lawson Co., Ltd. (the name was changed to Lawson Japan in 1979, is now Lawson, Inc., hereafter called Lawson Japan) as its own subsidiary.

The other *super*, Seiyu, took a slightly different path. An executive, Sueaki Takaoka, was actually involved in writing the *Convenience Store Manual* as a member of the Research Institute of the Distribution Industry (Tanouchi and Takaoka 1975: 1), and Seiyu started an experiment to introduce this format as early as 1972, rather earlier than Ito Yokado. Takaoka proposed a full-scale launch to the President, Seiji Tsutsumi, who hesitated initially because of his unique philosophy: if large-sized companies like Seiyu dominated this field, 'what could the petty retailers do to survive?' (interview cited from Hashimoto 1991: 175). Nevertheless, inspired by the distinct success of 7-Eleven Japan, Seiyu finally decided to inaugurate the convenience store, called Family Mart, in 1977, and established Family Mart Co., Ltd. in 1981 as its subsidiary. Although planning to develop the operating system by its own efforts, Family Mart introduced in 1980 some imported methods such as the system of procurement, order and delivery of goods, improvements on the contents of franchise agreements and training programmes from White Hen Pantry Inc., Illinois, which had developed a franchise chain of convenience stores (Hashimoto 1991: 175–83, see also Kawabe 2004: 13). Later in 2006–07, these stores were bought by Seven & i Holdings Japan (website 7-Eleven Inc.).

7-Eleven, Lawson and Family Mart were the 'big three' in the convenience stores industry in Japan, as shown in Table 7.1 below. Other large-sized *super* followed these three, such as Uni which established Circle K in 1979 under an agreement with Circle K, Inc., USA, and Nagasakiya which launched SunKus in 1980 (merged to Circle K SunKus in 2001). Jusco (now Aeon) also started Ministop from 1980. Meanwhile, a few food manufacturers went into

Table 7.1 Top 5 convenience stores in terms of sales volume (FY1978, FY1988, FY1998 and FY2008)

Ranking and store name	Parent company	Type of the parent company	Number of stores	Sales volume (mil. yen)	Type of the network
FY1978					
1 Kmart	Kittaka	Wholesaler of sweets	599	74,400	Voluntary chain
2 7-Eleven	Ito Yokado	*Super*	600	70,000	Franchise chain
3 Myshop Chain	Convenient Myshop	Retailer cooperative	300	39,030	Retailer cooperative
4 Sun Chain	T.V.B. Sun Chain	Drinking restaurant	360	24,200	Coporate chain
5 Coco Store	Yamaizumi Trading	Wholesaler of liquor	134	13,000	Voluntary chain
FY1988[1]					
1 7-Eleven	Ito Yokado	*Super*	3,653	686,356	Franchise chain
2 Lawson	Daiei	*Super*	2,150	244,689	Franchise chain
3 Family Mart	Seiyu	*Super*	1,502	220,490	Franchise chain
4 Sun Every, Yamazaki Daily Store	Yamazaki Bread	Manufacturer	1,982	203,090	Franchise chain
5 Sun Chain	Daiei	*Super*	1,035	105,009	Franchise chain
FY1998					
1 7-Eleven	Ito Yokado	*Super*	7,732	1,848,147	Franchise chain
2 Lawson	Daiei	*Super*	7,016	1,157,181	Franchise chain
3 Family Mart	Seiyu	*Super*	4,398	758,222	Franchise chain
4 Circle K	Uni	*Super*	2,289	406,769	Franchise chain
5 Daily Yamazaki	Yamazaki Bread	Manufacturer	2,782	381,127	Franchise chain
FY2008					
1 7-Eleven	Seven & i Holdings	*Super*	12,298	2,762,557	Franchise chain
2 Lawson[2]	Mitsubishi Trading Co.	General trading company	9,527	1,558,781	Franchise chain
3 Family Mart[2]	Itochu group	General trading company	7,404	1,334,048	Franchise chain
4 Circle K, Sunkus[2]	Uni	*Super*	6,166	1,095,201	Franchise chain
5 Mini Stop	Aeon	*Super*	1,772	302,911	Franchise chain

Source: *Nikkei Ryutsu Newspaper* ed. 1979, 1990, 1999; *Nikkei Marketing Journal* ed. 2009.

Notes: 1 The original ranking table includes the stores categorised to 'small-sized supermarkets (*mini super*)', which were eliminated in this table.
2 The number of stores and sales volume include those by local franchising licensees.

the convenience store business; for instance, Yamazaki Baking Co, the bread manufacturer, who distributed mass-produced bread on a nationwide scale through its *keiretsu* retailers (see Notes, Chapter 1, note 5), began to develop Sun Every in 1977 and Yamazaki Daily Store in 1980 (both were merged to Sun Shop Yamazaki in 1982, and the name changed to Daily Yamazaki from 1999), while Snow Brand Milk Products started Blue Mart from 1979. Their policy aimed to support their *keiretsu* bread shops and milk stores.

Thus, convenience stores powerfully backed up by *super* and manufacturers began to be the mainstream of this industry. The intensifying competition among them led to difficulties in the 1980s for some of the pioneers, who lacked competitive unity in strategy due to loose association in voluntary chains or retailer cooperatives. For instance, Myshop Chain, which had had more than 700 membership stores under 13 local headquarters, went down due to bankruptcy in 1986 (Abe 1993a). Kmart, with almost 1,100 member stores, which had been running at the top in terms of sales volume before 1979 (Deie 1995: 77–78), failed as the sponsoring wholesaler, Kittaka, went bust in 1993 (Abe 1993b). Among the pioneering examples of convenience stores mentioned above, only Seiko Mart and Coco Store are still in operation today.

Table 7.1 shows that in the late 1970s, the top five convenience stores in terms of sales volume were composed of various types; in contrast, after the 1980s onwards these positions were occupied by stores that the large-sized companies, especially *super*, controlled. These companies made full use of more manageable networks and franchise chains, instead of loosely tied networks of voluntary chains and retailer cooperatives.

Getting round the law

There was an easily understandable motive for *super* to enter the convenience store business. This format could elude the regulations of the Large-scale Retail Store Law, enacted in 1974, the same year of the opening of the first 7-Eleven store, and which began to be applied to the main shops of *super*.

The first (1937–47) and second (1956–74) Department Store Laws and the Large-scale Retail Store Law (1974–2000) with their ministerial ordinances defined regulations governing the minimum number of closing dates the stores would have per year and their latest closing times, as well as regulation in opening up new stores and expanding sales floor spaces. The enforcement ordinance of the second Department Store Law required four days' closure per month in metropolises (two days per month in other areas) and closure by 6.00 pm (Izumida 1996: 7). In the early 1970s, the regulation was about to be expanded to any formats of large-sized stores, whether they be department store, *super* or others. In fact, as was mentioned in Chapter 5, the enacted Large-scale Retail Store Law defined these premises as those of 1,500 m^2 or more total sales floor space (3,000 m^2 or more in the case of Tokyo and other ordinance-designated metropolises), and the Law was strengthened in 1978 by adding the 'type II large-scale retail store' definition, which included establishments with 500 m^2 to 1,500 m^2 (or 3,000 m^2 in metropolises) total sales floor space. In any case, the Law initially required 44 closing days per year (relaxed to 24 days per year in 1994) and closure by 6.00 pm (relaxed to 7.00 pm in 1990 and 8.00 pm in 1994), applying to any type of large-scale retail stores. If the large-scale store wanted to operate more than the defined closing dates and/or longer than the defined closing time, it could ask the Ministry, although assessment would take a prohibitively long time.

The convenience store, however, would only have about 100 to 200 m² of sales floor space, well below the 500 m² the Law and its ministerial ordinance defined as being 'large-scale'. This meant that convenience stores could freely operate longer hours without any closing dates and freely expand store networks. It was only natural for *super* to have a strong impetus to get involved in the convenience store format. In fact, in the middle of discussions for amendment of the second Department Store Law, Daiei openly announced that their strategy would be switched to focusing on smaller sized stores (*Asahi Newspaper* 1972b).

At the same time, public debates on protecting petty retailers also encouraged some *super* to choose the form of their networks carefully. As Table 7.1 shows, while the convenience stores based on voluntary chains and retailer cooperatives were defeated in competition with the convenience stores sponsored by *super*, these *super* adopted franchise networks rather than their own subsidiary networks. From the management point of view it was apparent (Takaoka 1999, Kim 2001: Chapter 2) that the franchising network was advantageous in terms of costs and speed of construction compared with the subsidiary network. Nevertheless, a few *super* decided to adopt this form by giving thoughtful attention to the political situation.

In the case of the leading marketer, 7-Eleven Japan, when they opened the first store in 1974 an internal controversy occurred about which organisational form would be better; an own subsidiary shop or a franchisee's shop. At the time, Southland Corp. recommended an own subsidiary shop first in order to control everything easily, and then to develop the franchise network gradually. Nevertheless, the executive, Toshifumi Suzuki, was fixed on starting their business with a franchisee's shop from the beginning. He thought that if they started the convenience store with their own subsidiary, the public would recognise Ito Yokado's business of convenience stores as aimed simply at escaping the regulations of the Large-scale Retail Store Law. In order to get the public to believe Ito Yokado's philosophy in which there was 'mutual prosperity' with existing small- and medium-sized retailers, it was thought that 7-Eleven Japan should start the first store as a franchisee's shop (7-Eleven Japan 1991: 30–32, Ito Yokado 2007: 153), and Suzuki realised his intention. This was in contrast to Southland Corp., which developed a network of its own stores first and did not adopt the franchise system until 1964 when they acquired Speed Mart, California, which had developed 126 convenience stores as franchised shops (Liles 1977: 163–5 and 169–70).

The discussions inside Family Mart were much more serious. According to interview research by Hashimoto (1991: 176–7), the eleventh-hour adjustments between Tsutsumi's unique philosophy that respected existing petty retailers and the recognition shared by other executives about the growing business of convenience stores defined the outline of the business strategy of Family Mart.

This emphasised a method of co-existence between Family Mart and the existing petty retailers, by defining Family Mart as a business that sold the method of business operations to the merchants who joined the firm's franchise system.

Location strategy as a basis of the Japanese system of convenience stores

It was often indicated that the convenience store could recommend itself as a time-saving system of shopping due to its nearness to consumers, plus its long opening hours and no closing days. The concept of 'nearness' was, however, largely different between the USA and Japan.

Many American convenience stores have been located at petrol stations, as shown by the fact sheet of the National Association of Convenience Stores (NACS) illustrating that about 80 per cent or 117,297 of the 146,341 convenience stores in the USA sold motor fuels in 2009 (NACS website). Southland Corp. also began to sell gasoline after the oil crisis in 1973; gasoline as a proportion of all sales increased from 2.7 per cent in 1974 to 21.6 per cent in 1991 (Kawabe 2003b: 5). The location at petrol stations meant that many customers came to the convenience stores by car. This macroenvironment was supported by the land-use law called 'zoning' set by the state and the local governments, which very often prohibited the store from locating in residential areas.

The situation was generally different in Japan. First of all, Japanese petrol stations were prohibited from running any retail stores by the Fire Service Law, as well as from self-service fuel sales, until 1998 when this regulation was relaxed.[2]

In addition, although Japan had a land-use planning system, it had not been so strict and many traditional neighbourhood retailers were located in residential areas. Therefore, many commentators believed in the early days that convenience stores might not have been needed in Japan because too many neighbourhood stores already existed (e.g. *Yomiuri Newspaper* 1971). This environment led the Japanese convenience stores to a unique location strategy which assumed that their customers came mainly on foot, rather than by car. The *Convenience Store Manual* published by the Small and Medium Enterprise Agency stated, 'there is no need to consider preparing a parking lot because almost all customers will come on foot' (SMEA 1972: 59).

Figure 7.1 shows the location strategy by 7-Eleven Japan. The company defined a circle with a radius of 500 m from the store as the 'primary trading area', which expected the consumers who lived within this area to come to the store anytime they wanted to buy something, even at midnight; however, those who lived outside this area would be too lazy to come, especially late at night. This idea clearly assumed that consumers generally visited convenience stores on foot, not by car. 'Nearness' had a totally different meaning between USA and Japan: near 'by car' and near 'on foot'.

The differences in the regulatory law and in location strategy would explain why Japanese convenience stores could compete successfully while their US counterparts could not. In American conditions, with strict zoning regulations to

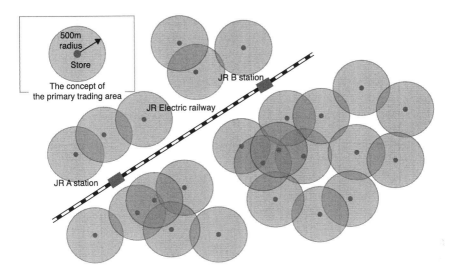

Figure 7.1 The strategy of dense location.

Source: Referring to Suzuki, Sekine and Yahagi 1997: 112. The picture was drawn by Akio Usui.

land use but no direct regulation in the working hours and the closing days of retail stores, many supermarkets could practise long opening hours and no closure dates, enjoyed by convenience stores. In fact it was reported (Kawabe 2003: 11) that more than 30 per cent of US supermarkets operated 24 hours a day in the 1980s. In this situation, even though the convenience stores were located at local petrol stations, those who came to fill up could easily drive further to supermarkets, where assortments of products were enormously wider and prices were generally lower. It was difficult for American convenience stores to gain competitive advantage over supermarkets.

In contrast in Japan, with less regulation on locations but direct regulation on retail operations, people came on foot to the nearest convenience stores that were located in residential areas, and there were no *super* nearby that operated longer hours due to the requirements of the Large-scale Retail Store Law. Although the traditional mom-and-pop stores were not regulated by the Law, they usually did not have the will to operate longer hours and without closing dates. In this situation, there was no format competing with the convenience store; and even if there was another convenience store operating near, people who came on foot rarely preferred to walk further.

This Japanese situation encouraged the marketers to compete to place many convenience stores nearer to consumers' residences. Figure 7.1 shows the so-called 'strategy of dense locations (*shuchu shutten senryaku*)' that 7-Eleven Japan adopted. This strategy meant that once a convenience store was opened in a certain area, the marketer did not place the next store far from the first but opened a succession of stores in the same area. As a result, many convenience stores, each with a trading area shown by a circle with 500 m radius, were densely located in certain areas adjacent to the Japan Railway (JR) electric railway line, even though some parts of the primary trading area were duplicated. This highly dense place-ment resulted in more 7-Eleven stores existing near many consumers' homes, compared to other competitors. This dense location also enhanced customer recognition of the same bannered convenience store in a certain area; if individual stores were far apart, they would be too small to be easily recognised by consumers. This location strategy had another advantage in terms of cost management, because as will be explored below, the frequent deliveries of products from ware-houses to each franchisee's shop and the heavy human support at each store were essential to the Japanese 7-Eleven and the dense location system could achieve efficient truck deliveries and less travelling by store helpers.

Thus, the location strategy of convenience stores itself represented a Japanese feature. The success of this strategy had a visible effect on the current Japanese urban scene, in which convenience stores were everywhere.

Changes in lifestyle as it became supportive to convenience stores

From the 1980s onwards, convenience stores rapidly became a representative retail format in Japan, an achievement fostered by several changes in consumers' lifestyle and demography.

First of all, the number of one-person households was increasing. They increased from 16.1 per cent of all 'ordinal households' in the Census of 1960 to 29.5 per cent in 2005 (calculated from SB website 1). The occupants of these one-person households varied, from the increasing numbers of students, workers posted away from their families ('*tanshin-funin*'), to isolated elderly people. The most enthusiastic shoppers in convenience stores were the young people, with elderly customers less regular.

Although the above data excluded students residing in dormitories because they were accounted as 'institutional households' (or 'quasi-households') in a different Census category from the 'ordinal households', those who lived in apartments reflected the increase of one-person homes and growing enrolment in universities and junior colleges. The enrolment increased from 10.1 per cent in 1955 to 32.3 per cent in 1973 (the final year of High Economic Growth); and since then the proportion has been steadily increasing, surpassing 50 per cent in 2005 (51.5 per cent) according to the records of the Ministry of Education and Science (SB website 1). These students became the most ardent customers of convenience stores located near their residences. Responding to this tendency, the assortments of products, the layout and atmosphere of stores were designed for the youngsters.

Meanwhile, another type of customer caught the public eye. The mass media (e.g. *Nikkei Ryutsu Newspaper* 1987a, *Yomiuri Newspaper* 1988) reported that pupils of junior high schools and even primary schools congregated at convenience stores on the way to or from their cram schools. While these pupils generally lived with their parents, they were also attracted to the convenience stores. Studying at cram schools after the end of the official school day has been very popular for primary and junior high school pupils in order to be successful in the severe entrance exams of universities or even high/junior high schools. 'The nearest cram school starts from about 4 pm. Soon after coming back from school, pupils either have refreshments or stop by at a convenience store, buy something like potato snacks and eat them there with their friends, and then go to the cram school', as mothers of primary school pupils reported in Megro Ward, Tokyo (*Asahi Newspaper* 1990). In an interview, a junior high school pupil in Tokyo reported, 'After cram school finishes a little before 9 pm, I buy and eat some fast foods at a convenience store, and enjoy chatting with my friends there' (*Nikkei Newspaper* 1991a). As a result, a nationwide sample survey indicated that 39 per cent of the customers of convenience stores were the young, from primary school pupils to university/college students. 'A major discovery in this survey is that convenience stores are deeply to do with education and culture', explained a commentator, Yukio Abe (*Nikkei Ryutsu Newspaper* 1990).

Younger working women also became an important segment of customers (e.g. *Nikkei Ryutsu Newspaper* 1995c). Despite the vestige of the traditional view that women should be homemakers, and despite there having been no radical growth in the ratio of 'employed' women (including all kinds of working women) among all workers as a whole,[3] younger working women, many of whom graduated from universities or junior colleges, were steadily increasing. According to Census data, the ratio of 'employed' (working) women of age 20–24 years, among all workers between those ages, expanded from 43.9 per cent in 1955 to 49.8 per cent in 2005 (calculated from SB website 1), although the proportion of working women in their thirties still decreased mainly due to marriage and child rearing. This trend was accelerated by enactment of the Equal Employment Opportunity Law for Men and Women in 1985 (by ratifying the Convention on the Elimination of All Forms of Discrimination against Women adopted by the United Nations in 1979) and the amendment of this law and the Labour Standard Law in 1997 (enforced in 1999) in order to permit late-night working (10.00 pm to 5.00 am) by women. The increase in female visitors to convenience stores was interpreted to be 'because of the increase in women who worked late at night, similarly to men' (*Nikkei Ryutsu Newspaper* 1995b). 'It is not rare that a woman comes to buy a late-night meal' at convenience stores (*Nikkei Ryutsu Newspaper* 1995a).

Corresponding to the above trends, the shift in the hours spent awake at night became apparent, and this was also an encouragement for convenience stores. NHK Broadcasting Culture Research Institute regularly investigated how Japanese people spent their hours in their ordinary life. It revealed that people awake after 11.00 pm on weekdays were increasing from 24 per cent in 1970, 30 per cent in 1980 to 39 per cent in 1990 among all people surveyed (NHK-BCRI 1991: 27). This tendency has continued until the present; 48 per cent in 2000 and 49 per cent in 2010 (calculated from NHK-BCRI 2011: 24). Meanwhile, the hours for sleep on average decreased from 7 hours and 53 minutes in 1980 to 7 hours and

39 minutes in 1990 (NHK-BCRI 1991: 51), and that trend continued: 7 hours and 23 minutes in 2000 and 7 hours and 14 minutes in 2010 (NHK-BCRI 2011: 22). The shift in hours spent awake at night tended to increase opportunities for accessing neighbouring convenience stores, especially during the period before 2000 when only those stores were allowed to open late at night.

The customer base of convenience stores was expanding, to include housewives, men posted away from home, working people especially at lunch time, and even elderly people. The expansion was a result of the assortment of products and services, which were suitable for Japanese consumers and culture.

Arranging assortments of goods and services the Japanese way

The assortments of the mainstream convenience stores operated under the direction of *super* were composed of four categories:[4] processed foods, fast foods, daily foods and non-foods (including printed materials like journals, newspapers and comics, everyday supplies like toiletry products, stationery and dry batteries, along with various services, etc.). While excluding the handling of perishable foods such as vegetables, fish and meats that were often sold by pioneering convenience stores in the late 1960s and the early 1970s, they were keen to provide other types of foods. At first, the dependence on processed foods, including sweets, snacks, instant noodles, frozen foods, canned or bottled soft drinks and alcoholic drinks, was heavy (see Kawabe 2007a: 102–3), but in due course, fast foods and daily products became strategically important.

'Fast food' at Japanese convenience stores usually meant products that could be eaten soon after purchase, in many cases at customers' homes or work places, and in some cases at the stores, although the definition was different in the case of Family Mart (see earlier note 4). An important feature was that fast foods were not mainly composed of foods bearing American or Western images like hamburgers (a McDonald's restaurant had been opened in Japan in 1971), but composed mainly of products with Japanese recipes, such as boxed lunches with rice (*obento*), rice balls (*onigiri*), *sushi*, *oden* (*daikon* radish, fish dumplings and others stewed in a thin soy soup), *an'man* (steamed bun filled with sweet beanpaste) and *nikuman* (steamed bun filled with meat) (see Figure 7.2). This category also included various types of bread, such as sandwiches, the Japanese sweet buns and stuffed bread, as well as canned coffee and soft drinks. 'Daily foods' included various kinds of cooked meals with both Western and Japanese ingredients and recipes, such as packed salad, Japanese pickles and ramen served cold.

In contrast to the field of processed foods, many of which were controlled by powerful manufacturers, the manufacturers in the categories of fast and daily foods were usually so small that the headquarters of the convenience stores could organise them themselves. In addition, convenience stores could get higher gross margins from fast foods; 'about a 10 per cent higher gross margin of products compared to other processed foods' (*Nikkei Newspaper* 1982a, see also Kawabe 2007a: 103). Therefore the field of fast foods and daily foods became a major battlefield in

(a) Lunch box with rice (*obento*)
This example is called '*makunouchi bento*', composed of a slice of salmon, a fried prawn, a Japanese flavoured omelette, boiled foods (right side), and rice with sesame and a pickled plum topping (left side).

(b) Rice ball (*onigiri*)
This rice ball has salmon roe (*ikura*) soaked in soy sauce inside, and is covered by a layer of seaweed (*nori*) outside (*right picture*). The left picture shows the package of this rice ball.

(c) *An'man* and *nikuman*
Chinese style steamed buns, which were modified to the Japanese style, and have been popular in Japan. *An'man* (upper left picture) means steamed bun filled with sweet beanpaste, and *nikuman* (lower right picture) is steamed bun filled with pork.

(d) *Oden*
The traditional recipe *oden* provides many kinds of ingredients in a thin soy soup. The customers can choose some of the ingredients to go in at the sales counter. This example includes *daikon* radish, fish paste (*chikuwa*) deep fried bean curd (*ganmodoki*), a piece of taro's jelly (*kon'njaku*), hard-boiled egg, and deep fried cake of ground fish (*satsuma age*).

Figure 7.2 The category of 'fast foods' at 7-Eleven Japan.

Pictures reproduced courtesy of Seven & i Holdings.

which each headquarters of a convenience store group was constantly involved in development of new products with original recipes to compete for consumers. Thus it came to be reported that 'the boxed lunches with rice were the highest saleable products at 7-Eleven, selling more than 200 billion yen per year and occupying about 20 per cent of the total sales' (*Monthly Food Retailing* 1994: 68).

On the side of the consumers, while the convenience stores generally sold processed foods at the manufacturers' recommended prices, general *super* and food *super* usually sold them at some discount, so the convenience stores were not so attractive in terms of prices. Nevertheless, the fast foods and daily foods were provided based on the original recipes that the headquarters had keenly developed and constantly renewed. These items became attractive home meal substitutes which were bought by various segments of customers; from the youngsters, the younger women, the housewives, the men posted away from their families, the working people on their break, to even the elderly people.

In the meantime, the convenience stores expanded their assortments to include intangible goods, as well as tangible products. In the case of 7-Eleven, it offered DPE (developing, printing and enlarging) services for films as early as 1974, the first year of starting the convenience store business. However, a turning point came when they began to accept payments for public utility charges, such as electricity bills (1987), gas bills (1988), viewing fees for NHK (1989), and telephone bills (1991) (7-Eleven Japan 1991: 211–12). These charges had been collected at home by special collectors, or paid at banks or post offices. However, collectors increasingly missed meeting the customers at home because of the rise in one-person households and the increasing chances of absence even for housewives, due to the increasing involvement in work, even though many of these were part-time jobs. In addition, the opening hours of banks and post offices were too short for those who worked on weekdays to use them. In contrast, the convenience stores operated longer hours or 24 hours, seven days a week; so these stores located nearest to the home were very convenient for customers in paying these charges. 7-Eleven had also begun to accept parcels under a contractual arrangement with a home delivery company (1981), and the payment of insurance bills by contract with insurance companies (1989) (7-Eleven Japan 1991: 211). Their competitors swiftly followed, resulting in many convenience stores becoming able to handle these services. By offering them, the convenience stores naturally earned handling fees from the contracted organisations and companies.

In this way the Japanese convenience stores became, as it were, a semi-public space offering various semi-public services, as well as selling tangible products. This function clearly attracted many people, even if they usually did not shop at convenience stores.

The management systems supporting the operations

Just-in-time delivery

The above features of Japanese convenience stores were supported by elaborate management systems. An outstanding case was what was called 'the system of frequent delivery of products in small lots (*tahindo shoryo haiso*)' or 'the just-in-time delivery system'.

In this system, the products each franchisee's convenience store ordered were delivered twice or three times a day. For instance, boxed lunches with rice, rice balls, *sushi* and various types of bread and buns (the so-called 'fast foods') were delivered to each store three times a day in the case of 7-Eleven, Lawson and

Family Mart; and daily foods were delivered twice a day to these three chains (see Yahagi 1992: 130). This system was to avoid the risks of surplus or insufficient stocks of products, and also to maintain the freshness of foods for sale.

The traditional method of delivery of products from vendors to retail stores had been in a large container or box, for instance, 30 bottles of soy source, 40 canned goods, or 20 packages of curry roux (see *Nikkei Sangyo Newspaper* 1982a, Yahagi 1992: 128). The size of the lot, usually defined by manufacturers, was often too large for retailers, so retailers had requested a smaller size. Some manufacturers and wholesalers had also sometimes cooperated in this in order to expand their sales (see e.g. *Nikkei Sangyo Newspaper* 1982a, *Nikkei Newspaper* 1982b, 1983a).

For convenience stores, the physical distribution system was streamlined by increasing the number of deliveries per day, accompanied by reducing the quantities of delivered products from large lots to individual items. In the case of 7-Eleven, it started delivery of rice-related foods twice a day in 1981, and three times a day in 1987 (Kim 2001: 98). This system not only aimed at reducing inventory, but also maintained freshness of foods. The executive, Suzuki, replied in a media interview, 'We deliver rice-related foods to each store three times a day. The taste is very different from when delivered only twice a day, even if the appearance may be similar' (*Asahi Newspaper* 1988). Such a radical reform of delivery focusing on a strategically important category of products for convenience stores exerted strong influences on its competitors. A survey conducted by *Nikkei Ryutsu Newspaper* (1988c) revealed that 17 chains of convenience stores (including small-sized *super*) had organised delivery three times a day for all member stores and the other 17 chains were using this system for part of their store groups, accounting for 32.6 per cent of all surveyed chains.

This system provoked some antagonism, however. Because the delivery costs were not borne by the convenience stores but by the vendors, some of them, such as Meijiya, a large-sized wholesaler of foods (*Nikkei Ryutsu Newspaper* 1989, Kawabe 2007b: 104), suspended its delivery to 7-Eleven. In addition, some media commentators indicated that the frequent delivery system caused an increase in traffic congestion and air pollution. In view of the dispute, the Fair Trade Commission issued guidelines for the distribution system and business practices and defined in which cases the frequent delivery system should be considered problematic (JFTC 1991). 7-Eleven argued in return that they had adopted the joint delivery system of vendors, which was bound to reduce the delivery costs significantly compared to the businesses in which this system was not being adopted (*Nikkei Newspaper* 1990, Nakada 1993: 161, Kawabe 2007b: 104).

Advanced information systems

Reform of the delivery system was also based on the welcome introduction of information technologies to convenience stores. 7-Eleven, and its parent company Ito Yokado, were known to be the state-of-the-art player in this field. Their competitors followed them to compete in the new information systems. As a result, the convenience stores sector developed a reputation for progressiveness in terms of information systems among the entire Japanese retail industry. After introducing the on-line ordering terminal in 1978 called Terminal Seven, 7-Eleven steadily developed and enhanced the information system through installing the EPOS (Electronic Point of Sales) System for all the stores in 1982–83, replacing Terminal Seven by the EOB (Electronic Ordering Book) System in 1982, and introducing enhanced information systems successively every five years (7-Eleven Japan 1991: Chapter 8).

Regarding the EPOS system, in which the bar code symbols on the products were scanned at cash registers to gather data on each individual item sold, the producers were rarely adding these symbols when 7-Eleven announced the introduction of this system to all the member stores in 1982. Although the Japan Article Number (JAN) code, which was compatible to the European Article Number (EAN) code used in Europe and upper compatible to the Universal Product Code (UPC) in North America, had already been defined as part of the JIS since 1978, the manufacturers at first were reluctant to print the JAN code symbols on the surface of their products during production, because the EPOS system was considered to be primarily for the sake of retailers and did not benefit manufacturers. Although the JIS was the national standard, the decision to adopt it was up to each private company; JIS did not have enough power to force private firms to adopt it. It became clear that the manufacturers' source marking of bar code symbols was largely behind the USA.[5]

In view of this, 7-Eleven Japan, collaborating with its parent company Ito Yokado, took a lead in introducing the EPOS System. This was soon followed by other convenience stores and *super*, resulting in enough group influence to make manufacturers observe the requirements from the retailers' side. According to the data by the Distribution Systems Research Institute (see DSRI website), which was established in 1972 as an extra-departmental body of the MITI to promote 'the systematisation of distribution' and has been a centre of the registration of JAN and other code symbols, the number of manufacturers who fulfilled the registration of the manufacturer's code for JAN code symbols was only 217 when 7-Eleven declared the EPOS system in 1982. At the time, only 91 stores were using the EPOS system and the total number of installed cash registers for the system was 406 in all Japan. After five years in 1987, however, the number of registered manufacturers rapidly increased to 26,440 (122-fold), the stores introducing the system to 11,711 (129-fold), and cash registers for the EPOS system to 40,691 (centuple). The increase in the number of registered manufacturers was so rapid, reaching 66,345 in 1992, and the apprehension on the inadequacy of the five-digit manufacturer's code – JAN was composed of a two-digit country code, five digits representing the manufacturer, five more for the item, and one digit for error checking – became so real that the DSRI made an application to the International Article Number Association in Belgium for an additional two-digit country code for Japan. As a result, Japan got the new country code of '45' in addition to the original '49' (*Nikkei Ryutsu Newspaper* 1992c).

Thus, a burst of adoption of the JAN code symbols and the EPOS system occurred from the latter half of the 1980s, triggered by the declaration by 7-Eleven. In

7-Eleven's opinion the introduction of the EPOS system was absolutely effective because it was a valid measure to recognise saleable and non-saleable items of a strategically important category of products, as *Nikkei Sangyo Newspaper* (1983a) reported: 'a large increase in profits was achieved by introducing the EPOS system, which could recognise individual saleable items in the category of fast foods such as boxed lunches with rice and rice balls, as well as the category of processed foods'.

As for the electronic ordering system, it was directly useful for achieving frequent delivery of products in small lots. The information system for buying operated in two ways (see Yahagi 1994 162–5): the headquarters of convenience stores defined the buyable products and the tradable vendors as the master file, and individual franchisees chose the items they sold from the master file and ordered every day. The ownership right of the products were held by franchisees, not the headquarters, so the actual decisions and operations of ordering were made by the franchisees, by telephone and ordering slips at first, but later electronically. Yahagi (1992: 131) stated, 'the short term cycle of ordering could not be realised without the electronic ordering system'. As a result of introducing this system, the cycle time from ordering to accepting the rice-related products and various cooked breads and buns from and to each franchisee's store was usually reduced to only 11 to 13 hours, and 31 hours at the longest, for the three leading convenience store chains (see Yahagi 1992: 130).[6]

Heavy support by humans

These systems were heavily supported by sales people who frequently travelled around the franchisees' stores. This was another feature of Japanese convenience stores.

In the case of 7-Eleven (the following descriptions will be based on 7-Eleven 1991: Chapter 6, Yahagi 1994: 177–82, Kawabe 2003a: 214–18), the supervisors of the stores, who were called the 'operating field counsellors (OFCs)', regularly visited the franchisees' stores. Each of them was responsible for seven to eight franchisees, and visited them at least twice a week, spending about two hours in each visit and calling at four franchisees' stores a day. They regularly:

- checked the selling and management conditions of each store by means of the checklist, which included investigating the attitude towards service to customers, the freshness of lunch boxes with rice and daily foods, the assortments of saleable goods, the conditions of out of stock products, cleanness of the floor and the frontage of each store; the conditions of the fluorescent lights of the store, etc.;
- supported each store by helping with manual work, transporting items from one store to another, collecting error records, etc.;
- relayed information and knowledge on the policies of the headquarters, on the saleable products according to the analysis of data from EPOS and other

sources, on how to utilise effectively the data obtained from the information systems and financial statements, etc. to each franchisee; and

• gave various consultations with the franchisees on their business.

There were also the District Managers (DMs), who managed seven to eight OFCs, and the Zone Managers (ZMs), who controlled seven to eight DMs. There were about 600 OFCs, 70 DMs and 8 ZMs as of March 1991 (7-Eleven 1991: 185).

All of these staff were summoned to the 7-Eleven headquarters in Tokyo every Tuesday. A general meeting was held first in the morning, followed by the field counsellor meeting, the zone meeting and the district meeting. General policies were defined, but the group also shared a lot of detailed information, such as successful examples of supervising the stores, how to exhibit saleable items of soft drinks and lunch boxes with rice at the shop fronts, how to reduce disposal losses due to leftovers, etc. Before these Tuesday meetings, several meetings of ZMs, DMs and board members were held in preparation. After the Tuesday meeting finished, everyone went back to their local areas by aeroplane or train. The total cost of these meetings was some hundred million yen per year (7-Eleven 1991: 160).

This thorough, hands-on human support system was significantly different from the Southland system, which respected the independent spirit of franchisees. The official historical record of 7-Eleven Japan indicates that the executive Suzuki did not think the American way of delegation of authority was suitable in Japan:

> [T]he national characteristics in Japan are different from the US. In Japan, people rely on each other in a group. There is not any cultural climate such that each individual independently takes full authority with full social responsibility, or that people have been trained to be independent.
>
> (7-Eleven 1991: 136)

The heavy support system was created intentionally as a very Japanese system from the outset.

Other competitors adopted supervisory systems, though not so thorough as 7-Eleven's. The increasing demand for nurturing supervision of franchisees encouraged the Japan Franchise Association to open a school in 1977 for training supervisors (Kawabe 2009: 101); the supervisory system became firmly rooted in Japanese business.

Some new trends in convenience stores

In the 2000s, Japanese convenience stores were approaching a crossroads. According to the Census of Commerce, the number of convenience stores[7] in 2007 was 43,684, accounting for 3.2 per cent of all retail stores, an increase from 0.6 per cent in 1991 and 1.8 per cent in 1999. Among them 36,868 were operating 24 hours, accounting for 84.3 per cent of all convenience stores, an increase from

40.7 per cent in 1991 and 65.5 per cent in 1999. The sales of convenience stores reached 4.6 per cent of the total sales volume by all retail stores in 2007, increasing from 1.1 per cent in 1991 and 3.2 per cent in 1999 (calculated from METI website 1). As the market share of convenience stores was increasing there was a growing sense that this format was becoming saturated, although this suggestion had sometimes been raised even in the late 1980s (e.g. *Nikkei Ryutsu Newspaper* 1987b, *Nikkei Newspaper* 1994b). Under this circumstance, some new methods were needed.

For instance a new formula appeared, called 'the fresh food convenience store (*seisen combini*)'. It sold the three categories of perishable goods, vegetables, fish and meat, at a unit price, 100 yen or less. The Japanese convenience stores had sold perishable goods in their earliest days, and small and medium-sized stores such as Myshop Chain in Shikoku Island and a voluntary chain of All Japan Foods had tried repeatedly to re-introduce the format (*Nikkei Ryutsu Newspaper* 1992a, *Daily Industrial Newspaper* 1996). However, as Shop 99 began to grow rapidly, which combined selling perishable foods with sales at a cheap unit price (99 yen) (started in 1996 by a newcomer Ninety-nine Plus Inc.), some large-sized chains were attracted to this formula, which they recognised could expand the market targets to housewives and elderly people. Lawson Store 100, Food Style (by am/pm), and 99 Market (by Circle K SunKus) followed in adopting this formula around the mid-2000s (e.g. *Nikkei Ryutsu Newspaper* 2005), while the pioneering company was bought by Lawson in 2007–08.

In order to expand the numbers of elderly customers, some leading convenience stores began delivery services of products to consumers' homes. 7-Eleven established a subsidiary, Seven Meal Service, in 2000 to deliver boxed lunches with rice and other cooked foods to individual homes according to the orders received in shops, on the phone, by fax or on the net (7-Eleven 1999, Seven & i Holdings 2011b). The competitors, such as Family Mart and am/pm, also launched a home delivery service (e.g. *Nikkei Newspaper* 2005b).

In the meantime, the convenience stores turned their hands to price competition, despite their history of observing the manufacturers' recommended prices. In 1999, 7-Eleven began the discounted selling of beer, followed by many competitors including Lawson and Family Mart (*Nikkei Newspaper* 1999) and in 2005 7-Eleven reduced the prices of famous brands of cola, green tea and other soft drinks (*Nikkei Newspaper* 2005a); again the competition followed suit. The change in pricing strategy not only extended to other products of manufacturers' or national brands, but also led to intensified price reductions on private or own brands. It also became apparent that 7-Eleven bypassed the lower-grade manufacturers to persuade only the top manufacturers to offer special brands for exclusive sale at the 7-Eleven stores as 'Seven Premium'. This was described as a new type of alliance between retailers and manufacturers, completely led by the retailers' side (e.g. *Nikkei Ryutsu Newspaper* 2008). These products were generally cheaper than the same graded manufacturers' brands.

Finally, convenience stores added new services. For instance, Ito Yokado and 7-Eleven Japan established its own bank, named I Y Bank, in 2000 (the name changed to Seven Bank in 2005), and installed automated teller machines inside the *super* and the convenience stores (Ito Yokado 2007: 491–506). This group also introduced *e*-money from 2007, named Nanaco, which was especially for payments to the Seven & i group. In addition, 7-Eleven, Lawson, Family Mart and other large-sized stores began to accept payment with other competing *e*-money, such as Eddy (managed by bitWallet Inc.), iD (by NTT DoCoMo), Suica (by Eastern Japan Railway Co.) and/or QUICPay (by Mobile Payment Promotion Association). As Japanese consumers preferred payments via mobile phone, the *e*-money was adapted for this system, as well as for cards. This payment form can be said to be unique to Japan.

Conclusion

A milestone in the rapid growth of Japanese convenience stores occurred in 1991 when 7-Eleven Japan and Ito Yokado acquired the bankrupted Southland Corporation. It was generally recognised by the Japanese media that the latecomer encroached on the originator. While Southland Corporation had individual difficulties in itself,[8] it is clear that this resulted from the general differences of social environments surrounding the convenience store format in Japan and the USA.

As this chapter illustrated, Japanese convenience stores developed rapidly thanks to the strict regulation of large-sized stores and the weak regulation of urban planning affording locations in residential areas, and as a result of changes in demography and lifestyle of consumers, such as the increasing number of one-person households, university/college students, pupils commuting to cram schools, and younger women working at night. It was also due to a general shift in the number of hours spent awake at night. In due course, housewives, men posted away from their families, working people (especially at lunch time), and even elderly people were also becoming customers of convenience stores.

The assortment strategies of goods and services taken by convenience stores were a selling point for these customers. They were beginning to focus on fast foods based on Japanese recipes, particularly rice-related products, and on cooked daily foods, which were developed by convenience stores as their original recipes. These products raised gross margins for the stores. Providing various services, especially accepting payments of public utility charges and arranging home deliveries of parcels, also attracted busy people to convenience stores, instead of to banks and post offices that were closed early in the day and at the weekend. Innovations in management, such as the arrangement of a frequent delivery system of small quantities from vendors to each convenience store, continuous advancement of the information systems, and providing heavy human support to franchisees, were effective supports for the operations of convenience stores. Thus, the development of this format was modified to a very Japanese method, although the basic format idea of the convenience store was born in America.

Notes

1   In addition to the instances mentioned above, Abe (1992) mentioned the example of Shell Garden (Tokyo) in 1966 as an early case of convenience stores.

2   In officially-regulated garage forecourt services, a very Japanese scene can be recognised; when people filled up at a petrol station, a few staff provided free services voluntarily, such as window and ashtray cleaning, in addition to the service of filling up. Even after regulations were relaxed, self-service petrol stations did not increase rapidly; only 21 per cent of all Japanese petrol stations adopted the self-service system by March 2010 (IEEJ 2011: 29), so such human services were still offered by many petrol stations.

3   The ratio of employed women was 39.1 per cent in 1955, 39.0 per cent in 1965, 37.1 per cent in 1975, 38.9 per cent in 1985, 39.9 per cent in 1995, and 41.9 per cent in 2005, even though the female population of 15 years old and over was always slightly larger than the male population (calculated from SB website 1).

4   As of FY2011, the composition of assortments of 7-Eleven Japan (Seven & i Holdings 2011a) was 28.1 per cent processed foods, 26.9 per cent fast foods, 12.2 per cent daily foods, and 32.8 per cent non-foods in terms of sales volume; in the case of Lawson (2011), 53.3 per cent processed foods, 19.1 per cent fast foods, 15.7 per cent daily foods, and 11.9 per cent non-foods; and in the case of Family Mart (2011), 28.0 per cent processed foods, 3.5 per cent fast foods, 29.6 per cent daily foods, and 38.9 per cent non-foods. However, the comparison should be treated with care because the definition of each category by the companies was slightly different. For instance, the ratio of fast foods by Family Mart looks small, but it excluded boxed lunches with rice, which were a large proportion of sales, and excluded cooked bread from fast foods and included it under daily foods.

5   For instance, *Nikkei Sangyo Newspaper* (1982c) reported that while the source marking proportion reached 97 per cent in the USA, the figure in Japan for the publishing industry still remained at 6 to 7 per cent. 7-Eleven required the publishers of magazines to add bar-code symbols in 1982.

6   Yahagi (1994: chapter 3) assessed the advantages of the system of convenience stores based on the principles of postponement and speculation advocated by Alderson (1957: 423–7) and Bucklin (1965). The principle of speculation holds that changes in form and movement of goods forward inventories should be made at the earliest possible time in the production and marketing flows, in order to realise economies of scale. However, it must increase the risk and uncertainty costs. The principle of postponement holds, on the contrary, that changes in form and the movement of goods forward inventories should be made at the latest possible time. However, it must expand the lead time. Yahagi indicated that the convenience stores found a new equilibrium point in this trade-off relationship. According to Yahagi's (1993: 29–31) detailed investigation on a subcontracted producer of boxed lunches with rice and other rice-related foods for 7-Eleven, production was divided into three rounds, one of which started from 4.00 am on the basis of speculation (cooking materials until around 8.00 am and then beginning the dishing up) and almost 80 per cent production was finished before the established orders came from the local headquarters at 11.00 am; then the production changed to fulfilling the orders and finished by noon. Another round of production started in the morning on the basis of tentative orders, and after the second established orders came at 2.00 pm, the production changed to fulfilling the orders. The third round of production was made entirely on order.

   Thus, boxed lunches and other rice-related foods were delivered three times a day via a joint-delivery centre to each franchisee's store. Under this system, the producers could complete operations with no unused stock remaining. Nevertheless, franchisers had to undertake the risk of surplus or shortage of stocks, although the products were delivered in very small amounts three times a day.

7   The Census of Commerce defines the convenience store as a store selling foods, adopting the self-service system, having a sales floor space of 35 m² or more up to 250 m², and operating 14 hours or more. It publishes two different types of tables; those based on the industries and those based on retail formats. The above definition applies to the retail format tables. The definition for the industrial tables is a little narrower; it defines the convenience store as one where foods comprise 50 per cent or more in all sales, as well as adopting the self-service system, having a sales floor space of 35 m² or more up to 250 m², and operating 14 hours or more.

8   Kawabe (2003a: 282–98, 2003b: 3–12) analysed that the Southland Corp. faced serious difficulties in 1980s because of the failure of backward integration towards oil refining businesses, the failure of urban development in Dallas, and the intensified competition among convenience stores and with different formats such as supermarkets, shopping centres and discounters.

Summing up

This book has explored how marketing played the role as a social medium to make the discourse of westernisation an everyday reality for consumers. As was frequently mentioned, accepting the discourse of westernisation never meant that Japan simply followed the Western way. On the contrary, new strategies of retail marketing, inspired by Western ideas but tailored to Japanese customs, have helped to shape consumers' lives in a mixture of Western and Japanese ways. A picture of the whole realised by interrelationships between marketing and consumption is the Japanese version of modernity.

Figure C.1 surveys how modern retail formats in Japan were influenced by Western concepts. The first retail format this book focused on was *keiretsu* retailing. Although this is not usually categorised as a retail format, the basic idea was extracted from the format of chain stores or multiples that spread in America and Britain. The gap between the necessity for nationwide distribution by modern manufacturers with mass production systems and a lack of knowledge and resources to develop national networks on the side of independent retailers induced the manufacturers to organise retail networks for mass marketing by

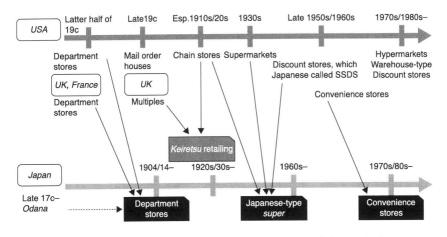

Figure C.1 International influence on development of major retail formats in Japan.

their own efforts. This was the case in the fields of Western-style sweets, Western-style cosmetics and household electrical products based on modern technologies.

The second focus was department stores. Some established merchants, who had sold *kimono* fabrics before the modern era, changed their shops to department stores based on their direct observations of American and European counterparts. Department stores became the place where many consumers encountered Western items for the first time. Only independent retailers were powerful enough to begin transforming their traditional retail format, called *odana*, to modern department stores. Followed by some newcomers who developed 'terminal department stores' built at railway stations, the department store format became predominant in the Japanese retail market, leading to the anti-department store movement by traditional merchants and enactment of the regulatory law. The tendency towards regulation restricting large-scale retailers continued until 2000.

The third focus was *super*, originally an abbreviation of supermarkets. This was the case in which new independent retailers were able to get the self-service idea from the USA. The arrangement was very Japanese, however: they developed what was called *super* or general *super*, selling not only foods but also clothing and many other items at cheaper prices in multi-storey buildings. Japanese consumers now bought outerwear and underwear entirely in the Western-style, in newly-developed synthetic fibres. General *super*, almost entirely originating in the garment trade, offered the new clothing in self-service discount department stores, rather than food supermarkets, although the proportion of food offerings gradually increased.

The final topic was convenience stores, which were born in America and matured in Japan. Under the regulatory law of large-scale stores, the general *super* companies organised their subsidiaries in this field and developed the Japanese strategy, such as dense location of shops near homes with presumption of consumers' coming on foot, development of Japanese-style fast foods, frequent delivery of products to each shop in order to maintain freshness and reduce the stock level, and heavy human support to every shop. While price-conscious formats such as hypermarkets and superstores became the mainstream in retailing in many Western countries from the 1970s–80s onwards, convenience stores, a service-oriented format without low-price appeal, grew as the main innovator in retailing in Japan. This feature represented a Japanese trait in itself.

Strategies in modern retail marketing mediated between the mode of consumption and individual consumer choice (see Figure 0.1). Marketing identified new factors influencing consumption – (1) the domain of availability of offerings and the places for purchase, and (2) the relationships of consumers with others during the act of consumption and with consumption itself – brought about by the progress of westernisation/Americanisation discourse in society, and shops presented their services in forms acceptable to Japanese consumers. In doing so, marketing solicited possible consumers in mixed Western and Japanese attributes in terms of the goods and services provided and the places for purchase. As a result, consumption in modern Japan bore very Japanese characteristics, as was explored in each chapter.

Modern Japanese marketing and consumption originally developed inspired by the discourse of westernisation/Americanisation, but also created the Japanese versions of them. Japan looks to be so close to the West, and yet so far away.

Bibliography

Abe, Yukio (1971a), *Growing Convenience Stores: A Rookie in Food Distribution in the USA* [*Hatten suru Convenience Store, America Shokuhin Ryutsu no Rookie*], Tokyo: Japan Provisions Newspaper Co. (in Japanese).

—— (1971b), 'Can the convenience store develop also in Japan?' Tokyo Chamber of Commerce and Industry, *Tosho* [*Tosho*], June: 36–40 (in Japanese).

—— (1971c), 'Convenience stores and small-sized stores in Japan', Shoko Chukin Bank Ltd., *Finances for Commercial and Industrial Companies* [*Shoko Kinyu*], 21 (9): 3–21 (in Japanese).

—— (1992), 'The history of convenience stores in Japan: past, present and future', *Japan Provisions Newspaper* [*Nihon Shokuryo Shimbun*], 25th June (in Japanese).

—— (1993a), 'Lessons from the bankruptcy of Nico Mart: entering into the new stage in the industry of convenience stores', *Japan Provisions Newspaper* [*Nihon Shokuryo Shimbun*], 20th August (in Japanese).

—— (1993b), 'Commotion from the bankruptcy of Kmart: are the voluntary chains unsuitable for the convenience stores?' *Japan Provisions Newspaper* [*Nihon Shokuryo Shimbun*], 8th October (in Japanese).

AERA (1996), 'All female high school girls are *bell-tomo* [friends on pagers], demand on *poke-bell* [pagers] is not defeated by that on mobile phones', *AERA*, 8th April: 62 (in Japanese).

Akiba, Yoshinobu (2003), *The Committee of Business in Ito Yokado: The CEO Toshifumi Suzuki is Appealing!* [*Ito Yokado Gyomu Iinkai, Suzuki Toshifumi CEO no Geki ga Tobu!*] Tokyo: Kodan-sha (in Japanese).

Akiya, Shigeo (1988), 'Consumer cooperative stores after breaking through the barrier of 1%: rallying of consumers to mutual buying activities', in Imamura, Naraomi and Yoshida, Tadashi (eds.), *The Way Eating Habits are Changing, Collective Works of Problems on Food and Agriculture, No. 17* [*Shoku Seikatsu Henbo no Vector, Shokuryo Nogyo Mondai Zenshu No. 17*], Tokyo: Nosan-gyoson Bunka Kyokai: 137–56 (in Japanese).

Akiyama, Hiromichi (2006), 'The process of development and transformation of the Nippon Electric Big-Stores Association (NEBA)', *Aoyama Journal of Social Science: Economics, Law and Business* [*Aoyama Shakai-kagaku Kiyo*], 35 (1), September: 75–101 (in Japanese).

Akutsu, Masahiro (2001), 'Historical transformation of the semiconductor industry and tasks in the future', The Society of Naval Architects of Japan, *Techno Marine* [*Nihon Zosen Gakkai-shi*], 860, March: 114–18 (in Japanese).

Alderson, Wroe (1957), *Marketing Behavior and Executive Action*, Homewood Illinois: Richard D. Irwin, 1957.

AOEB: Association for Open Education of Business ed. (1967), *The History of Retail Management in Japan* [*Nihon Kouri-gyo Keiei-shi*], Tokyo: The Association of Open Education of Business, Not for Sale (in Japanese).

—— ed. (1981), *The History of the Movements by Retailers in Japan, Vol. 3, The Period before the Second World War* [*Nihon Kouri-gyo Undo-shi 3, Sengo-hen*], Tokyo: The Association of Open Education of Business, Not for Sale (in Japanese).

—— ed. (1983), *The History of the Movements by Retailers in Japan, Vol. 1, The Period before the Second World War* [*Nihon Kouri-gyo Undo-shi 1, Senzen-hen*], Tokyo: The Association of Open Education of Business, Not for Sale (in Japanese).

Aoki, Hideo (1971), *The History of Western-like Hairstyles* [*Yohatsu no Rekishi*], *Selected Books on the History of Manners and Costumes, No. 3*, Tokyo: Yuzan-kaku Publisher (in Japanese).

Aoyama, Yoshiyuki (1991), *Household Electric Appliances, Social History of Industries in the Showa Era, No. 4* [*Kaden, Sangyo no Showa Shakai-shi 4*], Tokyo: Nihon Keizai Hyoron-sha (in Japanese).

APB: Association to Publish the Book on 100-Year Bread History (1970), *100-Year History of Bread from the Meiji Restoration* [*Pan no Meiji 100-nen-shi*], Not for Sale (in Japanese).

Arndt, Johan (1982), 'The conceptual domain of marketing: an evaluation of Shelby Hunt's three dichotomy model', *European Journal of Marketing*, 16 (1), 27–35.

Arisawa, Hiromi ed. ([1966] 1994), *The History of Japanese Industries* [Nihon Sangyo-shi], Tokyo: Nihon Keizai Shimbun-sha. Reprint as *The History of Japanese Industries, No.2*, Tokyo: Nikkei Bunko (in Japanese).

—— and Inaba, Hidezo (eds.) (1966), *Materials: 20 Year History after the War, Vol. 2, Economy* [*Shiryo: Sengo 20-nen-Shi, Vol. 2 Keizai*], Tokyo: Nihon Hyoron-sha (in Japanese).

Aruga, Ken (ed.) (1993), *Economics of Japanese-type Distribution: Analysis of New Entry and Regulation* [*Nihon-teki Ryutsu no Keizaigaku, San'nyu to Kisei no Kaimei*], Tokyo: Nihon Keizai Shimbun-sha (in Japanese).

Asahi Newspaper (1945), 'Removing the blackout curtains, revival of more and more street lights, gate lights and elevators; let's make our everyday life lighter', *Asahi Newspaper*, 9th September (in Japanese).

—— (1952), 'A never-ending problem of house famine; decreasing of the number of housing every year', *Asahi Newspaper*, 9th September (in Japanese).

—— (1957), 'Will the battle of electric rice cookers begin in the next year?' *Asahi Newspaper*, 30th May (in Japanese).

—— (1959), 'Housewives in the farming area were pleased with electrification of homes: emancipating from drawing water and reducing two hours of housework', *Asahi Newspaper*, 12th April (in Japanese).

—— (1966), 'Will a new era of "three sacred treasures" come? The business world is ready to sell personal automobile, colour TVs and coolers', *Asahi Newspaper*, 22nd March (in Japanese).

—— (1967), 'What are the next "three sacred treasures"? Travel abroad or swimming pools?' *Asahi Newspaper*, 7th August (in Japanese).

—— (1969a), 'Why can they sell at cheaper prices? Mass buying, mass selling, and cost-cutting of personnel expenses by reasonable management, a series of *super* viewing from the inside and the outside, No. 1', *Asahi Newspaper*, 31st October (in Japanese).

—— (1969b), 'Own brands: direct orders to manufacturers, some people tend to be concerned about the quality, a series of *super* viewing from the inside and the outside, No. 2', *Asahi Newspaper*, 1st November (in Japanese).

—— (1970a), 'Colour TVs sold at less than 60,000 yen, at last! Challenge by large-sized *super* to the industry of household electric equipment', *Asahi Newspaper*, 13th November (in Japanese).

—— (1970b), 'Fair Trade Commission issued a notice, show the new prices of new colour TVs within this year', *Asahi Newspaper*, 27th December (in Japanese).

—— (1971a), 'MITI's administrative guidance, 15% price reduction for new colour TVs', *Asahi Newspaper*, 12th January (in Japanese).

—— (1971b), 'Toward sorting out the double-standard pricing, Sharp leading the van, 20% price reduction, *Asahi Newspaper*, 14th January (in Japanese).

—— (1971c), 'Matsushita [Panasonic], 15–20% cut in prices, 3 types of colour TVs offered for sale on 21st', *Asahi Newspaper*, 17th January (in Japanese).

—— (1972a), 'Advertising own brands by *super*, low cost buying and large margins, welcomed even by manufacturers because of the stable sales agreements', *Asahi Newspaper*, 12th September (in Japanese).

—— (1972b), 'Switching the strategy to focusing on the smaller-sized stores: Daiei forestalling the amendment of the Department Store Law', *Asahi Newspaper*, 15th September (in Japanese).

—— (1988), 'A diagnosis of business conditions: Toshifumi Suzuki, the President of 7-Eleven Japan', *Asahi Newspaper*, 1st March (in Japanese).

—— (1990), 'Before and after joining the cram schools: signals from stressful society No.6, fat or slim', *Asahi Newspaper*, 14th May (in Japanese).

—— (2006), 'Handing down a story of the War: making up for the shortage of food by cultivating schoolyards', *Asahi Newspaper*, 15th September (in Japanese).

—— (2008), 'Training for business ethics, increasingthe sales outlets (a series of taking-off towards "Panasonic", No.2)', *Asahi Newspaper*, 27th September (in Japanese).

Azuchi, Satoshi (1987), *The Basic Principles of Japanese Supermarkets* [*Nihon Supermarket Genron*] Tokyo: Pulse Publishing (in Japanese).

—— (2006), *A Creative Theory on Japanese Supermarkets* [*Nihon Supermarket Soron*], Tokyo: Shogyo-kai (in Japanese).

Barthes, Roland ([1970] 1982), *The Empire of Signs*, New York: Farrar, Straus and Giroux, English translation by Richard Howard. (Japanese translation from the French version in 1970 by So, S., Tokyo: Shinchosha 1974; Ishikawa, Y., Tokyo: Misuzushobo, 2004.)

Baudrillard, Jean ([1970] 1998), *The Consumer Society: Myths and Structures*, London, Thousand Oaks and New Delhi: Sage Publications. (Japanese translation from the French version in 1970 by Imamura, H. and Tsukahara, F., Tokyo: Kinokuniya Shoten, 1979.)

Bell, Daniel (1973), *The Coming of Post-Industrial Society*, New York: Basic Books, Inc. (Japanese translation by Uchida, T. et al., Tokyo: Diamond-sha, 2 vols., 1975.)

Bonnet, Alastair (2004), *The Idea of the West: Culture, Politics and History*, New York: Palgrave Macmillan.

Braudel, Fernand (1994), *A History of Civilization*, London: The Penguin Press. (Translated from French into English by Richard Mayne.)

Broek, Andries van den (2002), 'Leisure across Europe', Paper to the International Association for Time Use Research (IATUR), Annual Conference 2002, October 15–18, Lisbon, Portugal, PDF version (http://pascal.iseg.utl.pt/~cisep/conferencias/conferencia_20021016/Papers/vandenbroek.pdf).

Bruma, Ian and Margalit, Avishai (2004), *Occidentalism: The West in the Eyes of its Enemy*, London: Penguin Books.

Bucklin, Luis P. (1965), 'Postponement, speculation and the structure of distribution channels', *Journal of Marketing Research*, 2 (1), February: 26–31.

Business Week (1962), 'Changing Fifth Avenue: I, discount house puts on airs' (cover story), *Business Week*, 10th February: 72–74.

Burt, Steve (2010), 'Retailing in Europe: 20 years on', *The International Review of Retail, Distribution and Consumer Research*, 20 (1): 9–27.

Cabinet Statistic Bureau (1939), *Report of the Temporary Census Survey in the 14th Year of Showa* [*Showa 14-nen Rinji Kokusei Chosa Kekka*], 1, Not for Sale (in Japanese).

Campbell, Colin ([1987] 2005), *The Romantic Ethic and the Spirit of Modern Consumerism*, [York:] Alcuin Academics.

Chandler, Jr., Alfred D. (1977), *The Visible Hand: The Managerial Revolution in American Enterprises*, Cambridge, Massachusetts and London: The Belknap Press of Harvard University Press.

—— (1990), *Scale and Scope: The Dynamics of Industrial Capitalism*, Cambridge, Massachusetts and London: The Belknap Press of Harvard University Press.

Chen, Xiaomei (1995), *Occidentalism: A Theory of Counter-Discourse in Post-Mao China*, New York and Oxford: Oxford University Press.

Choi, Sang Chul (2004), 'Household electric appliances: the conflicts and cooperation between manufactures and merchants of household electric appliances', in Ishihara and Yahagi 2004: 91–131 (in Japanese).

Chugai Commercial News (1927), 'Chain stores in America, selling 2.7 billion dollars of foods', *Chugai Commercial News* [*Chugai Shogo Shimpo*], 28th December, Kobe University Library Digital Archive (in Japanese).

—— (1928), 'Surprising chain stores in America, occupying 5% of total retail sales by 10 largest chain stores', *Chugai Commercial News* [*Chugai Shogo Shimpo*], 9th October, Kobe University Library Digital Archive (in Japanese).

—— (1929a), 'Where will chain stores in Japan be going to? No. 1. The organisation of Hongo Bar', *Chugai Commercial News* [*Chugai Shogo Shimpo*], 7th August (in Japanese).

—— (1929b), 'Where will chain stores in Japan be going to? No. 2. Miyoshino selling millet dough', *Chugai Commercial News* [*Chugai Shogo Shimpo*], 8th August (in Japanese).

—— (1929c), 'Where will chain stores in Japan be going to? No. 3. Kimura-ya sharing the store name nominally and Fugetsu-do bestowing the store brand', *Chugai Commercial News* [*Chugai Shogo Shimpo*], 9th August (in Japanese).

—— (1931a), 'The leading-edge management: 350 customers were handled per hour', *Chugai Commercial News* [*Chugai Shogo Shimpo*], 11th January, Kobe University Library Digital Archive (in Japanese).

—— (1931b), 'Comparing Chicago and Osaka from the point of view of retailing', *Chugai Commercial News* [*Chugai Shogo Shimpo*], 30th January, Kobe University Library Digital Archive (in Japanese).

—— (1931c), 'The law for promotion and regulation of cartels quite unique in the world: the industrial organisations targeted by the Law of Control over Important Industries', *Chugai Commercial News* [*Chugai Shogo Shimpo*], 28th February, Kobe University Library Digital Archive (in Japanese).

—— (1932a), 'The original bill of the Department Store Law drafted by the Ministry of Commerce and Industry: rigid articles of approvals and punishments', *Chugai*

Commercial News [*Chugai Shogo Shimpo*], 5th August, Kobe University Library Digital Archive (in Japanese).

—— (1932b), 'The Law to Control Goods Vouchers, the pain points are the obligatory deposits and the lien to be reimbursed', *Chugai Commercial News* [*Chugai Shogo Shimpo*], 9th September, Kobe University Library Digital Archive (in Japanese).

—— (1933), 'what is the department store? the definition by the Association of Department Store was decided', *Chugai Commercial News* [*Chugai Shogo Shimpo*], 10th September, Kobe University Library Digital Archive (in Japanese).

—— (1935), 'Voluntary chains', *Chugai Commercial News* [*Chugai Shogo Shimpo*], 21st to 27th March, a series of four articles, Kobe University Library Digital Archive (in Japanese).

Club Cosmetics Co., Ltd. (1983), *The 80-year History of Club Cosmetics: Founded as Nakayama Taiyo-do* [*Club Cosmetics 80-nen-shi: Sogyo Nakayama Taiyo-do*], Osaka: Club Cosmetics Co., Ltd., Not for Sale (in Japanese).

—— (2003), *All Sorts of Flowers: The 100-year History of Club Cosmetics* [*Hyakka Ryoran: Club Cosmetics 100-nen-shi*], Osaka: Club Cosmetics Co., Ltd., Not for Sale (in Japanese).

Corrigan, Peter (1997), *The Sociology of Consumption*, London: Sage Publications.

CSB: Cabinet Statistics Bureau, ed. ([1887] 1963a), *Statistical Yearbook of Imperial Japan* [*Teikoku Tokei Nenkan*], Vol. 6. (Reprint, Tokyo: Tokyo Reprint Co.) (in Japanese).

—— ([1896] 1963b), *Statistical Yearbook of Imperial Japan* [*Teikoku Tokei Nenkan*], Vol. 16. (Reprint, Tokyo: Tokyo Reprint Co.) (in Japanese).

—— (1939), *Special Census of Resources*, Not for Publication (in Japanese).

Daiei, Editorial Office of Company History ed. (1992), *35 Years Record of the Daiei Group* [*Daiei Grupu 35-nen no Kiroku*], Osaka: Daiei Inc., Not for Sale (in Japanese).

—— ed. (1997), *An Optimist, Develop Naturally and Never be Discouraged* [*Neaka, Nobi-nobi, Hekotarezu*] Osaka: Athine, Not for Sale (in Japanese).

Daily Industrial Newspaper (1996), 'All Japan Foods will standardise the members of convenience stores to "fresh food convenience store", aiming at establishing a new format', 1st June, *Daily Industrial Newspaper* (in Japanese).

Daimaru Co., Ltd. (1967), *The 250 Years History of Daimaru* [*Daimaru 250-nen-shi*], Osaka: Daimaru Co., Ltd., Not for Sale (in Japanese).

Dawson, John (2001a), 'Retailing at century end: some challenges for management and research', *The International Review of Retail, Distribution and Consumer Research*, 10 (2): 119–48.

—— (2001b), 'Is there a new commerce in Europe?' *The International Review of Retail, Distribution and Consumer Research*, 11 (3): 287–99.

—— (2005), 'New cultures, new strategies, new formats and new relationships in European retailing', *Journal of Global Marketing*, 18 (1): 73–97.

Deie, Kenji (1990), 'Problems in small- and medium-sized businesses: an analysis from the point of view of the historical development process of convenience stores', in Japan Academy of Small Business Studies ed., *The Japanese Small- and Medium-sized Businesses in the World* [*Sekai no nakano Nihon Chusho Kigyo*], Tokyo: Doyukan: 172–81 (in Japanese).

—— (1995), 'The historical process towards the maturity of convenience stores and their business strategies', Kumamoto-Gakuin University, *The Kumamoto-Gakuin Journal of Commerce* [*Kumamoto-Gakuin Shogaku Ronshu*], 2 (1), August: 73–96 (in Japanese).

Dicke, Thomas S. (1992), *Franchising in America: The Development of a Business Method, 1840–1980*, Chapel Hill, North Carolina and London: The University of North Carolina Press.

Dower, John W. (2000), *Embracing Defeat: Japan in the Wake of World War II*, New York: W. W. Newton & Company.

DTC: Daily Telecommunications Co., Ltd. (Shiotani, Yoshifumi ed.) (1979), *The True Faces of Large-sized Retailers* [*Sugao no Ryohan-ten*], Tokyo: Daily Telecommunications Co., Ltd. (in Japanese).

Economist (2007), 'The mass retailers of household electric appliances: changes favourable for the top company have occurred', *Economist* [*Economist*], 13th August: 72–73 (in Japanese).

Editorial Committee: Editorial Committee on the 50-year History of the Wholesale Market System (ed.) (1979), *50-year History of the Wholesale Market System Vol. 3, The Main Story Part 3* [*Oroshiuri-shijo Seido 50-nen-shi, Dai 3-kan, Honpen III*], Tokyo: Food Marketing Research and Information Centre (in Japanese).

Editors of Diamond-Freedman, *Supermarkets in Japan: Strategies of Growth by 10 Excellent Companies* [*Nihon no Supermarket, Yuryo 10-sha no Seicho Senryaku*] Tokyo: Diamond-sha (in Japanese).

EIAJ: Electric Industries Association of Japan (1979), *The 30-Year History of the Electric Industry* [*Denshi Kogyo 30-nen-shi*], Tokyo: Diamond, Not for Sale (in Japanese).

Ejiri, Hiroshi (1979), *The System of Returning Unsold Products: Strange Business Practices in Japan* [*Henpin-sei: Kono Fushigi na Nihon-teki Shoho*], Tokyo: Nikkei Ryutsu Book (in Japanese).

Enjoji, Kon (1917), *Policies to Increase Sales Power* [*Hanbai-Ryoku Zoshin-saku*], Tokyo: Sato Shuppan-bu (in Japanese).

Ennyū, Noboru (1987), *Fashion Apparel* [*Apparel*], Tokyo: Nihon Keizai Shimbun-sha (in Japanese).

EPA: Economic Planning Agency (1967), *An Outline of Economy 1967* [*Keizai Yoran 1967*], Tokyo: Ministry of Finance Printing Office (in Japanese).

—— (1977), *White Paper on Economy: Japanese Economy Adapting towards Steady Growth* [*Keizai Hakusho: Antei Seicho eno Tekio wo Susumeru Nihon Keizai*], Tokyo: The Ministry Finance Printing Office (in Japanese).

—— (1978), *Annual Report on National Income Statistics 1978*, Tokyo: Ministry of Finance Printing Office (in Japanese and English).

—— (1979), *White Paper on Economy: Superior Ability of Adaptation and a New Start* [*Keizai Hakusho: Sugureta Tekio-ryoku to Aratana Shuppatsu*], Tokyo: The Ministry Finance Printing Office (in Japanese).

—— (1985), *White Paper on Economy: New Growth Trajectory and its Tasks* [*Keizai Hakusho: Atarashii Seicho to Sono Kadai*], Tokyo: The Ministry Finance Printing Office (in Japanese).

Esashi, Akiko (1985), 'The social position of housewives', in the Group for Reconsideration of the High Economic Growth Period, ed., *The High Economic Growth and Japanese, Vol. 2, Homes: Lifestyle at Home* [*Kodo Seicho to Nihon-jin, Vol. 2 Kazoku-hen, Kazoku no Seilkatsu*], Tokyo: The Publishing Department of the Japan Editor School: 197–225 (in Japanese).

Family Mart Co., Ltd. (2011), *Annual Report 2011: Closed Relationship like a Family Forever* [*Family Mart Annual Report 2011: Korekara mo zutto Kazoku no yoni*], PDF Version (in Japanese).

Firat, A. Fuat (1977), 'Consumption patterns and macromarketing: a radical perspective', *European Journal of Marketing*, 11 (4): 291–8.

—— (1987), 'The social construction of consumption patterns: understanding macro consumption phenomena', in Firat, A. Fuat, Dholakia, Nikhilesh and Bagozzi, Richard P. (eds), *Philosophical and Radical Thought in Marketing*, Lexington, MA: Lexington Books: 251–67.

—— and Dholakia, Nikhilesh (1982), 'Consumption choice at the macro level', *Journal of Macromarketing*, 2 (2), Fall: 6–15.

—— —— (1998), *Consuming People: From Political Economy to Theaters of Consumption*, London and New York: Routledge.

Fisk, George (2006), 'Envisioning a future of macromarketing', *Journal of Macromarketing*, 26 (2), December: 214–18.

Flath, David (1989), 'Vertical restraints in Japan', *Japan and the World Economy*, 1 (2), March: 187–203.

Friends of Women (1937), 'A report of investigation on women's costume in 19 cities all over Japan', *Women's Friend* [*Fujin no Tomo*], June: 89–113 (in Japanese).

Fujii, Mitsuo (1971), *Business History of the Textile Industry: From Cotton Spinning to Synthetic Fibre in Postwar Japan* [*Nihon Sen'i Sangyo Keiei-shi, Sengo Boseki kara Gosen made*] Tokyo: Nihon Hyoron-sha (in Japanese).

Fujioka, Akiko (1999), 'Pioneering works of relationship marketing in Japan: focusing on the activities of Flower of Camellia Club of Shiseido before the Second World War', Kyoto University, *Research and Study: Special Issue of the Economic Review* [*Keizai Ronso Bessatsu: Chosa to Kenkyu*], 17, April: 75–92 (in Japanese).

—— (2000a), 'The Flower of Camellia Club and relationship marketing, No. 1: its birth and transformation before the Second World War (1937–1941)', Shiseido Corporate Museum, *Research Journal Eudermine* [*Eudermine*], 9: 54–67 (in Japanese).

—— (2000b), 'The Flower of Camellia Club and relationship marketing, No. 2: its revival and expansion after the Second World War', Shiseido Corporate Museum, *Research Journal Eudermine* [*Eudermine*], 10: 91–148 (in Japanese).

Fujioka, Rika (2006), *The Emergent Process of Department Stores* [*Hyakkaten no Seisei-katei*], Tokyo: Yuhikaku (in Japanese).

Fujisaki Co., Ltd. (1990), *Fujisaki: Progress for 170 Years* [*Fujisaki 170-nen no Ayumi*], Sendai: Fujisaki Co., Ltd. (in Japanese), Not for Sale.

Fujisawa, Ken (2007), *Distribution Keiretsu and the Anti-Monopoly Law: the Cosmetics Industry as a Clue for Research* [*Ryutsu Keiretsu-ka to Dokusen Kinshi-ho, Keshohin Gyokai wo Tegakari-toshite*], Tokyo: Hakuto-shobo (in Japanese).

Fujita, Teiichiro (1972), *Historical Research on the Modern Markets of Perishable Foods* [*Kindai Seisen Shokuryohin Shijo no Shiteki Kenkyu*], Tokyo: Seibun-do (in Japanese).

—— (1982), 'The transformation process of domestic commerce in the history of development of capitalism in Japan', *Historia* , 97: 150–164 (in Japanese).

—— (1986), 'Public markets in Japan', *Studies in Market History* [*Shijo-shi Kenkyu*], 3, October: 1–16 (in Japanese).

—— (1988), 'The Industrial Revolution and problems of markets', *Socio-Economic History* [*Shakai Keizai Shigaku*], 54 (1), April: 1–44 (in Japanese).

Fukuda, Tsuneari ([1955] 1982), 'The wrong argument of the emancipation of women', *Public Opinions for Women* [*Fujin Koron*]. Reprint, in Ueno 1982a: 48 60 (in Japanese).

Fukuhara, Shinzo (1924), 'On the organisation of chain stores', *Shiseido Monthly* [*Shiseido Geppo*], 1, 3rd November: 1 (in Japanese).

Furo, Tsutomu (1994), 'The marketing channel policy of manufacturers in pre-war Japan: the pioneering forms of vertical agencies and the system of sales companies', *Osaka Gakuin Business Review* [*Osaka Gakuin Daigaku Shogaku Ronshu*], 19 (3/4), March: 31–46 (in Japanese).

Gashu, Sanpei (1894), *The Commercial Directory in Tokyo, or The Shopping Guide* [*Tokyo Sho-eigyoino-roku, ichimei, Kaimono Tebiki*], Tokyo: Sanpei Gashu, Digital Version, National Diet Library, Digital Library (in Japanese).

Gay, Paul du, et al. (1997), *Doing Cultural Studies: The Story of the Sony Walkman*, London: Sage.

Gibson, James J. (1977), 'The theory of affordances', in Shaw, Robert and Bradsfold, John (eds), *Perceiving, Acting, and Knowing: Toward an Ecological Psychology*, New York: Halsted Press: 67–82.

Gluck, Carol (1993), 'The past in the present', in Gordon, Andrew (ed.), *Postwar Japan as History*, Berkeley and Los Angeles: University of California, 64–95.

Gordon, Andrew (2003), *A Modern History of Japan: From Tokugawa Times to the Present*, New York and Oxford: Oxford University Press.

GPB: Group to Publish a Book on the Progress of the Bread Industry ed. (1987) *The Progress of the Bread Industry* [*Pan Sangyo no Ayumi*], Tokyo: Mainichi Shimbun-sha, Not for Sale (in Japanese).

Grossick, Geoffrey and Jaumain, Serge (1999), 'The world of the department store: distribution, culture and social change', in Grossick, Geoffrey and Jaumain, Serge (eds), *Cathedrals of Consumption: The European Department Store, 1850–1939*, Aldershot: Ashgate: 1–45.

Habu, Kiyo (2004), *Dressing Herself, Living like Herself* [*Yosoou-koto, Ikiru-koto*], Tokyo: Keiso-shobo (in Japanese).

Hadley, Eleanor M. (1970), *Antitrust in Japan*, Princeton, NJ: Princeton University Press.

Hakuhodo: Hakuhodo Institute of Life and Living (1985), *The Birth of Divided Masses: What are the New Marketing Strategies to Grasp the New Type of People?* [*Bunshu no Tanjo*], Tokyo: Nihon Keizai Shimbun-sha (in Japanese).

Hamamura, Koichi (2007), *What Happened in the Industry of Video Game Consoles?* [*Game-ki Sangyo de Nani ga Okottaka?*], Tokyo: Ascii (in Japanese).

Haneda, Kazuhiro and Terauchi, Shin (1993), 'Research in development of the adjacent areas by electric railway companies: No. 2, the conditions of electric supply by Kei-Hanshin Electric Railway Co. before the Second World War', *Summaries of Technical Papers of Annual Meeting Architectural Institute of Japan* [*Nihon Kenchiku Gakkai Taikai Gakujutsu Koen Kogai-shu*], F. July: 821–4 (in Japanese).

Hankyu Department Store Co., Ltd. (1976), *The 25-year History of Hankyu Department Store* [*Hankyu Hyakkaten 25-nen-shi*], Osaka: Hankyu Department Store, Not for Sale (in Japanese).

Harada, Masami (1991), *Research on the History of Markets in Modern Japan* [*Kindai Nihon Shijo-shi Kenkyu*], Tokyo: Societe (in Japanese).

Harootunian, Harry (2000), *Overcoming by Modernity: History, Culture, and Community in Interwar Japan*, Princeton and Oxford: Princeton University Press.

Haruyama, Yukio (1989), *Hairstyle: Cultural History of Fashion, No. 2* [*Kami, Oshare no Bunka-shi 2*], Tokyo: Heibon-sha (in Japanese).

Hashimoto, Juro (1991), 'Encouragement of innovation in distribution and development of new business fields', in Yahagi, Toshiyuki ed., *The History of Saison, Vol. 2* [*Saison no Rekishi, Ge-kan*] Tokyo: Libro Port: 1–368 (in Japanese).

Hashizume, Shinya (1999), 'Buildings as department stores: consumer society and urban-scape', in Yamamoto, Taketoshi and Nishizawa, Tamotsu (eds), *The Cultural History of Department Stores: The Revolution in Consumption in Japan* [*Hyakkaten no Bunka-shi, Nihon no shohi Kakumei*], Kyoto: Sekai Shiso-sha: 273–88 (in Japanese).

—— and Nishimura, Akira (eds.) (2005), *The History of Electrification of Japan* [*Nippom Denka-shi*], Tokyo: The Newspaper Department of the Japan Electric Association (in Japanese).

Hatsuda, Toru (1983), 'The establishment of the exhibition house (*kankoba*) and the changes afterward', *Transactions of the Architectural Institute of Japan* [*Nihon Kenchiku Gakaki Ronbun Hokoku-shu*], 329, July: 125–34 (in Japanese).

—— (1993), *The Birth of Department Stores* [*Hyakkaten no Tanjo*], Tokyo: Sansei-do (in Japanese).

Hattori, Seiichi ([1914] 1992), *A Record of New Prosperity in Tokyo* [*Tokyo Shin Hanjo-ki*], Tokyo: Shuho-kaku (Reprint, Tokyo: Ryukeishosha) (in Japanese).

Hayashi, Kaori (1997), *Stories of Japanese American Journalists: A Lively Crowd of Japanese Born in the Meiji Era in Foreign Countries* [*Nikkei Journalist Monogatari, Kaigai ni okeru Meiji no Nihonjin Gunzo*], Tokyo: Shinzan-sha (in Japanese).

Hayashi, Reiko (1969), 'Commerce in the middle and end of early modern Japan', in Toyoda, Takeshi and Kodama, Kota (eds), *Ryutsu-shi I* [*The History of Distribution, Part I*], Tokyo: Yamakawa-shuppan: 187–250 (in Japanese).

—— (1992), 'Transition between the old and the new merchants', in Hayashi, Reiko ed., *Nihon no Kinsei, Vol. 5, Shonin no Katsudo* [*The Early Modern Age in Japan, Vol. 5, The Activities by Merchants*], Tokyo: Chuo Koron-sha: 43–88 (in Japanese).

—— (2001), *Women in the Large Merchant Houses in Edo and the Kyoto-Osaka Area* [*Edo-Kamigata no Odana to Machiya Josei*], Tokyo: Yoshikawa Kobun-kan (in Japanese).

Hayashi, Shuji (1962), *The Revolution of Distribution: Products, Channels and Consumers* [*Ryutsu Kakumei, Seihin, Keiro, Shohisha*] Tokyo: Chuokoron-sha (in Japanese).

Henmi, Toshie (2007), *Ito Yokado: Its Origin of Development* [*Ito Yokado, Seicho no Genryu*], Tokyo: Diamond-sha (in Japanese).

Hibi, Osuke ([1908] 1965), 'Requirements of the times and organisations of retail stores: three major factors of secret of success', in Shibusawa Eiichi (ed.), *The History of Commerce and Industry in the Meiji Period* [*Meiji Shoko-shi*], Tokyo: Hochi-sha, Reprint, *Chuo Koron, The Separate Volume: Issues on Business Management* [*Chuo Koron, Bessatsu Keiei Mondai*] 4 (1): 234–8 (in Japanese).

—— (1911), 'Requirements of the times and organisations of stores: three secrets for the success of department stores', in Shibsawa, Eiichi ed., *The History of Commerce and Industry in the Meiji Era* [*Meiji Shoko-shi*], Shobun-do: 247–52 (in Japanese).

Higuchi, Kiyoyuki (1960), *Nihon Shokumotsu-shi: Shoku-seikatsu no Rekishi* [*History of Food in Japan: History of Changes in Diet*], Tokyo: Shibata Shoten (in Japanese).

Hirajima, Yasuhisa (1985), *Grasping the "Small-sized Masses": Changing Markets! Changing Needs!* [*"Shoshu" o Tsukamu*], Tokyo: Jitsugo-no Nippon-sha (in Japanese).

Hiramatsu, Yumi (1989), *The Story of Aoyama Kinokuniya* [*Aoyama Kinokuniya Monogatari*], Tokyo: Shinshin-do Shuppan.

Hirano, Kiyoshi (2008), 'A study on the design development of the electric fan for home use in Japan', unpublished PhD thesis, Kyushu University (in Japanese). (PDF files at https://qir.kyushu-u.ac.jp/dspace/handle/2324/10325, January 2009.)

Hirano, Takashi (1999a), 'Entry into local cities by department stores and the small- and medium-sized shops', in Yamamoto, Taketoshi and Nishizawa, Tamotsu (eds), *The*

Cultural History of Department Stores: The Revolution in Consumption in Japan [*Hyakkaten no Bunka-shi, Nihon no shohi Kakumei*], Kyoto: Sekai Shiso-sha: 178–96 (in Japanese).

—— (1999b) 'Retailing in urban Japan, 1868–1945', *Urban History* 26 (3): 373–92.

—— (2005), 'Yoshio Takahashi and Osuke Hibi: the creators of the first department store in Japan', *Mita Hyoron* [*Mita Hyoron*] 1085, December: 32–38 (in Japanese).

—— (2008), 'The early development and the limitation of chain stores in pre-War Japan', Keio University, *Mita Business Review* [*Mita Shogaku*], 50 (6), February: 173–189 (in Japanese).

Hirano, Takeshi (1967), *Distribution of Food Hereafter: An Elucidation of Cold Chain* [*Korekara no Shokuhin Ryutsu, Cold Chain no Kaimei*], Tokyo: Diamond-sha (in Japanese).

Hirao, Taro (1929), *The 50-years History of Hirao Sampei Store* [*Hirao Sampei Shoten 50-nen-shi*], Tokyo: Hirao Sampei Store, Not for Sale (in Japanese).

Hirasawa, Teruo (1996), 'The Japanese electric lightbulb industry for export and its control problems in the first half of the 1930s', *Journal of Japanese History* [*Nihonshi Kenkyu*], No. 401, January: 1–26 (in Japanese).

—— (2004), 'The development of the Japanese electric lightbulb industry for export in the first half of the 1930s', *The Tsukuba University Economic Review* [*Tsukuba Daigaku Keizaigaku Ronshu*], 36: 37–69 (in Japanese).

Hiratsuka, Raicho ([1913] 1983a), 'The new woman', *Central Review* [*Chuo Koron*], January, in *The Collections of Raicho Hiratsuka's Writings* [*Hiratsuka Raicho Chosaku-shu*], Vol. 1, Tokyo: Ootsuki-shoten, pp. 257–9 (in Japanese).

—— ([1926] 1983b), 'My bobbed hairstyle', *Cloud, Grass and People* [*Kumo, Kusa, Hito*] Tokyo: Toe-Shoin, in *The Collections of Raicho Hiratsuka's Writings* [*Hiratsuka Raicho Chosaku-shu*], Vol. 4, Tokyo: Ootsuki-shoten, pp. 243–5 (in Japanese).

—— ([1955] 1984), 'My memory of Western-style clothing', *Newspaper of Women's Culture* [*Fujin Bunka Shimbun*], 10th June, in *The Collections of Raicho Hiratsuka's Writings* [*Hiratsuka Raicho Chosaku-shu*], Vol. 7, Tokyo: Ootsuki-shoten, pp. 302–4 (in Japanese).

Hisa, Tsutomu (1990), 'Frozen food', in Japan Food Journal Co., Ltd. (ed.), *History of the Food Industry in Showa Era* [*Showa no Shokuhin Sangyo-shi*] Tokyo: Japan Food Journal Co., Ltd.: 453–61 (in Japanese).

Hochi Newspaper (1939), 'A tremendous progress in a half century: the world highest spread ratio of electric lighting', 15th August *Hochi Newspaper*, Kobe University Library, Digital Archive (in Japanese).

Hofstede, Geert (2001), *Culture's Consequences: Comparing Values, Behaviors, Institutions, and Organizations across Nations*, 2nd edn, Thousand Oaks, CA: Sage Publications.

Hollander, Stanley C. (1960), 'The wheel of retailing', *The Journal of Marketing*, 25 (1), July: 37–42.

Hon'iden, Yoshio and Nakanishi, Torao (1938), 'The process whereby the Department Store Law was enacted', in Nakanishi, Torao (ed.), *Research in the Law of Department Stores* [*Hyakkaten-Ho ni kansuru Kenkyu*], Tokyo: Dobunkan: 83–128 (in Japanese).

Hori, Shin'ichi (1933a), 'Development of temporary sales exhibitions by department stores in Japan', Kyoto University, *Kyoto Economic Review* [*Keizai Ronso*], 36 (6), June: 101–22 (in Japanese).

—— (1933b), 'Conflicts between department stores and traditional retailers in terms of temporary sales exhibitions', Kyoto University, *Kyoto Economic Review* [*Keizai Ronso*], 37 (4), November: 114–34 (in Japanese).

—— (1934), 'The essential features of temporary sales exhibitions by department stores', Kyoto University, *Kyoto Economic Review* [*Keizai Ronso*], 38 (6), June: 134–46 (in Japanese).

—— (1935a), 'Conditions for the survival of temporary sales exhibitions by department stores, No. 1', Kyoto University, *Kyoto Economic Review* [*Keizai Ronso*], 40 (5), May: 108–20 (in Japanese).

—— (1935b), 'Conditions for the survival of temporary sales exhibitions by department stores, No. 2', Kyoto University, *Kyoto Economic Review* [*Keizai Ronso*], 40 (6), June: 118–30 (in Japanese).

—— (1937), *Research in the Problems of Department Stores* [*Hyakka-ten Mondai no Kenkyu*], Tokyo: Yuhikaku (in Japanese).

Hoshi Pharmaceutical Co., Ltd. (1923), *Hoshi: The Organization and its Business* [*Hoshi no Soshiki to Sono jigyo*], Tokyo: Hoshi Pharmaceutical Co., Ltd., Not for Sale (in Japanese).

Hoshi, Shin'ichi (1978), *People are Weak Whilst Government Officials are Powerful* [*Jinmin wa Yowashi, Kanri wa Tsuyoshi*], Tokyo: Shincho-bunko (in Japanese).

Hosoi, Wakizo ([1925] 1980), *A Tragic Story of Factory Girls* [*Joko Aishi*]. Reprint, Tokyo: Iwanami Bunko (in Japanese).

Hotta, Manabu (2005), 'Historical development and current issues of the school lunch system in Japan', *The Bulletin of Hiroshima Prefectural University* [*Hiroshima Kenritsu Daigaku Kiyo*], 17 (1), August: 79–84 (in Japanese).

Hunt, Shelby and Burnett, John J. (1982), 'The macromarketing/micromarketing dichotomy: a taxonomical model', *Journal of Marketing*, 46 (3), Summer: 11–26.

HBJ: Hypothec Bank of Japan, Research Department (1964), 'Tendencies of the electronic industry: focusing on consumer electronic appliances', *Research News Report* [*Nippon Kangyo Ginko, Chosa Jiho*], 18, October: 14–60 (in Japanese).

IBJ: Industrial Bank of Japan (1993), 'Trends in industries: recent trends in major industries and their outlooks, No. 1', *Research by the IBJ* [*Kogin Chosa*], 260: 2–200 (in Japanese).

Ichikawa, Koji (1999), *The Handbook of Video Game Consoles for Businessmen* [*Businessmen no tameno Computer Game-Dokuhon*], Tokyo: Locus (in Japanese).

Imai, Keiko (1999a), 'The history of the style of clothes in modern Japan, No. 1', Shiseido Corporate Museum, *Research Journal Eudermine* [*Eudermine*], 7: 120–6 (in Japanese).

—— (1999b), 'The history of the style of clothes in modern Japan, No. 2', Shiseido Corporate Museum, *Research Journal Eudermine* [*Eudermine*], 8: 127–32 (in Japanese).

—— (2000), 'The history of the style of clothes in modern Japan, No. 3', Shiseido Corporate Museum, *Research Journal Eudermine* [*Eudermine*], 9: 124–9 (in Japanese).

Inoue, Kiyoshi and Watanabe, Toru (1959), *Research on the Rice Riots* [*Kome Sodo no Kenkyu*], Vol. 1, Tokyo: Yuhikaku (in Japanese).

Inoue, Masato (2001), *Western-style Clothing and the Japanese: The Mode called Wartime Uniform* [*Yo-fuku to Nihon-jin, Kokumin-fuku toiu Mode*], Tokyo: Kosai-do Shuppan (in Japanese).

Inoue, Sanpo (1934), 'A united front of retailers', in RSSA 1934: 19–32 (in Japanese).

IEEJ: The Institute of Energy Economics, Japan (2011), *The Investigation Report on Improvements of Management and Structure of Petrol Stations, FY2010* [*Kyuyujo Keiei, Kozo Kaizen to Jittai Hokoku-sho, Heisei 22-nen*], PDF version (http://oil-info.ieej.or.jp/documents/index.php).

Isetan Co., Ltd. (1990), *The 100-year History of Isetan: Tracing the Path of 3 Generations of Tanji Kosuge* [*Isetan 100-nen-shi, 3-dai Kosuge Tanji no Kiseki wo Tadotte*], Tokyo: Isetan Co., Ltd. Not for Sale (in Japanese).

Ishida, Hideto ([1983] 1995), 'Anticompetitive practices in the distribution of goods and services in Japan: the problem of distribution *keiretsu*' (translated by Haley, John O.), *Journal of Japanese Studies*, 9 (2): pp. 319–34. Reprint, Ravenhill, John (ed.), *Japan, Volume II*, Aldershot, UK and Brookfield, US: Edward Elgar Publishing Co.: 101–16.

Ishihara, Takemasa (1989), *Birth and Development of Public Retail Markets* [*Kosetsu Kouri Ichiba no Seisei to Tenkai*], Tokyo: Chikura-shobo (in Japanese).

—— (1998), 'Establishment of foods *super* as the new retail format: a determination to get things right by Kansai Super', in Shimaguchi, Mitsuteru et al. (eds), *Innovations in Sales and Distribution, The Innovation Age of Marketing, Vol. 4* [*Eigyo Ryutsu Kakushin, Marketing Kakushin no Zidai, Vol. 4*] Tokyo: Yuhikaku: 143–69 (in Japanese).

—— and Yahagi, Toshiyuki (eds) (2004), *100 Year History of Distribution in Japan* [*Nihon no Ryutu 100-nen*], Tokyo: Yuhikaku (in Japanese).

Ishii, Junzo (1983), *The Power and Conflicts in Distribution* [*Ryutsu ni okeru Power to Tairitsu*], Tokyo: Chikura-shobo (in Japanese).

Ishii, Kanji (2003), *Nihon Ryutsyu-shi* [*The History of Market Distribution in Japan*], Tokyo: Yuhikaku (in Japanese).

Ishii, Kendo (1936), *Things Originated in the Meiji Period, Enlarged and Revised Edition* [*Zohtei Meiji Jibutsu Kigen*], Tokyo: Shunyodo (in Japanese).

Ishii, Takemochi (2000), *What is the 'iMode Revolution'? The Shocking IT Big Bang* [*iMode Kakumei toha Nanika: Shogeki no IT Big Bang*], Tokyo: Seishun-shuppan (in Japanese).

Ishikawa, Hiroyoshi (1989), *The History of Desires after the Second World War: A Profile of Japanese People Suffering from the 'Too Much Happiness' Syndrome* [*Yokubo no Sengo-shi*], Tokyo: Kobun-do Suppan (in Japanese).

Ishikawa, Kenji and Yasuoka, Shigeaki (1995), 'Accumulation of wealth by merchants and the forms of enterprises', Yasuoka, Shigeaki and Amano, Masatoshi (eds), *Development of Business in Early Modern Japan, Business History in Japan, Vol. 1* [*Kinsei Keiei no Tenkai, Nihon Keiei-shi 1*], Tokyo: Iwanami-shoten: 61–106 (in Japanese).

Ito, Kazuko (2005), 'Designing lifestyle', in the Group of Reconsideration of High Economic Growth (ed.), *High Economic Growth and the Japanese, Vol. 2, Lifestyle of Families* [*Kodo Seicho to Nihon-jin, Vol. 2 Kazoku-hen, Kazoku no Seilkatsu*] Tokyo, Tokyo: Publishing Division of the Japan Editor's School (in Japanese): 167–96.

Ito, Koichi (1984), 'The current situations of *keiretsu* retail stores under the distribution *keiretsu* and problems today: the case of cosmetics and household electric appliances', Osaka University of Economics, Institute of Small Business Research, *Quarterly Journal of Small Business* [*Chusho Kigyo Ki-ho*], 3: 9–17 (in Japanese).

Ito, Masatoshi (2003), *The Spirits of Trade by Masatoshi Ito* [*Ito Masatoshi no Akinai no Kokoro*] Tokyo: Nihon Keizai Shimbun-sha (in Japanese).

Ito, Shigejiro (1934a), 'Voluntary chains as a measure for rescuing petty retailers', in RSSA 1934: 1–18 (in Japanese).

—— (1934b), 'The organisation and business of the Association for Stores of Western-style Clothes in All Areas of Tokyo', in RSSA: 237–58 (in Japanese).

Ito Yokado (ed.) (2007), *Coping with Changes: Endless Seeking of Creation* [*Henka Taio: Sozo eno Akunaki Chosen*], Tokyo: Seven & I, not for sale (in Japanese).

Itozono, Tatsuo and Deie, Kenji (1983), 'The structural stagnation of small- and medium-sized retailers', in Itozono, Tatsuo et al. (eds.), *The Distribution Structure in Current*

Japan, A Series on the Distribution Economy in Current Japan, Vol. 3 [*Gendai Nihon no Ryutsu-Kiko, Koza: Gendai Nihon no Ryutsu Keizai, Dai 3-kan*] Tokyo: Otsuki-shoten: 157–185 (in Japanese).

Iwataya Co., Ltd. (1967), *Business History of Iwataya* [*Iwataya Keiei-shi*], Fukuoka: Iwataya Co., Ltd. (in Japanese), Not for Sale.

IWS: International Wool Secretariat in Tokyo (1978), *IWS Year Book of Clothing 1978* [*IWS Iryo Nenkan'78*] Tokyo: Research Department of the IWS (in Japanese).

Izumida, Eiichi (1996), 'The transformation process of the Large-scale Retail Store Law', Niigata University, *The Journal of Law and Politics* [*Hosei Riron*], 28 (3), February: 1–28 (in Japanese).

JACC: Japan Association of Chocolate and Cocoa (1958), *The History of the Chocolate Industry in Japan* [*Nihon Chocolate Kogyo-shi*], Not for Sale (in Japanese).

Japan Food Journal Co., Ltd. (ed.) (1990), *History of the Food Industry in Showa Era* [*Showa no Shokuhin Sangyo-shi*] Tokyo: Japan Food Journal Co., Ltd. (in Japanese).

Japan Provisions Newspaper Co. (ed.) (1967), *One Hundred Years of Tastes: Progress of the Food Industry* [*Aji 100-nen: Shokuhin Sangyo no Ayumi*], Not for Sale (in Japanese).

Japan Society of Lifology (ed.) (1999), *An Encyclopaedia of Lifology* [*Seikatu-gaku Jiten*], Tokyo: TBS Britannica (in Japanese).

JCCU: Japanese Consumers Co-operative Union (ed.) (2002), *The History of the Co-operative Movement in Modern Japan* [*Gendai Nihon Seikyo Undo-shi*], Vol. 1, Tokyo: JCCU, Not for Sale (in Japanese).

JCIA: Japan Cosmetic Industry Association (ed.) (1995), *Progress in 120 Years of the Cosmetic Industry* [*Keshohin Kogyo 120-nen no Ayumi*], Tokyo: Japan Cosmetic Industry Association, Not for Sale (in Japanese).

JCUD: Japan Commercial Union of Department Stores (1936), *The Declaration of Objection against the Department Store Law* [*Hyakkaten-ho Hantai Seimei-sho*], September, Tokyo: Japan Commercial Union of Department Stores, Brochure, Not for Sale (in Japanese).

Jefferys, James B. (1954), *Retail Trading in Britain, 1850–1950*, Cambridge: Cambridge University Press.

JFFA: Japan Frozen Food Association (2009), *Heisei 20th Year Statistics of Frozen Food* [*Heisei 20-nen Reito Shokuhin ni kansuru Sho-tokei*], Tokyo: Japan Frozen Food Association (in Japanese).

JFTC: Japan Fair Trade Commission (ed.) (1975), *Making Distribution Keiretsu: Administrated Prices and Resale Price Maintenance* [*Ryutu Keiretsu-ka, Kanri Kakaku to Saihanbai Kakaku Iji*], Tokyo: Printing Office of the Ministry of Finance (in Japanese).

—— (Noda, Minoru ed.) (1980), *Distribution Keiretsu and Anti-monopoly Law: The Report of the Research Meeting on the Anti-Monopoly Law* [*Ryutsu Keiretsuka to Dokusen Kihshi-ho: Dokusen Kinshi-ho Kenkyukai Hokoku*], Tokyo: The Printing Office, Ministry of Finance (in Japanese).

—— (1991), 'Guidelines concerning distribution systems and business practices', PDF Version (http://www.jftc.go.jp/e-page/legislation/ama/distribution.pdf).

Jiji News (1929), 'The problem of goods vouchers becomes the nation-wide issue: Tokyo and Osaka Trade Organisations of Kimono Fabric Retailers consider the countermeasure and tend to conclude it should be prohibited', *Jiji News* [*Jiji Shimpo*], 20 June, Kobe University Library, Digital Archive (in Japanese).

Jinbo, M. (2000), 'The sales organisations in the pharmaceutical industry before the Second World War in Japan', in Ozaki, Kunihiro and Jinbo, Mitsuhiro (eds), *A Historical*

Perspective to Marketing [*Marketing eno Rekishi teki Shikaku*], Tokyo: Dobunkan: 199–218 (in Japanese).

—— (2008), 'A pioneer sales organization in the Japanese Pharmaceutical Industry: a case of Hoshi Pharmaceutical Company', Business History Society in Japan, *Japan Business History Review* [*Keieishigaku*], 43 (2), September: 3–29 (in Japanese).

Jin'no, Yuki (1994), *The Birth of Taste: Shaped by the Department Store* [*Shumi no Tanjo, Hyakka-ten ga Tsukutta Taste*] Tokyo: Keiso-shobo (in Japanese).

—— (1999a), 'Department stores and interior decorations', in Yamamoto, Taketoshi and Nishizawa, Tamotsu (eds), *The Cultural History of Department Stores: The Revolution in Consumption in Japan* [*Hyakkaten no Bunka-shi, Nihon no shohi Kakumei*], Kyoto: Sekai Shiso-sha: 155–77 (in Japanese).

—— (1999b), 'Development of children's products: focusing on the case of Mitsukoshi', in Yamamoto, Taketoshi and Nishizawa, Tamotsu (eds), *The Cultural History of Department Stores: The Revolution in Consumption in Japan* [*Hyakkaten no Bunka-shi, Nihon no shohi Kakumei*], Kyoto: Sekai Shiso-sha: 178–96 (in Japanese).

Journal of Macromarketing (1982), 'Editor's working definition of macromarketing', *Journal of Macromarketing*, 2 (1), Spring: 3–4.

Jones, D. G. Brian and Monieson, David D. (1990), 'Early development of the philosophy of marketing thought', *Journal of Marketing*, 54 (1), January: 102–13.

JPC: Japan Productivity Centre (1957), *Marketing: A Report of the Special Mission for the Observation of Marketing* [*Marketing: Marketing Shisatsu-dan Hokoku-sho*], Tokyo: Japan Productivity Centre, Not for Sale (in Japanese).

JPCH: Japan Public Corporation of Housing, the Committee of the 20-year History of the Japan Housing Corporation (1981), *History of the Japan Housing Corporation* [*Nihon Jutaku Kodan-shi*], Tokyo: Japan Public Corporation of Housing, Not for Sale (in Japanese).

JSSA: Japan Self-Service Association (1975), 'Housewives' consciousness of buying and their behaviours', *Monthly Statistics Bulletin of Alcoholic Beverages and Foods* [*Shurui Shokuhin Tokei Geppo*], 17 (2), April: 58–61 (in Japanese).

Jusco Ltd. (2000), *The 30 Year History of Jusco* [*Jusco 30-nen-shi*], Chiba: Jusco Ltd. Not for Sale (in Japanese).

Kajima, Yasuko (1996), *Culture of Fashion: Considering Ready-made Clothing and Modern Consumer Society* [*Fashion Bunka: Kisei-huku to Gendaio Shohi-shakai wo Kangaeru*] Tokyo: Kasei Kyoiku Co. (in Japanese).

—— (2006), *Establishment of the Apparel Industry: Analysis on the Factors for its Establishment and Management of Companies* [*Apparel Sangyo no Seiritsu: sono Yoin to Kigyo Keiei no Bunseki*] Tokyo: Tokyo Tosho Publisher (in Japanese).

Kakizaki, Takao (2001), '85 years from establishment of the design department: toward innovation and creation of the Shiseido-style', Shiseido Corporate Museum, *Research Journal Eudermine* [*Eudermine*], 12: 11–20 (in Japanese).

Kanei, Akira (2000), 'The birth of *super* in Japan', in Ozaki, Kunihiro and Jinbo, Mitsuhiro (eds), *A Historical Perspective to Marketing* [*Marketing eno Rekishi teki Shikaku*], Tokyo: Dobunkan: 175–95 (in Japanese).

Kaneko, Yojiro (1942), *60 Years of Fukusuke Tabi: Cultural History of Split-toe Socks in the Early Modern Era* [*Fukusuke Tabi no 60-nen, Kinsei Tabi Bunka-shi*], Osaka: Fukusuke Tabi Co., Ltd., Not for Sale (in Japanese).

Kao Soap Co., Ltd., The Morgue Room (1971), *The History of Cleaning Culture in Japan* [*Nihon Senjo Bunka-shi*], Tokyo: Kao Soap Co. Not for Sale (in Japanese).

Kataoka, Mataichiro (1977), *Jusco: A Secret Story of Federal Management, An Advancing Large-sized Chain* [*Jusco Renpo Keiei no Himitsu, Yakushin suru Big Chain*] Tokyo: Shibata Shoten (in Japanese).

Kato, Husabumi (ed.) (1988), *Explications to the Systematic Materials of Business History in Japan, Vol. 6, Selling and Advertising* [*Nihon Keiei Shiryo Taiikei: Hanbai Kokoku*], Tokyo: Sanichi-shobo (in Japanese).

Kato, Kazutoshi (1997), *The Era of Group Migration as New Employees: The Supporters of High Economic Growth* [*Shudan Shushoku no Jidan: Kodo Seicho no Ninaite-tachi*], Tokyo: Aoki-shoten (in Japanese).

Kato Yoshitada (1989), 'The establishment process and the features of the First Department Store Law', Kansai University, *The Business Review of Kansai University* [*Kansai Daigaku Shogaku Ronshu*], 34 (3), August: 88–103 (in Japanese).

Kawabe, Nobuo (2003a), *Business History of 7-Eleven: Challenges for the Japanese-type Information-oriented Company, New Edition* [*7-Eleven no Keiei-shi, Nihon-gata Joho Kigyo e no Chosen, Shinban*], Tokyo: Yuhikaku (in Japanese).

—— (2003b), 'Business history of bankruptcy and reconstruction: a case study on Seven-Eleven Inc. (former Southland Corporation)', Waseda University, *Waseda Commercial Review* [*Waseda Shogaku*], 397, September: 1–53 (in Japanese).

—— (2004), 'Business history of convenience stores: 30 years history of convenience stores in Japan', Waseda University, *Waseda Commercial Review* [*Waseda Shogaku*], 400, September: 1–59 (in Japanese).

—— (2006), 'A complete history of convenience stores, No. 11: the vicissitude of Japanese-type convenience stores: the first convenience store as a phantasm and Mammy Toyonaka Store', *Monthly Convenience Stores* [*Gekkan Combini*], September: 87–91 (in Japanese).

—— (2007a), 'A complete history of convenience stores, No. 18: changes in the composition of product assortments', *Monthly Convenience Stores* [*Gekkan Combini*], April: 100–3 (in Japanese).

—— (2007b), 'the frequent delivery of small: a complete history of convenience stores, No. 26: the systems of frequent delivery of small-lots and joint-delivery', *Monthly Convenience Stores* [*Gekkan Combini*], December: 102–5 (in Japanese).

—— (2009), 'A complete history of convenience stores, No. 39: the operations of supervisors', *Monthly Convenience Stores* [*Gekkan Combini*], February: 100–3 (in Japanese).

Kei-Hanshin Kyuko Electric Railway Co., Ltd. (1959), *The 50-year History of Kei-Hanshin Kyuko Electric Railway* [*Kei-Hanshin Kyuko Dentetsu 50-nen-shi*], Osaka: Ke-Hanshin Kyuko Electric Railway, Not for Sale (in Japanese).

Kidachi, Manao (1996), 'Changes in the distribution system of wholesale markets', in Akiya, Shigeo and the Research Group of Food Distribution (eds), *Does the Future Await the Wholesale Markets?* [*Oroshiuri Shijo ni Mirai wa Aruka*] Tokyo: Nihon Keizai Shimbun-sha: 65–78 (in Japanese).

Kikkawa, Takeo (2004a), *Dynamism of Development in the Japanese Electric Power Industry* [*Nihon Denryoku Sangyo Hatten no Dynamism*], Nagoya: University of Nagoya Press (in Japanese).

—— (2004b), 'Competition for plant and equipment investment as an engine of economic growth: Japanese corporations during the High Growth Era', Institute of Social Science, Tokyo University, *The Journal of Social Science* [*Shakai Kagaku Kenkyu*], 55 (2), January: 155 77 (in Japanese).

Kikuchi, Ryoichi (1995), 'Supermarkets (mass retail shops) and wholesale markets of vegetables and fruits', Meiji University, *The Review of Economics and Political Science* [*Sei-Kei Ronsan*] 63 (1), February: 221–57 (in Japanese).

—— (2002), 'The public wholesale markets between 1923 and 1971', Meiji University, *The Review of Economics and Political Science* [*Sei-Kei Ronsan*] 70 (5/6), March: 49–105 (in Japanese).

Kim, Hyunchul (2001), *Innovations of the Format of Convenience Stores* [*Convenience Store Gyotai no Kakushin*], Tokyo: Yuhikaku (in Japanese).

Kimura, Kenji (2005), 'The Industrial Revolution and innovations in the distribution sector', in Ishii, Kanji (ed.), *The History of Distribution in Modern Japan* [*Kindai Nihon Ryutsu-shi*], Tokyo: Tokyo-do Shuppan: 30–51 (in Japanese).

Kimuraya General Head Store Co., Ltd. (1989), *The 120-Years History of Kimuraya General Head Store* [*Kimuraya Sohonten 120-nen-shi*], Tokyo: Kimuraya General Head Store Co., Ltd., Not for Sale (in Japanese).

Kinoshita, Akihiro (2004), 'The distribution system of clothing: from commodities to branded products', in Ishihara and Yahagi (2004): 153–72 (in Japanese).

—— (2011), *Marketing History in the Apparel Industry: Creating Brands and Subsuming the Retail Functions* [*Apparel Sangyo no Marketing: Brand Kochiku to Kouri Kino no Hosetsu*], Tokyo: Dobunkan (in Japanese).

Kita, Shunichi (2007), *Easily Understanding the Industry of Mobile Phones: The Newest Common Knowledge on the Industry* [*Yoku Wakaru Keitai Denwa Gyoukai: Gyoukai no Saishin Joshiki*], Tokyo: Jitsugyo no Nippon-sha (in Japanese).

Kitada, Uchizoshi (1931), *Department Stores and Chain Stores* [*Hyyakka-ten to Rensa-ten*], Tokyo: Seibun-do Shoten-kai-sha (in Japanese).

Kitagawa, Keiko (2002), *The Process of the Birth of Dinning Kitchen: What Miho Hamaguchi, the First Female Architect, Aimed At* [*Dinning Kitchen wa Koshite Tanjo shita: Josei Kenchikuka Miho Hamaguchi ga Mezashita mono*], Tokyo: Giho-do Shuppan (in Japanese).

Kitagawa, Keiko and Oogaki, Naoaki (2004a), 'Research in the establishment process of dining kitchen in Japan: analysis in assertions and proposals by architects in post-war Japan', Architectural Institute of Japan, *Journal of Architecture and Planning: Transaction of AIJ*, [*Nihon Kenchiku Gakkai Keikaku-kei Ronbunshu*], 576: 171–7 (in Japanese).

—— —— (2004b), 'A study on the establishment process of the post-war style of housing: analysis on the plan types of the competitions by the "Journal of New Housing" ', Architectural Institute of Japan, *Journal of Architecture and Planning: Transaction of AIJ*, [*Nihon Kenchiku Gakkai Keikaku-kei Ronbunshu*], 589: 153–9 (in Japanese).

Kitano, Shigeo (1969), *Modernisation of the retail structure in the USA* [*Beikoku ni okeru Ryutsu-kiko no Kindaika*], No Data of Publisher, Not for Sale (in Japanese).

Kitazato, Uichi (1962), 'A turmoil over the selling revolution in the USA: emergence of large-sized discount department stores', *Economist* [*Economist*] 28th August: 6–19 (in Japanese).

—— (1963), 'Department stores counterattacking the SSDDS: a dimension of the selling revolution in the USA', *Economist* [*Economist*] 1st/8th January: 54–62 (in Japanese).

—— (1967), 'A story of Ferkauf (the creator of SSDDS): success and failure of Korvette', *Economist* [*Economist*] 3rd January: 144–8 (in Japanese).

Kitazawa, Shuichi (1924), 'Modern girls', *Women* [*Josei*], August: 226–37 (in Japanese).

Kiyosawa, Kiyoshi (1926), *Modern Girls* [*Modern Girl*], Tokyo: Kinsei-do (in Japanese).

Klein, Thomas A. and Nason, Robert W. (2001), 'Marketing and development', in Bloom, Paul N. and Gundlagh, Gregory T. (eds), *Handbook of Marketing and Society*, Thousand Oaks, CA: Sage Publications: 263–97.

Kobayashi, Ichizo ([1935] 2000), *My Way of Life* [*Watashi no Ikikata*], Tokyo: PHP Bunko (in Japanese).

—— ([1953] 1997), *Kobayashi Ichizo: An Autobiography of Itsuo* [*Kobayashi Ichizo, Itsuo Jijoden*], Tokyo: Nihon Tosho Centre (in Japanese).

Kobayashi, Sumiko (1963), 'Reportage: SSDDS in Japan, pushing the discounting business', *Economist* [*Economist*], 1st and 8th January: 82–86 (in Japanese).

Kobayashi, Yoshihiro (1984), 'The new development of the policy of social education in the Taisho Period: focusing on the movement of improving lifestyles', in the Editorial Committee of 'A Series of the History of Education in Japan' (ed.), *A Series of the History of Education in Japan: Modern* [*Koza Nihon Kyoiku-shi*], Nos. 2 and 3, Tokyo: Dai-ichi Hoki Shuppan: 308–331 (in Japanese).

Kobayashi, Yoshimasa and Hattori, Shiso (1940), *The 50-years History of Kao Soap* [*Kao Sekken 50-nen-shi*], Tokyo: Kao Soap Co. Not for Sale (in Japanese).

Kobe City ([1936] 1987), *Investigation of Commerce* [*Shogo Chosa-sho*], Kobe: Kobe Municipal Office. Reprint, Tokyo: Hobunkaku Shuppan-bu (in Japanese).

Kobe Yushin Daily News (1929), 'New investigations on chain stores: a new institute for mass selling of mass produced products', *Kobe Yushin Daily News* [*Kobe Yushin Nippo*], 12 February–9 March, a series of articles, Kobe University Library, Digital Archive (in Japanese).

Kogo, Eriko (2006), 'Yoshio Takahashi and the Design Department of Mitsukoshi Kimono Fabric Shop', *Bulletin of the Graduate Division of Letters, Arts and Sciences of Waseda University* [*Waseda University Graduate School, Bungaku Kenkyuka Kiyo*], 51 (3): 161–74 (in Japanese).

Kohara, Hiroshi (1994), *History of Japanese Marketing: Historical Settings as a Basis of the Current Distribution System* [*Nohon Marketing-shi: Gendai Ryutsu no Shiteki Kozu*], Tokyo: Chuo Keizai-sha (in Japanese).

Kohashi, Reika (1993), 'Strategy and structure in the industry of software for home-use video game machines', Research Institute of Advanced Management, *Business Insight* [*Business Insight*], 1 (3), Autumn: 74–90 (in Japanese).

Komiya, Ryutaro, Takeuchi, Hiroshi and Kitahara, Masao (1973), 'The household electric appliances', in Kumagai, Hisao ed., *Industrial Organisations in Japan, Vol. 1* [*Nihon no Sangyo Soshiki I*], Tokyo: Chuo Koron-sha: 15–82 (in Japanese).

Komiya, Shigemi (2005a), 'Reiko Komai and Miss Shiseido: the birth and the history of their activities, Part 1', Shiseido Corporate Museum, *Research Journal Eudermine* [*Eudermine*], 19: 142–64 (in Japanese).

—— (2005b), 'Reiko Komai and Miss Shiseido: the birth and the history of their activities, Part 2', Shiseido Corporate Museum, *Research Journal Eudermine* [*Eudermine*], 20: 131–54 (in Japanese).

Kon, Wajiro (1925), 'A record on the costume on Ginza Street in the early summer 1925', *Public Opinions of Women* [*Fujin Ko-ron*], July: 78–105 (in Japanese).

—— (1967), *Forty Years of Wearing a Jumper* [*Jumper o Kite 40-nen*] Tokyo: Publishing Bureau of Bunka Fashion College (in Japanese).

—— ([1968] 1972), 'Japanese dress in everyday life', in *The History of Costume: The Collective Works of Wajiro Kon, Vol. 7* [*Fukuso-shi, Kon Wajiro Shu Dai-7-kan*], Toko: Domesu Publishing, 305–29 (in Japanese).

Kono, Yasunori (2005), 'Distribution and consumption in the interwar period: from recession and depression to business recovery, 1920–1937', in Ishii (2005): 58–88 (in Japanese).

Kotler, Philip (1972), 'Generic concept of marketing', *Journal of Marketing*, 36 (2): April, 46–54.

—— (2003), *Marketing Management,* 11th edn, Englewood Cliffs, New Jersey: Prentice Hall.

—— and Armstrong, G. (2000), *Principles of Marketing: An Introduction*, 5th edn, Upper Saddle River, New Jersey: Prentice-Hall.

—— and Keller, Kevin Lane (2009), *Marketing Management*, 13th edn, Upper Saddle River, New Jersey: Pearson Education, Inc.

—— and Levy, J. S. (1969), 'Broadening the concept of marketing', *Journal of Marketing*, 33 (1), January: 10–15.

——, Fahey, Liam and Jatusripitak, Somkid (1985), *The New Competition*, Englewood Cliffs, NJ: Prentice-Hall.

Kotter, John P. (1997), *Matsushita Leadership: Lessons from the 20th Century's Most Remarkable Entrepreneur*, New York: The Free Press.

Koyama, Shizuko (1991), *The Social Norm of a Good Wife and a Good Mother*, Tokyo: Keiso-shobo (in Japanese).

—— (1999), *Constructing the Concept of Home and Making Women a Member of the Nation*, Tokyo: Keiso-shobo (in Japanese).

—— (2008), 'The birth of female students', in Tsujimoto, Masao (ed.), *Social History of Education*, Tokyo: The Society for the Promotion of the University of the Air: 195–208 (in Japanese).

Koyama, Rika (1996), *Video Games and Restoration of Serenity: Life of Children Now and Here* [*Televi Game to Iyashi: Ima, Kokoni Ikiru Kodomo*], Tokyo: Iwanami-shoten (in Japanese).

Koyama, Shuzo (1991), 'Mature market and Saison Group', in Yui, Tsunehiko (ed.), *The History of Saison, Vol. 2* [*Saison no Rekishi, Jo-kan*], Tokyo: Libro Port: 369–630 (in Japanese).

Kuramoto, Choji (1924), 'Practical values of chain stores, attracting attention in the world of retail shops', *The Industrial World in Japan* [*Jitsugyo no Nihon*], 27 (9), 1st May: 12–16 (in Japanese).

Kuramoto, Hatsuo and Atsumi, Shun'ichi (1960), *Supermarkets in Japan* [*Nihon no Super-market*], Tokyo: Bunka-sha (in Japanese).

Kuroba, Ryoichi (1994), *The History of the Showa-period in Schools and Society* [*Gakko to Shakai no Showa-shi*], *Part 1*, Tokyo: Dai-ichi Hoki Shuppan (in Japanese).

Kuroda, Setsuko and Mogi, Shintaro (1985), 'Meal', in the Group for Reconsideration of the High Economic Growth Period (ed.), *The High Economic Growth and the Japanese, Vol. 2, Homes: Lifestyle at Home* [*Kodo Seicho to Nihon-jin, Vol. 2 Kazoku-hen, Kazoku no Seilkatsu*], Tokyo: The Publishing Department of Japan Editor School: 105–34 (in Japanese).

Kuroki, Yasuo (1990), *Walkman did Battle like this* [*Walkman Kaku Tatakaeri*], Tokyo: Chikuma-bunko (in Japanese).

—— (1999), *All Important Things were Taught by Akio Morita* [*Daiji na koto wa Subete Morita Akio ga Oshiete kureta*], Tokyo: KK Best Sellers (in Japanese).

Kuwata, Naoko (1998), 'A change in the sewing course in the process of spreading Western-style clothing among people and its dilemma: focusing on the idea of dress-making education by Jun Narita', Japan Society for the Study of Education, *Journal of Educational Study* [*Kyoiku-gaku Kenkyu*], 65 (2), June: 121–30 (in Japanese).

Kyu, Eikan ([1957] 1982), 'Theory of the division of labour between men and women', *Public Opinions for Women* [*Fujin Koron*]. Reprint, in Ueno 1982a: 148–62 (in Japanese).

Kyoto City ([1937] 1989), *Investigation of Commerce* [*Shogo Chosa-sho*], Kyoto: Kyoto Municipal Office. Reprint, Tokyo: Hobunkaku Shuppan-bu (in Japanese).

Kubo, Michimasa (1987), *The Lotus Flowers Bloom only in the Muddy Water* [*Hasu no Hana wa Doro-numa ni shika Sakanai*], Tokyo: Million-shobo (in Japanese).

Kurihara, Toyo ed. (1964), *Electric Power: The History of Modern Industry in Japan, Vol. 3* [*Denryoku, Gendai Nihon Sangyo Hatten-shi, III*], Tokyo: Toyo Keizai Shimpo-sha (in Japanese).

Kuwatani, Teiitsu (1912), 'Policy of retailers to expand the markets', *The Business World* [*Jitsugyo-kai*], 4 (2), February: 102–20 (in Japanese).

—— (1913), *Commercial Artifices* [*Sho-ryaku*], Tokyo: Dobunkan (in Japanese).

Lawson, Inc. (2011), *Annual Report 2011*, PDF Version (in Japanese) (http://tools.euro-land.com/arinhtml/jp-law/2011/ar_eng_2011).

Layton, Roger A. and Grossbart, Sanford (2006), 'Macromarketing: past, present, and possible future', *Journal of Macromarketing*, 26 (2), December: 193–213.

Lebhar, Godfrey M. (1959), *Chain Stores in America: 1859-1959*, New York: Chain Store Publishing Corporation.

Liles, Allen (1977), *Oh Thank Heaven! The Story of the Southland Corporation*, Dallas, Texas: The Southland Corporation.

Lion Toothpowder Co., Ltd. (1981), *The 80 Year History of Lion Toothpowder* [*Lion Hamigaki 80-nen-shi*], Tokyo: Lion Toothpowder Co., Ltd., Not for Sale (in Japanese).

Lowy, Dina (2007), *The Japanese 'New Woman': Images of Gender and Modernity*, New Brunswick, New Jersey and London: Rutgers University Press.

Lu, David J. (ed.) (1997), *Japan: A Documentary History, Volume II, The Late Tokugawa Period to the Present*, New York: An East Gate Book.

Maddison, Angus (1995), *Monitoring the World Economy 1820–1992*, Paris: Development Centre of the Organisation for Economic Co-operation and Development.

Maeda, Hajime (1928a), *A Story of Salaried Men* [*Salary-man Monogatari*], Tokyo: Toyo Keizai Shimpo Shuppan-sha (in Japanese).

—— (1928b), *A Story of Salaried Men, Second Series* [*Zoku Salary-man Monogatari*], Tokyo: Toyo Keizai Shimpo Shuppan-sha (in Japanese).

Maeda, Naomi (1985), 'Dwelling', in the Group for Reconsideration of the High Economic Growth Period (ed.), *The High Economic Growth and the Japanese, Vol. 2, Homes: Lifestyle at Home* [*Kodo Seicho to Nihon-jin, Vol. 2 Kazoku-hen, Kazoku no Seilkatsu*], Tokyo: The Publishing Department of Japan Editor School: 29–60 (in Japanese).

Makita, Tetsuo (2005), 'Changes in the way of viewing TV', in Tanaka, Yoshihisa and Ogawa, Fumiya (eds), *TVs and the Japanese: "The 50 Year History of TVs" and Japanese Life, Culture and Consciousness* [*Terebi to Nihonjin: "Terebi 50-nen-shi" to Seikatsu, Bunka, Ishiki*], Tokyo: The Public Office of Hosei University, 3–32 (in Japanese).

Mamada, Takao (2005), Where Consumer Society is Going: Consumption of Signs and Post-Materialism [*Shohi Shakai no Yukue: Kigo Shohi to Datsu-Bussitsu-shugi*], Tokyo: Yuhikaku (in Japanese).

—— (2007), *The Third Theory of Consumer Culture: Neither Modern Nor Postmodern Thought* [*Dai San no Shohi-Bunka-ron, Modern demo Postmodern demo Naku*], Kyoto: Minerva-shobo (in Japanese).

Manda, Kazuharu (1934), 'Organisation and performance of Morinaga Belt-Line Store: mentioning the issue of voluntary chain stores', in RSSA 1934: 33–48 (in Japanese).

—— (1935), 'The fundamental feature of the voluntary chain', *The Commercial World*, 1st August: 10–12 (in Japanese).

—— (1938), *Research in the Voluntary Chain: Theory and Practices of Management of the Comrade-oriented Organisation* [*Voluntary Chain no Kenkyu: Dantai Keiei no Riron to Jissen*]. Tokyo: Tohshin-sha (in Japanese).

Marui Imai Co., Ltd. (1992), *Marui Imai, Progress for One Century and Twenty Years* [*Marui Imai 1seiki to 20-sai no Ayumi*], Sapporo: Marui Imai Co., Ltd. Not for Sale (in Japanese).

Maruyama, Masayoshi (1988), *Economic Analysis of Distribution: Information and Trades* [*Ryutsu no Keizai Bunseki, Joho to Torihiki*], Tokyo: Sobun-sha (in Japanese).

Masui, Tokuo (1963), 'Towards the ideal of modernisation', in Nagato 1963: 169–82. (Original article was carried by *The Rtail Shop World* [*Shoten-kai*], July, 1963) (in Japanese).

Matsuda, Misa (2006), 'Discourses around *kehtai*', in Matsuda, Misa, Okabe, Daisuke and Ito, Mizuko (eds), *Mobile Phones in Japanese Life: Personal, Portable, Pedestrian* [*Kehtai no Aru Fukei: Technology no Nichijo-ka wo Kangaeru*], Kyoto: Kita Oji-shobo: 1–44 (in Japanese).

Matsunaga, Mari (2000), *The i-Mode Incident* [*i-Mode Jiken*], Tokyo: Kadokawa Shoten (in Japanese).

Matsuo, Takayoshi (2001), *Taisho Democracy* [*Taisho Democracy*], Tokyo: Iwanami Gakujutsu Bunko (in Japanese).

Matsushima, Harumi (1975a), 'Electric power and other new industries', in Oishi, Kaichiro and Miyamoto, Kenichi (eds), *Basic Knowledge on Development of Japanese Capitalism* [Nihon Shihonshugi Hattatsu-shi no Kiso Chisiki], Tokyo; Yuhikaku: 239–41 (in Japanese).

—— (1975b), 'Control over important industries and establishment of the Nippon Steel Corporation', in Oishi, Kaichiro and Miyamoto, Kenichi, (eds), *Basic Knowledge on Development of Japanese Capitalism* [Nihon Shihonshugi Hattatsu-shi no Kiso Chisiki], Tokyo: Yuhikaku, 368–9 (in Japanese).

Matsushita Electric Industry Co., Ltd. (1953), *The 35 Year History* [*Sogyo 35-nen-shi*], Osaka: Matsushita Electric Industry Co., Ltd. Not for Sale (in Japanese).

—— (1968), *An Outline of the 50 Year History of Matsushita Electric* [*Matsushita Denki 50-nen no Ryakushi*], Osaka: Matsushita Electric Industry Co., Ltd. Not for Sale (in Japanese).

Matsuya Co., Ltd. (1969), *The 100 Years History of Matsuya* [*Matsu-ha 100-nen-shi*], Tokyo: Matsuya. Not for Sale (in Japanese).

Matsuzakaya Co., Ltd. (1981), *The 70 Years History of Matsuzakaya* [*Matsuzakaya 70-nen-shi*], Nagoya: Matsuzakaya, Not for Sale (in Japanese).

Matsuzaki, Hanzaburo (1923a), 'A consideration of the confectionery industry, No. 2', *Morinaga Monthly* [*Morinaga Geppo*] 2, 15th June: 4–5 (in Japanese).

—— (1923b), 'A consideration of the confectionery industry, No. 3', *Morinaga Monthly* [*Morinaga Geppo*] 3, 15th July: 8–9 (in Japanese).

—— (1924a), 'A lecture at the Meeting for Chief Managers of Sales Companies by the Executive Director, Matsuzaki, No. 1, history and organisation of the company', *Morinaga Monthly* [*Morinaga Geppo*] 15, 15th August: 9 (in Japanese).

—— (1924b), 'Giving information and explanations on sales policy of our company to each retail store', *Morinaga Monthly* [*Morinaga Geppo*] 18, 15th November: 5 (in Japanese).

—— (1954), 'Just as my memories', in Morinaga & Co., Ltd. 1954: 67–204 (in Japanese).

Mayo, James M. (1993), *The American Grocery Store: The Business Evolution of an Architectural Space*, Westport, Connecticut and London: Greenwood Press.

McClain, James L. (2002), *Japan: A Modern History*, New York and London: W. W. Norton & Company.

McInerney, Francis (2007), *Panasonic: The Largest Corporate Restructuring in History*, New York: St. Martin's Press.

MCI: Ministry of Commerce and Industry, Division of Commerce (1935a), *Investigation of Chain Stores and Variety Stores* [*Rensa-ten oyobi Kin'itsu-ten ni kansuru Chosa*], The Materials for Improvement of the Conditions of Retailers, No. 3. March, Not for Sale (in Japanese).

—— (1935b), *On the Chain Store, Especially on the "Morinaga Belt-Line Store"* [*Rensa-ten, tokuni "Morinaga Belt-Line Store" ni tsuite*], The Materials for Improvement of the Conditions of Retailers, No. 4. March, Not for Sale (in Japanese).

—— (1936), *On Takashimaya 10-cen and 20-cen Stores*, The Materials for Improvement of the Conditions of Retailers, No. 17, July, Not for Sale (in Japanese).

McNair, Malcolm P. (1931), 'Trends in large scale retailing', *Harvard Business Review*, 10 (1), October: 30–39.

ME: Ministry of Education (1972a), *The 100-year History of the Educational System: The Volume for Explanations* [*Gakusei 100-nen-shi, Kijutsu-hen*], Teikoku Chiho Gyosei Co., Ltd. (in Japanese).

—— (1972b), *The 100-year History of the Educational System: The Volume for Historical Data* [*Gakusei 100-nen-shi, Shiro-hen*], Tokyo: Teikoku Chiho Gyosei Co., Ltd. (in Japanese).

Media Create (ed.) (2000), *White Paper on the Distribution of Video Game Consoles and Software* [*Televi Game Ryutsu Hakusho*], Tokyo: Media Create (in Japanese).

Meiji-ya Co., Ltd. (1958), *The 73 Year History of Meijiya* [*Meijiya 73-nen-shi*], Tokyo: Meiji-ya Co., Ltd. Not for Sale (in Japanese).

Messinger, Paul R. and Narasimhan, Chakravarthi (1997), 'A model of retail formats based on consumers' economizing on shopping time', *Marketing Science* 116 (1): 1–23.

—— (1955), *The History of Meiji Culture* [*Meiji Bunka-shi*], Vol. 12, *Everyday Life*, Tokyo: Yoyo-sha (in Japanese).

MIAC: Ministry of Internal Affairs and Communications, Economic and Social Research Institute (2004), *Tendencies in Consumption at Households: Annual Report of the Tendency of Consumption* [*Kakei Chosa Nenpo*], Tokyo: National Printing Bureau (in Japanese).

Miller, Michael B. (1981), *The Bon Marché: Bourgeois Culture and the Department Store, 1869–1920*, Princeton, New Jersey: Princeton University Press.

Minemura, Toshio (1931), 'A morphological consideration of women's magazines', in *A General Series of Lectures of Journalism* [*Sogo Jyanalizumu Koza*], Vol. 9, Tokyo: Naigai-sha: 63–67, Not for Sale (in Japanese).

MITI: Ministry of International Trade and Industry (ed.) (1957), *A White Paper on Rationalisation of Industries* [*Sangyo Gorika Hakusho*], Tokyo: Nikkan Kyogyo Shimbun Ltd. (in Japanese).

—— ed. (1980), *The Yearbook of the Electronic Industry 1980* [*Denshi Kogyo Nenkan 1980*], Tokyo: Dempa Publications (in Japanese).

—— Bureau of Heavy Industries (ed.), (1971), *Transfiguring the Structure of Distribution of Household Electric Appliances: A Research Report on the Actual Conditions of*

Distribution of Household Electric Products [*Henbo suru Kaden Ryutsu Kiko: Katei Denki Seihin Ryutsu Zittai Chosa Hokoku*], Tokyo: Research Institute of Trade and Industry (in Japanese).

—— Bureau of Industrial Policy (ed.) (1982), *Business Diagnosis of Japanese Enterprises, FY1982, The Edition for Analysis of Individual Companies, Vol.2* [*Wagakuni Kigyo no Keiei Bunseki, Showa 57-nendo, Kigyo-betsu Tokei-hen, Ge-kan*], Tokyo: MOF Printing Office (in Japanese).

—— —— (ed.) (1987), *Business Diagnosis of Japanese Enterprises, FY1987, The Edition for Analysis of Individual Companies: Non-Manufacturers* [*Wagakuni Kigyo no Keiei Bunseki, Showa 62-nendo, Kigyo-betsu Tokei-hen, Hi-Seizo-gyo*], Tokyo: MOF Printing Office (in Japanese).

—— —— (ed.) (1998), *Business Diagnosis of Japanese Enterprises, FY1998, The Edition for Analysis of Individual Companies: Non-Manufacturers* [*Wagakuni Kigyo no Keiei Bunseki, Heisei 10-nendo, Kigyo-betsu Tokei-hen, Hi-Seizo-gyo*], Tokyo: MOF Printing Office (in Japanese).

—— Corporate Bureau (ed.) (1964), *The Distribution Structure of Consumer Goods* [*Shohi-zai no Tyutsu Kiko*], Tokyo: Shoko Kaikan Foundation (in Japanese).

—— and SMEA: the Ministry of International Trade and Industry and the Small and Medium Enterprise Agency, (1972), *The Convenience Stores Manual* [*Convenience Store Manual*], Tokyo: Research Institute of the Distribution Industry (in Japanese).

Mitsui Bunko (1980), *The History of Mitsui Business, Main Series, Vol. 1* [*Mitsui Jigyo-shi, Honpen Dai 1-kan*], Tokyo: Mitsui Bunko, Not for Sale (in Japanese).

Mitsukoshi Co., Ltd. (1990), *The Record of the 85 Years of Mitsukoshi Co., Ltd.* [*Kabushiki-gaisha Mitsukoshi 85-nen no Kiroku*], Tokyo: Mitsukoshi Co., Ltd., Not for Sale (in Japanese).

—— (2005), *The 100 Years Record of Mitsukoshi Co., Ltd.* [*Kabushiki-gaisha Mitsukoshi 100-nen no Kiroku*], Tokyo: Mitsukoshi Co., Ltd., Not for Sale (in Japanese).

Miura, Ichiro and Koezuka, Hiroshi (1997), *The Management System of Nissin Food Co.: Creating Food Culture and Global Strategy* [*Nissin Sholkuhin no Management, Shoku Bunka no Sozo to Global Senryaku*], Kyoto: Ritsumeikan University, Research Centre on Business Strategy (in Japanese).

Miura, Toshiaki (1990), 'Retort-pouch food', in Japan Food Journal Co., Ltd. (ed.) (1990), *History of the Food Industry in Showa Era* [*Showa no Shokuhin Sangyo-shi*], Tokyo: Japan Food Journal Co., Ltd.: 441–8 (in Japanese).

Miyazaki, Giichi (1966), *The Economic Structure in Postwar Japan* [*Sengo Nihon no Keizai Kiko*], Tokyo: Shin-hyoron (in Japanese).

Mizuno, Manabu (2009), 'Innovativeness of foods *super*: the business system similar to manufacturers and the process of innovation', in Ishii, Junzo and Mukoyama, Masao (eds), *Innovation of Retail Formats, The Series of Systematic Study of Distribution, Vol. 1* [*Kourigyo no Gyotai Kakushin, Series Ryutsu Taikei, Vol. 1*], Tokyo: Yuhikaku: 99–124 (in Japanese).

Mizuo, Jun'ichi (1998), *The History of Cosmetics Brands* [*Kesho-hin no Brand-shi*], Tokyo: Cuko Shinsho (in Japanese).

Mizu'uchi, Toshio (2004), 'Formation and clearance of slums in Osaka from 1910 to 1975', *The Bulletin of the Institute of Humanities, Human and Social Sciences of Ritsumeikan University* [*Ritsumeikan Jinbun Kagaku Kenkusho Kiyo*] 83, February: 23–69 (in Japanese).

Molony, Barbara and Uno, Kathleen (eds) (2005), *Gendering Modern Japanese History*, Cambridge, Massachusetts and London: Harvard University Asia Centre.

Monthly Food Retailing (1994), *Everything about Convenience Stores, A Separate Volume of Monthly Food Retailing* [*Convenience Store no Subete, Gekkan Shokuhin Shogyo Bessatsu*], Tokyo: Shogyo-kai (in Japanese).

Morgan, Robert M. and Hunt, Shelby D. (1994), 'The commitment-trust theory of relationship marketing', *Journal of Marketing*, July, 58 (3): 20–38.

Mori, Rie (2008), 'Urban trends in middle-class women's dressmaking and clothing round 1950 Japan: an analysis of articles from *Fujin Asahi* Magazine', *Journal of Home Economics of Japan* [*Nihon Kasei Gakkai-shi*] 59 (3): 155–164 (in Japanese).

Morinaga & Co., Ltd. (1915), *The Eleventh Biannual Report, From 1st April 1915 to 30th September 1915* [*Dai 11-kai Hokoku-sho*] (in Japanese).

—— (1954), *Fifty-five Year History of Morinaga* [*Morinaga 55nen-shi*], Not for Sale (in Japanese).

—— (2000), *One Hundred Year History of Morinaga Seika: An Angel Flapping its Wings* [*Morinaga Seika 100nen-shi*], Not for Sale (in Japanese).

Morinaga Monthly (1924a), 'A young Morinaga Society for Mutual Prosperity born with new spirits', *Morinaga Monthly* [*Morinaga Geppo*] No. 9, 15th February: 15 (in Japanese).

—— (1924b), 'How to decorate display windows, No. 2', *Morinaga Monthly* [*Morinaga Geppo*] 11, 15th April: 17 (in Japanese).

—— (1925a), 'Beautifying the retailers in all areas in the metropolis of Imperial Japan: a wonderful sight made by the contest for decoration of shop windows involved more than 500 retailers', *Morinaga Monthly* [*Morinaga Geppo*] 21, 15th February: 12 (in Japanese).

—— (1925b), 'The Morinaga contest for decoration of shop windows beautified all areas of the metropolis', *Morinaga Monthly* [*Morinaga Geppo*] 22, 15th March: 8–9 (in Japanese).

—— (1925c), 'Morinaga will receive a request for designing a new store for refurbishment without a fee', *Morinaga Monthly* [*Morinaga Geppo*] 24, 15th May: 10 (in Japanese).

Morishita, Fujiya (1960), *Modern Economics of Commerce* [*Gendai Shogyo keizai-ron*], Toyko: Yuhikaku (in Japanese).

—— (1974), *The Current Distributive Structure* [*Gendai no Ryutsu-kiko*], Tokyo: Sekai Shiso-sha (in Japanese).

—— (1977), *Modern Economics of Commerce*, Revised edition [*Gendai Shogyo keizai-ron, Kaitei-ban*], Tokyo: Yuhikaku (in Japanese).

Morita, Akio (1986), with Reingold, Edward M. and Shimomura, Mitsuko, *Made in Japan: Akio Morita and Sony*, New York: E. P. Dutton (in English). (Japanese translation from the original English edition was made by Shimomura, Mitsuko, Tokyo: Asahi-bunko, 1990.)

MP: Memorial Project of 100 Years after the Opening-Up of Japan (ed.) (1954), *The History of Meiji Culture* [*Meiji Bunka-shi*], *Vol. 13, Manners and Customs*, Tokyo: Yoyo-sha (in Japanese).

Munakata, Heihachiro (1963), 'The revolution of distribution and the retail world of clothing', *Monthly Chemical Fibre* [*Kasen Geppo*] 173, February: 9–15 and 68 (in Japanese).

Muramoto, Fukumatsu (1938), 'The measures for rebirth and promotion of small- and medium-sized merchants and the Department Store Law', in Nakanishi, Torao (ed.), *Research in the Law of Department Stores* [*Hyakkaten Ho ni kansuru Kenkyu*], Tokyo: Dobunkan: 1–23 (in Japanese).

Nagao, Kiyomi (2002), 'Channel policy by manufacturers in the cosmetics industry before the Second World War: a comparative study of Shiseido, Nakayama Taiyo-do and Hirao

Sampei Shokai', *Journal of Market History* [*Shijo-shi Kenkyu*], 22, November: 111–35 (in Japanese).

Nagata, Toshio (1972), 'Lessons from American convenience stores', Shoko Chukin Bank Ltd., *Finances for Commercial and Industrial Companies* [*Shoko Kinyu*], 22 (3): 19–32 (in Japanese).

Nagato, Tsuyoshi (1963), *Supermarket* [*Supermarket*], Tokyo: Nihon Noritsu Kyokai (in Japanese).

—— (1991), *Innovations in Distribution: The Origins in Japan* [*Ryutsu Kakushin: Nihon no Genryu*], Tokyo: Doyukan (in Japanese).

Nagoya City ([1935] 1990), *Investigation of Commerce* [*Shogo Chosa-sho*], Nagoya: Nagoya Municipal Office. Reprint, Tokyo: Hobunkaku Shuppan-bu (in Japanese).

Nakada, Shinya (1993), 'Modernisation of the physical distribution system', in Nikkei Ryutsu Newspaper (ed.), *The Current History of Distribution* [*Ryutsu Gendai-shi*], Tokyo: Nihon Keizai Shimbun-sha: 150–65 (in Japanese).

Nakada, Yasunao (1959), *Takatoshi Mitsui, Biography Series, No. 17* [*Mitsui Takatoshi, Jinbutsu Sosho 17*], Tokyo: Yoshikawa Kobun-do (in Japanese).

Nakada, Yoshihiro (1986), *Marketing and Inter-Organisation Trades* [*Marketing to Soshiki-kan Kankei*], Tokyo: Dobunkan (in Japanese).

Nakagome, Shozo (1975), *The Clothing Industry in Japan* [*Nihon no Ifuku Sangyo*], Tokyo: Toyo Keizai Shimpo-sha (in Japanese).

Nakai, Nobuhiko (1966), 'The management system of Mitsui Family: the system of employees and its operation', *The Socio-Economic History* [*Shakai Keizai Shigaku*] 31 (6): 88–101 (in Japanese).

Nakagawa, Kiyoshi (1996), 'A life of Yoshio Takahashi, a business and literary man', Hakuho University, *Hakuo Review of Law and Politics* [*Hakuo Hogaku*], 6, October: 203–94 (in Japanese).

Nakajima, Kuni (1974), 'The "movement of improving lifestyles" in the Taisho Era', Japan Women's University, *Research in History* [*Shisou*] 15: 54–83 (in Japanese).

—— (1984), 'Institutionalisation of women's education: establishment of education centred on the idea on a good wife and a good mother and its historical evaluation', in the Editorial Committee of 'a Series of the History of Education in Japan' (ed.), *A Series of the History of Education in Japan* [*Koza Nihon Kyoiku-shi*], Nos. 2 and 3, Tokyo: Dai-ichi Hoki Shuppan: 101–26 (in Japanese).

Nakamura, Fumio (1989), *Isolation in a children's room: where the first generation of videogames will be going?* [*Kodomo-beya no Koddoku*], Tokyo: Gakuyo-shobo (in Japanese).

Nakamura, Masaru (2002), *Artificially Organised Markets: Traditional Markets and Public Markets in East Asia and in Modern Japan* [*Tsukurareta Shijo, Kindai Nihon to Higasi Asia no Zairai Shijo to Kosetsu Shijo*], Tokyo: Harvest-sha (in Japanese).

Nakamura, Takafusa (1971), *Analysis of Economic Growth in Japan Before the Second World War* [*Senzen-ki Nihon Keizai Seityo-no Bunseki*], Tokyo: Iwanami-shoten (in Japanese).

Nakanishi Torao (1938), 'The problem of department stores versus small- and medium-sized retailers', in Nakanishi, Torao (ed.), *Research in the Law of Department Stores* [*Hyakkaten-Ho ni kansuru Kenkyu*], Tokyo: Dobunkan: 25–48 (in Japanese).

Nakano, Yasushi (1974), *The Reorganising Process of the Wholesale Distribution Structure of Household Electric Appliances in Osaka* [*Osaka ni okeru Kaden Oroshi Ryutsu Kiko no Saihen Katei*], Osaka: Economic Research Institute of Osaka City University, Not for Sale (in Japanese).

Nakano, Yasushi (1983), 'Contemporary Japanese capitalism and the structure of distribution', in Itozono, Tatsuo et al. (eds), *A Series of Economy of Distribution in Current Japan, Vol. 3, The Structure of Distribution in Current Japan* [*Koza Gendai Nihon no Ryutsu Kiko, Dai 3-kan, Gendai Nihon no Ryutsu Kiko*], Tokyo: Otsuki Shoten: 7–43 (in Japanese).

—— (1984), 'Development of organisations to sell tangible products by large-sized retailers', Osaka City University, *The Quarterly Journal of Economic Studies* [*Kikan Keizai Kenkyu*], 6 (4), Spring: 16–32 (in Japanese).

—— (1995), 'The retail industry', in the Society for Industrial Studies (ed.), *The History of Industries in Japan after the Second World War* [*Sengo Nihon Sangyo-shi*], Tokyo: Toyo Keizai Shinpo-sha: 658–85 (in Japanese).

Nakauchi, Isao (1969), *Discount is My Philosophy* [*Waga Yasuuri Tetsugaku*], Tokyo: Nihon Keizai Shimbun-sha. (Reprint, *A Series of Works by Isao Nakauchi, Vol. I,* 2007, Tokyo: Chikura-shobo) (in Japanese).

—— (2000), *The Endless Revolution of Distribution* [*Rutsu Kakumei wa Owaranai*], Tokyo: Nihon Keizai Shimbun-sha (in Japanese).

Nakauchi Historical Resource Centre (2002), *The History of Daiei's PB: Continually Reducing the Prices of Good Quality Products* [*Daiei PB no Rekishi: Yoi Shina o Dondon Yasuku*] Kobe: University of Marketing and Distribution Science, Mimeo, Not for Sale (in Japanese).

Nakazawa, Shin'ichi (2004), *Wildness in a Pocket: Pokemon and Children* [*Pocket no nakano Yasei: Pokemon to Kodomo*], Tokyo: Shincho-bunko (in Japanese).

Narita, Ryuichi (2007), *Taisho Democracy, Series of the Modern and the Current History of Japan, No. 4* [*Taisho Democracy, Series Nihon Kin-Gendai-shi No.4*], Tokyo: Iwanami Shinsho (in Japanese).

Naryu, Tatsuhiko (1994), *Economic Theory of Distribution: Information, Keiretsu and Strategy* [*Ryutsu no Keizai Riron: Joho, Keiretsu, Senryaku*], Nagoya: The University of Nagoya Press (in Japanese).

—— and Torii, Akio (2000), 'Long-term manufacturer-distributor relationships', in Michael R. Czinkota and Masaaki Kotabe (eds), *Japanese Distribution Strategy: Changes and Innovations*, London: Thomas Learning: 135–53.

Nason, Robert (2006), 'The macromarketing mosaic', *Journal of Macromarketing*, 26 (2), December: 219–23.

Nasu, Yoshio (1935), 'The recent state of the genuine chain stores in our country', *The Retail Shop World* [*Shooten-kai*], 1st August: 13 (in Japanese).

Nasu, Yoshiro (1969), 'Development of monopoly capitalism and changes in people's lives', in Morisue, Yoshiaki et al. (eds), *The History of Lives, Vol. 3, A Systematic Series of Research in Japanese History, Vol. 17* [*Taikei Nihon-shi Sosho, Vol. 17: Seikatsu-shi, No. 3*], Tokyo: Yamakawa Shuppan-sha: 217–388 (in Japanese).

Natsuno, Takeshi (2003), *i-Mode Strategy*, translated into English by Ruth S. McCreery, Chichester: Wiley. (The Japanese version was published in 2000 by Tokyo: Nikkei BP Publishing.)

NBA: National Biscuit Association (ed.) (1951), *History of the Biscuit Industry* [*Biscuit Kogyo-shi*], Tokyo: National Biscuit Association, Not for Sale (in Japanese).

NHK-BCRI: NHK Broadcasting Culture Research Institute (ed.) (1991), *Survey on Time Use in Japanese Everyday Life, FY 1990, volume for All Japan, Use of Hours* [*1990-nendo Kokumin Seikatsu Jikan Chosa, Zenkoku. Jikan-hen*], Tokyo: NHK Broadcasting Culture Research Institute (in Japanese).

—— (2011), 'Sleeping time keeps decreasing, male homework time is increasing: from the 2010 NHK Japanese time use survey' (by Kobayashi, Toshiyuki et al.), NHK

Broadcasting Culture Research Institute, PDF Version (http://www.nhk.or.jp/bunken/english/reports/pdf/report_110401.pdf-290.0KB) (in English).

Nielsen (2008), 'Nielsen Reports TV, Internet and Mobile Usage among Americans' PDF version (http://www.nielsen.com/media/2008/pr_080708_download.pdf).

Nikkei Business (1986), *"The Hidden Mass" as the Leading Role: Looking for the Real Centre in the Market [Shuyaku wa "Kakure Taishu"]*, Tokyo: Nihon Keizai Shimbun-sha (in Japanese).

—— (1998a), 'Editor's interview: President of Shiseido, Mr. Akira Genma. Discount orientation is gradually returning to normal, bolstering up keiretsu stores to strengthen face-to-face retailing', *Nikkei Business*, 29th June: 84–86 (in Japanese).

—— (1998b), 'Special issue No.2, a counterattack by *super*, with a breaking away from practical use and general assortments' *Nikkei Business*, 17th August: 34–40 (in Japanese).

Nikkei Financial Newspaper (1996), 'A series of reading the FY1996 settlement of accounts: unusual figures, No. 11 Daiei–unsolved problem of reducing debts', *Nikkei Financial Newspaper*, 27th December (in Japanese).

Nikkei Marketing Journal (ed.) (2008), *Marketing Handbook 2009 [Nikkei MJ Trend Joho-gen 2009]*, Tokyo: Nihon Keizai Shimbun-sha (in Japanese).

—— (ed.) (2009), *Marketing Handbook 2010 [Nikkei MJ Trend Joho-gen 2010]*, Tokyo: Nihon Keizai Shimbun-sha (in Japanese).

Nikkei Newspaper (1953), 'American retailing in these days', *Nikkei Newspaper*, 29th January (in Japanese).

—— (1954), 'Self-service, a new sales method: appeal to "carefree shopping" without any interventions by sales clerks', *Nikkei Newspaper*, 10th February (in Japanese).

—— (1958a) 'Is the self-service age arriving?: also the appearance of a tendency to supermarket', *Nikkei Newspaper*, 11th July (in Japanese).

—— (1958b), 'Is the supermarket age arriving?: the present situation and prospective', *Nikkei Newspaper*, 21st October (in Japanese).

—— (1976a), 'Crown strengthening colour TVs with the cooperation of Sanyo, changing the brand name from Bubu to Crown', *Nikkei Newspaper*, 1st April (in Japanese).

—— (1976b), 'Individual consumption – turning away from tangible goods, orientation to leisure, and large increase in travel expenses, proved by the investigation by the Economic Planning Agency', *Nikkei Newspaper*, 21st July (in Japanese).

—— (1982a), 'Consideration on a company: 7-Eleven keeps increasing profits by leading the convenience store business: increase of 10 billion yen of ordinary profits', *Nikkei Newspaper*, 11th May (in Japanese).

—— (1982b), 'The new tendency in physical distribution: the attempts by Kao Soap, based on "small lots of various products"', *Nikkei Newspaper*, 25th October (in Japanese).

—— (1983a), 'Yamamoto, a wholesaler of foods, opens new shops to expand trades in cash: corresponding to requirements of trade with smaller lots', *Nikkei Newspaper*, 26th January (in Japanese).

—— (1983b), 'A withdrawal of Daiei from Crown, restructuring Crown is becoming a millstone of Daiei due to worsening of profitability in the main business', *Nikkei Newspaper*, 21st July (in Japanese).

—— (1984), 'MITI summoned the first Study Meeting on Service Industry', *Nikkei Newspaper*, 11th February (in Japanese).

—— (1985a), 'From household electric appliances (*ka-den*) to personal electric appliances (*ko-den*) in the case of Sharp: focusing on the post-baby boomer generation', *Nikkei Newspaper*, 3rd August (in Japanese).

—— (1985b), 'Le Printemps Ginza coming under the umbrella of ADS, Daiei's policy to remove deficit by non-reflection of it on the consolidated account', *Nikkei Newspaper*, 22nd August (in Japanese).

—— (1989), 'A ranking among top 10 *super* in terms of major management indices FY1987: expanding the gap in companies' financial standings', *Nikkei Newspaper*, 15th February (in Japanese).

—— (1990), 'Just before collapse of physical distribution: questions about surplus services, No. 2: wholesalers are dissatisfied with frequent delivery of small-lot products', *Nikkei Newspaper*, 9th November (in Japanese).

—— (1991a), 'Undermining the habit of three-time eating a day: university students tend to eat once a day as "today's rice", while primary and secondary pupils eat five times a day due to studying at the cram schools', *Nikkei Newspaper, Evening Paper*, 6th March (in Japanese).

—— (1991b), 'Voluntary restraint on dispatched sales clerks, called on by the Fair Trade Commission to each manufacturer of household electric appliances', *Nikkei Newspaper, the Evening Edition*, 19th August (in Japanese).

—— (1992), 'A dilemma of reorganising the sales network: dissolving the Association of National Shops of Matsushita (exploring a topic)', *Nikkei Newspaper, the Evening Edition*, 28th April (in Japanese).

—— (1994a), 'Explanation: Daiei is allying with large-sized manufacturers of household electric appliances, the re-attempt based on consumers' recognition of private brands', *Nikkei Newspaper,* 22nd April (in Japanese).

—— (1994b), 'Saturation of convenience stores: vying in low prices (a summary of the report)', *Nikkei Newspaper,* 22nd August (in Japanese).

—— (1995), 'Unrest of *keiretsu* stores of Matsushita: expansion of headhunting and quitting business, due to the gaps in ability to attract consumers against discounters', *Nikkei Newspaper*, 31st May (in Japanese).

—— (1997a), 'Home Videogame Consoles: Matsushita announced the withdrawal, abandoning development of the 64-bit console', *Nikkei Newspaper*, 4th July (in Japanese).

—— (1997b), 'Lonely even if he/she has the friends; figures fill up the empty space in his/her mind', *Nikkei Newspaper*, 10th November (in Japanese).

—— (1998a), 'Wandering around a general *super*, No. 1, "selling any old stuff" has no competitive power–focusing on particular customers and/or particular products', *Nikkei Newspaper*, 13th August (in Japanese).

—— (1998b), 'The face-to-face sales system of cosmetics is lawful judged by the Supreme Court, Shiseido and Kao finally win the suit', *Nikkei Newspaper, Evening paper*, 28th December (in Japanese).

—— (1999), 'Price competition began in convenience stores: many companies cut the prices of beer all at once, following 7-Eleven to boost sales', *Nikkei Newspaper*, 6th November (in Japanese).

—— (2005a), '7-Eleven cuts the prices of soft drinks: a turning point of pricing strategy at convenience stores, to compete with the stores selling at lower prices', *Nikkei Newspaper*, 2nd September (in Japanese).

—— (2005b), 'Convenience stores are delivering to homes: box lunches with rice, drinks and magazines, etc., utilised by elderly people and two-income households with expansion to local cities', *Nikkei Newspaper*, 14th December (in Japanese).

—— (2008a), 'The retraction order to Yamada Denki issued by the Fair Trade Commission, on a charge of abuse of superiority status, requiring the total of 60,000 unlawful dispatched sales clerks', *Nikkei Newspaper*, 1st July (in Japanese).

—— (2008b), 'The struggle for 7 trillion yen market of household electric appliances, No. 1: downturn of consumption thrusting into the war of attrition', *Nikkei Newspaper*, 21st November (in Japanese).

Nikkei Ryutsu Newspaper (1979), 'The wide back lanes, the routes of "unusual discounters [*batta-ya*]"', *Nikkei Ryutsu Newspaper*, 16th August (in Japanese).

—— (1982), 'Conflict on dispatching Helpers; the manufacturers consider reducing them, while the independent chains oppose as "a unilateral action"', *Nikkei Ryutsu Newspaper*, 17th May (in Japanese).

—— (1987a), 'The 27th survey of consumers: fourth-, fifth- and sixth year pupils feel that convenience stores are similar to the former penny candy stores, where they buy something after school', *Nikkei Ryutsu Newspaper*, 5th September (in Japanese).

—— (1987b), 'The survey of convenience stores, Showa 61st year: saturation of market, falling shortfall in new shop openings, fewer than planned', *Nikkei Ryutsu Newspaper*, 26th September (in Japanese).

—— (1988a), 'The large-sized super returning to discount pricing-orientation, Daiei's total penetration with the ethos of its origin', *Nikkei Ryutsu Newspaper*, 18th January (in Japanese).

—— (1988b), 'President of Shiseido Cosmenics, Mr. Akira Kaneko: what is the strategy for cosmetics sold under self-service? — strengthen the existing brands', *Nikkei Ryutsu Newspaper*, 26th March (in Japanese).

—— (1988c), 'Survey of convenience stores in FY Sowa 62nd year: streamlining by focusing on the information system and the frequent delivery system in physical distribution', *Nikkei Ryutsu Newspaper*, 24th September (in Japanese).

—— (1989), '7-Eleven suspended business with Meijiya: dissatisfaction with the delivery system', *Nikkei Ryutsu Newspaper*, 21st November (in Japanese).

—— (1990), 'The customers of convenience stores are shifting from the youngsters to the housewives: increasing market share of married people, and a problem to be solved is to promote children', *Nikkei Ryutsu Newspaper*, 30th January (in Japanese).

—— (1992a), 'Development of fresh food convenience stores by Myshop in Shikoku Island: an investment by Mitsubishi General Trading Co., etc.', *Nikkei Ryutsu Newspaper*, 21st January (in Japanese).

—— (1992b), 'Matsushita reorganising the *keiretsu* shops to "MAST", involving 18,000 shops', *Nikkei Ryutsu Newspaper*, 30th July (in Japanese).

—— (1992c), 'The Distribution System Research Institute will make an application of the additional country code in JAN code symbols in November', *Nikkei Ryutsu Newspaper*, 17th September (in Japanese).

—— (1992d), 'Changes of strategies by mass retailers, No. 2, organising the manufacturers' *keiretsu* retailers as franchisees', *Nikkei Ryutsu Newspaper*, 29th September (in Japanese).

—— (1992e), 'The Daiei Group strategy embracing many problems, No. 8, increasing interest-bearing debts–concerns on cash flow', *Nikkei Ryutsu Newspaper*, 1st October (in Japanese).

—— (1994), 'Matsushita supports the sales of *keiretsu* stores by setting up a special organisation, focusing on multi-media devices,' *Nikkei Ryutsu Newspaper*, 31st January (in Japanese).

—— (1995a), 'Favourable growth by opening new stores without experiencing any downturns, while boosting the existing shops is the task', *Nikkei Ryutsu Newspaper*, 9th May (in Japanese).

—— (1995b), 'Large increase in women's customers: the next task should be to atract elderly customers', Nikkei Ryutsu Newspaper, 26th September (in Japanese).

—— (1995c), 'From survey on convenience stores in FY1995, No. 2: the customers and a measure to handle the environmental issues, in order to attract the middle-aged and elderly people', *Nikkei Ryutsu Newspaper*, 3rd October (in Japanese).

—— (1996), 'Study series about the leaders: Daiei's President Isao Nakauchi–"moving ahead while continuing to think"', *Nikkei Ryutsu Newspaper*, 25th March (in Japanese).

—— (1998), 'Rallying by reorganisation of the distribution systems in the videogame market, Sega and Nintendo adopting direct sales or reducing the number of wholesalers to pursue the SCE', *Nikkei Ryutsu Newspaper*, 5th March (in Japanese).

—— (2003), 'Policy of sales as a way of thinking in reverse, small-sized electrical shops in towns transforming to mass retail stores, begin with supports from the manufacturers', *Nikkei Ryutsu Newspaper*, 11th March (in Japanese).

—— (2005), 'The 26th survey on convenience stores: developing borderless competition, succeeding one another to open fresh food convenience stores selling at 100 yen', *Nikkei Ryutsu Newspaper*, 17th July (in Japanese)

—— (2006), 'Hold on! The *keiretsu* retailers in towns survive; *keiretsu* stores dividing into two opposites, revival or atrophy–the number of petty retailers are more than that of convenience stores', *Nikkei Ryutsu Newspaper*, 27th January (in Japanese).

—— (2008), 'A shocking fact of private brands: Seven Premium as the retailer-led alliances between manufacturers and retailers, a succession of large-sized manufacturers enter', *Nikkei Ryutsu Newspaper*, 13th June (in Japanese).

—— (2011), 'Outlets for mobile phone handsets reduced by half over recent four years, concentration in large-sized shops due to the reduction of promotion allowances, also due to spread of smart phones,' *Nikkei Ryutsu Newspaper*, 2nd February (in Japanese).

Nikkei Ryutsu Newspaper (ed.) (1976), *The Guidebook of Distribution Economy: 1977 Edition* [*Ryutsu Keizai no Tebiki, 1977-nen-han*], Tokyo: Nikkei Newspaper Co. (in Japanese).

—— (ed.) (1979), *The Guidebook of Distribution Economy: 1980 Edition* [*Ryutsu Keizai no Tebiki, 1980-nen-han*], Tokyo: Nikkei Newspaper Co. (in Japanese).

—— (ed.) (1990), *The Guidebook of Distribution Economy: 1991 Edition* [*Ryutsu Keizai no Tebiki, 1991-nen-han*], Tokyo: Nikkei Newspaper Co. (in Japanese).

—— (ed.) (1999), *The Guidebook of Distribution Economy: 2000 Edition* [*Ryutsu Keizai no Tebiki, 2000-nen-han*], Tokyo: Nikkei Newspaper Co. (in Japanese).

Nikkei Sangyo Newspaper (1975a), 'The campaign by the All-Japan Federation of Electric Merchants to overcome the crisis in home electric distribution approaching the final stage, progressing the negotiations with manufacturers respectively', *Nikkei Sangyo Newspaper*, 23rd April (in Japanese).

—— (1975b), 'All-Japan Federal Association of Electric Merchants negotiated for increasing margins; they finally announced they would use force', *Nikkei Sangyo Newspaper*, 7th June (in Japanese).

—— (1979), 'Matsushita opens up the route to large-sized stores: establishing 4 local Sales Companies in order to unify the trading channel', *Nikkei Sangyo Newspaper*, 19th June (in Japanese).

—— (1982a), 'Kikkoman started delivery of corrugated boxes with smaller lots', *Nikkei Sangyo Newspaper*, 18th February (in Japanese).

—— (1982b), 'Matsushita going on the offensive in sales of PCs: entering into marketing by widening the variety and making full use of keiretsu stores,' *Nikkei Sangyo Newspaper*, 21st May (in Japanese).

—— (1982c), 'Tokyo Electronic offers for sale printers of EPOS labels: direct connection via computers to the headquarters', *Nikkei Sangyo Newspaper*, 1st October (in Japanese).

—— (1982d), 'The large-sized stores of electric products devising a strategy for breaking out of the recession, No. 4, expecting special supply of goods in exchange for handling PCs,' *Nikkei Sangyo Newspaper*, 15th December (in Japanese).

—— (1983a), 'A prompt report of P/L: 7-Eleven Japan, large increase of profits by large increase of the number of franchisees' stores', *Nikkei Sangyo Newspaper*, 16th May (in Japanese).

—— (1983b), 'Sony is strengthening the sales ability of its *keiretsu* retailers in order to emphasise the importance of domestic sales and secure stable growth: responding to the age of the new media', *Nikkei Sangyo Newspaper*, 2nd December (in Japanese).

—— (1984), 'A sales battle for telephone receivers has started: private companies versus NTT, along with the entrance of foreign companies', *Nikkei Sangyo Newspaper*, 3rd November (in Japanese).

—— (1985), 'One month after deregulation of telecommunications with reinforcement of the principle of competition: telephone handsets, new services, DDI, and VAN,' *Nikkei Sangyo Newspaper*, 6th May (in Japanese).

—— (1986), 'Matsushita Electric Industry: The plan to transform the shops (restore! *keiretsu* electric stores)', *Nikkei Sangyo Newspaper*, 23rd August (in Japanese).

—— (1992), 'Full swing in Toshiba chains, with cooperation for sales promotion and delivery: 100 chains will be established in this fiscal year', *Nikkei Sangyo Newspaper*, 19th May (in Japanese).

—— (1995), 'Series on the competition war in videogame business, No.3: declining compatible videogame consoles; Sanyo, IVC and Hitachi', *Nikkei Sangyo Newspaper*, 18th December (in Japanese).

—— (2006), '*Keiretsu* stores of Matsushita, transfiguring to advantage', *Nikkei Sangyo Newspaper*, 6th February (in Japanese).

Nishikawa, Shigeki et al. (1993), 'Development of suburban housing areas by Hankyu Electric Railway in the early Showa Era, No. 1, some features in development of houses adjacent to the Kobe Line', *Summaries of Technical Papers of Annual Meeting, Architectural Institute of Japan* [*Nihon Kenchiku Gakkai Taikai Gakujutsu Koen Kogai-shu*], September: 625–6 (in Japanese).

Nishimura, Eiji (1999), 'The historical significance of Masami Shimizu's marketing thought: a pioneer of the movement of modernisation of retail business', *Distribution* [*Ryutsu*] 12: 197–203 (in Japanese).

Nishino, Hajime (2006), 'Investments in plant and equipment in the electric apparatus industry during the reconstruction period in Japan', *Shizuoka University Economic Review* [*Keizai Kenkyu*] 10 (4), February: 99–122 (in Japanese).

Nishiyama, Uzo (1989), *Modernology of Dwellings* [*Sumai no Kogen-gaku*], Tokyo: Shokoku-sha. (in Japanese)

Nishizaka, Yasushi (1992), 'Metropolis and large merchant houses', in Yoshida, Nobuyuki (ed.), *The Pre-Modern Age in Japan, Vol. 9, The Urban Age* [*Nihon no Kinsei, 9, Toshi no Jidai*], Tokyo: Chuo Koron-sha: 173–220 (in Japanese).

—— (2006), *Research in Employees of Mitsui Echigoya* [*Mitsui Echigoya Hokonin no Kenkyu*], Tokyo: University of Tokyo Press (in Japanese).

Nishizawa, Tamotsu (1999), 'Tradition and innovation in management of department stores: a locus of Takashimaya', in Yamamoto, Taketoshi and Nishizawa, Tamotsu (eds), *The Cultural History of Department Stores: The Revolution in Consumption in*

Japan [*Hyakkaten no Bunka-shi, Nihon no shohi Kakumei*], Kyoto: Sekai Shiso-sha: 62–87 (in Japanese).

Noda, Mamoru et al. (1993), 'Development of suburban housing areas by Hankyu Electric Railway in the early Showa Era, No. 2, the case study of Muko-no-sho', *Summaries of Technical Papers of Annual Meeting, Architectural Institute of Japan* [*Nihon Kenchiku Gakkai Taikai Gakujutsu Koen Kogai-shu*], F. September: 627–8 (in Japanese).

NTT DoCoMo (2007), 'History of Pocket-Bell (now Quick-Cast) stirring up the boom in 'bell friends (*bell-tomo*),' *DoCoMo Report*, No. 55, 13th March, PDF Version (in Japanese).

Nye, David F. (1985), *Image Worlds: Corporative Identities at General Electric*, Cambridge MA and London: The MIT Press.

Ochanomizu University, The Committee to Publish the 100-years History (ed.) (1984), *The 100-years History of Ochanomizu University* [Ochanomizu Daigaku 100-nen-shi], Not for Sale, PDF Version (http://hdl.handle.net/10083/4567) (in Japanese).

Oe, Kenzaburo (1995), 'Japan, the ambiguous, and myself', in Kenzaburo Oe, *Japan, The Ambiguous and Myself: The Nobel Prize Speech and Other Lectures*, Tokyo: Kodansha International: 105–28. (Translated by Hisaaki Yamanouchi.)

Ogata, Tomoyuki ([1986] 1990), *Improvement of Business in Ito Yokado: What is the Super-excellent Company Doing?* [*Ito Yokado no Gyomu Kaikaku, Cho-yuryo Kigyo wa Nani o Shiteiru noka*], Tokyo: Mikasa-shobo (in Japanese).

Ogawa, Fumiya and Makita, Tetsuo (2005), 'A collection of information regarding the TV viewing', in Tanaka, Yoshihisa and Ogawa, Fumiya (eds), *TV and the Japanese: "The 50 Year History of TVs" and Japanese Life, Culture and Consciousness* [Terebi to Nihonjin: "Terebi 50-nen-shi" to Seikatsu, Bunka, Ishiki], Tokyo: The Public Office of Hosei University, 249–286 (in Japanese).

Ogita, Takeru and Limbon (1989), 'The historical process of public housing', in Mimura, Hiroshi (ed.) *Retrospect and Prospect of the Public Housing and Residential Movement* [*Koei Jutaku–Jukyosha Undo no Rekishi to Tembo*], Kyoto: Horitsu Bunka-sha, pp. 9–43 (in Japanese).

Oishi, Kaichiro (1975), 'An introductory discussion on modern Japan', in Oishi, Kaichiro (ed.), *A Series of Japanese History by Iwanami 14, Modern Japan 1*, [*Iwanami Koza: Nihon Rekishi, 14, Kindai, 1*], Tokyo: Iwanami-shoten: 1–64 (in Japanese).

Okada, Akio (1968), 'The civilisation and enlightenment movement and food', in Society on the Japanese History of Manners and Customs (ed.), *Kindai Nihon Huzoku-shi: Dai 5 kan, Shokuji to Shokuhin* [*The History of Manners and Customs in Modern Japan, Vol. 5, Dietary and Foodstuffs*], Tokyo: Yuzan-kaku: 15–52 (in Japanese).

Okada, Haruhiko (1975), 'Trends in the food *super* industry', *The Norin Kinyu: Monthly Review of Agriculture, Forestry and Fishery Finance* [*Norin Kinyu*] 28 (6), June: 10–22 (in Japanese).

Okada, Takuya (1983), *Put Wheels to the Central Pillar of a House: Management Thought Based on my Experiences* [*Daikoku-Bashira ni Kuruma wo Tsukeyo, Watashi no Taiken-teki Keiei-ron*], Tokyo: Toyo Keizai Shinpo (in Japanese).

Okamoto, Yasuo ed. (1973), *Corporate Behaviours in the Industry of Household Electric Appliances in Japan: Focusing on the Case of Matsushita Electric Industry* [*Matsushita Denki no Zittai Bunseki*], Not for Sale (in Japanese).

Okumura, Hiroshi (1978), *The Six Major Corporate Groups in Japan* [*Nihon no 6-dai Kigyo Shudan*], Tokyo: Diamond (in Japanese).

—— (1990), 'The "rationality" of *keiretsu* cannot be justified', *Weekly Economist* [*Ekono-misuto*], 68 (29) (July 10): 78–89 (in Japanese).

—— (2000), *Corporate Capitalism in Japan*, NY: St. Martin's Press. (Translated by Douglas Anthony and Naomi Brown).

Okumura, Makiko (1979), 'Dressmaking and clothing habits: focusing on women's clothing', Kyoto Prefectural University, *Annals of the Research Centre of Living Culture* [*Seikatsu Bunka Centre Nenpo*], 4: 33–58 (in Japanese).

Okuzumi, Masamichi (1958), 'Looking back on self-service stores in 1958', *Self Service* [*Self Service*] 1 (6), December: 36–38 (in Japanese).

—— (1960), 'The development and trends in self-service stores in 1960', *Self Service* [*Self Service*] 3 (11/12), December: 38–43 (in Japanese).

—— (1962), 'Looking back on the progress of self-service stores in 1961', *Self Service* [*Self Service*] 5 (1), January: 26–28 (in Japanese).

Onishi, Katsuaki (1994), *Research in the Industry of Semiconductors in Japan: the USA reversing Japanese Advantages* [*Handohtai Sangyo-ron*], Tokyo: Moriyama-shoten (in Japanese).

Oogushi, Matsuji (1924), 'Uniformity of prices and improvement of sales methods', *Morinaga Monthly* [*Morinaga Geppo*] 9, 15th February: 5 (in Japanese).

—— (1929) 'From manufacturing to selling, Part 2', *Studies on Selling* 17, August: 2–44 (in Japanese).

Ootake, Masayoshi (2001), 'The history of changes in the hairstyle in modern Japan', Shiseido Corporate Museum, *Research Journal Eudermine* [*Eudermine*], 11: 158–76 (in Japanese).

Ooyama, Esa (1959), *A Critical Bibliography of Hajime Hoshi: A Citizen of the World and a Hard Worker with Sturdy Faith* [*Hoshi Hajime Hyo-den*], Tokyo: Kyowa-shobo (in Japanese).

Ooyama, Masato (2001), *The Story of An-pan, Kimura-ya General Headquarters in Ginza* [*Ginza Kimuraya An-pan Monogatari*], Tokyo: Heibon-sha Shinsho (in Japanese).

Osaka Asahi Newspaper (1883), 'Bisen-ko' (advertisement by Kimura Otsuka-sha), *Osaka Asahi Newspaper* [*Osaka Asahi Shimbun*], 12th July, Kikuzo II Database (in Japanese).

—— (1885), 'Vogue of the bundled hairstyles for women', *Osaka Asahi Newspaper* [*Osaka Asahi Shimbun*], 10th September, Kikuzo II Database (in Japanese).

—— (1921), 'The plan of electrification of homes by Osaka Electric Light Co.', *Osaka Asahi Newspaper* [*Osaka Asahi Shimbun*], 13th August, Kobe University Library, Digital Archive (in Japanese).

—— (1932a), 'The Association of Department Stores decided on a self-control policy, to relax pressure on retail merchants, in return for the Department Store Law', *Osaka Asahi Newspaper* [*Osaka Asahi Shimbun*], 5th August, Kobe University Library Digital Archive (in Japanese).

—— (1932b), 'Will enactment of the Department Store Law delayed? There are both arguments for and against in the Ministry of Commerce and Industry', *Osaka Asahi Newspaper* [*Osaka Asahi Shimbun*], 6th August, Kobe University Library Digital Archive (in Japanese).

—— (1930), 'Department stores or chain stores?' *Osaka Asahi Newspaper* [*Osaka Asahi Shimbun*], 2nd March, Kobe University Library Digital Archive (in Japanese).

—— (1933a), 'The National Commercial Association of Department Stores will start soon at last', *Osaka Asahi Newspaper* [*Osaka Asahi Shimbun*], 31th March, Kobe University Library Digital Archive (in Japanese).

—— (1933b), 'Are there any measures to control the surplus of retailers?', *Osaka Asahi Newspaper* [*Osaka Asahi Shimbun*], 27th November, Kobe University Library, Digital Archive (in Japanese).

Osaka City (1937), *Investigation of Commerce* [*Shogo Chosa-sho*], Osaka: Osaka Municipal Office (in Japanese).

Osaka Jiji News (1922), 'Implementation of urban planning and improvement of citizens' life', *Osaka Jiji News* [*Osaka Jiji Shimpo*], 13th February, Kobe University Library, Digital Archive (in Japanese).

—— (1930), 'The disputes on improvement of retailers: what conclusion they will reach surrounding the proposal by the Council of Commerce and Industry, No. 1', *Osaka Jiji News* [*Osaka Jiji Shimpo*], 8th February, Kobe University Library, Digital Archive (in Japanese).

—— (1934), 'The voluntary chain system: supporting the rescue and development of 130,000 retailers', *Osaka Jiji News* [*Osaka Jiji Shimpo*], 16th May, Kobe University Library, Digital Archive (in Japanese).

Osaka Mainichi Newspaper (1929), 'The age of ordeal for retailers', *Osaka Mainichi Newspaper* [*Osaka Mainichi Shimbun*], 21 to 28 July, a series of articles by Taishiro Hirai, Kobe University Library, Digital Archive (in Japanese).

Osaki, Takanori (2008), *Mobile Phones in Japan and International Markets: Marketing Strategy in the Digital Age* [*Nihon no Keitai Denwa Tanmatsu to Kokusai Shijo: Digital Zidai no Marketing Senryaku*], Tokyo: Sosei-sha (in Japanese).

Otani, Koichi et al. (1998), 'Development of suburban houses by Hankyu Electric Railway before the Second World War, No. 2', *Summaries of Technical Papers of Annual Meeting, Architectural Institute of Japan* [*Nihon Kenchiku Gakkai Taikai Gakujutsu Koen Kogai-shu*], F. September: 165–6 (in Japanese).

Otsuka, Koichi (1934), 'The sales organisation of Shiseido and the features of Shiseido Chain Stores', in RSSA 1934: 101–12 (in Japanese).

—— (1926), 'The potency of chain stores dominant all over the world', *The Industrial World in Japan* [*Jitsugyo no Nihon*], 29 (13), 1st December: 64–73 (in Japanese).

Ouchi, Shujiro (2001), 'Marketing activities by Sanyo Electric in the early period of spread of the electric washing machine', in Research Group of Marketing at Kyoto University (ed.), *Development and Innovations in Mass Marketing* [*Mass Marketing no Hatten, Kakushin*], Tokyo: Dobunkan: 3–29 (in Japanese).

—— (2002), 'Development of marketing competition in the early period of spread of the electric washing machine', Kyoto University, *Kyoto Economic Review* [*Keizai Ronso*], 169 (3), March: 74–89.

Ozaki, Kunihiro (1989), 'Channel behaviours and corporate strategy by Matsushita before the Second World War', Shiga University, *Hikone Review* [*Hikone Ronso*], 257, June: 123–52 (in Japanese).

Ozaki, Kunihiro (1998), *Partnerships in Distribution* [*Ryutsu Partnership-ron*], Tokyo: Chuo Keizai-sha (in Japanese).

Ozawa, Masako (1985), *The Era of the "New Class-oriented Consumption": A New Concept to Grasp the Trend in Consumer Markets* [*Shin "Kaiso Shohi" no Zidai*], Tokyo: Nihon Keizai Shimbun-sha (in Japanese).

PASCO, Corporate Planning Divison (2009), *PASCO Corporate Profile*, PDF Version, at the web site: http://www.pasconet.co.jp/english/index.html (August 2009) (in English).

Peterson, Mark (2006), 'Focusing on the future of macromarketing', *Journal of Macromarketing* 26 (2), December: 245–49.

PRI: Pola Research Institute of Beauty and Culture (1986), *The History of Modern Makeup: 80 Year of Adornment* [*Modern Kesho-shi, Yosooi no 80-nen*], Tokyo: Pola Research Institute of Beauty and Culture (in Japanese).

Ponytail (ed.) (1994), *A Cryptogram Book for Pocket-Bells* [*Poke-Belu Ango Book*], Tokyo: Futaba-sha (in Japanese).

Porter, Glenn and Livesay, Harold C. (1971) *Merchants and Manufacturers: Studies in the Changing Structure of Nineteenth-Century Marketing*, Baltimore, Maryland and London: The Johns Hopkins Press.

Pyle, Kenneth B. (1969), *The New Generation in Meiji Japan: Problems of Cultural Identity 1885–1895*, California: Stanford University Press.

Retail Shop World (1929a), 'A general survey on chain stores in Japan: their organizations and conditions', *The Retail Shop World* [*Shooten-kai*], 9 (2), February: 59–75 (in Japanese).

—— (1929b), 'A series of biographies of successful chain stores in Japan', *The Retail Shop World* [*Shooten-kai*], 9 (3), March: 66–105 (in Japanese).

—— (1935), 'Research pages on chain stores', *The Retail Shop World* [*Shooten-kai*], 15 (8), August: 10–15 (in Japanese).

RGBA: Research Group of Business Administration (1957), 'The pioneer of the chain organisation: personality and works of Noboru Matsumoto' in *Theory and Practice of Chain Stores* [*Chain Store no Riron to Jissen*], Tokyo: Research Group of Business Administration: 217–321 (in Japanese).

RITI: Research Institute of Trade and Industry (ed.) (1990), *The Final Report of the Structural Impediments Initiative* [*Nichi-Bei Kozo Shoheki Kyogi Saishu Hokoku*], Tokyo: Research Institute of Trade and Industry (both in Japanese and English).

Research Laboratory on Food Science, Showa Women's University (ed.) (1971), *Kindai Nihon Shokumotsu-shi* [*The History of Food in Modern Japan*], Tokyo: Research Institute of Modern Culture, Showa Women's University (in Japanese).

RSSA: Research Society of Sales and Advertising, Rikkyo University (ed.) (1934), *A Measure to Revive Petty Retailers: Practical Research Focusing on Voluntary Chains* [*Kouri Kosei-saku: Voluntary Chain chushin no Jissho-teki Kenkyu*], Tokyo: Toyo Keizai Shimpo-sha (in Japanese).

Robun, Kanagaki ([1871] 1995) *Ushimise Zatsudan Agura Nabe* [*Idle Talks at a Beef Restaurant, Sitting Cross-legged Before a Pan Cooking Beef*], 1st Volume, Tokyo: Seinodo. (Reprint, Tokyo: The Museum of Modern Japanese Literature) (in Japanese).

Said, Edward W. (1979), *Orientalism*, New York: Vintage Books.

Saison Corporation (ed.) (1992), *Comprehensive Life Industry: A View for an Approach to Consumer Society* [*Seikatsu Sogo Sangyo-ron, Shohi Shakai e no Sekkin Shikaku*] Tokyo: Libro Port (in Japanese).

Saito, Hisao and Hashimoto, Tetsuro (1997), 'A centennial review of refrigerator, rice cooker and micro wave oven', *Journal of Japan Society of Mechanical Engineering* [*Nihon Kikai Gakkai-shi*], 100 (939), February: 39–44 (in Japanese).

Saito, Keisuke (1996), 'Visions of modern Japanese women through the images of Shiseido cosmetics 1872–1995', Shiseido Corporate Museum, *Research Journal Eudermine* [*Eudermine*], 1: 18–23 (in Japanese).

Sakaguchi, Hiroshi (1935), *Modernology of Mazda Lamp in a Red Package Box*, [*Akahako Matsuda Kogen-gaku*] Tokyo Electric Co., Ltd., Not for Sale (in Japanese).

Sakai, Haruo (1990), 'Instant noodles', in Japan Food Journal Co., Ltd. (ed.), *History of the Food Industry in Showa Era* [*Showa no Shokuhin Sangyo-shi*] Tokyo: Japan Food Journal Co., Ltd.: 240–3 (in Japanese).

Sakai, Yoneo (1949), *Letters from America* [*America Dayori*], Tokyo: Meikyoku-do Shuppan-bu (in Japanese).

Sakurai, Hide and Adachi, Isao (1973), *History of Provisions in Japan* [*Nihon Shokumotsu-shi*], Vol. 1, Tokyo: Yuzan-kaku (in Japanese).

Sankei Newspaper (2006), '*Keiretsu* stores of Matsushita attracting the middle-aged and the elderly customers, revival of popularity of electrical shops in town', *Sankei Newspaper*, 21st August (in Japanese).

—— (2007), 'The philosophical book by Nakauchi, the founder of Daiei, is gradually becoming popular, reprinted on the second anniversary of his death, "for the sake of consumers" evoking favourable responses', *Sankei Newspaper*, 16th December (in Japanese).

Sasaki, Satoshi (1995), 'Innovations in distribution in the cosmetics and soap industries: the cases of Shiseido and Kao', in Yui, Tsunehiko and Hashimoto, Juro (eds)., *Business History of Innovations: Innovative Behaviours by Japanese Firms before and after the Second World War* [*Kakushin no Keiei-shi, Senzen Sengo ni okeru Nihon Kigyo no Kakushin Kodo*], Tokyo: Yuhikaku: 1115–34 (in Japanese).

—— (2007), *Business History of the Japanese-type Distribution* [*Nihon-teki Rutsu no Keiei-shi*], Tokyo: Yuhikaku (in Japanese).

—— (2009), *Cosmetics and Hygiene that Changed Everyday Life, The Series of Japanese Business History of Passionate People, No. 3* [*Kurashi wo Kaeta Biyo to Eisei, Series Jonetsu no Nihon Keiei-shi 3*], Tokyo: Fuyo-shobo Publishing (in Japanese).

Sato, Barbara Hamill (1991), 'The emergence of modern girls and their relation to Intellectuals', *Review of History* [*Rekishi Hyoron*], 491, March: 18–26 (in Japanese).

—— (2003), *The New Japanese Women: Modernity, Media, and Women in Interwar Japan*, Durham and London: Duke University Press.

—— (2005), 'Commodifying and engendering morality: self-cultivation and the construction of the "ideal women" in 1920s women's magazines', in Molony, Barbara and Uno, Kathleen (eds)., *Gendering Modern Japanese History*, Cambridge, Massachusetts and London: Harvard University Asia Center: 99–130. (The article was translated into Japanese with a slight modification by Ueda, Miwa, in Sato 2007: 74–106.)

—— (ed.) (2007), *The Birth of Everyday Life: Transformation of Culture in Interwar Japan* [*Nichijo Seikatsu no Tanjo, Senkan-ki Nihon no Bunka Henyo*], Tokyo: Kashiwa-shobo (in Japanese).

Sato, Hajime (1971), *Industrial Revolution of Distribution: Lessons from the 100-year History of Modern Commerce* [*Ryutsu Sangyo Kakumei, Kindai Shogyo 100-nen ni Manabu*] Tokyo: Yuhikaku (in Japanese).

—— (1974), *The Distribution Structure in Japan* [*Nihon no Ryutsu Kiko*], Tokyo: Yuhikaku (in Japanese).

Seidensticker, Edward (1991), *Low City, High City: Tokyo from Edo to the Earthquake*, Cambridge, Massachusetts: Harvard University Press.

Sekishima, Hisao ([1956] 1982), 'Have confidence as a manager: the housewife is the first important job', *Public Opinions for Women* [*Fujin Koron*]. Reprint, in Ueno 1982a: 97–109 (in Japanese).

Seven & i Holdings Co., Ltd. (2011a), *Annual Report 2011: Focused Strength and Future Potential*, PDF Version (in English).

—— (2011b), 'On change in the scheme of delivery service by Seven Meal', News Release, PDF Version, 26th October (in Japanese)

7-Eleven Japan (1991), *7-Eleven Japan: Endless Innovation* [*7-Eleven Japan, Owarinaki Innovation*], Tokyo: 7-Eleven Japan Corporation (in Japanese). Not for Sale.

—— (1999), 'On the establishment of a joint corporation, Seven Meal Service', News Release, PDF Version, 7th August (in Japanese).

Shibahara, Takuji (1977), *Sekai-shi no nakano Meiji Ishin* [*The Meiji Restoration in the Context of the World History*], Tokyo: Iwanami-shoten (in Japanese).

Shibazaki, Kimio (1990), 'The form of consumption of foods and food safety', in Japan Food Journal (ed.), *The History of the Food Industry in the Showa Period* [*Showa no Shokuhin Sangyo-shi*] Tokyo: Japan Food Journal Co., Ltd.: 50–60 (in Japanese).

Shigekane, Yoshiko (1984), *A Rocking Chair for a Housewife*, Tokyo: Kodan-sha (in Japanese).

Shima, Hisayo (1975), 'How to sell electric products in the age of "personalised appliances"', *Central Public Opinions* [*Chuo Koron*], Special Issues on Business, Summer: 104–119 (in Japanese).

Shima, Masato (2007), 'Side businesses of electric railway companies before the Second World War', *The Journal of the Historical Society of Japan* [*Shigaku Zassi*], 116 (1): 112 (in Japanese).

Shimizu, Koshichiro (1935), 'My memory of Mazda Lamp in a Red Package Box', in Sakaguchi, Hiroshi, *Modernology of Mazda Lamp in a Red Package Box* [*Aka-Hako Matsuda Kogen-gaku*], Tokyo Electric Co., Ltd., Not for Sale: 1–6 (in Japanese).

Shimizu, Masami (1920), 'Retail shops in the USA and Japan, No.1', *The Newspaper of Current Events* [*Jiji Shimpo*], 3rd July, Kobe University Library Digital Archive (in Japanese).

—— (1923a), 'How to accept payments at stores, a series of articles of observations on world businesses, No. 9', *The Newspaper of Current Events* [*Jiji Shimpo*], 10th–16th January, Kobe University Library Digital Archive (in Japanese).

—— (1923b), 'Department stores in London, No. 2, a series of articles of observations on world businesses, No. 11', *The Newspaper of Current Events* [*Jiji Shimpo*], 21st December, Kobe University Library Digital Archive (in Japanese).

—— (1924a), 'Chain stores Nos. 1–6, a series of articles of observations on world businesses, Nos. 18–23', *The Newspaper of Current Events* [*Jiji Shimpo*], 10th–16th January, Kobe University Library Digital Archive (in Japanese).

—— (1924b), 'Shops without sales clerks Nos. 1–3, a series of articles of observations on world businesses, Nos. 34–36', *The Newspaper of Current Events* [*Jiji Shimpo*], 2nd–4th February, Kobe University Library Digital Archive (in Japanese).

—— (1928), 'The management method of chain stores that can be applied to Japan', *The World of Retail Shops* [*Shoten-kai*], 8 (7), July: 11–16 (in Japanese).

Shimokawa, Koshi (ed.) (1997), *The Chronological Table of the History of Households in the Showa and the Heisei Eras: 1926–1995* [*Showa, Heisei Katei-shi Nenpyo, 1926–1995*], Tokyo: Kawade Shuppan-sha (in Japanese).

Shimotani, Masahiro (1993), *Keiretsu and Corporate Groups in Japan: History and Theory* [*Nihon no Keiretsu to Kigyo Group, Sono Rekishi to Riron*], Tokyo: Yuhikaku (in Japanese).

—— (1994), 'Forming distribution *keiretsu* and the Matsushita Electric Industry Group', Kyoto University, *Kyoto Economic Review* [*Keizai Ronso*], 153 (1/2), June: 1–22 (in Japanese).

Shin, Ha-Kyoung (2003), 'Discourse of the "modern girl"', University of Tsukuba, *Tsukuba Studies in Literature* [*Bungaku Kenkyu Ronshu*], 21: 96–101 (in Japanese).

Shinobu, Seizaburo (1954), *The History of Taisho Democracy, Vol. 1* [*Taisho Democracy-shi, I*], Tokyo: Nihon Hyoron-sha.

—— (1958), *The History of Taisho Democracy, Vol. 2* [*Taisho Democracy-shi, II*], Tokyo: Nihon Hyoron-sha.

—— (1959), *The History of Taisho Democracy, Vol. 3* [*Taisho Democracy-shi, III*], Tokyo: Nihon Hyoron-sha.

Shintaku, Junjiro, Tanaka, Tatsuro and Yanagawa, Noriyuki (2003), *Economic Analysis of the Industry of Video Game Consoles: The Structure and Strategies for Development of the Industry of Contents for Video Game Consoles* [*Game-ki Sangyo no Keizai Bunseki, Contents Sangyo Hatten no Kozo to Senryaku*], Tokyo: Toyo Keizai Shimpo-sha (in Japanese).

Shirahige, Takeshi (1974), *Problems of Distribution in Modern Japan* [*Gendai Nihon no Ryutsu Mondai*], Tokyo: Hakuto-shobo (in Japanese).

Shirokiya Co., Ltd. (1957), *The 300-Year History of Shirokiya* [*Shirokiya 300-nen-shi*], Tokyo: Shirokiya, Co., Ltd., Not for Sale (in Japanese).

Shiseido Co., Ltd. (1972), *The 100-Year History of Shiseido* [*Shiseido 100-nen-shi*], Tokyo: Shiseido Co., Ltd., Not for Sale (in Japanese).

——— Department of Corporate Culture (ed.) (1993), *What has been Created and What should be Passed on: The 120-Year History of Corporate Culture in Shiseido* [*Tsukutte Kita Mono, Tsutaete Yuku Mono*], Tokyo: Shiseido Co., Ltd., Not for Sale (in Japanese).

Silberman, Charles E. (1962a), 'The revolution of retailing: the distribution upheaval I', *Fortune*, April: 99–102, 254, 256, 258, 260 and 265.

——— (1962b), 'The discounters choose their weapons: the distribution upheaval II', *Fortune*, May: 118–120, 186 and 188.

SMEA: Small and Medium Enterprise Agency (1966), *White Paper of Small and Medium Enterprises, 41st Year of Showa* [*Chusho Kigyo Hakusho, Showa 41-nen*], METI website: www.meti.go.jp/hakusho/chusyo/S41/01-03-02.html

——— Division of Commerce (1961), 'The actual state of supermarkets', *Monthly Small and Medium Enterprises* [*Gekkan Chusho Kigyo*] 13 (2), February: 27–31 (in Japanese).

Soma, Aizo (1934), 'Exploring the measure to revive petty retailers means exploring the countermeasure against the department stores', in RSSA 1934: 135–141 (in Japanese).

Son, Il Sun (1992), 'Structural changes in the distribution channels of home appliances during Japan's High Economic Growth Period: focusing on the vertical integration of wholesale distribution networks by home appliance manufacturers', Tokyo University, *The Journal of Economic Study* [*Keizai-gaku Kenkyu*], 35, December: 22–34 (in Japanese).

Sony Corporation (1996), *The Origin* [*Genryu*], Tokyo: Sony Corporation, Not for Sale (in Japanese).

Sony Corporate Communications (1998), *An Autobiography of Sony* [Sony Jijoden], Tokyo: WAC Co., Ltd. (in Japanese).

SB: Statistics Bureau, Management and Coordination Agency (ed.) (1987), *Historical Statistics of Japan* [*Nihon Choki Tokei Soran*], Vol. 1, Tokyo: Japan Statistical Association (in both Japanese and English).

——— (1988a), *Historical Statistics of Japan* [*Nihon Choki Tokei Soran*], *Vol. 4*, Tokyo: Japan Statistical Association (in both Japanese and English).

——— (1988b), *Historical Statistics of Japan* [*Nihon Choki Tokei Soran*], *Vol. 5*, Tokyo: Japan Statistical Association (in both Japanese and English).

Sparks, Lee (1995), 'Reciprocal retail internationalisation: the Southland Corporation, Ito-Yokado and 7-Eleven Convenience Stores', *The Service Industries Journal*, 15 (4): 57–96.

STA: Science and Technology Agency (1965), *White Paper of Science and Technology* [*Kagaku Gijutsu Hakusho*], the 40th Year of Showa, on the website of the Ministry of Culture and Science: http://www.mext.go.jp/b_menu/hakusho/html/hpaa196501/hpaa196501_2_033.html (in Japanese).

—— (1967), *White Paper of Science and Technology* [*Kagaku Gijutsu Hakusho*], the 42nd Year of Showa, on the website of the Ministry of Culture and Science: http://www.mext.go.jp/b_menu/hakusho/html/hpaa196701/hpaa196701_2_083.html (in Japanese).

Stores (2008), '2008 global power of retailing', *Stores*, January, section 2. (http://www.nxtbook.com/nxtbooks/nrfe/stores-globalretail08/) (September 2008).

Sugihara, Kaoru (1990), 'Journals focusing on commerce', in Sugihara, Shiro (ed.), *The Origins of Economic Journals in Japan* [*Nihon Keizai Zasshi no Genryu*], Tokyo: Yuhikaku: 221–51 (in Japanese).

Sugioka, Sekio (1977), 'Impacts by the convenience stores', National Finance Corporation, *Monthly Research Bulletin* [*Chosa Geppo*], 191, March: 16–42 (in Japanese).

Suzuki, Hideo (2000), 'The exhibition houses (*kanko-ba*) and culture in the Meiji period, No. 1', *Journal of Shizuoka Sangyo University* [*Shizuoka Sangyo Daigaku Ronshu*], 6 (2), December: 231–41 (in Japanese).

—— (2001), 'The exhibition houses (*kanko-ba*) and culture in the Meiji period, No. 2', *Journal of Shizuoka Sangyo University* [*Shizuoka Sangyo Daigaku Ronshu*], 7 (2), October: 1–20 (in Japanese).

—— (2002), *Research in the Exhibition Houses (Kanko-ba): Their Relationship with Culture in the Meiji Period* [*Kanko-ba no Kenkyu: Meiji Bunka tono Kakawari*], Tokyo: Soei-sha (in Japanese).

Suzuki, Reiji (1999), 'Development of the school lunch system and its present state', *The Monthly Journal of MONBUSHO* [*Monbu Jiho*], 1354, October: 46–53 (in Japanese).

Suzuki, Shigefumi (2004), *"51C": The Post-War Period and the Present Time of a Space where a Japanese Family Lives* [*"51C": Kazoku o Ireru Hako no Sengo to Genzai*], Tokyo: Heibon-sha (in Japanese).

Suzuki, Shinya (1978), *Challenges by the Sharp ATOM Force: An Amateur Group that Caused a Revolution in Sales* [*Sharp ATOM-tai wa Chosen-Suru, Hanbai ni Kakumei wo Okoshita Shiroto Shudan*], Tokyo: The Editing Project of Diamond Sales (in Japanese).

Suzuki, Yasuaki (1980), *The Problems of Retailers in the Early Showa Period* [*Showa Shoki no Koirisho Mondai*], Tokyo: Nihon Keizai Shimbun-sha (in Japanese).

—— (1991) 'Early development of *Super* in Japan', Aoyama University, *Aoyama Journal of Business* [*Aoyama Keiei Ronshu*], 26 (2), September: 313–323 (in Japanese).

——, Sekine, Takashi and Yahagi, Toshiyuki (1997), *Materials for the Analysis of Distribution and Commerce, 2nd edn* [*Material Ryutsu to Shogyo, Dai 2-han*], Tokyo: Yuhikaku (in Japanese).

Takamura, Naosuke (1992), T*he Rapid Increase of Firms: Establishment of Japanese Capitalism* [*Kigyo-bokko: Nihon Shihonsyugi no Keisei*], Kyoto: Minerva-shobo (in Japanese).

Tajima, Natsuko (1999), 'The display windows', in Yamamoto, Taketoshi and Nishizawa, Tamotsu (eds.), *The Cultural History of Department Stores: The Revolution in Consumption in Japan* [*Hyakkaten no Bunka-shi, Nihon no shohi Kakumei*], Kyoto: Sekai Shiso-sha, pp. 253–72 (in Japanese).

Tajima, Yoshihiro (1962), *The Revolution of Distribution in Japan* [*Nihon no Ryutsu Kakumei*], Tokyo: Nihon Noritsu Kyokai, Management Shinsho (in Japanese).

Takahashi, Masaki (2001), 'The emergence of "salaried men as a social representation": how can the union movements by the waged people before the Second World War be evaluated?' *The Journal of Ohara Institute for Social Research* [*Ohara Shakai Mondai Kenkyusyo Zassi*], 511, June: 16–30 (in Japanese).

Takahashi, Yasuo (1999), *Women Who Had Hair Cut Short: An Urban-scape of Modern Girls* [*Danpatsu suru On'na-tachi: Modern Girl no Fukei*], Tokyo: Kyoiku Publishing (in Japanese).

Takahashi, Yoshio (1933), *Broom Marks* [*Hoki no Ato*], No. 1, Tokyo: Shuho-do (in Japanese).

Takaoka, Mika (1997), 'Department store business in Japan between 1945 and 1955: formation of the Japanese style trade practices', Business History Society in Japan, *Japan Business History Review* [*Keieishigaku*], 32 (1), April: 1–35 (in Japanese).

—— (1999), 'Resource supplement mechanism of the convenience store business in Japan: selection of the franchise system', Business History Society in Japan, *Japan Business History Review* [*Keieishigaku*], 34 (2), September: 44–73 (in Japanese).

Takase, Mizue (1997), 'The 100-year history of Eudermine', Shiseido Corporate Museum, *Research Journal Eudermine* [*Eudermine*], 3: 37–51 (in Japanese).

Takashima, Tadashi (1976), 'Computers', in Kumagai, Hisao (ed.), *Industrial Organisations in Japan, Vol. 3* [*Nihon no Sangyo Soshiki III*], Tokyo: Chuo Koron-sha: 1–73 (in Japanese).

Takashimaya Co., Ltd. (1941), *The 100-Year History of Takashimaya* [*Takashimaya 100-nen-shi*], Osaka: Takashimaya Co., Ltd., Not for Sale (in Japanese).

—— (1968), *The 135 Year History of Takashimaya* [*Takashimaya 135-nen-shi*], Osaka: Takashimaya Co., Ltd., Not for Sale (in Japanese).

Takayanagi, Mika (1994), *The Story of Window Display* [*Show Window Monogatari*], Tokyo: Keiso-shobo (in Japanese).

Takebayashi, Yukichi (1973), 'Some problems in convenience stores', Osaka University of Economics, *Business Economy* [*Keiei Keizai*], 9, March: 28–41 (in Japanese).

Takemura, Manabu (1983), 'The resale price maintenance case of electronic toys', Japan Fair Trade Commission, *Fair Trade*, 396, October: 50–54 (in Japanese).

Takeuchi, Hiroshi (1966), *Series on Modern Industries: The Industry of Electric Appliances* [*Denki Kikai Kogyo*], Tokyo: Toyo Keizai Shimpo-sha (in Japanese).

Takeuchi, Yasukazu and Miyamoto, Mataji (eds.) (1979), *A Genealogy of Business Philosophy: An International Comparative Study* [*Keiei Rinen no Keifu: Sono Kokusai Hikaku*], Kyoto: Toyo Bunka-sha (in Japanese).

Tamai, Tetsuo (1986), *Edo: Understanding the Lost Space* [*Edo: Ushinawareta Toshi Kukan o Yomu*], Tokyo: Heibon-sha (in Japanese).

Tamaki, Akira (1967), 'The confectionery industry', in Nakajima, Tsuneo (ed.), *Development of Modern Industry in Japan, No. 18, The Food Industry* [*Gendai Nihon Sangyo Hattatsu-shi 18, Shokuhin*], Tokyo: Koshun-sha: 329–94 (in Japanese).

Tamaoki, Masami (1957), 'Analysis of actual conditions on the rebuilding process of *Konzern* [concern] during the postwar', in Ito, Taikichi (ed.), *Policies of Manufacturing Industry in Postwar Japan* [*Sengo Nihon no Kogyo Seisaku*], Tokyo: Nihon Hyoron-sha: 176–218 (in Japanese).

Tanabe, Mayumi (2010), 'Clothing in the modern age', in Masuda, Yoshiko (ed.), *The History of Clothing in Japan*, Tokyo: Yoshikawa Kobun-kan: 285–358 (in Japanese).

Tanaka, Seiji (1986), 'Establishment and development of the exhibition houses (kanko-ba)', The Society for Studies in Market History, *Studies in Market History* [*Shijo-shi Kenkyu*], 3, October: 17–33 (in Japanese).

Tanaka, Yoko (2004), 'Background to promoting education in dressmaking of Western-style clothing in sewing lessons in primary schools', *Journal of the Home Education Society of Japan* [*Nihon Katei Kyoiku Gakkai-shi*], 47 (1): 38–47 (in Japanese).

Taniguchi, Kichihiko (1933), 'Voluntary chains as a measure for rescuing petty retailers', Kyoto University, *Kyoto Economic Review* [*Keizai Ronso*], 37 (6), December: 56–74 (in Japanese).

—— (1936), 'Enactment of the Department Store Law', Kyoto University, *Kyoto Economic Review* [*Keizai Ronso*], 43 (6), December: 54–81 (in Japanese).

—— (1938), 'Enactment of the Department Store Law', in Nakanishi, Torao (ed.), *Research in the Law of Department Stores* [*Hyakkaten-Ho ni kansuru Kenkyu*], Tokyo: Dobunkan: 49–82 (in Japanese).

Tanimitsu, Taro (1994), *The Historical Tracks of the Industry of ICs* [*Handotai Sangyo no Kiseki*], Tokyo: Nikkan Kogyo Shimbun (in Japanese).

Taniwaki, Yasuhiko (2008), *Japanese Mobile Phones as the Strangest in the World* [*Sekai-ichi Fushigi na Nippon no Kehtai*], Tokyo: Impress R&D (in Japanese).

Tanouchi, Koichi and Takaoka, Sueaki (1975), *Convenience Stores: The New Retailers Challenging Super* [*Convenience Store, Super ni idomu Atarashii Kouri*], Tokyo: Nihon Keizai Newspaper Co. (in Japanese).

Tateishi, Yasunori (2008), *Grace of Yamada Denki* [*Yamada Denki no Hinkaku*], Tokyo: Kodan-sha (in Japanese).

Tateno, Kensei (1986), 'Emergence of *super* in Japan', Nagasaki Prefectural University of Economics, *Journal of Liberal Arts and Economics* [*Nagasaki Kenristu Kokusai Keizai Daigaku Ronshu*], 19 (3), February: 35–79 (in Japanese).

—— (1991), 'The concept of *super* and the process of its development', Nagasaki Prefectural University of Economics, *Journal of Liberal Arts and Economics* [*Nagasaki Kenristu Kokusai Keizai Daigaku Ronshu*], 25 (1), September: 25–54 (in Japanese).

—— (1994), *The Chronological Table of Development of Super in Japan* [*Nihon Super Hattatsu-shi Nenpyo*], Tokyo: Sosei-sha (in Japanese).

Tatsuki, Mariko (1991), 'The revolution of distribution and the formation of Seibu Distribution Group', in Yui, Tsunehiko (ed.), *The History of Saison, Vol. 1* [*Saison no Rekishi, Jo-kan*] Tokyo: Libro Port: 227–458 (in Japanese).

Teraoka, Hiroshi (2004), 'The principles to organise small- and medium-sized enterprises and union activities: consideration of the genealogy in Japan, No.1', Chukyo University, *Journal of the Faculty of Management* [*Chukyo Keiei Kenkyu*], 14 (1), September: 155–77 (in Japanese).

Terauchi, Shin and Haneda, Kazuhiro (1993), 'Research in development of the adjacent areas by electric railway companies: No. 1, the conditions of electric supply by Kei-Hanshin Electric Railway Co. before the Second World War', *Summaries of Technical Papers of Annual Meeting, Architectural Institute of Japan* [*Nihon Kenchiku Gakkai Taikai Gakujutsu Koen Kogai-shu*], F. July: 817–20 (in Japanese).

Time (1963), 'Everybody loves a bargain' (cover story), *Time*, 6th July: 45–49.

TISI: Trade and Industry Statistics Association (ed.) (1983), T*he Census of Commerce after the War* [*Sengo no Shogyo Tokei Hyo*], Vol. 1, *Statistics Classified to the Industries*, Tokyo: TISI (in Japanese).

Tobu Department Store Co., Ltd. (1993), *Progress in 30 Years of Tobu Department Store: A Good Store* [*Tobu Department Store 30-nen no Ayumi, Good Depart*], Tokyo: Tobu Department Store, Not for Sale (in Japanese).

Toffler, Alvin ([1980] 1981), *The Third Wave*: New York: Bantam Books. (Japanese translation by T. Tokuoka from 1980 edition published by Morrow & Co., Tokyo: Chuo Koron-sha, 1982).

Toko Electric Co., Ltd. (1984), *The History of Toko Electric Company* [*Toko Denki Shashi*], Tokyo: Toko Electric Co., Ltd. Not for Sale (in Japanese).

Tokyo Asahi Newspaper (1931), 'From free competition to control over firms: explanations of the new law concerning commerce and industry', *Tokyo Asahi Newspaper* [*Tokyo Asahi Shimbun*], 5th to 8th April, Kobe University Library Digital Archive (in Japanese).

—— (1932), 'Enactment of the Department Store Law', *Tokyo Asahi Newspaper* [*Tokyo Asahi Shimbun*], 3rd August, Kobe University Library Digital Archive (in Japanese).

Tokyo City (1933), *Investigation of Commerce* [*Shogyo Chosa-sho*], Tokyo: Tokyo Municipal Office (in Japanese).

Tokyo Electric Co., Ltd. (1940), *The 50 Year History of Tokyo Electric Co., Ltd.* [*Tokyo Denki Kabushiki Kaisha 50-nen-shi*], Tokyo: Tokyo Electric Co., Ltd. Not for Sale (in Japanese).

Tokyo Newspaper (2010), '65 years after the War: thinking of days long past with miserable memories of standing starvation', *Tokyo Newspaper*, 20th March (in Japanese).

Tokyo Shibaura Electric Co., Ltd. (1963), *The 85 Year History of Tokyo Shibaura Electric Co., Ltd.* [*Tokyo Shibaura Denki Kabushiki Kaisha 85-nen-shi*], Tokyo: Tokyo Shibaura Electric Co., Ltd., Not for Sale (in Japanese).

—— (1977), *The 100-Year History of Toshiba* [*Toshiba 100-nen-shi*], Tokyo: Tokyo Shibaura Electric Co., Ltd., Not for Sale (in Japanese).

Tomita, Hidenori (1997), 'The age of intimate strangers: "intimate unknown others" combined by *poke-bell* and *kehtai*', in Tomita, Hidenori et al., *Poke-Bell-and-Kehtai-ism* [*Pokebelu Kehtai shugi*], Tokushima: Just System: 14–30 (in Japanese).

Tsuganesawa, Toshihiro (1999), 'Events sponsored by department stores and urban culture', in Yamamoto, Taketoshi and Nishizawa, Tamotsu (eds)., *The Cultural History of Department Stores: The Revolution in Consumption in Japan* [*Hyakkaten no Bunka-shi, Nihon no shohi Kakumei*], Kyoto: Sekai Shiso-sha: 130–54 (in Japanese).

Tsutsumi, Seiji (1979), *A Perspective of Changes* [*Henkaku no Toshizu*] Tokyo: Nihon Hyoron-sha (in Japanese).

—— (1985), *A Perspective of Changes* [*Henkaku no Toshizu*], Rev. edn, Tokyo: Trouville (in Japanese).

—— (1996), *Criticism against Consumer Society* [*Shohi Shakai Hihan*], Tokyo: Iwanami-shoten (in Japanese).

Ueno, Chizuko (ed.) (1982a), *Readings of the Disputes about Housewives, Vol. 1* [*Shufu Ronso wo Yomu, No.1*], Tokyo: Keiso-shobo (in Japanese).

—— ed. (1982b), *Readings of the Disputes about Housewives, Vol. 2* [*Shufu Ronso wo Yomu, No.1*], Tokyo: Keiso-shobo (in Japanese).

—— (1991), 'Market of images: the "shrine" of mass society and its crisis', in Ueno, Chizuko et al. (eds.), *Saison's Way of Thinking* [*Saison no Hasso*], Tokyo: Libro Port: 5–136 (in Japanese).

Ueshima, Tadao (1990), 'Interview: 60 years with coffee, bringing a dream with an aroma of culture, in Japan Food Journal Co., Ltd. (ed.), *History of the Food Industry in Showa Era* [*Showa no Shokuhin Sangyo-shi*] Tokyo: Japan Food Journal Co., Ltd.: 1122–27 (in Japanese).

UMDS: University of Marketing and Distribution Science (ed.) (2006), *Isao Nakauchi's Reminiscences* [*Nakauchi Isao Kaiso-roku*], Kobe: University of Marketing and Distribution Science. Not for Sale (in Japanese). (Included in Nakauchi, Jun and Ozu, Takashi (eds.), *Collection of Isao Nakauchi, Vol. 2* [*Nakauchi Isao Series, No. 2*], Tokyo: Chikura-shobo, 2009: 113–363 [in Japanese].)

Un'no, Hiroshi (1978), *Art Nouveau in Japan* [*Nihon no Art Nouveau*], Tokyo: Seido-sha (in Japanese).

Uno, Kathleen (2005), 'Womanhood, war, and Empire: transmutation of "good wife, wise mother" before 1931', in Molony, Barbara and Uno, Kathleen (eds), *Gendering Modern Japanese History*, Cambridge, Massachusetts and London: Harvard University Asia Center: 493–519.

Usui, Kazuo (1992), 'Innovation and tradition in the Japanese marketing system: the information-oriented marketing system in Japan', *Proceedings, the First International Federation of Scholarly Associations of Management (IFSAM) Conference*, Tokyo: Japan Society of Business Administration: 43–46.

—— (1995), 'A brief history of the rise and fall of macro-level marketing studies (studies of *haikyu*) in Japan', in Rassuli, Kathleen M., Hollander, Stanley C. and Nevett, Terence R. (eds), *Marketing History: Marketing's Greatest Empirical Experiment*, East Lansing: Michigan State University: 155–73.

—— (2000), 'The interpretation of Arch Wilkinson Shaw's thought by Japanese scholars', *Journal of Macromarketing*, 20 (2), December: 128–36.

—— (2008), *The Development of Ideas in Marketing Management: The Case of the USA c1910–1940*, Aldershot: Ashgate Publishing.

—— (2009), 'The Historical Contexts Producing *Keiretsu* Retailing: The Four Major Industries in Japan 1910s–1930s', in Hawkins, Richard A. (ed.), *Marketing History: Strengthening, Straightening and Extending, Proceedings of the 14th Biennial Conference on Historical Analysis and Research in Marketing (CHARM)*, University of Leicester, Leicester, United Kingdom: 277–94.

Veblen, Thorstein ([1899] 1994), *The Theory of Leisure Class*, New York: Dover Publications, Inc.

Wakuda, Yasuo (1993), *The Handbook of the History of Private Railway Services* [*Shitetsu-shi Handbook*], Tokyo: Research Association on Electric Railway Trains (in Japanese).

Walsh, Clarie (1999), 'The newness of the department store: a view from the eighteenth century, in Grossick, Geoffrey and Jaumain, Serge (eds), *Cathedrals of Consumption: The European Department Store, 1850–1939*, Aldershot: Ashgate: 46–71.

Weekly Diamond (2008), 'Special feature: Yamada Denki–a strange appearance of the company selling two trillion yen', *Weekly Diamond* [*Shukan Diamond*], 21st June: 30–61 (in Japanese).

Wirgman, Charles ([1892] 1975), *The Japan Punch*. (Reprint, Tokyo: Yushodo.)

Yahagi, Toshiyuki (1991a), 'Development of retail competition and Japan's *keiretsu* system: a consideration on the distribution structure of the household electric alliances', Hosei University, *The Hosei Journal of Business* [*Keiei Shirin*], 27 (4), January: 59–88 (in Japanese).

—— (1991b), 'Series of current history of distribution, No. 37, a hard barrier of national brands for private brands', *Nikkei Newspaper*, 3rd August (in Japanese).

—— (1992), 'Thought on the convenience store system, No. 1', Hosei University, *The Hosei Journal of Business* [*Keiei Shirin*], 29 (2), July: 121–36 (in Japanese).

—— (1993), 'Thought on the convenience store system, No. 2', Hosei University, *The Hosei Journal of Business* [*Keiei Shirin*], 29 (4), January: 17–37 (in Japanese).

—— (1994), *Innovativeness of the Convenience Store System* [*Convenience Store System no Kakushin-sei*], Tokyo: Yuhikaku (in Japanese).

—— (1997), *The Origins of Retail Innovation: Interchanges of Retailers and Modernisation of Distribution* [*Kouri Innovation no Genryu: Keiei Koryu to Ryutsu Kindaika*], Tokyo: Nihon Keizai Shimbun-sha (in Japanese).

—— (1998), 'Establishment of general *super*: rise of Daiei', in Shimaguchi, Mitsuteru et al. (eds.), *Innovations in Sales and Distribution, The Innovation Age of Marketing*,

Vol. 4 [*Eigyo Ryutsu Kakushin, Marketing Kakushin no Zidai, Vol. 4*], Tokyo: Yuhikaku: 122–42 (in Japanese)

—— (2004), 'Chain stores: successive development of retail innovations', in Ishihara and Yahagi (2004): 217–61 (in Japanese).

Yamada, Shogo and Mori, Akihide (1983), *Stories of the Past and the Present of Household Electric Appliances*, Tokyo: Sansei-do (in Japanese).

Yamada, Yoshiharu (2001), *An Obsession of Land/House Ownership: The Problem of Housing in Japan and the UK* [*Tochi Mochi-ie Complex*], Tokyo: Nihon Keizai Hyoron-sha (in Japanese).

Yamaguchi, Kikuo (1983), *History of Diet Culture after the War* [*Sengo ni Miru Shoku no Bunka-shi*], Tokyo: Sanrei-shobo (in Japanese).

—— (1990), 'Signs of the Showa Era and transformation of eating habits', in Japan Food Journal Co., Ltd. (ed.), *History of the Food Industry in Showa Era* [*Showa no Shokuhin Sangyo-shi*], Tokyo: Japan Food Journal Co., Ltd.: 17–30 (in Japanese).

Yamamoto, Kagehide (1980a), 'The destitution of small retailers and their anti-department store movement in the early Showa Era, No. 1', *The Kokugakuin University Economic Review* [Kokugakuin Keizai-gaku], 28 (1), March: 1–25 (in Japanese).

—— (1980b), 'The destitution of small retailers and their anti-department store movement in the early Showa Era, No. 2', *The Kokugakuin University Economic Review* [Kokugakuin Keizai-gaku], 28 (2), September: 47–102 (in Japanese).

Yamamoto, Taketoshi (1999), 'Department stores and the revolution in consumption', in Yamamoto, Taketoshi and Nishizawa, Tamotsu (eds), *Cultural History of Department Stores: The Revolution in Consumption in Japan* [*Hyakkaten no Bunka-shi, Nihon no Shohi Kakumei*], Kyoto: Sekai Shiso-sha: 3–11 (in Japanese).

Yamamori, Toshihiko and Kazama, Akira (1991), *Takashimaya Group: Challenges towards the 21st Century* [*Takashimaya Group, 21-seiki eno Chosen*], Tokyo: Stores-sha (in Japanese).

Yamashita, Kazuyuki (2003), *A Recommendation for Overcoming the Myth of House Ownership: Seeking a Philosophy for Living* [*Datsu Mochi-ie Shinwa no Susume*], Tokyo: Heibonsha Shinsyo (in Japanese).

Yamauchi, Shizuko (1996), 'From Miss Shiseido to Beauty Consultants: its history and today's roles', Shiseido Corporate Museum, *Research Journal Eudermine* [*Eudermine*], 2: 30–7 (in Japanese).

Yamazaki Baking Co., Ltd. (2010), *Fiscal Year 2010 Results, Data Book (Time-series Data)*, PDF Version, in Yamazaki website (in English).

Yamazaki, Mitsuru (1971), 'Far distant from rationalisation of selling fresh fish', *Economist* [*Economist*], 30th March: 78–81.

Yamazaki, Seibun (1988), *Challenges by the Nichii Mycal Group* [*Nichii Mycal Group no Chosen*] Tokyo: Diamond-sha (in Japanese).

Yanagawa, Noriyuki (2003), 'Changes in business models', in Shintaku, Junjiro, Tanaka, Tatsuo and Yanagawa, Noriyuki (2003), *Economic Analysis of the Videogame Industry: Structure and Strategy of the Contents Industry* [*Game Sangyo no Keizai Bunseki*], Tokyo: Toyo Keizai Shimpo-sha: 15–40 (in Japanese).

Yano, Tsuyoshi (1923a), 'The turnover of funds in retailing, Part 1', *Morinaga Monthly* [*Morinaga Geppo*] 5, 15th October: 11 (in Japanese).

—— (1923b), 'The turnover of funds in retailing, Part 2', *Morinaga Monthly* [*Morinaga Geppo*] 6, 15th November: 12 (in Japanese).

Yasuda, Takashi et al. (1998), 'Development of suburban houses by Hankyu Electric Railway before the Second World War, No. 1', *Summaries of Technical Papers of*

Annual Meeting, Architectural Institute of Japan [*Nihon Kenchiku Gakkai Taikai Gaku-jutsu Koen Kogai-shu*], F. September: 163–4 (in Japanese).

Yokohama City ([1937] 1987), *Investigation of Commerce* [*Shogo Chosa-sho*], Yokohama: Yokohama Municipal Office. Reprint, Tokyo: Hobunkaku Shuppan-bu (in Japanese).

Yokota, Naomi (1999), 'Reconsideration of wartime fashions', *Journal of Japan Society of Environmental Research for Fashion* [*Fashion Kankyo*], 9 (2), October: 54–59 (in Japanese).

Yokoyama, Gen'nosuke (1899 [1985]), *The Lower Classes in Japan* [*Nihon no Kaso Kaikyu*]. Reprint, Tokyo: Iwanami Bunko (in Japanese).

—— ([1903] 1998), *The Conditions of Factory Workers* [*Shokko Jijo*]. Reprint, 3 vols., Tokyo: Iwanami Bunko (in Japanese).

Yomiuri Newspaper (1878a and 1878b), 'hair washing powders' (advertisement by Tokyo Ginza Nishinomiya Hachirozaemon), *Yomiuri Newspaper*, 9th and 12th June (in Japanese).

—— (1881), 'Himeyanagi hair washing powders' (advertisement by Fujiya Shohachiro), *Yomiuri Newspaper*, 21st May (in Japanese).

—— (1907), 'Making-up techniques by current women students: soap, white powder, lotion, perfume and scented oil, and rouges and cream', *Yomiuri Newspaper*, 12th April (in Japanese).

—— (1953), 'What is self-service?: decreasing the number of sales clerks and increasing turnover', *Yomiuri Newspaper*, 27th July (in Japanese).

—— (1958a), 'Arrival of the age of super market: the menace of entry of large-sized companies encouraging the "revolution of retail business"', *Yomiuri Newspaper*, 11st August (in Japanese).

—— (1958b), 'Regrettable split of "Stores for Housewives", supermarket retailing', *Yomiuri Newspaper*, 22nd December (in Japanese).

—— (1971), 'The convenience stores on the boom in America, necessary for development of the Japanese-style', *Yomiuri Newspaper*, 21st September (in Japanese).

—— (1988), 'Convenience stores as the 24-hour shops: No. 4, customer traffic does not decrease until midnight', *Yomiuri Newspaper*, 6th April (in Japanese).

—— (1989a), 'Is it enough to "blame videogames"?: the serial murder case of little girls: a simple regulation is not the real answer', *Yomiuri Newspaper*, 23rd August (in Japanese).

—— (1989b), 'How to deal with videogame consoles for children?: "Have real experiences rather than video experiences": discussed at the National Meeting of Motherhood', *Yomiuri Newspaper*, 27th August (in Japanese).

—— (1990), 'Series of "What is play" No.2: Playing videogames in an isolated room', *Yomiuri Newspaper*, 25th May (in Japanese).

—— (1997), 'The case of murder and abandonment of a corpse of primary 6 girl in Suma Kobe, a bizarre crime in the age of virtual reality, commented by an intellectual', *Osaka Yomiuri Newspaper*, 28th May (in Japanese).

Yoshida, Hideo (1982), 'The Origin of the Movement of "Housewives' Stores"', in The National Chain of Housewives' Stores Supermarkets (ed.), *With Pinwheels* [*Kaza-Guruma to Tomoni*], Osaka: Uniusu: 1–8 (in Japanese).

Yoshida, Kenkichi (1955), *Women's Manners and Costumes* [*Josei no Fuzoku*] Tokyo: Kawade Shinsho (in Japanese).

Yoshida, Masaki (2005), 'The historical role of Tokyo Dento in the formation of the early stage of the electric lighting industry,' *Mita Business Review* [*Mita Shogaku*], 48 (5), December: 147–64 (in Japanese).

Yoshida, Tadashi (1988), '"Westernisation" of eating habits: transformation from rice-centred diet', Imamura, Naraomi and Yoshida, Tadashi (eds), *A Direction of Transfiguration of Eating Habits, Collective Works of Problems on Food and Agriculture, No. 17* [*Shoku Seikatsu Henbo no Vector, Shokuryo Nogyo Mondai Zenshu No. 17*], Tokyo: Nosan-gyoson Bunka Kyokai: 72–91 (in Japanese).

Yoshikawa, Hiroshi (1997), *High Economic Growth: 6,000 Days that Changed Japan*, Tokyo: Kodan-sha (in Japanese).

Yoshimi, Shunya (2007), 'The imperial capital and modern girls: the political space of modernity and sex in interwar Japan', in Sato, Barbara (ed.), *The Birth of Everyday Life: The Transfiguration of Culture in Interwar Japan* [*Nichijo Seikatsu no Tanjo, Senkan-ki Nihon no Bunka Henyo*], Tokyo: Kashiwa-shobo, 2007: 228–250 (in Japanese).

Yoshino, M. Y. (1971), *The Japanese Marketing System*, Cambridge, MA: MIT Press.

Yoshioka, Yutaka (1956), 'Acceptance of the gifts of flours and skimmed milk from the USA for the purpose of school lunches', Food Control Agency, *Monthly Bulletin of Food Control* [*Shokuryo Kanri Geppo*], 8 (9), September: 18–21 (in Japanese).

Yui, Tsunehiko (1991), 'From Musashino Department Store to Seibu Department Store', in Yui, Tsunehiko (ed.) (1991), *The History of Saison, Vol. 1* [*Saison no Rekishi, Jo-kan*], Tokyo: Libro Port: 1–72 (in Japanese).

—— (ed.) (1991b), *The History of Saison, Vol. 2* [*Saison no Rekishi, Ge-kan*], Tokyo: Libro Port (in Japanese).

——, Tatsuki, Mariko and Ito, Osamu (2010), *Collapse and Resuscitation of Saison* [*Saison no Zasetsu to Saisei*], Tokyo: Sanai-shoin (in Japanese).

Yumoto, Goichi (1996), *Explanatory Pictures: Dictionary of Things Originating in the Meiji Period* [*Zusetsu: Meiji Jibutsu Kigen Jiten*], Tokyo: Kashiwa-shobo (in Japanese).

Young, Louise (1999), 'Marketing the modern: department stores, consumer culture, and the new middle class in the interwar Japan', *International Labor and Working-Class History*, 55, Spring: 52–72. (Translated into Japanese by Okamoto, Koichi, in Sato, Barbara (ed.), *The Birth of Everyday Life: The Transfiguration of Culture in Interwar Japan* [*Nichijo Seikatsu no Tanjo, Senkan-ki Nihon no Bunka Henyo*], Tokyo: Kashiwa-shobo, 2007: 228–30).

Websites:

Aeon: http://www.aeon.info/en/aboutaeon/history.html (in English)
Amaguri Taro: http://www.amaguritarou.co.jp/rekishi/index.html (in Japanese).
Bunka Gakuen: http://www.bunka.ac.jp/contents/en_history.htm (in English)
Daily Yamazaki: http://www.daily-yamazaki.co.jp/index.html (in Japanese)
Deodeo: http://www.deodeo.co.jp/index01.html (in Japanese).
DSRI (The Distribution System Research Institute):
A fact-finding survey on introduction of the JAN-type EPOS system in 2009. http://www.dsri.jp/invres/index.htm (in Japanese).
Ferris University: http://www.ferris.ac.jp/aboutfs/history.html (in Japanese)
Fugetsudo: http://www.tokyo-fugetsudo.co.jp/gaiyou/ENKAKU.html (in Japanese)
Fukusuke Corporation:
http://www.fukusuke.com/museum/index.html (in Japanese)
Hoshi University: http://www.hoshi.ac.jp/english/history.htm (in Japanese)
Isetan Co., Ltd.:
http://www.isetan.co.jp/icm2/jsp/isetan/company/history.jsp (in Japanese)

Ito Yokado: http://www.itoyokado.co.jp/company/history.html (in Japanese)
JFTC (Japan Fair Trade Commission): http://www.jftc.go.jp/
  'Guidelines concerning distribution systems and business practices', 1991
  http://www.jftc.go.jp/e-page/legislation/ama/distribution.pdf (in Japanese)
Kao Corporation:
  http://www.kao.com/jp/corp_about/history_01.html#1890_1950 (in Japanese)
Kobe University Library, Digital Archive:
  http://www.lib.kobe-u.ac.jp/sinbun/ (in Japanese)
LaOX: http://www.laox.co.jp/laox/kigyo.html#05 (in Japanese)
Matsuya Co., Ltd.: http://wwwMatsuya.com/co/enkaku/index.html (in Japanese)
Meiji-ya Co., Ltd.:
  http://www.meiji-ya.co.jp/company/history/meiji.html (in Japanese)
METI (Ministry of Economy, Trade and Industry) website 1:
  Census of Commerce (in Japanese)
  http://www.meti.go.jp/statistics/tyo/syougyo/result-2.html
  Census of Commerce, Time-series data (in Japanese)
  http://www.meti.go.jp/statistics/tyo/syougyo/result-2/jikei.html
—— website 2:
  Current Survey of Commerce (*Shogyo Dotai Tokei Chosa*), Historical Data, Large-scale
  retail store sales value by type of business, by goods and ratio to the same month/term of
  the previous year (in Japanese)
  http://www.meti.go.jp/statistics/tyo/syoudou/result-2/index.html
ME (Ministry of Education):
  The 13th Proclamation of the Ministry of Education (in Japanese)
  http://www.mext.go.jp/b_menu/hakusho/html/hpbz198102/hpbz198102_2_012.html
  The 1886 Order of Primary Schools (in Japanese)
  http://www.mext.go.jp/b_menu/hakusho/html/hpbz198102/hpbz198102_2_044.html
NSAJ (New Supermarket Association of Japan):
  http://www.super.or.jp/?page_id=27 (in Japanese)
NACS (National Association of Convenience Stores) Online:
  http://www.nacsonline.com/NACS/News/FactSheets/Pages/default.aspx (in Japanese)
Nakamuraya Co., Ltd.:
  http://www.nakamuraya.co.jp/history/index.html (in Japanese)
National Diet Library, Digital Library:
  http://kindai.ndl.go.jp/index.html (in Japanese)
Nintendo: http://www.nintendo.com/
  http://www.nintendo.co.uk/NOE/en_GB/index.html (in Japanese)
Ochanomizu University:
  http://www.ocha.ac.jp/introduction/history.html (in Japanese)
Panasonic:
  http://panasonic.net/history/corporate/chronicle/1964-01.html (in Japanese)
  http://panasonic.net/history/corporate/chronicle/1965-01.html (in English)
SB (Statistics Bureau), Ministry of Internal Affairs and Communications, website 1:
  Historical Statistics in Japan
  http://www.stat.go.jp/english/data/chouki/index.htm (in Japanese and English)
—— website 2:
  Family Income and Expenditure Survey, 14th Year of Heisei (in Japanese)
  http://www.stat.go.jp/data/kakei/2002np/gaikyo/141gk.htm
—— (2009b) http://www.stat.go.jp/english/data/jinsui/2.htm (in English)

7-Eleven Inc:

http://corp.7-eleven.com/AboutUs/DomesticLicensing/tabid/443/Default.aspx (in English)

http://corp.7-eleven.com/AboutUs/InternationalLicensing/tabid/115/Default.aspx (in English)

Accomplishments and milestones

http://corp.7-eleven.com/AboutUs/Milestones/tabid/76/Default.aspx (in English)

Shiseido: http://www.us.shiseido.com/about/story/origins/index.htm (in English)

Shiseido Beauty Saloon:

'Stories of Shiseido Beauty Saloon, 50th Anniversary' (in Japanese)

http://www.shiseido.co.jp/biyoushitsu/whatsbs/index.htm

Sony Global:

Sony History   http://www.sony.net/SonyInfo/CorporateInfo/History/SonyHistory/ (in English)

Takashimaya Department Store:

http://www.takashimaya.co.jp/corp/info/history/index.html (in Japanese)

TCA (Telecommunications Carriers Association):

http://www.tca.or.jp/database/index.html (in English)

Uny:

http://www.uny.co.jp/corporate/about/history.html (in Japanese)

Yamada Denki Co., Ltd.:

http://www.yamada-denki.jp/company_e/index.html (in English)

Yamazaki Baking Co., Ltd.:

http://www.yamazakipan.co.jp/english/c_profile/index.html (in English)

Yamazaki Shop:

http://www.yamazakipan.co.jp/shops/yshop/ (in Japanese)

Index

Page numbers in **bold** refer to tables, in *italic* refer to figures and followed by a letter n refers to end of chapter notes.